D1282819

THE APPEAL
OF FASCISM

A STUDY OF INTELLECTUALS
AND FASCISM
1919-1945

THE
APPEAL
OF
FASCISM

ALASTAIR HAMILTON

A STUDY OF INTELLECTUALS
AND FASCISM
1919-1945

FOREWORD BY STEPHEN SPENDER

ANTHONY BLOND

FIRST PUBLISHED 1971 BY ANTHONY BLOND LTD
56 DOUGHTY STREET LONDON WC 1

© Copyright 1971 by Alastair Hamilton

SBN 218 51426 3

Made and printed in The Republic of Ireland
by Cahill and Company Limited
Parkgate Printing Works Dublin 8

ACKNOWLEDGEMENTS

Of the many people who have provided me with advice and information for this book I would like to thank particularly Professor Renzo De Felice, Dottor Piero Melograni and Monsieur Dominique de Roux. I am also most grateful to Conte Giacomo Antonini, Professor Carlo Bo, Herr Arno Breker, Avvocato Ugo Castelnuovo Tedesco, Dottor Benedetto Gentile, Mrs St John Hutchinson, Mr Arthur Koestler, Monsieur Jacques de Lacretelle, Monsieur Michel Mohrt, Professor Gioacchino Volpe and Mr Henry Williamson. For permission to quote I am indebted to the following: Messrs. Allen and Unwin for quotations from Arthur Helps' translation of the *Spengler Letters;* Messrs. Jonathan Cape for quotations from I.F.D. Morrow's translation of Ernst von Salomon's *The Outlaws;* Messrs. Cassell & Co. and Mrs Eva Alberman for quotations from Stefan Zweig's *The World of Yesterday*; Messrs. Hamish Hamilton for quotations from A.J.P. Taylor's *The Course of German History*; Messrs. A.D. Peters for quotations from *The Letters of Hilaire Belloc* and Robert Speaight's *Life of Hilaire Belloc;* to Messrs. A.M. Heath and to Mr Henry Williamson for quotations from Mr Williamson's novels; to Messrs. Thomas Nelson & Sons Ltd. for quotations from Sir Oswald Mosley's *My Life;* to Messrs. Methuen & Co. Ltd. for quotations from Christopher Seton-Watson's *Italy from Liberalism to Fascism;* to Messrs. Curtis Brown for quotations from Julian Symons' *The Thirties;* to Dr. S.J. Woolf for quotations from *European Fascism;* to The London School of Economics and Political Science for quotations from Beatrice Webb's *Diaries;* to Stanford University Press for quotations from Eugen Weber's *Action Française: Royalism and Reaction in Twentieth-*

Century France; to Mr Michael B. Yeats and Miss Anne Yeats for permission to quote from W.B. Yeats' *Letters, Senate Speeches,* and *A Vision.* Finally, I would like to express my deepest gratitude to Mr Tom Rivers.

PHOTOGRAPHIC ACKNOWLEDGEMENTS

The author and publishers wish to thank the following for permission to reproduce the photographs in this book: Foto Adelmann, Paris, for the photograph of Martin Heidegger (p. 136); Radio Times Hulton Picture Library, London, for the photographs of Henry Williamson (p. 264), Roy Campbell (p. 264), Percy Wyndham Lewis (p. 280) and Thomas Stearns Eliot (p. 281); L'Herne for the photographs of Louis-Ferdinand Céline (p. 239) and Ezra Loomis Pound (p. 265); Herr Arno Breker for the photographs of Otto Abetz & Robert Brasillach (p. 184), Arno Breker & Pierre Drieu La Rochelle (p. 200) and Jean Cocteau & Arno Breker (p. 185); The John Hillelson Agency Ltd., London for the photograph of Sacha Guitry (taken by Henri Cartier-Bresson) (p. 201) and Ullstein Bildedienst, Berlin, for the photographs of Ernst Jünger (p. 121) and Arnolt Bronnen (p. 137).

CONTENTS

ILLUSTRATIONS

FOREWORD

by STEPHEN SPENDER

During the thirties many people identified the politics of the intellectuals with the orthodoxy of the anti-Fascist left. Fascism meant dictatorship, censorship, the persecution of the Jews, the destruction of intellectual freedom. To be anti-Fascist was to be on the side of humanity. Conversely, to be Fascist was to be against it. This being so, it seemed incredible that there were intellectuals— philosophers, poets—who intermittently or, even, consistently, were Fascist. Yet some of the greatest modern writers sympathised with Fascism.

In this comparative study of Fascism in Italy, Germany, France and England, Alastair Hamilton throws a great deal of light on its appeal to writers. Fascism offered political answers to criticisms of modern technological society made by the cultured and the lovers of past civilisation. These answers appealed in one way to anarchist Futurists and in another to reactionary traditionalists. A Futurist like Marinetti and a classicist like Ezra Pound had in common their hatred of the bourgeois and their contempt for democracy. Marinetti saw in Mussolini the nationalist who released energies which had been repressed for hundreds of years as the result of Italy being regarded as the cultural museum and the political maidservant of other European countries. Ezra Pound saw him as the economist who, given a little instruction by the social creditors, might find the contemporary means to restore or re-invent a society where it was possible to purify language and the arts. He believed that Mussolini shared with Jefferson "the sense of the 'root and the branch', readiness to scrap the lesser thing for the thing of major importance, indifferent to mechanism as weighed against the main purpose without regard to abstract ideas, even if the idea was proclaimed the week before last." In Pound's view, Jefferson and Mussolini were opposed to usury. In Italy—as he saw it— Pound could perfect his vision of a pre-Renaissance Italy which was an "organic community" in which the artist's hand that painted the outline of a profile or dress was not corrupted by usury and he could believe that there was a relation between this imagined past and the envisioned Fascist future.

In the minds of writers who thought that their first obligation in their art was to keep open lines of communication with the dead, Fascism represented order, a return to the past tradition, opposition to Communism and social decadence. On account of the enthusiasm which the first years of Mussolini's and Hitler's régimes inspired in young Italians and Germans, it also seemed vitalist, an expression of the forces of life, the blood, and thus had a momentary appeal even for D. H. Lawrence.

However, it must be said that most writers who supported Fascism did so more because they were against other politics than because they were for it. To some extent it fulfilled their prophecies which were also prophecies of doom : Oswald Spengler saw in it a period of Caesarism which was the last phase of a declining civilisation, and Yeats perhaps, a spirited march by tragic heroes who preserved their gaiety in the last lunar phase which completed the cycle of Western civilisation. Men like Yeats and Wyndham Lewis were liable suddenly to withdraw their support from leaders whom they half regarded as puppets or masks when they appeared in more sordid roles.

Alastair Hamilton raises the interesting question whether Charles Maurras or any other French writer can really be considered a Fascist. He points out that "Maurras was a classicist. He had always regarded romanticism as a foreign import which distorted the French spirit, a barbarous and confused patchwork of ideas and emotions. The French, he claimed, must return to *their* tradition, in which order, hierarchy and discipline were essential". These views, which T. S. Eliot shared, are not so much political as a vision of civilisation. Men who held them regarded Fascism at best as a vehicle which might carry them towards a society which came closer to the greatness of the past. They saw in Fascism more order than in liberal or Socialist movements, but there was nothing in the way of philosophy, ideology or sense of order which they had to learn from it. Even Gentile, despite his complete loyalty to Mussolini, saw Italian Fascism as a means for the realisation of his own ideas which he regarded, perhaps justly, as liberal.

W. B. Yeats expressed admiration for Hitler and Mussolini and he wrote songs for General O'Duffy's Blue Shirts. But Yeats had grown up (to quote Richard Ellman) " with Villiers de l'Isle Adam's epigram ringing in his ears, 'As for living, our servants will do that for us'." He regarded Hitler and Mussolini perhaps as liveried major domos and his expression of admiration for them did not impose on him the slightest obligation to refrain, at a moment's notice, from kicking them downstairs.

Stefan George, from whom the Nazis learned so much and whom Hitler was so anxious to shower with honours, regarded the Nazis with contempt. Oswald Spengler thought Hitler a crude play actor. All this is not to say that the reactionaries and Fascist sympathising writers did not give aid and comfort to Hitler and Mussolini as the Communist leftists gave aid and comfort to Stalin. Yet there is no symmetry balancing the anti-Fascist intellectuals against the Fascist ones.

The anti-Fascist found in Marxism a system which was not a reflection or expression of their own aesthetic attitudes. It was an ideology which explained society to them as a conflict of forces external to their concerns with their art. They saw a struggle going on in society between oppressors and oppressed and in order to take sides in this (as the Fascist threat forced them to do) they had to unlearn their aesthetic attitudes and relate their art and themselves to the social context of struggle.

The difference between these positions make it difficult to judge the writers who supported Fascism as having accepted a Fascist ideology in the way in which the anti-Fascist had accepted a Marxist one. The reactionary traditionalists stood outside Fascism while supporting it. What they believed in was civilisation. They saw Fascism as a means of defending civilised standards. However mistaken they may have been, this did mean that the standards remain intact in their work and unaffected by the cause they supported. Personally, of course, they bear responsibility for the things Hitler and Mussolini did, just as Stalinists bear responsibility for the acts of Stalin. Some of them paid dearly for this, as Alastair Hamilton makes clear in his study of Gentile. Pound also

paid dearly. But I think that Hamilton is right scarcely to touch
on the question of culpability. His objective way of presenting the
facts provides a sufficient basis of judgement, where condemnation
is required. The men who are judged most severely turn out to be
the inferior artists. Here for example, there is a portrait of Malaparte which is damning enough. But the fact that men like Maurras,
Ernst Jünger, Yeats and Pound observed standards in their work
which were independent of their politics, makes them tragically
mistaken but does not affect their art. One can feel a special debt
of gratitude for those who kept alive the tradition during the terrible
inter-war years.

INTRODUCTION

The consequences of Hitler's ideas, the victims of persecution and discrimination, the disgrace incurred by Mussolini because of his early influence on the German dictator and his subsequent alliance with him, tend to obscure the atmosphere in which Fascism developed and to becloud that period when hardly anyone imagined to what it could lead. They distort beyond recognition the time when writers, known for their hatred of democracy, had little reason to believe that their apologies for violence would go farther than the paper on which they expressed them. The purpose of my study is to give an account of the ideas of some of these writers, in Italy, Germany, France and England; to examine the appeal which Fascism, that thoroughly ambiguous ideology, had for them; and to establish what their dealings were with Fascist movements in their own and other countries. I do not, I hasten to say, propose to accuse them, any more than I intend to defend them, for who am I to pass judgement? I simply wish to examine, through them, some of those illusions which hung over Europe until the collapse of the Third Reich, some of those myths which now, less than thirty years after the war, seem so unreal, so absurd, so profoundly alien to us.

I shall do no more than allude to the so-called precursors of Fascism, who died before Fascism was born, for I agree that it is "misleading to suppose that Fascism itself can be understood in terms of certain theoretical 'roots' ".[1] But just as it is impossible to prove that Fascism had its undisputed forerunners in the nineteenth century, so I believe it impossible to prove that the thought

---

[1]Maurice Cranston, *Sunday Times*, February 8, 1970.

of a writer led him inevitably to Fascism. This was a fantasy—
a somewhat dangerous fantasy, I cannot help feeling—both of the
left-wing and of the Fascists themselves. The situation was by no
means clear cut. A number of men who were hailed as Fascist
thinkers would either have nothing to do with the movement, or
approved it briefly and reluctantly. Others amazed their contemporaries by welcoming Mussolini and Hitler to power—and
although I have not extended this study to the phenomenon of the
intellectual who committed himself to Communism, the barrier
between those who chose Communism and those who preferred
Fascism seems to me, in many cases, so slim that we are less than
ever entitled to say that a certain type of man, a certain type of
psychology tended towards Fascism. If I have occasionally suggested, as with Céline and Gottfried Benn, that a writer's profession
and environment might be partially responsible for his political
sympathies, this is no more than a suggestion: I am aware that
many writers of the same profession and from a similar background
could be produced as evidence against it.

One of the features that emerges from a study of political commitment between the wars is inconsistency. And if, as I think in
most cases we must, we regard the intellectual's decision to back
a particular political movement as a relatively disinterested decision,
taken in the hope that this political movement will produce a
better, happier world and ultimately lead to the improvement of
social conditions, we see that the events between 1918 and 1939
often threw men in search of the right solution into wholly incongruous positions. They witnessed two economic crises of unprecedented violence which led to riots, to unemployment, to the threat
of starvation for millions of families. They feared that the Great
War, with all its horrors, might be repeated; and, in the thirties,
Hitler's determination to fulfil his expansionist ambitions—his
withdrawal from the League of Nations and the Disarmament Conference, the occupation of the Rhineland, the annexation of Austria,
the occupation of the Sudetenland—suggested that peace would
only last as long as the democratic powers continued to betray their
principles. Yet in order to avoid a repetition of the Great War people
found themselves supporting régimes for which they had no natural
sympathy and defending points of view which, at any other time,
they would have deplored. In order to find some way out of the
economic and social crises in which the world was steeped, they

came to advise political solutions the practice of which would, in other circumstances, have revolted them.

Even the pattern of political alliances was paradoxical. From Hitler's rise to power in 1933 to his invasion of the Soviet Union in 1941 there were three possible combinations in Europe : the first —the one which only prevailed with the breach of the Nazi-Soviet pact—was an alliance between the Fascist States, Italy and Germany, against the European "democracies", including the Soviet Union. The second was an anti-Communist alliance between the Fascist States and the "democracies" against the Soviet Union. And the third was an "anti-democratic" alliance—an alliance between the Fascist States and the Soviet Union against the democracies. These three combinations, sustained alternately by a variety of politicians, were reflected in the views of the European intelligentsia. There were the democrats, who opposed every form of totalitarianism, and there were the Nationalists who, if they were Italian or German, tended to support a Fascist alliance against Communism and democracy, but who, in all events, put their own country first. There were the anti-Communists—the intellectuals who, though they had no particular sympathy for Fascism, preferred it to, and regarded it as the best defence against, Communism. And finally there were the "anti-democrats", those who wanted a revolutionary and authoritarian State, who looked with far more sympathy at the Soviet Union than they did at the liberal democracies. It is this last category which, to my mind, provided the true Fascists, the men like Malaparte and Drieu La Rochelle— and which also produced a great many intellectual Communists. These were the rebels whose main enemy was the *status quo,* the quiet, peaceful, complacent and somewhat hypocritical liberal State. The Fascists saw Communism and Fascism running parallel to each other. They believed not only that Fascism was revolutionary, but that it was left-wing. Indeed, even if Fascism turned out to be reactionary in practice, its adherents were rarely willing to recognise it as such—and for this reason we are not entitled to dismiss it as purely conservative or to interpret it in terms of the traditional right-wing. Fascism purported to be a third solution, biased to the left, which was to run its course between Communism and liberalism, closer to the former. It intended, if not to eliminate capitalism, at least to break the hold of the capitalist oligarchy. It was, in theory, to introduce "bourgeois Socialism".

B

This bourgeois Socialism had, both in theory and practice, little in common with proletarian, Marxist Socialism. The differences between the various forms of Fascism and the very considerable transformation which they underwent in the course of their existence, should appear clearly enough from my study and must be examined in their historical and national context, so I will here merely outline some of the points they had in common, some of the "images" which, in the twenties and thirties, people associated with the word "Fascism". Fundamentally it was an ideology intended to recruit those lower middle classes who were embittered by the economic and social crises, frightened by the idea of Communism, disappointed by the world which had emerged from the Great War, and who were dissatisfied with the traditional left- and right-wing parties. That Fascism, in the original sense of the word, was a phenomenon restricted exclusively to the period between the two wars, is indicated fairly clearly by the structure and outlook of the true Fascist movements—Mussolini's *Partito Nazionale Fascista*, Hitler's *N.S.D.A.P.*, Georges Valois' *Faisceau*, Mosley's British Union of Fascists. For these movements were originally designed to attract the ex-servicemen, the trench fighters of the First World War, to recreate the atmosphere of youthful comradeship, heroism and idealism that had developed in the trenches—or, it would be safer to say, that had developed in the myth of the trenches which the Fascists created. The Fascist leaders, therefore, organised parades, devised uniforms, provided their followers with songs, emblems and slogans, and emphasised such military qualities as hierarchy, leadership and discipline.

Yet Fascism was not intended solely for the ex-serviceman; it was, as I have said, intended for an entire class which felt its social status threatened, which feared the collapse of the traditional institutions, family, religion and nation, scorned by Marxism. In the Fascist States, therefore, these "eternal values", more the family and the nation than religion (for Fascism purported to be a religion in itself), became the object of a cult, and seemed to guarantee that the new world would be illuminated by familiar beacons. At the same time Fascism was presented as the only ideology which could do away with the class struggle and ultimately disprove the Marxist concept of the irreconcilability of the proletariat and the bourgeoisie. So, on a practical level, it offered corporativism—the corporate State where the old Socialist trade unions would be abolished, and the manpower of the nation would be reorganised in corporations, submitted to the authority of the State, in which the employer could come to terms with his employee on an egalitarian, and, above all, on an amicable and comradely, basis.

Anti-semitism, it should be emphasised, played no part in the essence of Fascist doctrine : the conservation of racial purity was Hitler's own myth, shared neither by Mussolini nor by many of the other Fascist leaders. But it is also true to say that the organised violence offered by Fascism—even after it had officially been put to an end—required an object; Fascist activism needed to be directed *against* something. To start with, in Italy and elsewhere, this object was constituted by the Socialists, accused of being traitors to their country in the service of some international organisation, tainted by defeatism in the Great War and responsible for disrupting national unity and prolonging the economic crisis with their strikes and riots. To the Socialists Hitler added the Jews, in the belief that he could fire the petty bourgeoisie still more by inspiring in them a truly physical revulsion for another race.

In substance Fascism was a "myth" in the Sorelian sense of the word, a "system of images" defying logical definition or rational analysis, filled, if submitted to either, with contradictions. From myth to reality, from theory to practice, the gulf, as is often the case, was exceedingly wide. If examined with any degree of objectivity, if its course was traced and its achievements compared with its principles, Fascism was less than a myth : it was a hoax. Although the enthusiasm which it inspired is indisputable, and although this enthusiasm, in Germany if not in Italy, did more to diminish class antagonism than any reform undertaken by a democratic state, Fascism's claims to be revolutionary turned out to be false once it became a régime. In neither Italy nor in Germany did it succeed in changing the class structure, or in destroying capitalism. In both countries the revolutionary core of the movement, the *squadristi* and the S.A., were rendered ineffectual as soon as the dictator had the chance to suppress them. Corporatism was never implemented in Germany and failed in Italy. Subject itself to so many different interpretations, it turned out, in Italy, to be no more than a means of retaining the former hierarchy.

If we examine Fascism outside Italy and Germany, still more discrepancies and contradictions come to light: most Fascist movements took either the Germans or the Italians as their model, thereby renouncing any claims to national tradition or originality. Strictly speaking Fascism was a Nationalist movement, but many French Fascists liked to think of it as international, while those who collaborated with the Germans during the Second World War in the name of Nationalism found themselves in a situation analogous to that of the Jacobite squire in *Tom Jones* who, after hearing the news that reinforcements for the Young Pretender had disembarked in England, " with great joy in his countenance, shook the landlord by the hand, saying, 'All's our own, boy, ten thousand honest Frenchmen are landed in Suffolk. Old England for ever! ten thousand Frenchmen, my brave lad!' "

What, then, was the appeal which Fascism, for however short a time, had for so many eminent men of letters, some of whom were in a perfectly good position to see through the myth? One of the advantages of the vagueness of Fascist doctrine and of its lack of a generally accepted originator was that a number of writers, who had very little in common with one another, could regard themselves as the precursors of a political movement which had triumphed. The ambiguity of the ideology allowed those who supported it to read into it what they pleased; they could twist it this way and that, according to their whim. And, for all its malleability, Fascism did constitute a phenomenon which artists found aesthetically satisfactory : it had turned anarchy into order. For Fascism, the Fascism of the intellectuals above all, had its origins in sheer rebelliousness, in an anarchistic revolt directed against the established order. I shall in this study be examining the relationship between Fascism and those artistic movements which developed before the Great War—Futurism in Italy, Expressionism in Germany, Vorticism in England. On the one hand these movements started as a reaction against the legacy of the nineteenth century—a traditionalist legacy which threatened to smother the arts as much as it inhibited the individual; but on the other they originated in a need to escape. The complacency of the despised, hard-working bourgeois was accompanied by a threat which struck the intelligentsia as equally distasteful and far more frightening— the threat of anonymity, due to the speed at which industry and mechanisation were advancing and the progressive rise of masses who could at last participate in the administration of a world in which they had previously been voiceless. It appeared, therefore, that the rôle of the individual was over: he was either to be enslaved

by the ever more powerful machine, or he was to be engulfed in
mass society.

To this threat of anonymity Fascism seemed to offer a solution,
for it conciliated the cult of the hero with a mass movement. It
defied social transformation by its deliberate protection of traditional values and attempted to impose a social structure which,
though aristocratic in form, was based on individual merit regardless of social origin. Here was none of the sinister equality offered
by the Communists : here was a society where each man was given
his due, where he could retain his individuality, where the machine
age was attractively draped in myths of mediaeval heroism and
chivalry. And that Mussolini and Hitler should have "tamed the
revolt"[1] at the expense of the revolution was found to be less dis-
turbing than the orderly State which rose up under their dictatorship was found impressive.

It is a mistake, no doubt, to transpose certain aesthetic ideals on to
the level of politics—an error frivolously made by Salvador Dali
when, at a Surrealist meeting in 1934, he proclaimed that Hitler's
Surrealist personality was as admirable as that of Sade or of
Lautréamont, and a mistake which proved of greater consequence
when a number of writers sought, in a totalitarian régime, the
discipline which they associated with their own, private, creative
process. The difficulties implicit in such an attitude were well
expressed by André Gide, who preferred to commit himself to
Communism. "The notion of liberty such as it is taught us,"
he wrote in October 1931, "seems to me false and pernicious in
the extreme. And if I approve Soviet constraint I must also approve
Fascist discipline. I believe ever more firmly that the idea of liberty
is nothing but a hoax. I would like to be sure that I would think
the same if I were not free myself, I who value my own liberty of
thought above all else : but I also believe more and more firmly that
man does nothing valid without constraint, and that those capable
of finding this constraint within themselves are very rare. I believe,
too, that the true colour of a particular thought only assumes its
full value when it is thrown into relief against an unperturbed
background. It is the uniformity of the masses which enables certain
individuals to rise up and stand out against it. The 'Render unto

---

[1]The phrase is George Mosse's. G. L. Mosse, *The Genesis of Fascism*
in *The Journal of Contemporary History*, vol. 1, No. 1, 1966, p. 14-26.

Caesar the things which are Caesar's; and unto God the things that
are God's' of the Gospel seems to me wiser than ever. On God's side
we have liberty—the liberty of the spirit; on Caesar's side there is
submission—the submission of our acts."[1]

Fascism combined the idea of discipline with another prospect
which was found equally exciting intellectually, although we now
have some difficulty in dissociating it from the genocide which,
however indirectly, descended from it. This was the prospect of the
"new man", the élite of heroic supermen, "*artist*-tyrants", of whom
Nietzsche had dreamt. But this élite should not be understood in
terms of anti-semitism, for hardly any intellectual did so. One should,
instead, place it on the vague and artistic level which attracted Gottfried Benn and Martin Heidegger. It was, in a way, a poetic fiction
—a fiction which, despite the general repugnance felt by the Anglo-
Saxons for Fascism, enchanted two of the greatest poets in the
English language, Yeats and Ezra Pound.

The myth of the "new man" was connected, in its turn, with the
desire for renewal, for revival, for invigoration, with those misleading but popular interpretations of history which came into fashion
with the revolt against positivism at the end of the nineteenth
century. I shall be mentioning the implication of the "cyclical
theory" with reference to Oswald Spengler—there was nothing new
about it, nothing original about it, nor was there anything new
or original in the idea that civilisation had reached a point of
crisis. Whether this belief became more acute or more widespread in the first thirty years of this century than it has ever
done before, I hesitate to say; but it did pervade intellectual circles,
and it was provided with the semblance of confirmation by the
Great War and the Depression. More and more writers began to
find the apocalypse not only inevitable but desirable. Partly in
order to forestall it, partly in order to survive it, they chose to
commit themselves to totalitarian ideologies and to support régimes
that would hasten the destruction of the civilisation which they
believed in a state of putrefaction. There was, of course, a profoundly self-destructive streak in this attitude of theirs, which we
find most apparent in Gide. In 1932 he informed Dorothy Bussy
"that he had played all his life with false chips; that nothing for
which he had lived had any value any more; that *art*, free *thought*,

---

[1]A. Gide, *Journal 1889-1939*, Paris, 1939, p. 1084.

even truth, would no longer count, *should* no longer count in the new world which Communism was opening for us. That we should side with the men who made Socrates drink hemlock, that art and the spiritual values of *Andromaque* were out of date and no longer concerned us. . ."[1]

Here again Fascism seemed a solution. It claimed to be anti-intellectual—and most intellectuals agreed that the new world, beyond the apocalypse, would have no place for intellectuals anyhow—but at the same time it claimed to uphold those spiritual values which Communism would, in all likelihood, destroy. To believe such a blatant lie (as far, at least, as National Socialism was concerned) it was necessary to overlook the remarkable similarity between the official works of art which issued from the Third Reich and from the Soviet Union; but this was easily done, particularly by men who were living neither in the Soviet Union nor in the Third Reich. In all events it seemed that under Fascism the death of the old world and the birth of the new would be relatively painless. Indeed, so painless did they believe it to be, that we can almost detect a greater sense of self-preservation in the writers who chose Fascism than in those who chose Communism.

The other reasons which induced writers to commit themselves to the ideology of Mussolini and Hitler should appear in the course of this book—there was opportunism in the countries where Fascism triumphed; a desire, in the liberal democracies, to provoke popular opinion, to emphasise the individuality of the artist by taking an unpopular political line. There were purely personal motives—caprice, affections, perversions. There was chance—the chance by which one man might witness the atrocities committed by the Fascists, while another might see those committed by the Communists. There were, in short, a hundred reasons : and there was no one rule that regulated them any more than there is any one rule by which we can judge them.

---

[1]André Gide-Roger Martin du Gard, *Correspondance 1915-1934*, Paris, 1968, p. 731.

ITALY

Section One

The Great War, welcomed by so many with enthusiasm, was followed by a widespread conviction that it had inaugurated a new era. It is therefore curious to establish how few problems it actually solved and how few were the innovations to which it led. Rather than being the cause or the beginning of a crisis, it appears more as one of innumerable stages in an historical movement to which it is hard to give a starting point and impossible to foresee an end. The Great War acted as a catalyst for some of the elements which were to form the movement known as Fascism, but these elements, the intellectual reaction, the political discontent, the social transformation, had emerged more or less clearly by the end of the first decade of this century.

In Italy the most extreme form of this intellectual reaction was Futurism, a movement limited both in originality and constructive capacity, but nevertheless influential. Its instigator, Filippo Tommaso Marinetti, who was born in Alexandria in 1876 and had studied in Egypt and France, had at his disposal a certain wit and a conspicuous amount of money. Charming, obstreperous and exhibitionistic, he travelled from one capital city to another, scandalising and provoking his contemporaries. It was in a Milanese flat of sybaritic aspect that, together with three painters, Carlo Carrà, Umberto Boccioni and Luigi Russolo, he drew up the Futurist Manifesto in February 1909, exhorting the young to " sing the love of danger, the habit of energy and boldness." "Literature," the Futurists believed, "has hitherto celebrated contemplative immobility, rapture and slumber. We want to exalt aggressive motion, feverish insomnia . . . We affirm that the magnificence of the world has been enriched by a new beauty: the beauty of speed. A racing car, its bonnet decked with great tubes like serpents with explosive breath . . . a roaring motor car which seems to run on machine gun fire, are more beautiful than the Victory of Samothrace." The

3

Futurists' intention, the manifesto proclaimed, was to destroy "museums, libraries, academies of every type" for "we, young and strong Futurists, wish to have nothing to do with the past."[1]

Marinetti's assertion that art could "only be violence, cruelty and injustice", his contempt for every form of cultural heritage, his view of war and destruction as satisfactory aesthetic experiences, owed no small debt to Nietzsche, to the nineteenth-century anarchists, even to Alfred Jarry, and his particular interpretation of currents of thought which were gaining popularity throughout Europe, had an undeniable fascination for an entire generation of artists who were attempting to divest themselves of the musty clothes of the nineteenth century and to skip from the festering Belle Epoque into a world of polished and glittering machinery—a world that was new, clean and fresh. In a comfortable and cosmopolitan society Marinetti offered the ingredients for the explosives which would destroy it: the cult of violence, the cult of war, "the sole hygiene of the world", the cult, finally, of aggressive nationalism, and it is this last aspect of Marinetti's thought which must be examined in the context of "modern" Italy.

The whole Italian intelligentsia was tormented by the dissatisfaction and contradictory ambitions which so frequently undermine the members of a new nation. Italy had been united in 1870. What, the Italians asked themselves, was her rôle now to be? As the Neapolitan philosopher, Benedetto Croce, wrote, Italy's "mission . . . usually remained undetermined". "For some it was the duty of a land which had been among the oppressed to encourage and accomplish the liberation of all oppressed peoples of the world; for others it was the duty of a country which had broken the temporal power of the Church to free the world from its spiritual yoke and create a new, more human religion. Still others wanted to found a 'third Rome', which was to emulate in world eminence and surpass in the quality of its thoughts and works, ancient Rome and Christian Rome."[2]

Until 1870 Italian Nationalists had one principal aim—the country's unity, but after this had been achieved, their ambitions became more aggressive and the organisations which they formed increasingly popular. On the one hand there were the Irredentists, the men who believed that Italian unity would only be complete

[1]*Le Figaro,* February 20, 1909.
[2]B. Croce, *Storia d'Italia dal 1871 al 1915,* Bari, 1967, p. 2.

after Trieste and the Trentino (and in some cases Istria, Fiume and Gorizia) had been wrested from Austrian rule. The largest Irredentist organisation, the Dante Alighieri society, doubled its membership from 1905 to the outbreak of the Great War; Ettore Tolomei, the geographer, elaborated theories of the *italianità* of the south Tyrol; scientists endeavoured to put convincing cases in favour of Italy's "natural" frontiers which covered areas with minute Italian-speaking minorities. Then there were the Nationalists whose ambitions went far beyond Venezia Giulia. They wanted Italy to be treated as an equal by France, Germany and Great Britain, and to have an empire of her own. For the empire they looked to Africa: but here it was evident that Italy's territorial demands depended on the whims of the larger powers. She had hoped for Tunisia, but by the Treaty of the Bardo in 1881, Tunisia went to the French. All Italy had managed to obtain was Eritrea, a vulnerable strip of land along the Red Sea, and even here hopes of large scale settlement had to be renounced when, in 1896, the Italian garrison was defeated by the Emperor's forces at Adowa, in the Ethiopian province of Tigré.

The defeat at Adowa was decisive in arousing the patriotism of Enrico Corradini, one of the leading representatives of the younger Nationalists, his subsequent visits to the communities of Italian emigrants in Tunisia, South America and the United States convincing him of the importance of Italian colonialism. The emigrants, he felt, were exploited: everywhere they were put to build roads and railways and to drain marshlands, but to the advantage of foreigners. Italy was being sapped of her manpower. African colonies alone would solve this problem, and give the Italians an imperialistic spirit instead of the subservience which they developed in the slavery of alien countries. Italy, Corradini claimed, was a proletarian nation, exploited by the world plutocracies. She must assert herself, and the only means of doing so was to fight a war. In 1903 Corradini founded the first Nationalist review, *Il Regno*, with the intent "to stir the Italian bourgeoisie, 'decadent but not irremediably decadent', from its torpor; to mould an élite that would create wealth, cultivate self-discipline and aspire to power and conquest."[1] The Nationalist Association was formed in

---

[1]Christopher Seton-Watson, *Italy from Liberalism to Fascism 1870-1925*, Methuen & Co., 1967, p. 351.

1911; on the anniversary of Adowa, Corradini started another paper, *L'Idea Nazionale;* and two years later the Nationalists became a political party which managed to send six deputies to parliament.

As a party the Nationalists never had a mass appeal, but they had numerous admirers among the intellectuals, most of Italy's leading writers contributing, at one point, to *L'Idea Nazionale*. In Corradini's paper the cry for African colonies combined not only with Irredentism, but also with the determination to snatch the Dalmatian coast from Austro-Hungary—a claim which had little justification. In the Trentino the Italians formed ninety-seven per cent of the population, in Trieste sixty-two per cent, but in Dalmatia they barely formed three per cent. Nationalist demands were based on historical nostalgia, on the traditions of Venice and ancient Rome, and were encouraged in their romantic irrationalism by the publication in 1908 of *La Nave,* a play by a man whose influence as a writer was formidable, Gabriele d'Annunzio.[1]

What so many Italians found in the writings of d'Annunzio, what Marinetti and his followers yearned for and failed to find in contemporary Italy, was heroism. Although artful compromise had been one of the main weapons of the great statesman, Camillo Benso di Cavour, the process known as *trasformismo,* compromise with parties of the left and the right in order to obtain a political majority, was generally regarded as the heritage of the comparatively left-wing Prime Minister, Agostino Depretis. With unscrupulous compromise went corruption. Under Giovanni Giolitti, the leading political figure in Italy from 1890 to 1915, votes were bought and electors tricked: everything was "rigged". "The truth is that under a democratic banner we have imperceptibly arrived at a dictatorial régime," complained an independent Socialist, Orazio Raimondo, in 1913. "The Honourable Giolitti has four times conducted elections, in 1892, 1904, 1909 and 1913. Moreover, in his long parliamentary career he has nominated practically all the senators, practically all the councillors of state, all the prefects and all the high officials in our administrative, judicial, political and military hierarchy. With this formidable power of his he has drawn parties together by means of reforms, and individuals together by means of personal attentions. Now, Honourable Giolitti, when

---

[1]See *infra,* p. 25.

parties forget their programmes, when those who arrive at the threshold of the chamber discard the rags of their political convictions at the door, it is necessary to create a majority by other means . . . with trickery and corruption. In this way parliamentary institutions are annulled, parties are annihilated, and *trasformismo* is achieved."[1]

Giolitti was an able politician, wily and cautious, aware of the defects of his countrymen and ready to exploit them. Although he failed to satisfy the aspirations of the intellectuals with his home policy and his parliamentary manoeuvres, it was he who declared war on Turkey at the end of September 1911 and enabled the Italians to conquer the colony of Libya. Despite the ill organisation of the campaign Marinetti's comment in 1912 reflected a certain current of nationalist opinion. "We are proud to feel that the warlike fervour which inspires the whole country equals our own," he wrote, after joining the Italian forces in Tripoli as a reporter, "and we invite the Italian government, which has finally become Futurist, to magnify all the nation's ambitions, to despise stupid accusations of piracy, and to proclaim the birth of Panitalianism."[2]

The resentment of parliamentarianism was accompanied, in the world of ideas, by what, for want of a better term, I shall call "the revolt against positivism". This phenomenon was common, to a greater or lesser extent, to most countries in western Europe, but, in the north of Italy, positivism survived longer than elsewhere, under the influence of Roberto Ardigò, a former priest who lectured at the University of Padua and did not die until 1920, "his ideas twenty years out of date".[3] He was, Benedetto Croce tells us, "a philosopher of 'facts'. Few had the courage to oppose his ideas and those who did merely denied, or rather, pointed out, certain childish philosophical blunders and wild inaccuracies, but proved unable to construct or to reconstruct. The name 'philosopher', the word 'philosophy', which had been revered for centuries for the idea which they conveyed of serenity and moral superiority, fell into discredit : they were either taken as signs of insanity or made the object of jokes and mockery. Hardly anyone

---

[1] Quoted in C. Seton-Watson, *op. cit.*, p. 390.

[2] Quoted in James Joll, *Intellectuals in Politics*, Weidenfeld & Nicolson, 1960, p. 151.

[3] Eugenio Garin, *Cronache di filosofia italiana 1900-1943*, I, Bari, 1966, p. 1933.

dared say that he was undertaking philosophical research or performing philosophical meditations, while everyone prided himself
on studying 'science' and behaving like a 'scientist'."[1] The revival
of idealism started in the south. The Hegelian tradition had
been sustained in Naples by Bertrando Spaventa and Francesco
De Sanctis, and when, in the 1890s, the doctrine of Herbert
Spencer was replaced in popularity by that of Karl Marx, two
younger philosophers came to the fore and established their
reputation with critiques of historical materialism—Benedetto Croce
(Spaventa's nephew) and the Sicilian Giovanni Gentile. In 1902
they founded a review, *La Critica,* due to remain, even after Gentile
had left it, the most distinguished expression of Italian philosophy
in the first forty years of the twentieth century.

Despite the influence of neo-idealism, however, the thought of
Nietzsche and William James had a greater and more spontaneous
appeal for a quantity of intellectuals lacking the philosophical training necessary to understand the complexities of Croce. The Nietzschean concept of a powerful élite was eagerly assimilated by the
readers of d'Annunzio, while James' pragmatism was a doctrine
favoured by the contributors to the Tuscan review *Leonardo* and the
youthful editors of *La Voce,* Giovanni Papini and Giuseppe Prezzolini. In its most unimaginative form positivism had been a strictly
rational movement, but, in the enticing writings of Nietzsche, man
was recognised as an irrational creature dominated by a lust for
power. Among Nietzsche's followers irrationalism and violence became a cult in themselves, and the pragmatists completed the desire
for self-assertion with their insistence on the importance of action.
"Intellectualism", they believed, was something of the past. It was
now time to "act". The world had reached a point of unprecedented
technical development : what it required were engineers and technicians who could impose themselves on it, rather than intellectuals.

The Futurists' call for movement, for speed, for action, and,
indeed, for war, were therefore heard with relish; Marinetti's determination to burn all gondolas and "fill the stinking little canals" of
Venice "with the ruins of crumbling, leprous palaces"[2] was regarded
with approval. It all represented a break with the past, an expedition into a new and exciting future. The Italy that Marinetti longed

---

[1]B. Croce, *op. cit.,* p. 124.
[2]F. T. Marinetti, *Contro Venezia passatista* in *Teoria e invenzione
futurista,* Milano, 1968, p. 30.

for was an heroic technocracy where "the energy of distant winds and rebellious seas, transformed into millions of kilowatts by the genius of man, would be distributed everywhere . . . regulated by keyboards vibrating under the fingers of the technicians"[1], who would practice "the religion of extrinsic Will and daily Heroism."

The failure of the Italian left wing in 1922 was due both to the refusal of the various parties to unite against Fascism, and to the Socialists' inability to agree on any one policy. At the time observers were surprised, and yet the Italian left had split at an early stage. "Middle class intellectual leadership," as Christopher Seton-Watson wrote of the Italian Socialists, "Latin ebullience and the restricted size of the industrial proletariat made the party peculiarly liable to heresies and deviations."[2] By 1903, just over ten years after its foundation, the Italian Socialist Party was torn between the "reformists" and the "revolutionaries". The reformists, philanthropic intellectuals like Filippo Turati and Leonida Bissolati, represented Socialism in its most respectable form. They were prepared to compromise with the liberal government and accept the monarchy: indeed, they did not aim at the immediate overthrow of the Italian régime, but wanted to steer it towards greater democracy. Thus, Turati imagined, the proletariat would one day find itself in power—by a gradual and bloodless process of evolution. To the left of Turati stood Enrico Ferri, who had replaced Bissolati as editor of the party paper, *Avanti!*, in May 1903. He was not prepared to accept Turati's compromises with Giolitti and, with his exceptional gifts as an orator, managed to arouse his audiences against reformism. But even Ferri did little more than vociferate. By far the most active and extreme elements of left-wing Socialism were the syndicalists.

Syndicalist ideology was derived primarily from the writings of a French engineer, Georges Sorel, an individual whose thought contained a number of elements which could be reconciled, without too much difficulty, with the theories of both Nationalists and Futurists, and whose influence on the subsequent formation of Fascist doctrine was as decisive as that of any Italian. Sorel believed that the men who participated in the social movements of which

---

[1] F. T. Marinetti, *La guerra elettrica* in *op. cit.*, p. 274.
[2] C. Seton-Watson, *op. cit.*, p. 160.

C

history is composed did so under the guidance of "myths". These were "not descriptions of things, but the expression of the will," they were "systems of images" which corresponded to the basic reality of an ideology. Now Sorel himself, it is important to recall, was a Marxist—an orthodox Marxist by contemporary unorthodox standards, an unorthodox Marxist by subsequent orthodox standards—and the myth which he proposed should be adopted by the revolutionary syndicalists was "the general strike". This, he considered, was the best expression of Marxist doctrine, for in it was contained the idea of the class struggle, of the irremediable division of the population into two hostile camps—the employers and the employed. And yet Sorel's theory had further implications. One of them was the benefits of violence. Writing as a Marxist Sorel believed that the proletariat could only be forced to resort to violence and to summon up the heroism of which it was capable by the presence of an equally ruthless, violent and heroic class of capitalists. Indeed, Sorel deplored the lack of heroism in modern society. It grieved him to see his own country debilitated by humanitarian principles. Violence alone, he felt, would save France —either a "great foreign war which could revive our energy and would in all events, allow those men with a will to govern to rise to power"[1] or proletarian violence which would brace the bourgeoisie—and Sorel was later prepared to admit that the reinvigoration of the capitalists would be much to the advantage of the nation.

To start with the Italian syndicalists used the most left-wing of Sorel's ideas: parliamentary democracy was to be overthrown by means of a general strike, and a proletarian state was then to be formed and run by trade unions. For the syndicalists Costantino Lazzari and Arturo Labriola, the first and most important part of their plan was "action". In theory they were to train a proletarian élite for the revolution by organising a series of strikes, but in practice they only succeeded in organising strikes, and, however often they struck, the unions never managed to triumph over the employers and landlords. Their funds merely diminished and the workers wearied. The peak of syndicalist activity was realised in 1907 and 1908, and the reformists watched with relief their failure to accomplish the revolutionary strike of which

---

[1]G. Sorel, *Réflexions sur la violence,* Paris, 1912, p. 180.

they had boasted. Then, for two years, from 1908 to 1910, there was a lull. Ferri had antagonised the syndicalists by his attempts to mediate with Turati, and even Labriola started moving towards reformism. At the Milan party congress in October 1910, however, Lazzari ranted once more against Turati's men, and was now supported in his attacks on parliament and democracy by a young Socialist from Romagna, Benito Mussolini.

The son of an anarchist blacksmith, Mussolini was by temperament violent and rebellious. Behind him lay a somewhat louche past. Contemptuous of authority, he had never hesitated to oppose the established order, whether it was in Switzerland, where he had worked for two years as a journalist, or in Trento, where he had been secretary of the Chamber of Labour. In 1911, when the syndicalists declared a general strike in protest against the invasion of Libya, Mussolini distinguished himself together with Pietro Nenni by encouraging a crowd to destroy tramlines and block the troop trains on their way south. Mussolini's rise in the Socialist Party coincided with a sudden strengthening of the revolutionary left wing. In July 1912, despite Turati's attempts to preserve party unity, Bissolati, Bonomi and Cabrini, who had congratulated the King on having escaped assassination by the anarchist D'Alba in March, were expelled. The days of compromise were over. The Socialists now insisted on the importance of pursuing the class struggle. They pronounced themselves against the monarchy and refused any form of participation in the government. Lazzari became party secretary; Mussolini was elected to the executive, and, in December, was appointed editor of *Avanti!* Within a year he was aiming at the leadership of the Italian proletariat. He wanted to head a revolutionary movement, but his "revolutionarism . . . had little to do with Socialism."[1] "He was, and appeared to want to remain, plebeian," wrote Pietro Nenni. "But he had no love for the plebs. He did not see the workers he addressed as brothers, but as a force which he could use to overthrow the world."[2] In short Mussolini was hampered by few principles : what he wanted was power and the means by which he obtained it were indifferent to him.

On June 28, 1914, the Archduke Ferdinand of Austria was

---

[1]Renzo De Felice, *Mussolini il rivoluzionario* 1883-1920, Torino, 1965, p. 216.
[2]Quoted *ibid.* p. 219.

assassinated in Sarajevo. A month later Austria-Hungary declared war on Serbia and within a week Russia, Germany, France, Belgium and England were also at war. Italy's position was equivocal. She was bound to Austria and Germany by the Triple Alliance, which had been renewed in 1912, but for some time Italian politicians had been eager to improve relations with France and England. Fighting, however, was another matter. Aware of the country's lack of military preparation, the liberal followers of Giolitti cautiously avoided commitment.

To start with only a few conservatives favoured intervention—and that on the side of their allies, Austria and Germany. After a few weeks, however, other factors came into play. The Italian intelligentsia tended to regard France as their natural ally and German aggression increased their friendship for her. For the Irredentists the possibility of war against Austria came to mean that Italy could at last conquer Trieste, Trento and the South Tyrol, while the Nationalists soon believed that Italian participation was essential if Italy was to be taken seriously by the other powers. Finally, a convincing case was put for left-wing interventionism by the new hero of revolutionary syndicalism, Filippo Corridoni. Transposing Sorel's concept of class from social to national values, Corridoni claimed that it was the Italian nation, an oppressed, proletarian nation, rather than a certain class, which was to establish itself by fighting against the German and Austro-Hungarian "plutocracies": the experience of war was to be a catalyst for class rivalries, invigorate the country, and provide the proletariat with a national consciousness.

Like his fellow Socialists Mussolini had at first opposed intervention. In July he had insisted on neutrality. "Either the government must accept this necessity [of neutrality] or the proletariat will force it to do so. The moment for assuming responsibility has arrived. Will the Italian proletariat let itself be led to the slaughter once more? We do not think so. But we must move: we must act before it is too late. We must mobilise our forces. Let one cry arise from our political clubs, our economic organisations, the communes and provinces where our Party has its representatives, let one cry arise from the proletarian masses and echo in every street and square in Italy: 'Down with war!' "[1] The reasons for Mussolini's

---

[1] Quoted in R. De Felice, *op. cit.* p. 222.

decision to support the war and his subsequent expulsion from the Socialist Party were multiple. Although he had never really been an internationalist—his stay in Trento in 1909 had left him with a distinct strain of Irredentism—he had opposed the Libyan campaign and, to start with, the Great War, in accordance with the policy of the Second International. He had put his faith in the solidarity of the world proletariat. In August, 1914, however, the German Social Democrats, together with the rest of the German parliament, voted for war credits; the Belgian Socialist, Vandervelde, joined a wartime coalition government; in France Gustave Hervé, the syndicalist who had but shortly before recommended a general strike as a protest against mobilisation, volunteered as a private. "In the name of the syndicalist organisation," said Léon Jouhaux, the head of the C.G.T., "in the name of all the workers who have joined their regiments and those, including myself, who go tomorrow, I declare that we go to the field of battle willingly to repel the aggressor."[1]

As the German and French workers marched off to the trenches the illusion of proletarian solidarity dissolved, and patriotism, rather than internationalism, appeared to be the driving force behind the Socialist parties of Europe. The Italians, alone, insisted on neutrality. In these circumstances Mussolini, who had the greatest admiration for Corridoni both as a man and a thinker, found the new ideology of the revolutionary syndicalists appealing: even if international proletarian solidarity was dead, it was Italy's duty, as a proletarian nation, to assist France, Belgium and Serbia, against the "plutocratic" aggressor.

In all of Mussolini's decisions, personal ambition must be taken into account. His aim was to lead a revolutionary movement, and hitherto he had had to accept as his ideology a traditional form of Socialism. In the theories of the syndicalists, however, he found a far more original revolutionary policy. According to his biographer De Felice he "was under the illusion . . . that the revolutionary masses would follow him. He thought that the revolutionary conjunction for which he had searched and waited so long, would be provided by war—not by opposition to the war, as his fellow Socialists thought, but by the 'revolutionary war'."[2] In this he was mistaken.

---

[1] Quoted in Barbara W. Tuchman, *The Proud Tower*, Hamish Hamilton, 1966, p. 462.
[2] R. De Felice, *op. cit.*, p. 182.

He was not followed by the masses, and certainly not by the proletariat : throughout the war the Italian industrial workers continued
to abide by the pacifism of the Italian Socialists. On his expulsion
from the party in November Mussolini found himself in a small
but vociferous minority—the interventionist left. He received a
telegram from Prezzolini, to whose *Voce* he had contributed a
couple of articles in 1910: "The Socialist Party expels you: Italy
welcomes you."[1] Gaetano Salvemini, another renegade Socialist,
wrote to congratulate him, and, on November 15, with the financial
support of Filippo Nardi, the editor of the Bolognese paper *Il Resto
del Carlino,* Mussolini launched his own daily paper, *Il Popolo
d'Italia.*

The influential group of men campaigning for Italian entry
into the war on the side of France was composed largely of
intellectuals—d'Annunzio, Marinetti, Prezzolini, Salvemini, syndicalists, Nationalists and Futurists—and, on March 31, 1915,
Mussolini first campaigned publicly with Marinetti in Milan. That
April they were both arrested for organising a demonstration in
Rome, and the Futurists, who had scorned Mussolini ever since he
had opposed the invasion of Libya, now welcomed him as a man of
suitably "Futurist" persuasion.

As mounting pressure was exerted on the Italian government by
the interventionists at home and by the belligerent powers abroad,
Giolitti's successor, Antonio Salandra[2] came to believe that there
was no alternative for Italy but to fight. On April 26, 1915, there-
fore, the Foreign Minister, Sidney Sonnino, signed the Treaty of
London which committed Italy to enter the war with France,
England and Russia, and stipulated certain territorial concessions
in the event of an Allied victory—the Brenner frontier, Istria,
Valona and its hinterland, Central Dalmatia and its islands. On
May 24, Italy went to war against Austria.

It was inevitable that the enthusiasm of the Italian interventionists should soon be dampened by the reality of trench warfare.

---

[1] R. De Felice, *op. cit.,* p. 283.
[2] Salandra replaced Giolitti as Prime Minister in March, 1914.
With the exception of the war years, from 1915 to 1918, Giolitti retained
a sufficient quantity of supporters and enough prestige to be the most
influential figure in Italian politics even when he was out of power.
Italian political life was permanently haunted by the expectation that
Giolitti would return "a few months later".

They had hoped for a war which would unite the nation, but it rapidly appeared that they were curiously isolated from the rest of the army. There was strong prejudice against them. The conservative High Command regarded these impulsive (and often left-wing) amateurs with the utmost suspicion, forbidding any kind of propaganda and refusing to allow the formation of brigades of volunteers. The other troops detested them, in the belief that it was owing to them that they had been torn from their homes to fight.[1]

The interventionists had looked forward to a brief and colourful experience, but the Great War was no such thing. It dragged on, in the squalor of the trenches. Discipline was enforced by General Cadorna, the Commander-in-Chief, with brutality. Decimation was frequent. The only forms of entertainment accorded the troops were brothels and wine, and at one point even singing was forbidden, "out of respect for the dead".[2] Finally, not only were Italy's military successes minimal, but the inhabitants of Venezia Giulia and other territory wrested from Austria, for whose liberation Irredentists and Nationalists believed they were fighting, made it plain that they preferred Austrian rule to Italian.

Despite the initial antagonism felt by the reluctant conscripts for the interventionists, a somewhat negative type of solidarity gradually developed among the servicemen. Like every country that fought in the Great War, Italy found herself divided between the men in the trenches and the men behind the lines, between the soldiers and the civilians, who had no idea of the conditions on the front and, more often than not, showed no interest in them. One thing, however, was found particularly galling by the Italian soldiery: the exemption of the vast majority of the industrial proletariat from military service. By a law of April 29, 1915, all men who had been working for at least one month in any factory providing material for the army or navy, were exempted from fighting. This covered the metal workers in addition to workers producing textiles, foodstuffs and chemicals. Of those who were called up,

[1]Shortly after Corridoni had been killed, Mussolini was accosted in the trenches by a soldier: "I've a good piece of news for you: they've killed Corridoni. That's what he deserves and I'm glad about it. I wish all the interventionists would end up like that!" (R. De Felice, *op. cit.*, p. 323.)

[2]For the conditions in the Italian Army, see Piero Melograni, *Storia politica della grande guerra 1915-1918*, Bari, 1969.

few were actually sent to the front: they were mainly kept behind the lines, where they repaired weapons, motor vehicles, and other mechanical or electrical equipment.

Even if their physical safety was guaranteed, the workers were just as dissatisfied with their fate as the soldiers. In the factories military discipline was enforced; compulsory arbitration was introduced; and they found themselves having to work up to sixteen hours a day while real wages sank twenty-seven per cent below their level in 1913. The losses suffered by the Italian navy produced a shortage of vital supplies, so their families often went without bread, and their opposition to the war was not unnaturally whole-hearted.

The official policy of the Italian Socialists was announced by Lazzari in 1915: *non aderire nè sabotare,* neither support nor sabotage. As usual Turati was less intransigent. He was prepared to approve some of the Allied war aims, and, on June 16, 1918, during the battle of the Piave, appeared still readier to compromise with the government. To the applause of his fellow deputies he said that the Socialists shared "the trepidation, hopes and wishes" of all the other parties.[1] But Turati was in a minority. Most of the Socialists encouraged the discontented workers in their hostility to the war, and in March 1917 the Russian Revolution raised the hopes of the extremists. In the spring and summer a series of riots, frequently led by the womenfolk, took place all over northern Italy. Although they were directed primarily against the rising cost of living and the bread shortage, Socialist agitators managed to turn them into anti-war demonstrations, and, that August, the riots reached a point of such violence in Turin that the government called in troops who had no scruples about firing on the mob.

The main burden of the war fell upon the peasantry and the lower middle classes—those, in other words, who had to fight. The peasants had the greatest difficulty in obtaining temporary exemption to bring in their harvests: it was their wives who had to do most of the work and indeed, thanks to them, agricultural production sunk barely ten per cent below the pre-war norm. Besides, life in the country was even harder than in the towns: grain and cattle were constantly being requisitioned for the army; agricultural wages fell further than industrial wages; and the inflation which accompanied the war hit the small landowners and householders,

---

[1]P. Melograni, *op. cit.,* p. 538.

the men at the front who had left their families with what little money they had managed to put aside.

The resentment which the soldiery felt for all the *imboscati*[1] reached its climax with the Italian defeat at Caporetto in October 1917. The principal causes of the rout were, of course, military. For the first time in the war German troops fought on the Italian front and employed the new tactics which were to be so successful when used against the French and the British in the spring of 1918. The Italian General Staff, on the other hand, proved outrageously incompetent, ignoring information from the enemy lines and taking inadequate measures to ensure communications. It was also true, however, that Italian morale was low, and to this the interventionists attributed the defeat. Demoralisation, they claimed, was the fault of the Socialists and the pacifists. It was the fault of the Vatican, for Pope Benedict XV, who had succeeded Pius X in September 1914, had always urged neutrality and described the war as a "useless slaughter", *inutile strage*. In short Caporetto was the fault of all who were not entirely in favour of the war. "Everyone agrees on this point," wrote the Futurist painter Ardengo Soffici. "The main reasons for Caporetto are : the moral depression caused in the country and consequently among the soldiers by the defeatist propaganda of the Socialists, Giolitti's followers and the priests; the bestial sluggishness of the government which tolerated, provoked and almost encouraged that propaganda; the inadequate training and the parade-ground dogmatism of certain leaders."[2] After Caporetto the Italian attitude started to alter. Benedetto Croce wrote at the time that "the war, which has so far been an international affair and could only partially be considered ours, has now really become a war of our own."[3] Foreign troops were on Italian soil and now, for the first time, the Italians believed that they were fighting a defensive battle. While the Italian soldiers felt a greater incentive to fight, the High Command saw the necessity of improving conditions and raising morale. To the relief of the Government Cadorna was replaced by General Diaz, who proved more humane; permission was accorded the interventionist intellectuals to launch a propaganda campaign amongst the troops;

---

[1]*Imboscato* means, literally, someone who lies in ambush. But during the Great War it came to mean a "shirker", a man who evaded active military service.

[2]A. Soffici, *Battaglia fra due vittorie*, Firenze, 1923, p. 3.

[3]B. Croce, *Pagine sulla guerra*, Bari, 1966, p. 233.

rations were increased; soldiers were issued with free life insurance policies; and those exempt from military service were obliged to pay a tax. Finally, government promises to redistribute land amongst the servicemen became one of the principal causes of the conviction that the war would be followed by utopia.

Filippo Corridoni had been killed in the first year of combat. According to his followers, however, Caporetto was the signal for the defeated soldiery to unite and plan a seizure of power for their return from the trenches. One of the exponents of this theory was a young writer called Curt Erich Suckert. The son of a Saxon dyer, he had run away from his father's house in Prato at the age of sixteen to fight with the Italian volunteers in France, and returned to Italy a year later to serve as a private in the Brigata Alpi. Shortly before Caporetto (at which he was not present), he became an officer, ending the war on the French front, where he was wounded at the battle of Bligny. In 1925, when his enemies accused him of being a Polish Jew, he changed his name to Curzio Malaparte.

In Malaparte's eyes what had previously been a divergence of ideas between pacifists and interventionists became a "class war" after Caporetto. "The phenomenon of Caporetto" was "an essentially social phenomenon", "a revolution", "the revolt of a class (the infantry), of a mentality, of a state of mind, against another mentality, another state of mind".[1] "I was certain," he wrote, "of an imminent national revolution in Italy, brought about by the real warriors, that is, by the infantrymen: a revolution, in other words, of the peasants ... An anti-proletarian, anti-bourgeois revolution ... a reconciliation of the rural, georgic peasant spirit with the heroism of noble blood; an anti-political return of the Vendée, a new natural and terrestrial spirit of the Counter-Reformation. The most Christian soldiers returned from the trenches . . . would unite around the *patres familias* as they had been united around their officers in war . . ."[2]

Though Mussolini took a more sober and practical view of the situation, for him, too, Caporetto was a turning point. Until October 1917 he had believed in "left-wing interventionism". Two years

[1] C. Malaparte, *La Rivolta dei Santi maledetti in L'Europa vivente e altri saggi politici,* Firenze, 1961, p. 93.
[2] *Ibid.,* pp. 187-188.

of war, however, had proved to him the extent to which the interventionists were not only disliked, but were actually cut off from the mass of the soldiery. Caporetto established a form of solidarity and it was at that moment that Mussolini realised what invaluable political material could be provided by the ex-servicemen in general. "Until Caporetto Mussolini had behaved ... like an agitator, a propagandist of left-wing interventionism, but after the defeat, when he understood the important psychological and political transformation to which this episode had led, he became, above all, a politician."[1] By deciding to use the ex-servicemen rather than the left-wing interventionists as his vehicle for seizing power he found himself obliged to satisfy far more conflicting, in many cases far more conservative, aspirations—and this, as we shall see, was to force him further and further to the right. He had no definite plan of action. Indeed, when the war ended he had no precise idea of how to devise a programme which would captivate the ex-servicemen. All he knew was, that if he was to rise to power, they were the men to enable him to do so. It was in this frame of mind, therefore, that he took his first ideas from those radical founders of ex-servicemen's organisations, the Futurists.

True to their bellicose principles nearly all the Futurists had distinguished themselves in the war. The architect Sant' Elia was killed, and Luigi Russolo wounded. Marinetti, who had joined the Alpini, was also wounded and was decorated for gallantry. Early in 1918 he started to formulate a political programme for the revolutionary state which was to emerge after the cessation of hostilities, the Manifesto of the *Partito Politico Futurista*. "We must carry our war to total victory," he announced in February, "that is, to the partitioning of the Austro-Hungarian empire and the security of our natural borders on land and sea, without which we cannot have our hands free to clear, clean, renovate and enlarge Italy."[2] Uncompromisingly opposed to monarchy, he advocated, instead, a "technical government of thirty or forty competent young directors with no parliament, to be elected by the whole nation through the trade unions." There was to be nationalisation of mines and water, confiscation of uncultivated or ill-cultivated lands and of two-thirds of any extra profits made during the war, heavy death duties and a

---

[1] R. De Felice, *op. cit.,* p. 393.
[2] F. T. Marinetti, *Democrazia futurista, dinamismo politico,* Milano, 1919, p. 18.

system of taxation which would enable the government to purchase and redistribute land among the ex-servicemen. Conscription was to be gradually abolished and a small volunteer army created for use in the colonies. Workers were to have the right to strike and organise public meetings. Freedom of the press was stipulated, as was education for all. The Manifesto demanded the eight-hour working day, equal salaries for men and women, collective bargaining, social assistance, "the gradual abolition of marriage through very easy divorce, the vote for women and their participation in national activity."

Marinetti also recommended the abolition of the police and prisons, for which he had developed an aversion since his arrests in 1914 and 1915. "Prisons," he wrote, "are ghastly traps which pre-suppose the most savage Cat-order directed against extremely agree-able and ingenuous Rat-temperaments."[1] If more time were devoted to physical training than to the study of Latin and Greek, every man, according to Marinetti, would be able to defend himself against potential criminals. And finally, he urged "the most intran-sigent anti-clericalism to liberate Italy from churches, priests, friars, nuns, candles and bells."[2] But despite the philanthropic measures contained in the Futurist programme, Marinetti's ideal state was not egalitarian. Marinetti considered himself a superior being, and egalitarianism implied mediocrity. "It is only with violence that we can restore the idea of justice . . . that hygienic, healthy idea which consists in the right of the bravest, of the most disinterested: only then can we restore heroism."[3]

The Great War terminated, for the Italians, on November 4, 1918, and less than a week earlier they had compensated, to some extent, for the defeat of Caporetto by routing the demoralised Austrian forces at Vittorio Veneto. In December the Futurists revived the *Fasci*, as the interventionist groups had called themselves in 1914 and 1915:[4] for what had

---

[1]*Ibid.*, p. 237.
[2]*Ibid.*, p. 21.
[3]*Ibid.*, p. 224.
[4]The interventionists assembled in groups called the *Fasci di Azione Rivoluzionaria*. *Fascio*, meaning "group" or "association" (literary "bundle"), had long been used by the Italian left. In 1872 Garibaldi had founded a *Fascio Operaio* in Bologna, and in 1891 the extreme left-wing Sicilian leader, Giuseppe De Felice Giuffrida, had founded a *Fascio dei Lavoratori* in Catania.

now become ex-servicemen's associations, they managed to recruit veterans from the Italian shock troops, the black-shirted *Arditi,* and some four months later, on March 23, 1919, Mussolini continued their initiative by founding his own *Fasci di Combattimento* in Piazza San Sepolcro in Milan. His fellow-founders included Marinetti and the poet Giuseppe Ungaretti, while his political programme was based entirely on that of the Futurists. He demanded the abolition of the monarchy and the Senate, confiscation of war profits and all the goods belonging to the Church, redistribution of the land to the peasants. He wished to abolish all titles and impose a capital levy. He wanted to do away with the political police and conscription, to prevent speculation on the stock exchange, and bring about complete individual liberty—freedom of the press, freedom of conscience, freedom of expression in every form. He urged a share in factory management for the workers, the introduction of the eight-hour working day and prohibition of work to anyone under sixteen. In short, his programme had everything to appeal to idealistic ex-servicemen but little that greater realists could take seriously. In the autumn of 1919 Marinetti persuaded Arturo Toscanini to stand as Fascist candidate in the national elections, but neither Toscanini nor any of the other nineteen candidates were elected.

Within a few months of the celebration of victory Italy was hit by the worst crisis since unification. The war had totally disrupted Italian economy. The lira was devalued; inflation was rampant; and the budget deficit had risen to huge figures. As the cost of living ascended the first riots broke out in Emilia, in June 1919. In many towns local citizens' committees assumed control of distribution and announced fifty per cent price reductions. Shops were sacked and shopkeepers, suspected of hoarding, assaulted. In the south, first in Lazio and then in Sicily, peasants, determined to seize the property they had been promised by the government after Caporetto, occupied land and evicted landowners. In the Po valley, the *braccianti* or day labourers, who had been cruelly exploited before the war, formed themselves into leagues at the instigation of the Socialists and the left wing of the *Partito popolare.*[1] The brutality of their methods was notorious: landowners employing labourers unattached to the leagues were boycotted, had their

---

[1] See *infra,* p. 22.

property burnt and their cattle slaughtered, and the members of the leagues who transgressed union orders were fined and ostracised.

It is impossible to understand the growth and subsequent triumph of Fascism unless one has an idea of the loathing and contempt which developed for the left wing from its first great electoral victories in 1919 to its defeat in 1922. The revolutionary core of the left consisted of three groups: the anarchists led by Enrico Malatesta, and the two factions of Communists, one under Amedeo Bordiga, the other under Antonio Gramsci, who broke away from the Socialists to found the Italian Communist Party in September 1920. Otherwise the left contained two large parties. The *Partito popolare italiano,* the first Catholic party of united Italy, was founded in 1918 by Don Luigi Sturzo with the consent of the Vatican. It was divided between a right-wing faction under Agostino Gemelli, a left-wing under the pacifist trade unionist Guido Miglioli, and the largest, centre group headed by Alcide De Gasperi and Sturzo himself. Their demands focused on fiscal and land reform, social legislation, decentralisation of government and proportional representation.

The Socialists still formed the biggest left-wing party but they too were divided, fatally as it turned out, between the reformists and the "maximalists". After the war Turati wished to continue political action on traditional lines, a policy directly opposed to that of the maximalist leader, Giacinto Menotti Serrati, Mussolini's successor as editor of *Avanti!,* whose declared intention was to overthrow the existing government and establish a dictatorship of the proletariat based on the Soviet model. Not only was this unacceptable to Turati: it was unacceptable to the majority of Italians.

In retrospect the most obvious reason for the failure of the Socialist Party was its lack of any politician of sufficient calibre. But to this must be added the uncertainty caused by the split, the Socialists being unable to decide whether to follow Serrati's programme or Turati's. Officially the Party demanded the dictatorship of the proletariat, for a maximalist executive had been elected at the Party congress in Rome in September 1918. In practice, however, the reformists remained strong enough to prevent the Party from either establishing or taking the steps necessary to accomplish it. "The Party," wrote Pietro Nenni, "did not have a plan. It did not even bother to explain what it meant by dictatorship of the proletariat. In Italy the industrial proletariat is a minority. Did it want the dictatorship of this minority? Certainly not. But then it should have reassured the other classes—the petty bourgeoisie, the bureaucracy, the small land-owners and tradesmen, and the returning soldiers, for their interests were not in contrast to those of the proletariat. The Party never reassured them. It simply professed itself against democracy and parliamentarianism, but never said on what basis it would organise the State. The press could therefore easily accuse the heads of the revolutionary faction of attempting to establish a personal dictatorship, a red terror. This aroused the mistrust and hostility of those intermediate sections of the working classes who can be of decisive political importance."[1]

Ultimately the maximalists were responsible for the refusal to collaborate with the other left-wing parties, and, to some extent, for the attacks on ex-servicemen. Decrying the war on every occasion, they prevented the latter from joining the Socialist Party. Socialist and anarchist fanatics insulted officers in the streets, and tram and engine drivers often refused to work if there was an officer in uniform on board, thereby antagonising the police force, the regular army and large groups of homecoming soldiers. Above all their behaviour lost the Socialists friends who might have been invaluable and earned them enemies who proved formidable.

Throughout the first nine months of 1920 the combined effort of the anarchists, Communists, Socialists and left-wing *popolari* reduced the country to a state of paralysis. Strike followed strike, riot followed riot. Between April 1919 and September 1920 there were 140 clashes with the police and over 320 deaths. Although the lack of co-ordination of these various attacks against the State and the vagueness of the Socialist programme rendered the agitation ineffectual, these same defects made it appear unnecessarily irritating to those "sections of the working classes" excluded from the Socialist Party. The strikes reached a climax in the summer of 1920. In March a strike ordered by the F.I.O.M., the metal-workers' union, which had immobilised the motor-car and engineering industry in Turin, developed into a general strike, affecting the whole city. The issue at stake was the recognition of the workers' factory councils; the pretext, the

---

[1]P. Nenni, *Storia di quattro anni,* Rome, 1946, p. 16.

introduction of summer time in the factories. Owing to the divergences between the various groups of Socialists, trade union leaders and politicians, the strike was called off, with the result that the perturbed industrialists were doubly determined to yield no further to the workers' demands. The talks between the F.I.O.M. and the employers broke down, and again the F.I.O.M. ordered a strike. This time the members of two other unions, the U.S.I. and U.I.L., joined in, and factories were occupied, red guards posted at their gates, in Milan, Turin and Genoa. Soon half a million workers were involved. In accordance with the tactics he had used with the strikers in 1904 Giolitti, who had returned to power in June 1920, did nothing for a week, refusing to turn them out of the factories by force. He saw the flaws in the Socialist Party and realised that the strike would not lead to the proletarian revolution which Gramsci was urging in Turin. He claimed the Socialist leaders were too cautious and, indeed, when the industrialists eventually agreed to a rise in wages and recognition of the factory councils, the trade unionists ordered the peaceful evacuation of the factories.

In the countryside the situation was similar. In October 1919 the Socialist Federation of Land Workers refused to negotiate collective wage agreements with the landowners' association in the province of Bologna, demanding, instead, separate agreements with each landowner. These demands were found unacceptable, and in February 1920 the *braccianti* and *mezzadri* went on strike. By May all the other peasants had joined them. The harvest rotted, and the strike lasted until October 25, when the landowners' association agreed to accept the Federation's conditions. Despite the appearance of victory, however, both the agricultural and industrial strikes turned out to be failures. In theory the workers were in a position to seize power, and it was the official policy of the Socialist Party that once they were in this position they should do so. But the maximalists stated their policy, while the reformists thwarted it. The workers, frustrated and disillusioned, lost faith in their unions, and the General Confederation of Labour lost half its members between the autumn of 1920 and the end of 1921.

The main result of the strikes was to leave the industrialists and the landowners longing for revenge, but the social category which had suffered most from the economic crisis, prolonged and aggravated by left-wing agitation, was again the lower middle class.

Filippo Tommaso Marinetti

Benedetto Croce

Before the war they had experienced a certain security under Giolitti's government, but when the post-war crisis broke out they were virtually defenceless. The proletariat was protected by trade unions and the Socialist Party; the industrial workers had been in a strong position, and in February 1919 metal workers had been accorded the eight-hour working day and a pay rise; the lower middle classes had no unions, and the Socialist Party, acting on maximalist principles, tended to spurn them as members of the bourgeoisie and ex-servicemen. The upper middle classes, on the other hand, the industrialists, financiers and traders who had either made fortunes during the war or had put enough money aside to be relatively sheltered from the inflation, enjoyed privileges to which the lower middle classes could not accede. It was the savings of the small investor, who had generously given money during the war, which now vanished; the new rent control hit the small landlords; shopkeepers had had their premises ransacked and had been the direct victims of the price reductions announced by the Socialist committees; peasant proprietors and tenant farmers had suffered from the tyranny of the red leagues and were frightened by Socialist threats of land nationalisation. These were the men who turned to Fascism in self-defence and in the hope that it would enable them to dominate the new society which had emerged from the war. They believed Fascism to be *their* movement; they believed that through it they would impose *their* form of democracy, *their* form of Socialism. Opposing the upper middle classes, the heinous profiteers, just as much as they did the proletariat which prolonged the crisis at their expense, they were Mussolini's tools in turning Fascism into a mass movement.

There was one man who, more than any other, aroused the nationalism of his compatriots and made so many of them look towards a *coup d'état* as something both glamorous and desirable— Gabriele d'Annunzio. As an influence on Fascism d'Annunzio can be placed on a level of equal importance with Marinetti, but if we compare the two men one of the first differences which comes to mind is d'Annunzio's popularity. Since the 1890s he had exercised a mass appeal which Marinetti never attained. For hundreds of thousands of readers it was d'Annunzio's novels, plays and poems rather than the esoteric writings of Marinetti that evoked boldness and virility. Indeed, d'Annunzio's personal qualities, his lascivious-

D

ness, his caddishness, his snobbery, his vanity, his extravagance, met with greater approval by far than the high-principled trucu-lence of Marinetti. D'Annunzio's art was decadent, as Croce pointed out, "but generally European, rather than specifically Italian: so much so that d'Annunzio had a wider and more favour-able reception the world over than Italian literature had known since the times of Metastasio, and his decadence was hailed in France as a *renaissance latine.*"[1] Nor can the importance and quality of d'Annunzio's writing be dismissed, now that he has fallen from fashion. At the age of seventeen James Joyce declared that *Il Fuoco* was the greatest achievement in the novel since Flaubert, going still further than Flaubert; and at the age of fifty-six he reaffirmed his admiration.[2]

D'Annunzio's passion for aristocratic decadence and comfort, fine houses, thoroughbred horses and greyhounds, was regarded by Marinetti as deplorably *passatista*; his interest in eroticism, un-healthy; his contempt for women, according to Marinetti "the essential condition for the existence of the contemporary hero", plagiarism of Futurist ideas. "Gabriele d'Annunzio followed us at a distance," wrote Marinetti, "a converted *passatista* who never had the courage to give up his immense clientèle of erotic maniacs and elegant archaeologists."[3] To start with d'Annunzio had affected an aesthete's indifference to politics, scandalising patriotic opinion by his reference in *Il Piacere*, his first novel, to the Italian soldiers killed by the Ethiopians at Dogali in 1887, as "four hundred brutes, brutally butchered". But in 1896, yielding to the insistence of his friends, he agreed to stand as right-wing candidate for the town of Ortona in his home region, the Abruzzi. What were his politics? D'Annunzio refused to commit himself. "My undertaking may seem rash and alien to my art and style of life," he wrote to his publisher, "but . . . people must realise that I am capable of doing anything."[4] His attitude was characteristic: politics were yet another game in which d'Annunzio could impose his will and come a little closer to the supermen of his novels. After his election he dis-played his contempt for the Chamber of Deputies by appearing

---

[1]B. Croce, *Storia d'Italia dal 1871 al 1915,* p. 151.

[2]Richard Ellmann, *James Joyce,* Oxford University Press, 1959, pp. 60, 673.

[3]*Teoria e invenzione futurista,* p. 202.

[4]Quoted in Guglielmo Gatti, *Vita Gabriele d'Annunzio,* Firenze, 1956, p. 163.

rarely at the sessions, and behaving unpredictably when he did. In March 1900, at a meeting of the extreme left, he declared himself in favour of their opposition to a law proposed by the Government which would set severe limitations on political liberty. "I congratulate the extreme left," he said, "on their energy and determination in defending their ideas. After today's spectacle I know that on one side a great many dead men are shouting, and that on the other there are a few men who are alive and eloquent. As an intellectual I shall go towards life."[1] Some days later he crossed the Chamber to sit with the members of the left.

At this stage d'Annunzio's interest in politics was too superficial to last. Nicknamed *il deputato della bellezza,* "the deputy of beauty", he watched the parliamentary debates as an artist rather than a participant, and was always ready to leave them to attend to his love affairs. When he stood again in Florence in June, 1900, he was not re-elected. During the next decade he restricted his political activity to literary evocations of Italy's former glories, concentrating on his mistresses and his art, and attempting unsuccessfully to pay off his vast debts. It was therefore from France, whither he had been driven by his creditors the year before, that he ardently supported the Libyan campaign in 1911, and it was as much because of his Francophilia as his patriotism that he returned to Italy in 1915, one of the most impassioned and influential interventionists, greeted in Rome on May 12 by some hundred thousand admirers.

During the war d'Annunzio was as gallant as his admirers expected. Aged fifty-two he volunteered for active service in the trenches. In 1915 he made reconnaissance flights over Trento and Trieste, lost an eye early in the following year as the result of an aeroplane accident, and in 1917 led bombing raids over Pola and Kotor. Finally, in August 1918, he accomplished his most heroic gesture : he flew as far as Vienna and there dropped propaganda pamphlets from his aeroplane. D'Annunzio was transformed. He had now become the hero he had formerly written about. The men who joined him in the march on Fiume had not read his books : they had merely followed his exploits. It was enough for them to see d'Annunzio as the heroic alternative to the sedentary parliamentarians they despised.

In an article in *Il Corriere della sera* of November 24, 1918,

[1]*Ibid.,* p. 181.

d'Annunzio first referred to the "mutilated victory", *la vittoria mutilata,* a phrase which was to be almost as cherished in Italy as the *Dolchstoss* in Germany. And if we consider the extent of the Nationalists' claims after the Italian victory in November 1918 we see that any policy based on the proposals of President Wilson would make that victory appear "mutilated". Not only did the Italian Nationalists claim their share of Dalmatia and Albania (Italy had been promised Valona and its hinterland at the Treaty of London), but they also "dreamt of Italian influence spreading through the Balkans and Asia Minor to Armenia, the Levant and, with the church's blessing, even down into Palestine."[1]

Little aroused the indignation of so many Italians as much as the question of Fiume. At the Treaty of London their claim to the port had not been recognised : Fiume, the Hungarian coast-line and southern Dalmatia, were to be assigned to Croatia, Serbia and Montenegro by the Allied powers. As the end of the war approached, however, and the Italians were faced with the prospect of a united Yugoslavia, their aspirations to Fiume grew more insistent. And, indeed, these claims were not wholly unjustified, for forty-nine per cent of the population of Fiume was Italian, as opposed to the 2.8 per cent in Dalmatia. Besides, Fiume was of great strategic importance: on the one hand it would strengthen the frontier between the Italians and the Yugoslavs, whom they considered as a military danger, and on the other they feared that, if Fiume were Yugoslav, it would draw the trade to and from Central Europe and constitute a formidable rival to Trieste.

At the Peace Conference in 1919 the Italian delegation under Vittorio Emmanuele Orlando advanced the claim to Fiume on the grounds of self-determination. On February 7, President Wilson recognised the existence of Yugoslavia as a national unit, and, while he agreed to give Italy the Brenner frontier and a large part of the Istrian peninsula (including Pola and Trieste), he regarded Fiume as economically vital to Yugoslavia. For the Italians this was an unpleasant blow. They had had great hopes in Wilson. His Fourteen Points, which stipulated free navigation and free trade, the abolition of secret diplomacy and a League of Nations to guarantee world peace, might have provided the basis for a safer, happier Europe, and his ninth point, that "a readjustment of the frontiers

---

[1] C. Seton-Watson, *op. cit.,* p. 509.

of Italy should be effected along clearly recognisable lines of nationality", seemed entirely to Italian advantage. Wilson's stand over Fiume was therefore the first indication that post-war Europe would not be what nationalistically-minded Italians had hoped for. Feeling turned sharply against the American president, and everything he now proposed fell under suspicion.

Fiume was occupied by Allied troops while its status remained unsettled, and the situation was aggravated in July 1919 when nine French soldiers were lynched by Italian Nationalists. To mollify the French, the Italian government decided to reduce the Italian garrison, dissolve the volunteer battalions occupying the port, replace the National Council by a municipal council and admit an Allied police force and control commission. At this point a group of young officers, determined to prevent the evacuation of Fiume by the Italian garrison, begged d'Annunzio to invade. On September 12 he marched from Ronchi at the head of a thousand "legionaries"; the Allied troops withdrew and d'Annunzio, who announced his intention of remaining in the city until it was annexed by Italy, assumed dictatorial powers.

Within a few weeks some seven thousand legionaries and four hundred sailors had joined him. The Futurists and the Nationalists were exultant. The weakness of the Prime Minister, Francesco Saverio Nitti, who hesitated to eject d'Annunzio by force, led the Comandante, as he was now called, to believe that the time had come for a "march on Rome" and the overthrow of democracy in Italy. For many spectators, and above all for d'Annunzio's legionaries, the Comandante's Fiume became "the symbol of a moral, political and social rejection of the entire established order, of the order identified with Rome and with the budding League of Nations and the Allies."[1] It is hard to specify the aims of the legionaries. They tended to support the cause of the "oppressed peoples" and they regarded the Soviet experiment in Russia with benign interest. They were open to the idea of an alliance with the syndicalists, anarchists and Socialists; but above all they wanted something new, and this they found in the constitution which d'Annunzio had drawn up for Fiume in September 1920 together with the syndicalist Alceste De Ambris. By the *Carta del Carnaro* all the citizens of Fiume were to belong to one of ten corporations, accord-

---

[1] Renzo De Felice, *D'Annunzio e la vita politica italiana dal 1918 al 1936*, Quaderni Dannunziani, Fascicolo XXXVIII-XXXIX.

ing to their profession. There was to be universal suffrage and a people's government, while supreme powers were to be given the Comandante in moments of danger.

By the time it was issued the *Carta del Carnaro* appealed only to an idealistic minority. At a relatively early stage d'Annunzio had shown that he was no politician and had started to lose the sympathy which he had originally aroused among the Italian army. In December 1919, after the Comandante had reached an agreement with the Italian government, through the intermediary of General Badoglio, that Fiume's right of self-determination be officially affirmed and that the port be occupied by regular forces until a decision be reached at the Peace Conference, he suddenly changed his mind, annulled the plebiscite which had approved the agreement, and broke off relations with Rome. Many of d'Annunzio's early followers deserted him. His legionaries who remained led a flamboyant and dissolute life which disgusted the local inhabitants. "Fiume," Nitti told Turati in March 1920, "has become a brothel, the refuge of the underworld and *prostitute più o meno high life.*"[1] D'Annunzio himself became increasingly unpopular. In Fiume there was a shortage of food, mass unemployment and a total lack of trade, and in April 1920 the Comandante had no alternative but to yield the internal administration of the port to the National Council. By the Treaty of Rapallo in November Fiume was made a free state and Italy renounced all her claims to Dalmatia except for Zara and four Dalmatian islands. As a last defiance of the Italian government d'Annunzio ordered his legionaries to raid Susak and seize Krk and Rab. When the regular army refused to support him, he declared war on Italy. On Giolitti's orders General Caviglia's troops started to move in to Fiume on December 24, and on January 18, 1921, d'Annunzio was forced to leave.

Although Mussolini gave the Fiume venture the maximum amount of publicity and encouragement in *Il Popolo d'Italia* his own attitude towards it turned out to be highly equivocal. It is interesting to observe that d'Annunzio's political evolution was in a direction completely opposed to Mussolini's. When he marched from Ronchi on September 12, 1919, d'Annunzio enjoyed invaluable support amongst the conservative army officers, and it was

---

[1]F. Turati – A. Kuliscioff, *Carteggio, V, Dopoguerra e fascismo 1919-1922,* Torino, 1953, p. 294.

largely on account of this that Nitti never dared ask the Army
to evict him. Then he lost this support, and, in so doing, turned to
the left. He established contacts with Sean O'Kelly, the future
President of Eire, who then represented the Sinn Fein in Paris;
with the Egyptian Nationalist Zaghlul Pasha; and with the Soviet
Government of Russia. Lenin referred to him as one of the only
revolutionaries in Italy, and in April 1920 d'Annunzio approached
the Socialists in Trieste with the intention of proclaiming a Soviet
Republic in Fiume and Venezia Giulia. Mussolini, on the other
hand, who had been in correspondence with the Comandante
since December 1918, had always advised caution. He flew to
Fiume on October 8, 1919, stayed barely twelve hours, and
although no record of his conversation with d'Annunzio was ever
made, he appears to have pronounced himself against any revolutionary exploit.

Mussolini's electoral failure in November 1919 increased his
wariness of supporting or undertaking a *coup d'état*, and was
an indication of the inability of the "interventionist left"—
for so the Futurists and Fascists still remained—to obtain votes. It
was essential, Mussolini now thought, to attract some of the more
conservative elements of the bourgeoisie and to come to terms with
the most powerful of Italian institutions, the Papacy, and even the
monarchy. For Marinetti Mussolini, with his "square champing
jaws, prominent, scornful lips, which spit arrogantly and aggres-
sively on everything that is slow, pedantic, analytical, whimper-
ing", had been a Futurist ideal, but when Marinetti, who had proposed that the Pope should be banished to Avignon, heard
Mussolini proclaim his intention to compromise at the Fascist
Congress in May 1920, he left the *Fasci* while Mussolini referred to
him as "this extravagant buffoon who wants to dabble in politics and
whom nobody, not even myself, takes seriously".[1] The Fascist
programme issued at the end of the Congress contained
a new clause "in favour of a working bourgeoisie", *per una
borghesia del lavoro*. "The Fasci recognise the immense value
of that 'working bourgeoisie' which, in every field of human activity
(from industry to agriculture, from science to the liberal profes-

---

[1]G. Pini and D. Susmel, *Mussolini L'Uomo e l'Opera, II*, Firenze
1954, p. 68.

sions), constitutes the precious and indispensable element for the development of progress and the triumph of national fortunes."[1] The programme insisted on the Fascists' opposition to "political Socialism" and "the desire to support any initiative of those minority groups of the proletariat who can conciliate class interests with national interests". Mention was no longer made either of abolishing the Senate or of introducing universal suffrage. A capital levy was still demanded, however, together with the confiscation of ecclesiastical property, the eight-hour working day and a share in factory management for the workers, and, in August and September 1920, Mussolini supported some of the demands of the workers occupying the factories in *Il Popolo d'Italia.*

Marinetti was not the only member to leave the movement after the May Congress. From their electoral failure in 1919 to the latter half of 1920 the *Fasci* lost a quantity of former Socialists, syndicalists, anarchists and Republicans, and gained, instead, members with very different political convictions. Students and young ex-servicemen were drawn by the vagueness of the Fascist programme and the very fact that it should be opposed to Socialism and the government. Besides, by the winter of 1920, Fascism offered these young men something else : the possibility of indulging in organised violence. Not only did the Fascists state their opposition to Socialism : they were prepared to challenge the Socialists in the streets. The first "punitive expedition" had been organised by Marinetti and Mussolini on January 11, 1919, when they disrupted a meeting held by Leonida Bissolati, the former Minister of Pensions and Military Welfare who was ready to renounce Italian claims to the Dalmatian coast. In April they elaborated on this by leading the *Arditi* to the offices of the Socialist paper, *Avanti!,* in Milan, and the building was set on fire, although Marinetti himself appears not to have taken part in the burning of the premises. If Marinetti regarded these exploits as protests against the established order, Mussolini saw that they had further possibilities. Fascism could oppose the government, but it could also be used to safeguard "order", and it was this aspect that ultimately endeared the movement to the conservative sectors of the bourgeoisie.

In July 1920 Fascist violence, organised on a larger scale and in a different field, broke out in Trieste. Young Fascists,

---

[1] R. De Felice, *op. cit.,* p. 746.

calling themselves *squadristi,* burnt down the headquarters of the Slovene organisations in response to the assassination of two Italian officers in Split by Slav separatists, and in November *squadrismo* spread to Emilia after a Nationalist deputy had been shot in a riot between Socialists and Fascists in Bologna at the opening session of the newly elected city council. Henceforth the Po valley, with its landowners embittered and frightened by the strike which had lasted from May to October, proved an ideal ground for what came to be known as "agrarian Fascism".

The *squadre* were recruited by Mussolini's local *ras* or "chieftains"—Italo Balbo in Ferrara, Dino Grandi in Bologna, Roberto Farinacci in Cremona. Their object was to break the peasant leagues and destroy the left-wing unions, and their method was a more brutal type of "punitive expedition". Truckloads of Fascists would arrive in villages in the middle of the night. "From twenty to a hundred *squadristi,* armed with guns and revolvers, assemble before a house and surround it," said the Socialist deputy, Giacomo Matteotti. "They call for the leader of the league, threatening to burn down his house with his wife and children inside. When he comes to the door they tie him up, put him in their truck, torture him, often pretending to kill or drown him, and then leave him tied naked to a tree."[1] *Squadrismo,* though remaining essentially an agrarian phenomenon, spread to the towns, and the Socialists retaliated with a violence as distasteful as that of their opponents. Tuscany, in 1921, was the scene of an incident which aroused particular indignation. In Florence, on February 27, a bomb was hurled at a procession of Fascists, who took their revenge the same evening by murdering a Communist leader, Lavagnini. On the next day the Socialists ordered a general strike, and a group of workers captured a young Fascist, Giovanni Berta, the son of a rich industrialist, stabbed him and flung him into the Arno. After erecting barricades in the suburbs to defend their union offices, the workers opened fire on the Fascists, who arrived supported by the *carabinieri.* The *squadristi* and the police returned to the attack with armoured cars and artillery, and finally managed to break down the barricades and demolish the *casa del popolo* with cannon. Meanwhile, in Empoli near Florence, it was rumoured that the

---

[1]Quoted in Angelo Tasca, *Nascita e avvento del fascismo,* Bari, 1965, p. 213.

Fascists had planned a raid. The inhabitants started shooting at the first two trucks they saw, set one of them on fire, lynched eight of the passengers and wounded ten others. When a victim asked for a glass of water he was clubbed to death and thrown into the river. It later transpired that the trucks were not carrying Fascists, but some innocuous army technicians on their way to Florence to replace the railwaymen on strike.

With the growth of *squadrismo* in the provinces Mussolini found himself at the head of a mass movement. At the end of 1919 there had been thirty *Fasci* with 870 members; at the end of 1920, eighty-eight *Fasci* with 20,600 members; and by the end of 1921 there were 834 *Fasci* with 249,000 members. The flux of new members brought monarchists, Catholics, Republicans, united by their nationalism and their hatred of Socialism. In many cases former syndicalists like Dino Grandi continued to prevail, and in February 1921 the first Fascist agricultural labour union was founded in Ferrara, and was joined by numerous *braccianti* whose "red" leagues had been crushed and who now looked to the Fascists for the protection they had previously expected from the Socialists. So much had the landowners come to rely on the *squadristi* to break strikes and enforce new contracts, that they were in a strong position when it came to making these same landowners accept their terms and those of their protégés. "There were Fascists who took their syndicalism seriously," wrote Seton-Watson. "Having destroyed their enemies, they found themselves responsible for grappling with land hunger and unemployment, and forced to adopt many of the Socialists' methods. It was now the Fascists who operated minimum labour quotas and lobbied the ministries for subsidies and public works. But they were able to promise something that the Socialists couldn't. Early in 1921 Mussolini announced that Fascism meant 'land for those who till it', and this proved an effective slogan for winning rural recruits."[1]

While the *squadristi* represented the most violent side of Fascism, Mussolini stood for prudence and calculation. His aim was to seize political power, and to do so it was necessary for him to gain admission to political circles. Though the responsibility of Giolitti, is frequently exaggerated where the triumph of Fascism is con-

---

[1] C. Seton-Watson, *op. cit.,* p. 574.

cerned, he was admittedly irritated by the Socialists' refusal to join his National Bloc. Nor was he averse to the idea of allowing the Fascists to break the Socialists' strength and force a split between reformists and maximalists. To say that he actually encouraged Fascism, however, is mistaken: he simply looked on while the two rivals, the *squadristi* and the left wing, fought it out between themselves. Although the majority of his followers were intransigently opposed to Giolitti, Mussolini saw the Prime Minister's favour as his best chance of entering parliament. In November 1920, therefore, he committed his first great betrayal of d'Annunzio: he approved the Treaty of Rapallo, by which Fiume was made a free state. Giolitti, on the other hand, convinced that he could ultimately control Fascism and put it to his own use, saw it as the most opportune means of effecting a compromise between the old liberal Italy, which he represented, and the new Italy which had emerged from the Great War. In this spirit he invited Mussolini to join his National Bloc in the 1921 elections.

Not only did the growth of *squadrismo* turn Fascism into a mass movement: it constituted a serious threat to Mussolini's authority. It soon became clear that Mussolini had little control over the provincial *squadre* : even financially the *ras* managed to obtain a certain autonomy by retaining the money levied from the landowners' and farmers' associations in Lombardy and Emilia for the headquarters of the Fascist movement in Milan. The latent antagonism between "provincial" and "political" Fascism reached a peak in the summer of 1921 when Mussolini signed a "pact of pacification" with the Socialists. Ideally, the truce was to be the first of a series of political "alliances" which would have brought Fascism to power without a *coup d'état,* but the opposition which Mussolini met with from his own men put paid to this hope. At the first protests by the *squadristi* Mussolini went as far as to resign from the executive of the movement, observing: "Fascism can get along without me? Undoubtedly, but I can also get along without Fascism." When Grandi and Balbo organised a march on Ravenna by some three thousand men, however, Mussolini revised his opinion. *Squadrismo* and he were interdependent : if Mussolini wanted to come to power he could not afford to antagonise the *squadristi* : they, for their part, would never come to power without him. As a guarantee of his loyalty to

Fascist "ideals" Mussolini turned the movement into a party, the
Partito Nazionale Fascista, and, after the Fascist congress in Rome
in November, issued his new programme.

By comparison with the two previous programmes, that of 1921
was conservative in the extreme. It no longer suggested that ecclesiastical property be confiscated. Private property was now described
as a "right and a due". Telephones and railways were to be returned
to private ownership; the State was to "renounce the monopoly
of the postal and telegraph services so that private initiative
should . . . eventually replace State services"; and corporations
were to be founded "as an expression of national solidarity and a
means of developing production". The programme also contained
a list of public works to be performed, and sustained obligatory
military service. In the course of 1922 Mussolini shed his few
remaining left-wing principles. In January he affirmed that "the
world is moving to the right" and that he considered Fascism a
right-wing movement. He made overt advances to the Vatican and,
in August, to the monarchy. Until 1922 the main financial backers
of his movement had been the landowners, but in 1922 both the
bankers and the industrialists started providing him with funds.
The *ras,* in the meantime, had become so powerful that they were
in a position to occupy entire towns. In May Balbo occupied
Ferrara for a brief period, and in July proceeded to invade
Ravenna. Either out of fear or preference the local authorities
refused to obey the orders of Giolitti's ineffectual successors,
Bonomi[1] and Facta[2]. Rather than arrest the Fascists in possession
of fire-arms, they hounded out the Communists and Socialists.

The black-shirted *squadristi* had effectively succeeded in exhaust-
ing the country. The liberal government was unable to cope with
them and there was an increasing tendency to believe that the only
way to solve the crisis and to end the continual punitive expeditions,
was to give Mussolini the power he sought. No party was strong
enough to resist him. The Socialists had been in decline since 1920,
and the *Popolari* provided no viable alternative to them : the stand
that the Catholics had taken against the war disqualified them from
the ex-servicemen's point of view, and besides, as in the case of the
Socialists, it was the rifts in the Party which made it ineffectual.
The left and centre wings were soon at odds with the Vatican,

---

[1]Prime Minister from July 1921 to February 1922.
[2]Prime Minister from February 1922 until the March on Rome.

while the right-wing refused to collaborate with any left-wing party and showed itself frankly sympathetic to Fascism. And indeed, even the new Pope, Pius XI, who had succeeded Benedict XV in January 1922, was as favourable to Mussolini as he had been when he was Archbishop of Milan.

The liberals were divided between a few enlightened individuals, like Alfredo Frassati, Francesco Coccu-Ortu and Giovanni Amendola, who were aware of the danger that Fascism represented, and the older men, Giolitti, Salandra, Nitti, and Orlando, who looked to Fascism as a means of support to themselves. Among the Italian Royal Family Mussolini enjoyed the approval of the Queen Mother, Margherita, and of the King's cousin, the Duke of Aosta, ready, it was rumoured, to let the Fascists proclaim him regent if the King opposed them. And even in the army, Mussolini's movement was regarded with tolerance : both officers and Fascist leaders were members of the same masonic lodges, and it had long been Mussolini's claim that he was avenging the honour of the soldiers.

One important figure with whom Mussolini had to reach a settlement before he could be sure of eliminating the obstacles on his way to power was d'Annunzio. Although the Comandante's withdrawal from Fiume to his villa on Lake Garda was an anticlimax, he still retained a large number of supporters. He managed to *appear* as one of the only alternatives to Mussolini, and in 1921 some of the most intransigent *squadristi* had contemplated turning to him as a leader. Fascism owed much to d'Annunzio and his Fiume venture—Roman salutes, songs, slogans, uniforms and parades. Mussolini exploited those currents of public opinion which d'Annunzio had aroused. It was therefore found especially annoying by the Comandante that a number of his legionaries should join the *Fasci* when, in the latter half of 1921, it grew evident not only that Mussolini was the true leader of his movement, but that there was no other organisation which could compete with Fascism. D'Annunzio frankly disapproved of the violence of the punitive expeditions and described the effects of provincial *squadrismo* on the peasants as "agrarian slavery". In the spring of 1922 he held discussions with various trade unionists, including Gino Baldesi and Ludovico D'Aragona of the C.G.T., and that summer received a visit from the Soviet Commissar for Foreign Affairs, Georgi Chicherin. The Fascists thought it quite possible that d'Annunzio might try to organise a left-wing bloc against Mussolini, and when they tricked him into haranguing a crowd in Milan as their spokesman in August, d'Annunzio confirmed their suspicions by making no mention of Fascism in his speech, but simply pleading for national unity.

Even the liberal government seems to have envisaged d'Annunzio as a means of foiling Mussolini, but a plan to form a coalition between the Comandante, Nitti and Mussolini failed in that same August when d'Annunzio fell out of his window in ambiguous circumstances and had to spend some weeks in bed. In September, however, he was again threatening to mobilise those of his legionaries who remained loyal to him and seize dictatorial powers himself. How real his political ambitions were, is open to doubt. It should have been obvious to him, at this point, that he stood no chance against Mussolini, and it is probable that d'Annunzio's true ambition was to become the spiritual rather than the political leader of a national movement. Nevertheless he was unable to resist capricious plunges into the world of politics. According to his biographer, Guglielmo Gatti,[1] it was in a last attempt to deal with Mussolini "on an equal footing" that d'Annunzio identified himself with the cause of Giuseppe Giulietti's Genoese seamen's union which had supported him in Fiume. With the intention of neutralising d'Annunzio Mussolini signed an agreement with the Comandante and Giulietti on October 16, stipulating the suppression of the Fascist seamen's corporation in Genoa and the recognition by the shipowners of Giulietti's national syndicates. Although the terms of this agreement were to remain a source of contention between Mussolini and d'Annunzio until 1924, the Comandante was temporarily satisfied.

In the summer of 1922 there had been a revulsion of public opinion against Fascism. The punitive expeditions had reached a climax of brutality and were directed ever more frequently against the most innocuous and exhausted elements of the left. In August, however, the Socialists rashly organised yet another strike, thereby enabling the *squadristi* to secure public approval by breaking it. Many members of the Socialist and Catholic unions capitulated and joined the Fascists and, in October, when Mus-

---

[1] G. Gatti, *op. cit.*, p. 385.

solini was sure that he would meet with no opposition, he ordered his *squadre* to converge on Rome. They could have been dispersed by the regular army, but the King refused to proclaim a state of siege and, on October 30, appointed Mussolini Prime Minister.

At the age of thirty-nine Mussolini was the youngest Prime Minister Italy had yet had. While the youth of its members was one of the main attractions of Fascism as a movement, the youth and political inexperience of its leader seemed to guarantee that he would rely on the advice of the older liberal politicians and would not remain in power for long. Hardly anyone thought he would survive more than a few months, and when, in November, the new government was accorded one year's plenary powers to carry out fiscal and administrative reforms, the scepticism with which Gaetano Salvemini received the news expressed a common state of mind: "There is nothing new about Mussolini's 'dictatorship'. The Italian parliament has produced nothing but dictators for as long as I can remember . . . Crispi was a dictator . . . Giolitti was a dictator . . . Salandra . . . Boselli . . . Orlando . . . The Italian Chamber has always been only too pleased to accord full powers to the Prime Minister."[1]

Few people wanted an all-Fascist government, and Mussolini's first cabinet was reassuring. It included two *popolari*, Tangorra and Cavazzoni, two army officers, Generals Diaz and Thaon di Revel, the democrats Carnazza and Rossi, the Nationalist Federzoni, the *demo-sociale* Colonna di Cesarò, the liberal De Capitani, and three Fascists, De Stefani, Minister of Finance, Oviglio, Minister of Justice, and Giuriati, Minister of Liberated Territories. There were nine Fascist under-secretaries, four *popolari*, two Nationalists and *demo-sociali*, and one liberal. Every effort was made by the new Prime Minister to please the conservative electorate. In February 1923 he persuaded the Nationalists to merge with the Fascist Party. He took several steps to satisfy the church: crucifixes were once again hung in schools and law courts; according to Gentile's plan for educational reform religious instruction was made compulsory in elementary schools; the Chigi Library was presented to the Vatican; money was accorded by the State for the restoration of churches damaged during the war; and Mussolini announced his intention of proceeding against free-

---

[1]G. Salvemini, *Scritti sul fascismo, II,* Milano, 1966, p. 20.

masonry. At the same time he opened the negotiations which were to lead to the conciliation between Church and State. "What we know of Mussolini," Cardinal Gasparri, the Papal Secretary of State, told the Belgian Ambassador to the Holy See, "is that he is a remarkable organiser—Fascism is there to prove it—and a great character."[1] The Belgian Ambassador himself was delighted by the results of Mussolini's administration: "The eighteen months that followed the March on Rome were a period of relief and security, the usual result of the establishment of a strong government. Fascism restored order wherever it could make its iron hand felt, in the countryside as well as in the towns. The Communist attacks were repressed, the strikes suppressed. The railways were closely watched by the Black Shirts, and the passenger no longer travelled in dread of having his luggage stolen. All the public services functioned perfectly . . . A new era had commenced."[2]

In January 1923 Mussolini "legalised" the *squadristi* by forming them into a Voluntary Militia which was later absorbed by the regular army. The powers of the police was increased. The organisation of the non-Fascist trade unions had been shattered by the *squadristi,* so their members were in no position to bargain, and while this resulted in a decrease in strikes and the punctual arrival of trains—all the more remarkable after a period when they often failed to depart—Mussolini kept up democratic appearances by recognising the independence of the non-Fascist General Confederation of Labour and by giving assurances to the Catholic *Confederazione Italiana del Lavoro.*

Gradually the financiers and industrialists lost their reservations about the new régime. In accordance with his 1921 programme Mussolini upheld free enterprise. He returned the telephone system to private ownership, abolished rent control, reduced death duties and put an end to the commission of enquiry into war profiteering which Giolitti had set up in 1920. The *Confindustria,* the largest industrial employers' association was recognised as the sole representative of the industrialists. The Minister of Finance, De Stefani, firmly opposed any scheme to introduce state syndicalism and dealt with the Italian economy along traditional lines. Partly owing to the general economic improvement throughout Europe, and partly

---

[1]Baron Beyens *Quatre ans à Rome 1921-1926,* Paris 1934, p. 136.
[2]*Ibid.,* p. 226.

Giovanni Gentile

a Fracchia, in ricordo del mio duello con Carli, affettuosamente, Malaparte.

Curzio Malaparte (*left*)

because of his administration he was able, in March 1924, to announce the first budget surplus for sixteen years.

The deeply contradictory nature of the various intellectual streams that were to form the ideology of Fascism began to appear with a certain clarity when Giovanni Gentile tried to reform the Italian educational system. Aiming "to concentrate the greatest minds and talents in Italy in his government, without any prejudice or sectarian ostracisms,"[1] Mussolini had appointed the Sicilian philosopher, as Minister of Education—a post which Gentile accepted on condition that he could implement his plan for school reform. The enthusiasm which this appointment met with outside the Fascist Party was almost as great as the opposition which Gentile's ideas aroused within the Party. Croce, we shall see, looked upon it most favourably, while even Salvemini, who had been opposed to Fascism from the first, wrote in his diary: "It will be necessary to help Gentile, and, if I am invited to co-operate, I shall do so—unofficially, on a friendly basis, and on condition that nobody ever thinks I am adhering to Mussolini's régime."[2] Giolitti's first plans for reforming Italian education had been interrupted by the war, and when he subsequently appointed Benedetto Croce Minister, Croce's staff went on strike, so Gentile at last found himself in the position to effectuate the reform for which the liberals had been waiting.

The corruption and mediocrity of the Italian governments since the Risorgimento, the low morale of the Italian army and the defeat at Caporetto, were, according to Gentile, largely due to the educational system. For Gentile conceived education as an essential part of his ideal state. "There can never be real pupils," he maintained, "where masters are lacking." His main object was to grant the school teachers greater autonomy and to increase the importance of philosophy. Religion was to be taught in the elementary schools, thereby serving as a training for the younger children who would then study philosophy, instead of religion, in the secondary schools. In addition to certain alterations in the curriculum, Gentile increased the teachers' salaries, raised the school-leaving age, and established a state examination for both private and public schools,

---

[1] R. De Felice, *Mussolini il fascista, I,* Torino, 1966, p. 376.
[2] G. Salvemini, *op. cit.,* p. 62.

E

to give all children an equal opportunity of proceeding to secondary schools.

The strongest opposition to the reform came from the Fascists themselves. Marinetti described it as "*passatista* and anti-Fascist".[1] Others, who objected to the German influences in Gentile's philosophy, found it un-Italian, and many pupils and teachers resented the change in syllabus that it entailed. So disheartened was Gentile that he offered to resign, and it appears to have been a letter from Croce to *Il Giornale d'Italia*[2] that made Mussolini realise the full importance of the plan and insist on carrying it through. To forestall further criticism he described it as "the most Fascist of the Fascist reforms," and in May 1923 Gentile joined the Fascist Party. "I have become convinced," he wrote to Mussolini, "that liberalism as I understand it and as the men of the glorious right who led Italy in the Risorgimento understood it, the liberalism of freedom within the law and therefore within a strong State, a State conceived as an ethical reality, is not represented in Italy today by the liberals who are more or less openly opposed to you, but in actual fact by yourself."[3]

Benedetto Croce's attitude towards Fascism at this early stage is of some interest since he later came to represent the strongest opposition to Mussolini inside Italy. In 1923, however, he still held the opinions of Giolitti's faction. Liberalism and democracy are vague terms, vaguer even than Fascism : thus we find that Giovanni Gentile regarded Fascism as the continuation of liberalism, and the Fascist State as "the democratic state *par excellence*." One thing was certain, however; for the older Italian liberals, for men like Vilfredo Pareto and Benedetto Croce, the liberal State was, by definition, strong. Both Croce and Pareto saw history as a process

---

[1] See Croce's article in *La Stampa,* May 15, 1924.

[2] "How long is it since we have had as willing and competent a Minister as Gentile, and how long will it be before we have another one? I am sure that the furious attacks to which Gentile's work is exposed will be to no avail, but I would like those who indulge in them or who approve of them to consider that if their opinion prevailed they would assume a serious responsibility and a heavy weight on their conscience." (*Giornale d'Italia,* November 3, 1923.) According to Croce this article was written at Gentile's request. When Croce visited him in 1923 Gentile assured him that what remained of Fascist violence would soon cease and that liberty would be restored. (B. Croce *Nuove pagine sparse,* Bari, 1966, p. 83.)

[3] *Giornale d'Italia,* June 1, 1923.

created by élites, and revolution as the struggle between a new élite seeking to replace the old. Thus in 1917 Croce had written that the study of Karl Marx brought him back "to the best traditions of Italian political science, thanks to the firm assertion of the principle of force, of struggle, of power, and the satirical and caustic opposition to the anti-historical and democratic insipidities of natural law doctrine—to the so-called ideals of 1789."[1] The survival of any parliamentary institution, therefore, depended on the strength of the governing class. Weakness was death. This Croce believed as much in 1922 as he did in 1937, when he wrote that liberalism was "opposed to democracy when democracy substitutes quantity for quality, because, by so doing, it is laying the basis for demagogy, and, without wanting to, for dictatorship and tyranny, thereby destroying itself."[2] In Italy the hold of the liberal élite (if such a thing ever really existed) had been broken by the war: the strikes and the riots, the Fascist punitive expeditions and the Socialist retaliations, were proof of this. Even if Mussolini and his *squadristi* did not constitute an élite which Croce was prepared to acknowledge, their very violence showed up the weakness of the liberals, and, Croce hoped, would inject some life into the governing class. In an article in *La Stampa* in May 1924 Croce approvingly described the Futurists' influence on Fascism as "that determination to come out in the streets and impose one's ideas, stopping the mouths of those who disagree and braving riots, that thirst for novelty and that eagerness to break with every tradition, that glorification of youth, so typical of Futurism, which appealed to the homecoming soldiers disgusted by the squabbles of the old parties and their listlessness before the violence and sabotage raging against the nation and the State."[3]

Together with Gentile, Croce had founded *La Critica* in 1902, and although they had diverged owing to differences in their philosophies, they remained on cordial terms. Croce refused Gentile's offer to join his Ministry, but referred to him as "the right man in the right place"[4] and was gratified that Gentile's plan

---

[1]Quoted in H. Stuart Hughes, *Consciousness and Society,* MacGibbon & Kee, p. 249.
[2]B. Croce, *Nuove pagine sparse,* Bari, 1966, p. 523.
[3]*La Stampa,* May 15, 1924.
[4]*Carteggio Croce-Vossler 1899-1949,* Bari, 1951, p. 28.

for school reform was the one which he himself had tried to carry out in 1920.

To a reporter from *Il Giornale d'Italia* in October 1923 Croce said that it would be difficult "to overcome the sum of the atrocities committed in Italy in the first years following the war. So in fact there is no question of liberalism or Fascism, but simply of political forces. Where are the forces which can oppose or succeed the present government? I do not see them. All I can see is a terror of returning to the anarchy of 1922. It is because of this that no man of good sense wishes for a change in régime." "Is there not a contradiction between your faith in liberalism and your acceptance and justification of Fascism?" the interviewer asked him. "None whatsoever. If the liberals lacked the force and ability to save Italy from the anarchy which was rampant, they have only themselves to blame. In the meantime they must accept and acknowledge the cure, whatever its source, and prepare themselves for the future."[1]

In February of the following year, on being asked about Mussolini's plan for revising the electoral system to a single list, Croce affirmed that it was essential for a politician to be able to govern with a clear majority. Mussolini, he believed (and even certain members of the opposition like Nitti and the Socialist Anna Kuliscioff agreed with him), must be given a fair chance to rule. "I consider so excellent the cure to which Fascism has submitted Italy that my main worry is that the convalescent may leave her bed too soon and suffer a serious relapse." "The heart of Fascism," he added, "is love of Italy; it is the feeling of her salvation, the salvation of the State; it is the just conviction that the State without authority is no State at all."[2]

"People have written that I was one of the precursors of

---

[1] *Giornale d'Italia*, October 27, 1923.

[2] *Corriere italiano*, February 1, 1924. Vilfredo Pareto, the economist whose courses Mussolini had followed in Lausanne, referred to the Prime Minister as "the man invoked in my *Sociologia*". (T. Giacalone Monaco, *Vilfredo Pareto nel carteggio con C. Placci*, Padova, 1957, p. 105), and in his turn Mussolini, who always acclaimed Pareto as one of the greatest influences in his life, conferred a senatorship on him. Pareto died ten months after Mussolini's appointment as Prime Minister, but just before his death he wrote him a letter of advice. Active opponents of the régime, he suggested, should be struck down without hesitation, but opponents who had done no more than express their

Fascism," Luigi Pirandello told Benjamin Crémieux in 1934. "I think one can say that I was a precursor to the extent in which Fascism has been the refusal of every preconceived doctrine, the will of adaptation to reality, the will to modify an action according to the modifications of reality . . . There must be a Caesar and an Octavian for there to be a Virgil."[1] With a mixture of opportunism and conviction, Pirandello adapted Fascism to his aesthetic theories, but at least Fascism was the negation of democracy, which, in the ingenuous words of a character in one of his novels, was "the true cause of all evils," "because when the power is in the hands of one man, this one man knows that he is alone and must satisfy many; but when many men govern, they only want to satisfy themselves, and that is when we have the most idiotic and odious tyranny: tyranny wearing the mask of liberty."[2]

Born in 1867, near Agrigento in the most backward part of Sicily, Pirandello inherited from his father an attitude of intransigent anti-clericalism, of conservative opposition to such innovations as the emancipation of women, and a belief in the myth of the Risorgimento. From his surroundings he gathered and developed the scepticism, so common in Sicily, to the reforms imposed by the mainland. Although he studied in Palermo, went to university in Bonn, and settled in Rome in his early twenties, Pirandello carried with him, wherever he went, the closed world of nineteenth-century Agrigento.

Politics had never been his concern and became still less so as he concentrated on the evolution of his dramatic theories. He had briefly believed in Sicilian Socialism, in the *Fasci siciliani* of the 1890s which play so important a part in his novel *I vecchi i giovani;* for Giolitti he had felt a certain admiration, and he shared the enthusiasm of his fellow intellectuals for Italian intervention in the First World War. He found it unfortunate, however, that one of the men he despised most, Gabriele d'Annunzio, should be leading

---

views should not be harmed. Censorship concealed public opinion, it did not change it. "Let the crows craw," wrote Pareto, "but BE MERCILESS when it comes to ACTS. . . A system's worst enemies are those who push it to extremes." (*Vita italiana,* September 1923.)

[1] *Le Journal,* December 1, 1934.
[2] L. Pirandello, *Il fu Mattia Pascal* in *Tutti i romanzi,* Milano, 1957, p. 368.

the interventionist campaign.[1] Pirandello himself participated in no public demonstration and continued to lead an isolated existence in Rome, writing, teaching in a girls' school, and suffering from the attacks and accusations of his wife.

At the time of the March on Rome Pirandello was solely concerned with the production of his play *Vestire gli ignudi*. In a letter to his daughter on October 29 he made no mention of politics. And yet his Nationalist friends must have known of his sympathy for the new movement and arranged for the meeting which he had with Mussolini at Palazzo Chigi in October 1923. Pirandello was one of many intellectuals to be seduced by Mussolini's charm, for the Duce knew the art of telling his visitors exactly what they wanted to hear. He made them believe that they could count on his personal loyalty, and it was only on closer acquaintance that they found he broke his promises as easily as he gave them, and would contradict himself entirely if he thought he could endear himself to someone by doing so. Besides, Mussolini knew how to flatter artists. When Ezra Pound met him in 1933 he found a copy of his *Cantos* lying on Mussolini's desk, while Hilaire Belloc was delighted to establish how well read the Italian Prime Minister was.[2]

To this kind of flattery Pirandello was particularly susceptible. He was having his first great theatrical successes abroad and Mussolini expressed an intelligent admiration for his plays at an effective moment. He offered him a decoration as a token of the esteem of the government, "which, as you know, is a new government," he added engagingly. In a series of interviews Pirandello told of the appeal that Fascism had for him. "I have always had the greatest admiration for Mussolini and I think I am one of the few people capable of understanding the beauty of this continuous

---

[1] The contempt was reciprocal. D'Annunzio is said to have caught two frogs, tied them together by their back legs, and christened them *Sem Benelli* (see *infra.* p. 47) and *Luigi Pirandello,* as they hopped about on the floor squabbling. Croce, too, hated Pirandello, who had unwisely attacked his *Estetica* and tried to involve him in polemics. The philosopher riposted by boycotting his words at the Biblioteca Nazionale in Naples.

[2] Even the rational Benedetto Croce was impressed by Mussolini's personality when he first saw him at a Fascist meeting in Naples shortly before the March on Rome. When Luigi Russo, who accompanied him, asked him if he found Mussolini histrionic, Croce replied that all politicians had to be actors and Mussolini seemed a particularly good one. Nobody could say of Musssolini, as Spengler did of Hitler, that he was insignificant.

creation of reality performed by him : an Italian and Fascist reality, which does not submit itself to anyone else's reality. Mussolini is one of the few people who knows that reality only exists in man's power to create it, and that one creates it only through the activity of the mind."[1]

Pirandello's problem, his aesthetic problem and, for that matter, his personal problem, is expressed in a preface he wrote to his *Six Characters in Search of an Author.* "Without wanting to, without knowing that they are doing it, in the confusion of their minds, each one of them, in order to defend himself from the accusations of the others, expresses as his own passion and torment what, for so many years, have been the travails of my spirit : the deceit of mutual understanding, based irremediably on the empty abstraction of words; the multiple personality of everybody according to the various possibilities of being which exist in each of us; and finally the tragic conflict immanent between life, which is constantly moving and changing, and the unchangeable form which determines and immobilises it."[2] By emerging from the confusion of the punitive expeditions and restoring order, Mussolini had managed to impose his own reality on life : this was more than any of Pirandello's characters, tormented by the loss of their own identity, had been able to do. Furthermore, Pirandello considered that Mussolini had solved the antinomy between life and form. "Mussolini can only be blessed," he asserted, "by somebody who has always felt the immanent tragedy of life, which, in order to exist in some way, requires a form, but which senses death in any form it assumes. For, since it is subject to continual change and motion, it feels itself imprisoned in any form. It rages and storms inside it and finally escapes from it. Mussolini has clearly shown that he is aware of this double and tragic necessity of movement and form, and hopes to conciliate the two. Form must not be a vain and empty idol. It must receive life, pulsating and quivering, so that it should be for ever recreated and ready for the act which affirms itself and imposes itself on others."[3]

---

[1]*Idea Nazionale,* October 23, 1923.

[2]L. Pirandello, *Sei Personaggi in cerca d'autore,* Milano, 1963, pp. 10-11.

[3]*Idea nazionale,* October 28, 1923. For Pirandello's attitude to Fascism see also Gaspare Giudice, *Luigi Pirandello,* Torino, 1963, pp. 413-464, and Leonardo Sciascia, *Pirandello e la Sicilia,* Caltanissetta, 1961.

By his rise to power Mussolini conciliated a number of intellectuals who had previously resented his compromises. Marinetti forgot his quarrels and welcomed him loyally. "The coming to power of Fascism constitutes the realisation of the minimum Futurist programme," he wrote in 1923. "Prophets and forerunners of the great Italy of today, we Futurists are happy to salute in our not yet forty-year-old Prime Minister a marvellous Futurist temperament."[1] In *La Rivoluzione Liberale* Giuseppe Prezzolini admitted pragmatically that success was a criterion of quality. "Are we historians?" he asked. "Then we must give up sheer anti-Fascism. I do not see how one can oppose Fascism without renouncing every historical consideration. Fascism exists, it has won: for us historians this means that there are adequate reasons for its victory."[2]

In the last months of 1922 the problem of d'Annunzio's attitude to the régime arose yet again. There was a desire among some of the leading left-wing trade unionists, including D'Aragona, Baldesi and the reformist Socialist Zaniboni, to form a single trade union organisation which would be independent of every political party and would have d'Annunzio as its head. On December 5 Baldesi and Zaniboni met d'Annunzio to discuss the matter. But although Mussolini himself does not seem to have been averse to the proposal, opposition came from the maximalist Socialists on the one side and from the Fascist syndicalists, led by the *ras* of Cremona, Farinacci, on the other, who believed that any attempt to form a single, politically independent union organisation would be fatal to Fascism and Mussolini, fearing a repetition of the 1921 crisis, yielded to the pressure of their opinion.

D'Annunzio came reluctantly to heel. In reply to a telegram from the Prime Minister begging him to deny rumours in France that he opposed Fascism and warning him to beware of those of his followers who were against the new régime, d'Annunzio wrote, on January 7, 1923 : "Your telegram has that odd tone which may be fundamental to 'Fascism' but which remains totally alien to my mentality . . . Nobody can influence . . . any of my opinions or decisions. From the day of my birth I alone have been my leader . . . It is you who must rid yourself of supporters who are leading you

[1]Quoted in J. Joll, *op. cit.*, p. 176.
[2]*Rivoluzione liberale*, December 7, 1922.

astray . . . The best of the 'Fascist' movement has surely been gener-
ated by me . . . So how can I be your rival?"[1]

Once he realised how decisive Mussolini's victory had been,
d'Annunzio withdrew from politics, determined to be respected as
the greatest poet in Italy, if not as the greatest politician. Few
Prime Ministers have conferred as many honours on a writer as
Mussolini on d'Annunzio. He presented him with a sea-plane; in
1923 he sent him a bodyguard (who also served as a government
spy); and in March 1924, when Fiume was annexed to Italy, he
persuaded the King to make d'Annunzio Prince of Montenevoso.
Yet these favours did not prevent the Comandante from sharing the nation's indignation over the murder of Matteotti
in June 1924. He described it as *una fetida ruina* and
Mussolini's spies had to reassure him that the Comandante's main
fear was that the Fascist government would fall. At the same time
the playwright Sem Benelli[2] left the Fascist Party and tried to form
an opposition movement, *La Lega italica*. It was erroneously
rumoured that d'Annunzio had joined it, and Mussolini, in yet
another attempt to mollify him, purchased his manuscripts. A year
later his bodyguard reported that d'Annunzio "is now entirely
against any form of opposition and says that it must be treated
with the utmost intransigence."[3]

The murder of Giacomo Matteotti, the Socialist deputy who
spoke against Mussolini in the Chamber, was a decisive moment in
the history of Italian Fascism. Matteotti was kidnapped and killed
(probably unintentionally) by a group of Fascist extremists under the
leadership of Amerigo Dumini. Mussolini himself appears to have
had no direct connection with the crime, but the opposition
accused him of it, and some of his closest acquaintances
were implicated—Cesare Rossi, the head of the Prime Minister's

---

[1]G. Gatti, *op. cit.*, p. 405.

[2]Benelli was one of the many intellectuals to claim to be a precursor of Fascism: "You know that I was one of the precursors of
this movement against the ignorant, bestial, levelling tyranny of the
reds," he said in December 1922. "Benito Mussolini has the greatest
task in the world: Italy will once again be able to set an example
to the world. . . By breaking the chains of our recent history he has
conquered new currents of ambitions which lacked his stout heart
and immense will-power. . . Apart from him, to tell you the truth,
I see nothing but darkness." (*Popolo d'Italia*, December 27, 1922.)

[3]Nino Valeri, *D'Annunzio davanti al fascismo*, Firenze, 1963, p. 124.

press office, and Giovanni Marinelli, the Party treasurer. That Mussolini should so nearly have fallen as a result of the murder is proof of how precarious his position still was, and the fact that he remained in power is proof of the ineffectiveness of the opposition. In the next few months of uncertainty and anxiety Mussolini, it is said, developed the stomach ulcer which was to torture him for the rest of his life. "My worst enemies," he told the Neapolitan novelist Matilde Serao, "could never have done what my friends have just done to me."[1]

Fascism lost what mass popularity it had acquired. The circulation of Fascist newspapers dropped; Gentile and three other cabinet ministers resigned, advising moderation and suggesting that Mussolini collaborate with the opposition. The members of the opposition, on the other hand, said that they would have nothing to do with a government of murderers and withdrew from active politics on the assumption that the tension created by Matteotti's assassination and the revival of *squadrismo*[2] would suffice to ruin Mussolini. The opposite occurred. The strain proved unbearable, and soon the nation wished for any solution. The cost of living was again rising, the stock exchange was uncertain, and what was most desired was a return to normalcy. As in 1922, the man who promised it was Mussolini. There was a mounting tendency to dissociate him from the violence of his followers, and, a month after the murder, the Senate gave him a vote of confidence. "You know I have always considered the Fascist movement devoid of new institutions, and incapable of moulding a new type of State, as its propagandists had boasted," Benedetto Croce told an interviewer in July. "In my opinion it could only be a bridge to the restoration of a stricter liberal régime within a stronger State. It should give up the claim of inaugurating a new historical epoch, but it can well be satisfied with the by no means inconsiderable glory of bringing colour and vigour back into Italian political life . . . We could not expect, or even hope, that Fascism should suddenly fall. It has not been an infatuation or a prank. It has satisfied some serious requirements, and has done much good, as every fair mind must admit. It advanced with the applause and consent of the nation. So on one side there is a desire to preserve the benefits of Fascism and not to return to the exhaustion and inconclusiveness

---

[1]Paolo Monelli, *Mussolini piccolo borghese,* Milano, 1950, p. 161.
[2]See *infra.,* p. 52.

which preceded it; and on the other there is the feeling that the interests created by Fascism, even the less laudable and beneficial ones, are also a reality and cannot be tossed away. We must therefore give Fascism time to complete its process of transformation. This is the reason for the Senate's prudent and patriotic vote."[1]

In September Luigi Pirandello joined the Fascist party and gave his reasons to the editor of *L'Impero*. He was shocked by the behaviour of the opposition and refused to believe that Mussolini had anything to do with Matteotti's murder. His gesture earned him an attack from the Socialist press, and gave rise to a lengthy polemic between the radical Giovanni Amendola writing in *Il Mondo*, supported by the paper's dramatic critic, Adriano Tilgher, and Telesio Interlandi in *L'Impero*. Pirandello was accused of owing his entire inspiration to Tilgher and indeed, if he took anything from Tilgher, it was precisely the antinomy between Life and Form, with which he justified his adherence to Fascism. A number of Italian intellectuals rallied in his defence and signed a protest,[2] but shortly after the incident Pirandello denied all interest in politics. "My life is work and study. . .I am isolated from the world and have only my work and my art. Politics? I have nothing to do with them and have never had anything to do with them. If you are referring to my joining the Fascist Party, I can tell you that I did so to help Fascism in its task of renovation and reconstruction."[3]

However noxious its effect on public opinion, the Matteotti crisis revived the hopes of those Fascist revolutionaries who had been distressed by the respectability the new régime was assuming. The Futurists hoped at last to be able to impose their programme of 1919, *diciannovismo*. In November 1924, at the end of a Futurist congress in his honour, the participants approved Marinetti's political declarations: "The Italian Futurists, the first interventionists and the first soldiers, the first of the first *diciannovisti*, more than ever devoted to ideas and art, far removed from politics, say to their old comrade Benito Mussolini: 'Free yourself from parliament with one necessary and violent stroke. Restore to Fascism and Italy

---

[1]*Giornale d'Italia,* July 10, 1924.
[2]Antonio Beltramelli, Massimo Bontempelli, Ugo Ojetti, C. E. Oppo, Ottorino Respighi, Soffici, Malaparte, Ungaretti, etc.
[3]*Il piccolo,* October 21, 1924.

the marvellous, disinterested, bold, anti-Socialist, anti-clerical, anti-monarchical, *diciannovista* spirit . . . Refuse to let (monarchy) suffocate or anaesthetise the greatest, most brilliant and just Italy of tomorrow. Do not imitate Giolitti, imitate the great Mussolini of 1919 . . . Quell the clerical opposition . . . with a steely and dynamic aristocracy of thought which can replace the present demagogy of arms without thought . . .' "[1]

Lacking a specific ideology, the *squadristi* were motivated and united by little more than what they termed, somewhat vaguely, "dynamism". As long as Fascism was a movement which had to be brought to power this dynamism had an immediate object, but once Mussolini had been appointed Prime Minister it was obviously threatened. The formation of the Voluntary Militia tied the hands of the *squadre* : by obtaining respectability they lost their life force. They were resented by the regular Army and they feared their absorption by it. "Fascism", in short, was rapidly escaping from their control: it had become a political régime in which they had no place. The *squadristi*, like the Futurists, believed that the Matteotti crisis would give them the opportunity of perpetuating the revolution, of resuming the punitive expeditions, and of bringing on "the second wave" of Fascism.

The intrigues which took place on every level of the Militia and the Fascist Party from June 1924 to January 1925 are too complicated to be analysed here. It was at this time and in this context, however, that Curzio Malaparte reappeared as a representative of a certain state of mind which culminated in one of the most unpleasant events of the period. In the years immediately following the war Malaparte had been away from Italy—until 1921 he had been attached to the Italian Military Legation in Warsaw—and according to the "liberal revolutionary" Piero Gobetti he was initially undecided about his political attitude. He seemed too much of an internationalist to subscribe to the strictly nationalistic views of the Italian Fascists, and he never hesitated to declare his interest in Russia and Communism. At the same time, however, his quest for heroism kept him from joining the Italian Socialists who continued to pride themselves on the fact that they had been the only Socialist Party in Europe to remain pacifist throughout the war. Whether Malaparte

[1]Quoted in Luigi Scrivo, *Sintesi del Futurismo,* Roma, 1968, p. 21.

joined the Fascists in 1921, as he claimed under the Fascist régime, or in 1922, as he maintained after the Second World War, is still a matter of doubt. He informed Gobetti of his decision, saying: "I think this is the time to prove that the Italian intelligentsia is capable of putting itself at the service of the proletariat with more than words. Of that same proletariat which was red yesterday and is red, white and green today. Intelligent and cultured young Italians must be the first to put themselves at the head of the people. The greatness of humanity means that Italy too must be great. We Italians must start with Italy, that's logical. Then we shall think of humanity."[1]

Resting on the philosophy of Giambattista Vico, Malaparte saw Fascism as an heroic revival : "Stern, calm men raise their heads from the long sleep and lend their hands to the reconstruction of the earth; they are always the same, they always have the same aspect, only their names change. Vico's law of returns comes true, both for the events and the heroes."[2] Yet at the same time he believed Fascism to be revolutionary—an anti-intellectual, revolutionary movement which would lead Italy back to her true nature : "Our revolution is more against Benedetto Croce than against Buozzi[3] and Modigliani[4] . . . I am not one of those men who are prepared to overlook strength, courage, violence and ferocity and ask the true Fascists to give way graciously to the intellectuals . . . The Fascist revolution (is) a whole process of revision of the present civil, cultural, political and spiritual values, a radical and objective criticism of the present form of civil life, of everything modern . . . the final goal of the Fascist revolution is the restoration of our natural and historical civilisation which has been degraded by the triumphant rise of the barbarism of modern life."[5]

At first Malaparte occupied a succession of minor posts in the Fascist Party, and in 1923 went to Paris as correspondent for the syndicalist Edmondo Rossoni's *Il Lavoro d'Italia*, contributing, furthermore, to Amendola's *Il Mondo* and to Piero Gobetti's left-wing *Rivoluzione Liberale*. Now, although Gobetti and Malaparte represented enemy parties, Malaparte retained Gobetti's esteem:

---

[1]P. Gobetti, *Scritti politici,* Torino, 1960, pp. 566-567.
[2]C. Malaparte, *Europa vivente e altri saggi politici,* p. 476.
[3]A trade unionist.
[4]A Socialist.
[5]C. Suckert, *Ragguaglio sullo stato degli intellettuali rispetto al fascismo,* in Ardengo Soffici, *Battaglia fra due vittorie,* pp. 27-29,

indeed, Gobetti referred to him as "the best theoretician of Fascism" and "the most open-minded of Mussolini's writers."[1] The two men shared an ineffable contempt for parliamentarianism in the traditional sense of the word, and all that Gobetti scathingly called "Giolitti's old methods", and they both admired one of the most violent representatives of provincial *squadrismo,* Roberto Farinacci. Even Gobetti agreed that what Italy needed was the symbol of the punitive expedition, *il manganello,* the cudgel. "If a kind of Fascism could be of some use to Italy," he wrote in 1923, "it is the Fascism of the *manganello* . . . There are too many opportunists: Baroncini[2] and Farinacci are men . . . (They) defend personal positions which may be illegitimate but which were conquered by sacrifice and brawn: behind them they have a hundred thousand young men who have not become Fascists in order to earn money or get themselves a job, but because of their exasperation, their disgust with the compromises and the opportunism. We must respect, in their ignorance and barbarity, a sense of dignity and a proof of sacrifice. The theoreticians of Rome are another race: they want to get rewarding positions for themselves by writing articles and confusing people's ideas. But they have nothing to teach the Italians: Farinacci and Baroncini are more cultured, a hundred times more cultured than Massimo Rocca, just as a clerk is a hundred times more cultured than a former anarchist."[3]

The following year Gobetti still believed Farinacci to be "the most complete and respectable type of man which has yet been produced by the Fascist movement", his qualities to be "personal disinterest and austerity". It was shortly after Matteotti's murder that Malaparte founded a review, *La Conquista dello Stato,* in which he expressed views to which Farinacci fully subscribed. In the first number Malaparte deplored political Fascism "with its liberalising tendencies", and affirmed that "the safety of Fascism rests in the provinces, in the revolutionary spirit which wants to conquer the State for Italy and absorb itself in this State".[4] Three weeks later he wrote that the time had come for Mussolini to dissolve parliament as an institution, set about forming technical works councils, and introduce total Fascist syndicalism. Every step

---

[1]P. Gobetti, *op. cit.,* p. 568.
[2]A *squadrista.*
[3]P. Gobetti, *op. cit.,* p. 527.
[4]*Conquista dello Stato,* July 10, 1924.

which Mussolini took to appease public opinion about the
Matteotti murder was, according to Malaparte, a blow against
the revolution. If Fascism *was* revolutionary, as it claimed to be,
it "must be carried all the way through, with no regard for anyone, even for those Fascists or anti-Fascists who think they can
end Fascism by sending it to jail".[1] At a meeting with Mussolini,
Malaparte suggested that any compromise (like the reform of the
electoral system) was the sign of "a policy of the liquidation of
Fascism as a doctrine and as a party". "My dear Suckert,"
Mussolini is said to have replied, "if we weaken now we will never
come back, never. Do you understand, yes or no?"[2]

The sinister *fatti di Firenze* which took place on December 31
were the most horrifying results of the type of mentality represented
by Malaparte. After a mass rally in Florence armed groups of
Militiamen destroyed the printing presses of two newspapers,
Fanteria and *Il Nuovo Giornale,* raided the masonic lodge, the
circolo della cultura, and the offices of several anti-Fascist lawyers.
This did more than appal the Italian public : it brought home
to Mussolini the necessity of acting against the *squadre.* On
January 3, therefore, after assuming full responsibility for the
murder of Matteotti, or, as he said, "for all that has happened",
Mussolini promised an immediate return to normalcy. "Italy,
gentlemen, wants peace, she wants quiet and calm. We promise
to give her this peace, quiet and calm with love, if possible,
and with force, if necessary. You can be sure that within forty-
eight hours of my speech the situation will be cleared up."[3]
The Prime Minister declared a state of emergency.
The Minister of the Interior, Federzoni, ordered strong police
measures to be taken against anyone who contributed to the disorder, and Mussolini himself sent personal instructions to the heads
of police to proceed energetically against any Fascists breaching the
peace. Inevitably the opposition suffered most from these measures.
Arms were confiscated from extremist groups, certain newspapers
were suppressed and Communists were watched by police spies.
Although the opposition parties were to survive for another two
years, their existence became increasingly precarious. Their clubs

---

[1]*Conquista dello Stato,* December 21, 1924.
[2]Quoted in Adrian Lyttleton, *Fascism in Italy: The Second Wave,*
Journal of Contemporary History, vol. I, 1966, p. 93.
[3]R. De Felice, *op. cit.,* p. 722.

were closed down, their more dangerous members had their houses searched and were placed under arrest, or, like Piero Gobetti and Giovanni Amendola, were assaulted and injured. Only certain individuals, of whom Antonio Gramsci is a striking example, had the courage to appear in the Chamber of Deputies.

But for the Fascist extremists, too, the January measures meant the end of their ambitions. Malaparte expressed his unqualified disapproval. He attributed the responsibility for this step more to Federzoni than to Mussolini himself, and, in a number of *La Conquista dello Stato* which was banned by the censor, he wrote : "We do not like the government's measures against the opposition. They are not revolutionary measures but reactionary police measures. . . Doesn't the Minister of the Interior realise that in addition to Leninist methods of suppressing his opponents and the present means of silencing them, there is a third, revolutionary way, worthy of a nation as progressive as our own?"[1] Malaparte's provincialism, *strapaese,* as he called it, was due to remain a purely literary phenomenon—the ideology of Mino Maccari's review, *Il Selvaggio.* The "dynamism" of the *squadristi,* on the other hand, was to perish altogether. By 1926 all punitive expeditions had ceased and over the next three years the most violent elements were systematically expelled from the Fascist Party. Roberto Farinacci was replaced as Party Secretary by Augusto Turati[2] and, with Mussolini's encouragement, Turati purged and devitalised the Party so thoroughly that it came to be regarded merely as a convenient means for securing a job or gaining promotion. Of the vague and somewhat crude dynamic idealism of the first *squadristi* it contained not a jot.

In March 1925 a congress of Fascist intellectuals was held in Bologna. It concluded with a manifesto drawn up by Giovanni Gentile which approved the January measures and the state of emergency. "All constitutional liberties in the most liberal states have been suspended when particular reasons proved it necessary, and all theoreticians and defenders of liberty have recognised the legitimacy of similar measures." The manifesto went on to give a short account of Mussolini's rise to power, to stress the vitality of

---

[1]*Conquista dello Stato,* January 4, 1925 quoted in R. De Felice, *op. cit.,* p. 274.
[2]See *infra.* p. 69.

Benito Mussolini (*centre*) & Gabriele d'Annunzio (*right*)

Gabriele d'Annunzio's membership card of the
Fascio Fiumano di Combattimento

Luigi Pirandello (*centre*)

Fascism and to exalt the Italian nation. It was signed by Luigi Barzini, Antonio Beltramelli, Francesco Coppola, Enrico Corradini, Carlo Foà, Marinetti, Malaparte, Ugo Ojetti, C. E. Oppo, Sergio Panunzio, Alberto Panzini, Camillo Pellizi, Ildbrando Pizzetti, Enrico Prampolini, Soffici, Ugo Spirito, Gioacchino Volpe, and several others. Pirandello, who had not cared to attend the congress, sent a letter from Rome which illustrated an ever more current tendency among Italian writers to pay to the régime a homage which did not go beyond the written word. After asking to be included among the signatories he wrote : "I have always fought against words. I am well aware of your reasons for meeting. But it is precisely for those reasons that, even today, I must stay at home and work."

Gentile emerged from the Congress as the official philosopher of Fascism, and Mussolini honoured him more as the philosopher of the régime than Hitler ever did Alfred Rosenberg. Indeed, it was Gentile who wrote the standard definition of Fascist doctrine which appeared, bearing Mussolini's signature, in the *Enciclopedia italiana*. As we shall see later, however, there was remarkably little unanimity among Fascists in the acceptance of Gentile's views.

In Gentile's philosophy the idea of the Risorgimento was of primary importance. It constituted a philosophical category of an importance comparable to that of the Revolution for Marx. But Gentile refuted the philosophical value of the Revolution. Materialism, he believed, led to the negation of society. This concept appears in all his work, from his first studies on Marx, Rosmini and Gioberti in 1897 and 1898 to his last writings in 1944. For Gentile the Risorgimento was the revival of a spiritual tradition, evolution rather than revolution, and with this he equated Fascism. So Fascism, in Gentile's eyes, was *not* revolutionary.[1] It was the revival of an idealist tradition which had been in decline since the last representative of the "glorious Right", Marco Minghetti, was succeeded as Prime Minister by Agostino Depretis in 1876. With the accession to power by Depretis there was a turn to the left in Italian politics : while the right had "moved from the State to the individual", the left "moved

---

[1] Augusto Del Noce, *L'idea di Risorgimento come categoria filosofica in Giovanni Gentile* in *Giornale critico della filosofia italiana*, Aprile-Giugno, 1968.

from the individual to the State". Depretis and his successors concentrated on economic development, on the campaign against
illiteracy, and on social reforms which would facilitate the rise of a
lower class inevitably neglected in the course of the Risorgimento.
During this process, according to Gentile, the authority of the State
had been undermined, and with it, the liberty of the individual, for
the supreme entity was the State, a State which embodied the
citizen's ethical personality, and the stronger the State, the freer the
individual. "Liberty is certainly the supreme end and rule of
every human life, but only so far as individual and social
education make it a reality by embodying the common will,
which takes the form of law and hence of the State, in the particular individual. . . From this point of view State and individual
are identical, and the art of government is the art of so reconciling
and uniting the two terms that a maximum of liberty harmonises
with a maximum of public order not merely in the external sense,
but also and above all in the sovereignty ascribed to the law and
its necessary organs. For the maximum liberty always coincides
with the maximum force of the State."[1]

At last, in Fascism, Gentile saw the true realisation of Mazzini's
axiom *pensiero e azione*, thought and action, the negation of the
"intellectualism" which had developed since the Risorgimento and
which constituted the main force in opposition to Mussolini's
régime. In Fascism, thought and action "coincide perfectly, and
no value is attributed to the thought that has not been transposed
or expressed in action, hence every form of anti-intellectual polemic
which is one of the most recurrent themes of the Fascists. This
polemic, I must emphasise, is profoundly Mazzinian, since intellectualism is thought divorced from action, science divorced from
life, the brain from the heart, theory from practice".[2] Already at the Bologna Congress of 1925, however, a group of young
men, led by G. A. Fanelli, who had been formerly expelled from the
party for his violence but recently readmitted on Farinacci's request,
refused to sign the manifesto and maintained that the Fascist State
was absolute and transcended the individual. They could not accept

---

[1]Quoted in H. S. Harris, *The Social Philosophy of Giovanni Gentile*,
University of Illinois, 1960, p. 174.
[2]G. Gentile, *Origini e dottrina del fascimo* 1927 in *Il Fascimo,
Antologia di scritti critici*, a cura di Costanzo Casucci, Bologna, 1961,
pp. 37-38.

Gentile's concept of Nation and State mirroring a reality only created by each individual for himself. Gentile, claimed Fanelli, was a liberal heretic, tolerant to opposition and a danger to the state: true Fascism regarded his philosophy "as an enemy of its religious and political faith, of its morality and of its nation".[1]

Italian Fascism was little more than a set of individual attitudes, and the attitude which happened to prevail over the régime was not that of Gentile, but that of the Nationalists. Gentile refuted both the Nationalists' theory of the aristocratic State and their acceptance of the nation as "a natural, anthropological or ethnographical fact". This, according to Gentile, was a denial of man's freedom to create history. "The nation only exists as far as it is created," he insisted. "And it is what we make it, with our serious work, our efforts, never believing that it is already there, thinking, rather, that it is never there, that it must always be created."[2]

By 1926 former Nationalists held two key posts in Mussolini's cabinet: Luigi Federzoni had been appointed Minister of the Interior in June 1924, and from 1925 to 1932 Alfredo Rocco was Minister of Justice. Ever since Fascism had emerged as a movement likely to come to power the Nationalists had tried to turn it into a conservative counter-revolution. They had always opposed the idea of confiscating profits made during the war or of expropriating land: the aristocratic élite which they hoped would emerge after the Fascist seizure of power was to consist of the financiers, industrialists and large landowners. For Mussolini the Nationalists were a valuable means of securing the support of those powerful categories on whom the survival of Fascism initially depended. It was with the intention of pleasing the conservative electorate that he persuaded the Nationalists to merge with the Fascists early in 1923, and that he nominated Federzoni Minister of Colonies in his first cabinet and Minister of the Interior immediately after Matteotti's murder. For the same reason he appointed Rocco Minister of Justice in January 1925.

In an article which appeared in *Gerarchia* in the month of Rocco's appointment Enrico Corradini gave a succinct account of the Nationalist view of Fascism. Fascism, he wrote, was "a revolution taking place within the established order", and its programme was to

---

[1] G. A. Fanelli, *Contra Gentiles—Mistificazioni dell'idealismo attuale nella rivoluzione fascista,* Roma, 1933, p. 183.

[2] G. Gentile, *Guerra e fede,* Napoli, 1919, pp. 48-52.

"overtake old-fashioned liberalism, democracy and Socialism in order to become a régime in which the State, the active means of national unity, would prevail over the parliamentary parties". Acting on this premise Rocco was responsible for the final warrant of Mussolini's dictatorship. And, however idealistic his determination to subjugate every organisation in the country to the State, it proved effective in breaking the old liberal institutions. In October 1926 he reformed the Constitution, subordinating the Grand Council (the Fascist "cabinet") to Mussolini, and the Fascist Party to the Grand Council. In November, after the fourth attempt to murder the Prime Minister in twelve months, Rocco passed his State security laws : they introduced the death penalty and a special tribunal for crimes against the State, stipulated the revision of all passports and the suppression of newspapers containing any statement damaging to the régime, outlawed opposition parties and revived the *confino*, banishment to a town or island in southern Italy, as a punishment.

Rocco's influence went still further. It has recently been established, by Renzo De Felice, that Rocco, and not, as has hitherto been supposed, Mussolini's Minister of Corporations Giuseppe Bottai, was responsible for the final draft of the Fascist Charter of Labour in April, 1927.[1] The underlying principle of the Charter which provided the ideological basis of the Corporate State, was class collaboration. Bargaining was to be done through "the collective labour contract" in which "the solidarity between the various factors of production finds its concrete expression, by means of the conciliation of the opposed interests of employers and employees and their subordination to the higher interests of production". Labour disputes were to be regulated by special Labour tribunals, while "the legally recognised professional associations assure legal equality between employers and employees, maintain the discipline of production and labour and promote their increasing perfection. The corporations constitute the unitary organisation of the forces of production and integrally represent its interests. In virtue of this integral representation, the interests of production being national interests, the corporations are recognised by law as organs of the State". Finally, and this is where Rocco's hand appears most strongly, private initiative was to prevail over State intervention :

---

[1] R. De Felice, *Mussolini il fascista, II,* Torino, p. 293. See also Paolo Ungari, *Alfredo Rocco e l'ideologia giuridica del fascismo,* Brescia, 1963.

"The corporate State regards private initiative in the field of production as the most effective and useful instrument of the national interest. Since the private organisation of production is a function of national interest, the organiser of an enterprise is responsible to the State for the directions its production takes. From the co-operation of the productive forces it follows that they have mutual rights and duties. The employee, whether a technical expert, clerk or labourer, is an active co-operator in the economic enterprise, the direction of which belongs to the employer who is responsible for it. . . . The intervention of the State in economic production takes place only when private initiative is lacking or insufficient, or when the political interests of the State are at stake. Such intervention may assume the form of control, encouragement or direct management."[1] The Charter of Labour was, of course, a compromise. Mussolini had to produce a document acceptable both to the General Confederation of Fascist Unions and to the employers' association, the *Confindustria*. The State, therefore, reserved the right to intervene, and when the corporations were formed it was this intervention which the *Confindustria* most resented.

By 1927 left-wing opposition to Mussolini's régime had been effectively silenced. The opposition parties were dissolved. Nenni, Sturzo, Turati, Treves and Bordiga were all in exile. Gramsci was in prison, and Gobetti and Amendola were dead. The most effective, though cautious, opposition to the régime within Italy, came from Benedetto Croce, who had publicly disclaimed his support of Fascism after the publication of Gentile's manifesto in the spring of 1925. He replied with a counter-manifesto in which he expressed a view Julien Benda was to hold two years later in *La Trahison des clercs*: intellectuals should try to raise "all men and parties to a higher spiritual level". They should act as moral arbiters, condemn violence whatever its source, and defend freedom of expression. Their place was not at the battlefield, but at the writing desk and the pulpit.[2]

[1] Reproduced in Herbert W. Schneider, *Making the Fascist State,* New York, 1928, pp. 332-336.

[2] Croce's manifesto was originally printed in *Il Mondo* on May 1, 1925, and was signed by a couple of dozen of Italy's leading writers and professors. Two more numbers of *Il Mondo,* on May 10 and 22, carried further lists of sympathisers who far exceeded the Fascist signatories in quantity, if not in quality. They included Giovanni Amendola, Roberto Bracco, Sem Benelli, Carlo Cassola, Emilio

The liberals, Croce realised after the *fatti di Firenze* and the January measures, could no longer control Mussolini. If the violence of the Fascists had been justified initially by that of the Socialists, it had now become unnecessary. Mussolini had been slow in mastering it, and when he did so, the liberals disapproved of his methods. Throughout the Fascist period Croce remained in Italy, occasionally speaking against Mussolini in the Senate and conducting a guarded campaign against the régime in *La Critica*. In 1926 some Fascist thugs ransacked his house in Naples. A detective always lingered on his doorstep; his mail was censored; he was followed wherever he went; and his acquaintances were liable to have their houses searched. Subsequently he described Fascism as a parenthesis in Italian history. When surprise was expressed that Italy should have fallen ill so suddenly and unexpectedly, and should have remained ill for so long, he pointed out that even the healthiest men can contract a humiliating disease.[1]

But what was Fascist Italy in reality? It was neither the vital creation of which Gentile dreamt nor the monolith for which Rocco hoped. Apart from the fact that there was very little agreement about the ideological principles of Fascism, Mussolini's compromises accumulated and quickly ruined all possibilities of forming a totalitarianism. Fascism survived partly because of the Duce's accomplishments on a national level, and partly because, after the dissolution of the opposition, there was simply nothing else.

One of the many indications of the hopelessness of implementing Gentile's or Rocco's ideals was the signature of the Lateran Pacts

---

Cecchi, Guido De Ruggiero, Luigi Einaudi, Giustino Fortunato, Piero Giacosa, Tommaso Gallarati Scotti, A. C. Jemolo, Giorgio Levi della Vida, Luigi Salvatorelli, Matilde Serao, Francesco Ruffini, Luigi Albertini, Arturo Labriola, Gaetano Salvemini, Michele Saponaro, Adriano Tilgher and Gaetano Mosca. For a full list of signatories and the texts of the two manifestos see Emilio R. Papa, *Storia di due manifesti*, Milano, 1958.

[1]This became one of the three "classic" interpretations of Fascism. According to the Marxists, Fascism was purely a product of capitalism—a reaction against the proletariat. According to the Liberals (Giustino Fortunato and Piero Gobetti) Fascism was a "revelation", the logical and inevitable product of Italy's historical development. This latter interpretation was much favoured by foreign historians. See Renzo De Felice, *Le interpretazioni del fascismo*, Bari, 1969, and Nino Valeri, *Premessa ad una storia dell'Italia nel Postrisorgimento* in *Orientamenti per la storia d'Italia nel Risorgimento*, Bari, 1952.

with the Pope in February 1929. For the first time since the Unification of Italy the Italian government recognised the Pope's sovereignty over the Vatican City, while the Pope recognised "the Kingdom of Italy under the dynasty of the House of Savoy, with Rome as the capital of the Italian State". Restitution was paid for the Vatican property which had been seized between 1861 and 1870. The Italian government undertook to exclude apostate or censured priests from any public office and to recognise the "sacrament of marriage as regulated by canon law". The Pope was at liberty to veto any political or religious event of which he disapproved in Rome; the Catholic religion was to be taught in every school; and the Vatican was accorded full powers to cater for the religious welfare of Roman Catholics.

The Conciliation secured Fascism the approval of the Church and ensured for Mussolini a quantity of sincere Catholic votes when elections were held a few months later. But to many Italian intellectuals—to Pirandello, to Marinetti, to d'Annunzio—one of the more progressive aspects of the Risorgimento had been the breaking of clerical power.[1] For Rocco the Conciliation was a disappointment because it provided yet another object of allegiance. The King retained a large following who only justified their loyalty to Mussolini by his admission of the monarchy to the Fascist State —this was the case of the "official" Fascist historian, Gioacchino Volpe—and the Concordat with the Vatican undermined the integralism of Fascism still more. Gentile, on the other hand, had always claimed that it was against the Church's interests to accept corporal existence at the hands of a national State, and against the State's interests to share its sovereignty with the Pope. Although he subsequently acknowledged Mussolini's skill in coming to terms with the Vatican, the fact that religious education should now be enforced in the secondary schools put a major obstacle before the completion of his plan for school reform and ended his hope of replacing religion by philosophy.

In a period when Fascism was becoming bureaucratic and list-

---

[1]"I always disapproved of the Conciliation because I know how irreducible the mercantile, intrusive spirit of the Vatican is," d'Annunzio wrote to Mussolini in 1931. This passage, quoted by De Felice in *D'Annunzio e la vita politica italiana dal 1918 al 1936*, was censored, when their correspondence was published.

less Gentile's calls for vitality sound singularly ineffectual. In March 1931 he deplored the complacency of the Fascist Party. "The party card is only an honour for those who regard the party as a militia," he wrote, "a militia in which every member fights, even risking his life, for love of his country, a militia whose members morally accept obedience to that strict discipline which keeps an army marching behind its flag."[1] Three weeks later he was deprecating the foibles of the Italian character. "Today there are many, too many people who murmur against the régime, not because they have reason to do so, but because of an increasing tendency which, were it to prevail, might present a considerable danger to the Italian character. In the past Italians have always withdrawn into a private life and watched the State from outside, as if it were alien to their own interests. It was more the object of negative spite than of effective, constructive criticism. Fascism is the revolution of a new, positive and active Italy, against the old Italy of gossips and complaints . . . the Italy of the brave against the Italy of the cowards."[2]

It was clearly impossible for as pure an ideal as that of Gentile to be realised, yet Gentile remained oddly unaware of this fact. All his life he retained his faith in Mussolini and his belief in *his* Fascism. He did his best to remain true to his principles, but he also had to watch these principles miscarry. He had frequently begged Mussolini to allow greater freedom to the press, and had suggested the foundation of an opposition paper after the Bologna congress in 1925. As editor of the Italian Encyclopedia—the *Enciclopedia Treccani,* still one of the best reference works in existence, which owes its political impartiality to Gentile—he enlisted for his staff a number of intellectuals who had signed Croce's counter-manifesto. After 1931 he employed some of the professors who had refused to take the oath of loyalty to Mussolini, but the oath was the distortion of an idea originally put forward by Gentile himself—in 1923 he had suggested an oath of loyalty to King and Constitution : in 1931 the oath was sworn to King, Constitution and the Fascist régime.[3]

With as much loyalty as Gentile, Marinetti sustained his support

---

[1] *Corriere della sera,* March 11, 1931; see *Corriere della sera, 1919-1943,* a cura di Piero Melograni, Bologna, 1965, p. 416.

[2] *Corriere della sera,* April 1, 1931, *op. cit.,* p. 418.

[3] Of 1,225 professors eleven refused to take the oath and had to give up their teaching posts.

of Mussolini, and although he repeated his pre-war Futurist slogans and cherished the myth of *diciannovismo,* he accepted election to the Italian Academy, which had been announced in January 1926 but was not inaugurated until October 1929. According to anti-Fascist sources Mussolini decided to found the Academy as a result of the quantity of signatures to Croce's manifesto in 1925 and in an attempt to "corrupt" the Italian intelligentsia.[1] Indeed, Mussolini did endeavour to persuade both the Neapolitan poet Roberto Bracco and Benedetto Croce to join, and their refusal may well have been one of the reasons for the delay in the inauguration. When this event at last took place the scientist Guglielmo Marconi was President of the Academy, the historian Gioacchino Volpe secretary, and the members included the composers, Mascagni, Respighi and Giordano, the scientist Enrico Fermi, the writers Beltramelli, Panzini, Pirandello and, of course, Marinetti. They were accorded a substantial monthly salary, they could travel free in the first class and be called "Your Excellency", and they appeared at public ceremonies wearing Academic uniforms and mock swords.

Marinetti said that personally he did not much care, "but it is important that Futurism be represented in the Academy,"[2] and if Mussolini can ever be said to have had a cultural policy which went beyond the myth of ancient Rome and a classical revival, it was the very antithesis of ancient Rome, Futurism: in the same year as he was elected to the Academy Marinetti became Secretary of the Fascist Writers' Union and therefore the official representative of Fascist culture.

In every way as distressed as Gentile by the lethargy of his compatriots, Marinetti attributed it to more material factors—to spaghetti. In a Manifesto of Futurist Cooking in the *Gazzetta di Torino* of December 28, 1930, and in his book *La cucina futurista* which appeared two years later, he deplored the national diet of *pastasciutta,* to the distress of Mussolini's corpulent wife, Donna Rachele. "Once more," he exclaimed, "Italian Futurism braves unpopularity with a programme for the renovation of Italian

---

[1]See Alessandro Bonsanti *La Cultura degli anni trenta dai Littoriali all'antifacismo,* Terzo Programma, No. 4, October 1963, pp. 183-217. These suggestions are denied by the former Secretary of the Academy, Gioacchino Volpe, in *L'Italia che fu,* Milano, 1961.

[2]Walter Vaccari, *Vita e tumulti di F. T. Marinetti,* Milano, 1959, p. 363.

cuisine. . . Cod, roast-beef and pudding may be all right for the English; meat cooked with cheese for the Dutch; *sauerkraut*, smoked lard and sausages for the Germans; but *pastasciutta* is bad for the Italians. . . By eating it they develop that typical ironical and sentimental scepticism which all too often damps their enthusiasm."[1]

Both in Germany and Italy intellectuals became the object of intrigues within the Fascist Party, and were alternately supported and attacked by the various representatives of conflicting streams of Fascist thought. While Farinacci continued to pursue the intransigent line which later led him to admire Hitler, Bottai, who had started as a syndicalist close to the Malaparte-Farinacci faction of the party, became a liberal protector of the younger writers, and in the thirties Mussolini's son-in-law and Foreign Secretary, Galeazzo Ciano, patronised Malaparte and a number of his friends.

Despite his avowed lack of interest in politics Pirandello was often regarded as the playwright of the régime. In 1925 Mussolini offered to subsidise his new theatre in the Sala Odescalchi in Rome, and attended the inauguration in person, and in 1929 Pirandello was elected to the Academy. But his success aroused the jealousy of his rivals. In 1927 he accompanied his troupe to Brazil, where he told some Italian journalists : "Abroad there are neither Fascists nor anti-Fascists, but we are all Italians." On his return he discovered that the envious Enrico Corradini had denounced him on the strength of this statement for "anti-Fascist activity abroad". When the Party Secretary, Augusto Turati, upbraided him, Pirandello tore up his party card and threw it in his face, and seven years later Farinacci, who had supported Corradini from the outset, arranged for his followers to hiss Pirandello's opera put to music by Malipiero, *La Favola del figlio cambiato,* which had been banned in Nazi Germany.

The liking which Pirandello had taken to Mussolini diminished in January 1935. He had just returned from Stockholm, where he had received the Nobel Prize, and the Duce was eager to congratulate him in person. Pirandello, for his part, believed that any interview with the Duce might be to the advantage of his ambition to found a National Theatre, but Mussolini proved insensitive on this occasion. Pirandello had fallen platonically in love with his

---

[1]Quoted in L. Scrivo, *op. cit., pp.* 188-189.

leading actress, Marta Abba, and Mussolini, who had heard of the matter, said humorously and somewhat coarsely : "When you love a woman you don't beat about the bush, you throw her onto the sofa."[1]

However much at variance the numerous concepts of Fascism were with one another, they all met in their admiration for Mussolini. And the accomplishments of the Duce and the government, magnified by every means of propaganda—the press, the radio and the cinema—were considerable. With the assistance of his able Minister of Finance, De Stefani's successor, Count Volpi, Mussolini managed to revalue the *lira* in 1926. His campaign to relaunch Italian agriculture was successful. Marshland was reclaimed all over the peninsula, and in 1932 and 1933 two towns, Littoria and Sabaudia, rose up on what had previously been the malaria-ridden Pontine Marshes. Roads, bridges, hospitals and schools were built; archaeological excavations were led in Rome, Herculaneum and Pompey, and in Libya, at Leptis Magna, Sabratha and in Cyrene. The trans-Atlantic flights of Del Prete, Ferrarin, De Pinedo and Balbo were triumphs for Italian aviation, and the advance in national industry enabled the country to produce ships and motor-cars admired throughout the world.

"Italy," Mussolini told a journalist a few days after his rise to power, "wants to be treated by the great nations of the world as a sister, not as a chamber-maid."[2] His aim was to gain Italy international recognition as a great power. He had obtained some slight acknowledgement by the Allies for his support of French occupation of the Ruhr, and had impressed the Italians by the energy with which he briefly occupied Corfu in August 1923. In 1925 he signed the Treaty of Locarno guaranteeing the Franco-German frontier, and Italy's status seemed ensured. The Duce had numerous admirers abroad: Ramsay MacDonald wrote to him cordially, Austen Chamberlain exchanged photographs with him and Winston Churchill praised him, and in July 1933 he proposed and signed the Four Power Pact with England, France and Germany by which Italy became part of a European directory legislating to the smaller states and peacefully revising European policy. Mussolini now appeared as

---

[1]Gaspare Giudice, *op. cit.*, p. 460.
[2]R. De Felice, *Mussolini il fascista I*, p. 560.

one of the main champions of world peace. That September he signed a non-aggression pact with the Soviet Union. The following July he mobilised his troops on the Brenner after the assassination of the Austrian Chancellor Dollfuss, thereby becoming the only European statesman actively to oppose German expansion, and at Stresa, in April 1935, he confirmed his excellent intentions, and Great Britain and France their faith in him.

This faith was somewhat shaken, however, by the one action of Mussolini that filled the whole of Italy with enthusiasm: the invasion of Ethiopia. At last Italians, both Fascist and anti-Fascist, could combine the prospect of an empire with a crusade and a war of liberation. The Ethiopians, it was pointed out by the Italian Government, lived in squalor, suffered the worst injustice and were ruled by the most feudal of monarchs. To emphasise the benefits of the campaign pictures of attractive Ethiopian women were widely circulated, while the newspapers reminded the Italians that Italy was overpopulated, and needed both the living space and the "place in the sun" which Ethiopia would provide.

Ethiopia had joined the League of Nations at the instigation of the Italians, against the wishes of the British, in 1925. Any aggression on Italy's part would therefore be in defiance of the League. Plans for mediation, put forward variously by Hoare, Laval, and Eden, failed. In September 1935 the British Home Fleet sailed menacingly into the Mediterranean, and in November sanctions were ordered by the League which consisted of an embargo on arms and ammunition, the refusal of monetary loans, the banning of Italian imports and partial prohibition of exports to Italy. Although they were never effectively enforced, the sanctions aroused the greatest antagonism amongst the Italians, and, still more than the prospects of an Empire, kindled their patriotism and determination to fight. Numerous anti-Fascists volunteered in the name of the nation rather than the régime. The former liberal Prime Minister, Vittorio Emmanuele Orlando, put himself at Mussolini's service; Arturo Labriola returned from exile; Sem Benelli, who had opposed Mussolini ever since Matteotti's murder, hastened to join his regiment in Africa. "Our venture does not extort, it offers," he wrote. "It is performing a mission. . . This is not even imperialism : we are holding out a hand to those outside civilisation."[1] He added

---

[1] S. Benelli, *Io in Affrica*, Milano, 1936, p. 226.

in his memoirs that he "thought Italy had the right to a great colony because she was overcrowded and all nations, even those much smaller than herself, had colonies and always wanted more."[1]

D'Annunzio congratulated Mussolini on "fighting an unknown people in an unknown land",[2] Marinetti volunteered; Gentile rejoiced and Pirandello said of Mussolini: "The Author of this great feat is also a Poet who knows his trade. A true man of the theatre, a providential hero whom God granted Italy at the right moment, he acts in the Theatre of the Centuries both as author and protagonist."[3] The sanctions were exploited to the full. In the winter of 1935, a month after they had been imposed, Mussolini appealed to the Italians for their gold and silver. In Rome alone, on December 18, a quarter of a million Italians gave their wedding rings. Benedetto Croce and Luigi Albertini sacrificed their Senators' medals, and Pirandello—to the indignation of the Swedes—his Nobel Prize Medal.

Mussolini's great talent lay in accomplishing short term reforms that had an immediate appeal and could be easily publicised. By so doing he managed to give the Italians the confidence which they had lost in the years after the war, and by his very presence at the head of it he managed to give the country a stability which it initially needed. On the other hand the longer term reforms for which the more progressive elements of the Fascist Party had hoped either failed or did not take place. The syndicalists had hoped that the Fascist régime would be to the advantage of the peasants and the workers, but it was not. It was to the advantage of the propertied classes. Even after his rise to power Mussolini continued to pass from compromise to compromise, and had he not done so he might well not have remained in power so long. One of the most striking indications of this was the purge of the Fascist Party between 1926 and 1928, when the new Party Secretary, Augusto Turati, systematically expelled those *squadristi* and early Fascists who had constituted the revolutionary core of the movement. Mussolini's compromises were also evident in his reforms. Thus the drainage of the marshland was primarily to the advantage of the large landowners, and the agricultural campaign, the *battaglia*

---

[1]S. Benelli, *Schiavitù*, Milano, 1945, p. 122.
[2]G. Gatti, *op. cit.*, p. 450.
[3]*Quadrivio*, November 3, 1935.

del grano, to the disadvantage of the small fruit-growers.[1] Fascist labour policy favoured the industrialists, the corporations, the employers. Fascism, the much vaunted "revolution", left the Italian social structure substantially unchanged. Mussolini carried out his reforms through the bureaucrats and financiers of the previous régime. No new governing class emerged from Fascism, even if some of the Fascist officials, or *gerachi,* struck as superficial an observer as Corrado Alvaro by their youth and good looks. "The governing class," he wrote after a night at the opera in 1933, "is well-built, well-fed, dark and athletic. One usually associates a governing class with a class of intellectuals. But here physical fitness and a commanding presence are the first requisites."[2]

Although the workers did derive certain benefits from Fascist labour policy, they were outweighed by the disadvantages. The Fascist trade unions had obtained paid holidays and indemnities in the case of dismissal. Men kept their jobs if they were ill, received family allowances and health insurance, while the *Opera Nazionale del Dopolavoro* organised trips and mass entertainment. Strikes, however, had been outlawed by the Pact of Palazzo Vidoni in 1925. By 1927 the non-Fascist trade unions had been dissolved. Discipline had become stricter than before and the workers had no means of protecting their wage packets.

Corporativism, on which the originality of the Fascist experiment was based, never worked. The corporations were announced by Rocco in 1926, but were not formed until 1934. At the base of the corporative "pyramid" were 160 national federations of employers' and workers' syndicates and professional associations. Then came twenty-two corporations, sixteen of which represented the workers and employers in different branches of production, while the six others represented the professions. At the head was a National Council of Corporations and a Ministry of Corporations, responsible for all problems of production, labour relations and social welfare. The system satisfied neither the employers, who resented State intervention in their affairs, nor the workers, who were under-represented. The main benefits of corporativism were the theories

---

[1]Vittorio Foà, *Le strutture economiche e la politica economica del regime fascista* in *Fascismo e antifascismo, 1918-1936, Lezioni e testimonianze,* Milano, 1962.

[2]C. Alvaro, *Quasi una vita, giornale di uno scrittore,* Milano, 1951, p. 101.

and debates to which it gave rise and which reached the height of controversy at a meeting in Ferrara in May 1932 when the philosopher Ugo Spirito presented a plan by which the capital would pass, within the corporations, from the shareholders to the workers, thereby abolishing class distinction and the antagonism between employers and employees.[1]

Mussolini's dictatorship was more clement than most. Both because of Mussolini's own reluctance to cause unnecessary bloodshed, and the natural tendency of the Italians to be humane even in dealing with their enemies, Fascist Italy was free of the atrocities associated with Hitler and Stalin, until the German occupation during the war years. Although capital punishment had been introduced in 1926, from 1926 to 1943 there were only twenty-five executions, twenty-one of which were of Slav terrorists. Over the same period of time about 10,000 Italians were sent to the *confino*—the islands of Tremiti, Lipari, Ponza and Ventotene being the principal places of banishment—where they enjoyed relatively good treatment. In 1927 Mussolini had founded a secret police force, the OVRA, which was organised by an astute Neapolitan named Arturo Bocchini. What the letters stood for, Mussolini told no one, not even Bocchini. Their main purpose, he said, was to arouse fear, and curiosity, and a sense of intangible omnipotence and vigilance. The OVRA differed considerably from the Gestapo : it never tortured, and it appears to have been better organised. It had spies in every branch of the country's political, economic and social life, as well as in the communities of Italian exiles abroad, and its functionaries, who fulfilled their duty coldly and dispassionately, were probably better informed than any other policemen in Europe. They preferred to threaten rather than arrest. And the threat of the *confino* was most effectual. A man could be *confinato* without trial, sometimes without even knowing why, and, once he was banished, his sentence could be prolonged at the whim of the government and the local head of police. If, and when, he returned, people hesitated to employ him. Wherever he went he was regarded with suspicion and, if a Fascist official visited the town where he was living, he was kept under arrest for the length of the visit.

---

[1]See Alberto Aquarone, *L'organizzazione dello stato totalitario,* Torino, 1965, p. 198 *ff.*, and Ruggero Zangrandi, *Il lungo viaggio attraverso il fascismo,* Milano, 1962, p. 461 *ff.*

Censorship was relatively lax, except where the daily newspapers were concerned. There was an underworld of literary magazines in which every current of Fascist opinion was expressed, respect for the Duce and the nation being the only necessary premise for freedom of opinion.[1] Fiction and poetry were subject to still less censorship, for, as the censor well knew, the Italians were not avid readers, and certain writers who later prided themselves on their anti-Fascism, were able to have their works published without too much difficulty. The theatrical censor, an obtuse individual named Zurlo who understood little about politics and nothing about literature, has written his memoirs, which he justly qualified as useless.[2] His criteria of censorship were primarily moral: he discouraged mentions of adultery, banned references to homosexuality, and changed all suicides to accidents. Otherwise his instructions were not to pass any play containing attacks on King, Pope or government, or disparaging remarks about southern Italians.

On the whole, therefore, just as Fascism left the social structure unaffected, so it allowed Italian middle class life to continue no less comfortably than before the First World War. Italy even seemed to survive the economic Depression of the early thirties with remarkable ease. Despite the fact that there were about 1,300,000 unemployed in 1933 Mussolini disguised the situation. The prohibition of strikes enabled the government to lower wages more or less indiscriminately, and in December 1930 they were decreased by twelve per cent. The full statistics of the unemployed were never revealed; women and pensioners demanding work were not allowed to enter their names in the employment records; and a law was enforced which prevented the peasants from leaving their land for the crowded cities.[3] But to these must be added two psychological factors : confidence in Mussolini was high, and Italian morale had risen owing to the dexterity with which he had saved the country from the previous crisis. The impressions of a foreign observer were favourable. "I had been to a first night at

---

[1] See Giorgio Luti, *Cronache letterarie tra le due guerre, 1920-1940,* Bari, 1966.

[2] Leopoldo Zurlo, *Memorie inutili—La censura teatrale nel ventennio,* Roma, 1952.

[3] See Paola Sylos Labini, *La politica economica del fascismo e la crisi del 29* in *Nord e Sud,* No. 70, October 1965, pp. 59-66, and Alberto Aquarone, *Italy: the crisis and corporative economy* in *Journal of Contemporary History,* vol. 4, No. 4, October 1969, pp. 37-58.

Ardengo Soffici

Giovanni Papini

the opera," wrote Emil Ludwig in 1932, "and had seen in the boxes more resplendent gowns and had noted the flashing of more jewels than had been visible in the opera-houses of Paris and New York of late years. The numberless cars, only half of which could be parked in the square, the abundance of liveried servants, the whole setting, seemed to negate the notion that the world was sick of a fever. Rome, to all appearances, was resolved to deny that a social revolution was in progress."[1] All Fascism had managed to impose were the Saturday parades, Fascist uniforms, patriotic rhetoric and the endless publicity devoted to Mussolini. Italy was a dictatorship, but for the first thirteen years Fascism did not weigh too heavily on the individual, especially if he was prepared to keep away from politics and pay that lip service which Mussolini might demand.

While Gentile and Marinetti proved ready to compromise with the régime, Malaparte could not resist the temptations of illegality for long. To start with he realised the importance of adapting himself to the course taken by Fascism in 1925. In January, in order to remedy the disorder into which the Fascist Party had fallen after the Matteotti crisis, Mussolini had appointed Roberto Farinacci Party Secretary. But from Mussolini's point of view the danger in keeping Farinacci as Party Secretary for too long was that he would not only put the party in order, but that he would strengthen it to such a degree that it would become uncontrollable. What Mussolini wanted was a disciplined, obedient party which he could manipulate as he liked, and in March 1926 he replaced Farinacci by the more reliable and devoted Augusto Turati. As soon as Farinacci had lost his post, Malaparte, with the unspoken consent of Mussolini, attacked him in *La Conquista dello Stato*. It was at this point, according to Malaparte, that he invented a "Fascist past" for himself, claiming to have joined the party in 1921 instead of 1922, and to have participated in the punitive expeditions and the March on Rome. As a result of Malaparte's attacks Farinacci sent Mario Carli, Emilio Settimelli, Silvio Maurano and several other of his friends from *L'Impero* to assault Malaparte in Via Sistina, and Malaparte responded by challenging each one of them to a duel.[2]

Farinacci's fall marked the beginning of a period in which

---

[1] E. Ludwig, *Talks with Mussolini*, translated by Eden and Cedar Paul, G. Allen and Unwin, 1933, p. 148.

[2] In the same year Malaparte fought a duel with Pietro Nenni who had insulted him in *Avanti!*

G

Malaparte served the régime. This was fully in character. Gobetti had already pointed out that Malaparte "was always an undaunted admirer of regicides and courtiers, that politics for him are a game, the cult of surprises."[1] Malaparte's rôle as a regicide was over : with facility he became the court hero, the master of intrigue and conspiracy, and his career as a journalist thrived accordingly. In 1926 he became editor of the literary review *La Fiera Letteraria,* then of *Il Mattino* in Naples, and in 1929 he was called to Turin to direct Senator Giovanni Agnelli's newspaper *La Stampa.* Handsome and entertaining, a skilful teller of alluring lies as well as an able maker of mischief, Malaparte had no difficulty in entering the coterie surrounding Mussolini, and became a close friend of Mussolini's Minister of Aviation, Italo Balbo. Balbo seconded Malaparte in one of his innumerable duels, while Malaparte, together with Enrico Falqui, wrote a sycophantic biography of him, " *chevalier sans peur et sans reproche,* whose generous restlessness and vivid fantasy have made a champion of modern Italy, determined to wage war and master the globe, whatever the price."[2]

As the years passed Malaparte became more cynical and more cunning. And yet the appeal that the permanent revolution had had for him never really waned. Having seen that Fascism could not provide it he believed that Communism might. He had always regarded Russian Bolshevism with respect. Although he made it clear that it was not suited to the individualistic spirit of the Italians, he considered it the only viable alternative to Fascism, and had written in *La Rivolta dei santi maledetti*: "I believe that the phenomenon of the Russian revolution, which proceeds parallel to the Italian revolution in its hatred for and struggle against the modern spirit (which for us is the north western spirit and for the Russians the European spirit), is the complement of the phenomenon of the Italian revolution. Both are helping each other in their common task of destroying *modernity,* and one is not conceivable, possible or *right* without the other."[3] In 1929 Malaparte was sent by *La Stampa* to visit the Soviet Union, and he recorded his experiences in *Intelligenza di Lenin,* which appeared the following year. Impressed by the ruthlessness of the Soviet régime and what he con-

---

[1]P. Gobetti, *op. cit.,* p. 465.
[2]Malaparte-Falqui, *Vita di Pizzo-di-Ferro detto Italo Balbo,* Roma, 1931, p. 7.
[3]Malaparte, *Europa vivente,* p. 135.

sidered to be the single-minded devotion of its citizens, he was optimistic about Stalin's Five Year Plan, and more than ever fascinated by the possibilities of totalitarianism.

The reasons for which Malaparte resigned as editor of *La Stampa* in January 1931, left the Fascist Party and emigrated to France in March remain as obscure as the reasons for his arrest two years later. According to him, he disagreed with Senator Agnelli about certain innovations in the Fiat factory in Turin and refused to dismiss an editor who had issued a mistaken report. It was in Paris, in all events, that Malaparte established his reputation as a European writer with the publication of *Technique du coup d'Etat*. Subscribing to Trotsky's theory that a revolution was just as possible in a civilised country like England as it was in a country undermined by rival political factions, Malaparte, by giving examples of successful and unsuccessful *coups d'état*, intended to demonstrate that the problem both of conquering and defending the State was technical rather than political. It was possible for a relatively small group of determined men to overthrow any government provided they could gain control of certain strategic points—the railways, post offices, telephones, banks and radio.

Technique du coup d'Etat was indeed "seminal in the thinking of the extreme right in Europe during the thirties".[1] Yet Malaparte stressed the ambiguity of its reception.[2] Charles Maurras, Léon Daudet and Jacques Bainville of the *Action Française* were as pleased with it as Malaparte's Communist friend Jean-Richard Bloch. Both the Austrian Vice-Chancellor Prince Starhemberg and the Chancellor Dollfuss had copies of it in their libraries. In 1932, on account of *Technique du coup d'Etat* and a second book on Russia, *Le bonhomme Lénine,* Malaparte was officially invited to visit the Soviet Union again. Finally for the dissident members of the *Action Française,* the future *Cagoulards, Technique du coup d'Etat* was a manual.

Malaparte sent a copy of his book to the Chief of the Paris police, Jean Chiappe, whose dismissal was to cause the riots in Paris on February 6, 1934. It was dedicated *"A Monsieur Jean Chiappe, technicien du coup d'arrêt"*, and Chiappe wrote back saying that it

---

[1]Eugen Weber, *Action Française—Royalism and Reaction in Twentieth-Century France,* Stanford, California, 1962, p. 275.

[2]Malaparte, *Que la défense de la liberté ne rapporte pas!,* Introduction to *Technique du coup d'Etat,* Paris, 1948.

was as dangerous for "enemies of liberty" to possess the book as it was precious for the statesmen "defending democratic liberties". "You teach statesmen," added Chiappe, "to understand the revolutionary phenomena of our time, to foresee them and to prevent seditious elements from seizing power with violent methods."[1] In *Kaputt* Malaparte tells of his meeting with Oswald Mosley in Paris. "He had brought with him the English edition of *Technique du coup d'Etat* and wanted me to write a dedication on the frontispiece. He probably expected me to write something heroic, so, in order to delude him, I cunningly copied out two phrases from my book: 'Hitler, like all dictators, is nothing but a woman,' and 'Dictatorship is the most complete form of jealousy.' "[2]

Technique du coup d'Etat was banned in Italy and burnt in Germany after Hitler's rise to power. The latter measure is understandable because the final chapter, written in the Spring of 1931, contained statements which the National Socialists found difficult to forgive. "Hitler is only a caricature of Mussolini . . . In the National Socialist Party freedom of thought, personal dignity, intelligence and culture are persecuted with that stupid and brutal hatred which characterises third-rate dictators . . . (Hitler) is a weak man who seeks refuge in brutality to hide his lack of energy, his amazing weaknesses, his morbid egoism, his resourceless pride."[3] But Malaparte's claim that his attack on Hitler caused his arrest when he returned to Italy in October 1933 can hardly be taken seriously. Nor can his suggestion that Ugo Ojetti denounced him to Mussolini for frequenting Gaetano Salvemini in Paris. The more likely reasons are less flattering for Malaparte—his mercenary behaviour in an involvement with the daughter-in-law of a powerful Italian industrialist, and his quarrel with Italo Balbo.[4] Mussolini, as those close to him knew, was jealous of anyone who threatened to overshadow him. The glamour and prestige which Balbo had assumed, heightened after his flight from Rome to Rio de Janeiro in 1931, seemed excessive, so in 1933 Mussolini appointed him Governor of Libya. Thinking he could do to Balbo what he had done to Farinacci in 1926, Malaparte accused him and the editor of his paper, *Il Corriere padano,* Nello Quilici, of plotting to over-

---

[1]Malaparte, *ibid.,* p. 6.
[2]Malaparte, *Kaputt,* Napoli, 1944, pp. 171-172.
[3]Malaparte, *Technique du coup d'Etat,* pp. 160, 163, 170.
[4]Franco Vegliani, *Malaparte,* Venezia, 1957, p. 86.

throw Mussolini, and, on Balbo's insistence, Mussolini decided to punish him.

Officially Malaparte was sentenced to five years *confino* for "anti-Fascist activity abroad". His treatment in exile, however, was by no means as bad as he subsequently claimed. He was first sent to the island of Lipari, where he was allowed to live with his mistress, and within a year his new protector, Mussolini's son-in-law Galeazzo Ciano, arranged for his transfer to Ischia, and thence to Forte de' Marmi, where he was permitted to write articles for *Il Corriere della sera* under the pseudonym of *Candido*.

In spite of the threats of arrest and the suspicion which weighed on him, Malaparte's "anti-Fascism" after his return from the *confino* remains of dubious quality. In 1937 he managed to found a review, *Prospettive*, in which obsequious praise of the régime and articles devoted to the heroism of the Italian Fascists in the Spanish Civil War were accompanied by short stories, literary and art criticism of a consistently high standard. For Malaparte *Prospettive* was the last utterance of a generation. "The Alexandrian age of Europe is ending," he wrote in one of the last numbers, in 1940. "(And that, alas! is our age.) And we are starting to stink. Fortunately we all stink, and our only consolation is that we don't all stink in the same way. Some stink more than others. Some are more dead than others. But the only conclusion that can be drawn from any discussion of contemporary Italian and European literature is that our literary generation has finished its task. It was a necessary, very important task, but it's finished."[1]

The Duce's elevation above the Fascist Party and the Fascist Grand Council had been confirmed by the reform of the Constitution in 1926. In the years that followed he rose still higher. By laws passed in December 1928 and December 1929 his dictatorship was given legal form, and, knowing that his image alone held the multiple types of Fascism together, he soared to even greater heights, beyond all the practical possibilities of temporal power, until he became an idol, praised day in and day out, on the radio, in the papers, in every school text book. He was totally cut off from the reality of public opinion and nourished on the flattery of Fascist officials. Formerly an able judge of character, those he now chose

---

[1]*Prospettive,* No. 6-7, 1940.

as his collaborators were sycophants. Although no logical sequence of events led from the triumph in Ethiopia to the rapprochement with Germany which started in 1936 Mussolini's willingness to form an alliance with Hitler must be regarded, to a large extent, as the consequence of a megalomania which would have been unthinkable in the days when the Duce was still a shrewd and wary politician.

The view which Malaparte expressed of Hitler in *Technique du coup d'Etat* was widely shared in Italy. The Führer's person was considered ridiculous, his sexual tastes suspect, his anti-semitism loathsome, d'Annunzio, in a letter to Mussolini of October 10, 1933 describing him as a "ferocious clown" of "ignoble countenance".[1] But what was resented most about Italo-German friendship were the bigger and gaudier parades with compulsory attendance, organised by Achille Starace, the Party Secretary who had been bewitched by his visits to Germany. His aim was to abolish afternoon tea, top hats, gaiters, stiff collars, striped trousers and evening dress, substitute *lei* as a means of address by the "more virile" *voi,* and oblige the Italians to do the goose-step, called, by Starace, the Roman step.

Admiration for Nazi Germany was originally restricted to a group of men concentrated round Farinacci and a Neapolitan defrocked priest, Giovanni Preziosi. After Farinacci's dismissal as Party secretary he had started to look elsewhere for a more vital and violent régime, while Preziosi, a former Nationalist who edited *La Vita italiana,* was one of the few Italians to be sincerely anti-semitic.[2] Both Farinacci and he, therefore, found satisfaction in National Socialism. Soon after 1933 they began to launch an anti-semitic campaign together with the editor of *Il Tevere,* Telesio Interlandi. But they found little response in Italy, where Hitler's treatment of the Jews was generally condemned. Not only were the 45,000 Italian Jews perfectly assimilated, but they had fought

---

[1] R. De Felice, *D'Annunzio e la vita politica italiana dal 1918 al 1936,* pp. 30-31.

[2] Preziosi seems to have developed his conviction that the Jews were responsible for the world's evils after a visit to the Italian emigrants in the United States in 1905. He attributed the misery of the emigrants to the ruthlessness and rapacity of the New York Jews. See R. De Felice, *Giovanni Preziosi e le origini del fascismo 1917-1931,* Milano, 1962.

courageously in the First World War and in Ethiopia, several of
them occupying high posts in the army and the government. Nevertheless, after 1936, the anti-semitic campaign met with the approval
of Mussolini himself. "What saddens me most," wrote the critic Ugo
Ojetti in his diary in August 1938, "is this appearance of copying,
or rather obeying the Germans in everything: the Roman step, the
persecution of the Jews. There was no better way of making
Germany unpopular."[1]

It was at this point that the Italians began to turn against the
régime, timidly, gradually, silently but inexorably. Fascism had
been a label which they had been able to attach to national achievements. It had meant the glory of Italy, the assertion of Italy as a
great power. When Hitler was appointed Chancellor in 1933 it was
with pleasure that the Italians perceived Mussolini's high-handed
treatment of him, and the Duce's mobilisation of troops after
Dollfuss' murder had been a gesture of which they were proud. But
the anti-semitic laws meant that Mussolini's relationship with
Hitler was changing. No longer a paragon of skill admired by the
"Bohemian corporal", he was now taking orders from the corporal.
This spectacle was humiliating. Yet as the centralisation of power
continued, as the strength of the OVRA increased, it became more
and more difficult for the individual to express his disgust at the
turn Fascism was taking. Besides, there was no alternative to
Fascism. The Italians had to wait for the Fascist Grand Council to
eliminate their own leader in 1943 and for the King to arrest him.
Except for a minority and the few intellectuals I shall now be
dealing with Mussolini's anti-semitism lost him the support which
had reached its climax with the invasion of Ethiopia.

The first anti-semitic laws were passed before the Grand Council
in October 1938. They were frivolously advanced by Mussolini in
order to please Hitler—he had all the less excuse since the Germans
exerted no pressure on him until they actually occupied Italy in
1943,[2] and he was one of the only politicians for whom
Hitler had enough respect for him to adopt as independent
a policy as he chose. His belief was that there were so few Jews in
Italy that discrimination against them was a cheap way to satisfy

---

[1] U. Ojetti, *I Taccuini 1914-1943*, Firenze, 1954, p. 495.
[2] A subsidiary, but equally unsatisfactory, reason was Mussolini's
desire to instil a "racial consciousness" into the Italian forces in
Ethiopia, engaged, at the time, in copulating with Ethiopian women.

one of Hitler's whims and with this nearly all the other members of the Grand Council agreed. Only three of them, De Bono, Federzoni and Italo Balbo, voted against the laws, although the King protested against them and the Pope dissociated himself from them.

By the October measures foreign Jews were to be expelled from the country, while Italian Jews were prevented from going to school and joining the army or the Fascist Party. Subsequently Italian Jews found themselves unable to exercise most liberal professions or to have Aryan servants and own land or property, and in 1942 further laws were passed by which they were interned or set to work in factories, on roads and river beds. The authorities tended to be lenient in the application of these measures. In many cases the Jews excluded from schools could take private lessons from priests. Care was taken not to hand foreign Jews over to Nazi-occupied countries; Bocchini did his best to facilitate their passage to Palestine; and during the war the Italian soldiers in occupied territory regularly protected the Jews from the Germans.

Anti-semitism was not an integral part of Fascist doctrine. In Italy the Nazi myth of racial superiority corresponded to the myth of the rights of the "young", "proletarian" nation, against those of the "old" and "plutocratic" nations. This was the myth with which the revolutionary syndicalists and the Nationalists had justified Italy's intervention in the First World War, and it was to be the myth which Papini used to justify her entry into the Second World War. Otherwise, if we rest on Gentile's actualist philosophy of Fascism, it was a loose ideology open to anyone who believed in it. Admittedly Ardengo Soffici had, in his early writings, associated Jews with Socialism; admittedly Malaparte had gone to some lengths to prove that he himself was not only Aryan, but also basically unsympathetic to the Jewish cause; admittedly the Fascist press had, on various occasions, expressed a traditional suspicion of international Jewish finance; but until 1936 the majority of the various Fascisms which existed in Italy had simply not adopted a position towards the Jews, and the proof of the absurdity of the attempt to graft anti-semitism on to Fascism was the opposition it met with from those two well-established Fascists, Gentile and Marinetti. In 1938, hearing that Hitler wanted to include Futurism in an exhibition of "degenerate art" to be held in a railway carriage that would travel through Europe, Marinetti had persuaded Mussolini to refuse to let the train enter Italy, and that December he protested against the anti-semitic measures. "I wonder, with ever increasing perplexity," he complained in his review *Artecrazia*, "whether it is not you, instead of the Jews who, with these recurrent campaigns, have undertaken to sweep away those few, very few genuine Fascists of the first hour who are still in circulation and who oppose, unacknowledged and starving, the triumphant march of the countless opportunists and profiteers of the last moment."[1]

banned/
Censored

The prospect of Italy's entry into the Second World War as Germany's ally was a further indication of Mussolini's subservience to Hitler. The police reports on the nation's attitude towards the war are a good indication of the profound reluctance of the Italians to fight in 1939—a reluctance which was only slightly alleviated by the prospect of a rapid victory in 1940.[2] The vast majority of the Italians feared that Germany would not hesitate to impose her will on her weaker ally. Those few who favoured intervention had, primarily, the country's reputation at heart. "We must hope in the war to save our reputation and our seriousness," asserted Ugo Ojetti in August 1939. "We are rather like those braggarts who, thirty or forty years ago, were advised by their seconds to fight a duel at all costs in order to regain their good name and put an end to malicious gossip."[3]

Mussolini entered the war in June 1940 convinced that the Germans had already won and that they would deal more kindly with an ally than with a sympathetic spectator. Once Italy was definitively committed certain old loyalties, like that of Marinetti who joined his regiment on the Don in 1942, were aroused. Giovanni Papini, however, was a more recent supporter of Fascism. A former editor of *La Voce*, he had dabbled in Nationalism, Futurism and Pragmatism before becoming a devout Catholic. Initially he had been wary of Mussolini, but he warmed to him in the early thirties and became an ardent admirer after his election to the Academy in 1937. In his plea for Italian intervention in the war, *Italia mia,* he described Fascism as "the last battle for Italy's spiritual independence. It has torn ill-fitting clothes from our

---

[1]This number of *Artecrazia* was banned by the censor, see Renzo De Felice, *Storia degli Ebrei italiani sotto il fascismo,* Torino, 1962, p. 357.

[2]Alberto Aquarone, *Lo spirito pubblico in Italia alla vigilia della seconda guerra mondiale* in *Nord e Sud,* January 1964, pp. 117-125.

[3]U. Ojetti, *op. cit.,* p. 513.

back, it has burnt masks which hid our true face, it has restored the principles on which were based our ancient artistocratic republics and our dominions: the authority of the State and unity of command."[1]

The war, according to Papini, was to reunite Europe with Italy at its head. This he deduced from the fact that Italy was unquestionably the greatest country in the world. "Every other country lacks something. England lacks sculpture and music; France lacks the gift of mechanical invention; Russia lacks philosophy; Spain lacks political ability, and so on. Italy lacks nothing, absolutely nothing of that which constitutes the greatness and strength of the human mind."[2] But the war was also a struggle between poor countries and rich countries, Papini maintained, repeating the Nationalist-syndicalist views of 1914: "England—which is the supreme committee of the intercontinental community for the exploitation of the planet—has no European feeling or intentions and has always opposed any effort to assemble the nations which could prepare and lead to such a unity. So when Italy fights, she fights against British hegemony; she does not fight for herself alone, but above all for the good of Europe . . . This war is a war against the revolting democratic comedy, against the plutocratic domination, against the corrosive forces of the free-masonic and Judaic spirit, against the last degeneration and putrefaction of romanticism . . . A war of the working nations against the rich nations, of the revolutionaries against the conservatives, of the good Europeans against the conservatives, of the good Europeans against the cosmopolitans, of the compact nations against the molecular nations; of the future against the past. And finally, for us, also a national war."[3] Germany had offered Italy Nice, Corsica, Tunis and Savoy in the event of victory, so the war was the final stage of the Risorgimento. "Whoever does not think that Italy is fighting for a just cause and for her very existence," concluded Papini, "whoever does not feel that Italy must win at all costs and that she will win, is not worthy of being called an Italian—he despises his mother, betrays his brothers and allies himself with his country's enemies."[4]

In 1941 Italy lost her Empire and in July 1943 Sicily fell to the

---

[1]G. Papini, *Italia mia*, Firenze, 1941, p. 48.
[2]*Ibid.*, p. 152.
[3]*Ibid.*, pp. 176-186.
[4]*Ibid.*, p. 289.

Allies. On July 25 nineteen members of the Grand Council approved Dino Grandi's vote of no confidence in Mussolini. The Duce was placed under arrest and the King asked Marshal Badoglio to form a new ministry. Fascism had suddenly ended. The general delight with which most of the Italians received the news is a better indication than any other of the superficiality of the régime's appeal. With relief people returned to their former loyalties, the Catholics to the Pope, the monarchists to the King. The head of the Fascist press agency, Senator Morgagni, who shot himself, leaving a note expressing distress at Mussolini's fall, was considered risibly eccentric.

Just over six weeks after Mussolini's arrest, on September 8, the Italian army surrendered unconditionally to the British and the Americans, and the Allies landed in Salerno, while the German commander Kesselring, occupied Rome and Naples. The King fled to Brindisi with Badoglio, and the unexpected proclamation of a new Fascist government in the north was followed by news of Mussolini's liberation by the Germans.

The Italian Social Republic, or the Republic of Salò, as Mussolini's new State was called, stretched from the northern frontiers to the Allied lines, Mussolini himself living in Villa Feltrinelli at Gargnano on Lake Garda. At first sight there was nothing attractive about the Republic of Salò and few people adhered to it of their own free will. The majority of the Italian officers who had been captured by the Germans after the signature of the armistice chose to remain in concentration camps rather than sign a document which would enable them to return to Italy and join the Republican army, and most of the men of fighting age, who found themselves in Italy from November 1943 to the end of the war, joined the partisans whose growing power in the north rendered allegiance to Salò still more undesirable.

The new Republic was set up by the Germans, and two of its nominal founders, Farinacci and Preziosi, represented the most unpleasant aspects of Fascism—violence and anti-semitism. And yet the Republic retained a certain ambiguity. From a distance it was difficult to tell the extent to which Mussolini was manipulated by Hitler. Now that he was free of the King, who had fled to Brindisi, and of the Pope, who refused to recognise the Social Republic, might he not return to the origins of Fascism, to the Fascism of 1919? This was what Mussolini hoped, and this was what drew former Communists, liberals and anti-Fascists like Nicola Bombacci, Edmondo Cione, and Concetto Pettinato to Salò.

Proposing to give the Social Republic a truly progressive aspect, Mussolini concocted the Manifesto of Verona together with Nicola Bombacci. Based on a combination of the Charter of Labour of 1927 and the Fascist programme of 1919, the Manifesto was an attempt to institute a working form of corporativism. A republic was proclaimed; no citizen was to be kept under arrest for more than a week without a special order from the judicial authorities; individually earned property was to be respected, public services nationalised, and the trade unions amalgamated in a General Confederation of Labour. Italy's object was to create a European community which would guard the continent from the intrigues of the British, world capitalism and world plutocracy. "Members of the Jewish race" were designated as "foreigners", "during this war they belong to enemy nationality."

It was the apparent purity of the new Fascism which attracted the former Futurist Ardengo Soffici. He had long complained about the corrupt opportunists who were turning Fascism off its original course, and in January 1944 Galeazzo Ciano and four other members of the Grand Council[1] who had voted against Mussolini in July 1943 were executed in Verona at the behest of the new Fascist Party Secretary, Pavolini. The elimination of Ciano, undoubtedly a representative of one of the most corrupt trends in Fascism, was regrettable in itself, but meant, from Soffici's point of view, that Mussolini could start anew.

For all his ingenuousness Soffici did sincerely believe in the importance of liberty—and had much resented the intrusive and dominating attitude taken by Marinetti towards his fellow Futurists in 1914 on this account. He also realised that Fascism had developed into an oppressive force, and his opinion of the Soviet invasion of Finland in December 1939 displays a grudging acceptance of the "logic of the situation". "The Russian attack on Finland," he noted, "seems to me a logical consequence of previous facts. Less logical is the attitude of the Fascist press. There may be many reasons to show our aversion for the USSR and our sentimental sympathy for this tiny nation which defends itself heroically . . . But Fascist ideology is such that the pietistic mawkishness over

---

[1]De Bono, Pareschi, Gottardi and Marinelli.

poor innocent Finland, a small nation that has indeed been attacked, is in complete and absurd contrast to this ideology. Fascist Italy, which claims to be anti-democratic and anti-liberal, should realise that with the end of democracy and liberalism also ends the right of the small nations to remain what they were under those régimes. When individual rights have to yield before the totalitarian, authoritarian State, the rights of the smaller nations have to yield before the vital necessity of the larger ones. It was on the basis of this concept that we invaded Albania."[1] The scepticism, the "realism" with which Soffici accepted what he considered to be the inevitable course of events is similar to the attitude which some of the French collaborators held towards the Germans: the Germans had won, the larger nations had conquered the smaller ones, it was all in the logic of history and any resistance would be as futile as it would be absurd.[2]

Soffici had always had unbounded confidence in the Duce. In his diary Corrado Alvaro records a meeting with him at Papini's[3] house in Florence, on which occasion Soffici had remarked candidly: "Since there is no reason to believe that Mussolini is mad he will certainly lead us to greatness; of course, if he were mad, he would lead us to our ruin."[4] And in September 1939, Soffici confirmed his faith in Italy and Fascism. "Italy cannot remain humiliated. Nothing can stop her ascent, which I believe to be historically destined."[5] The brief experience of Marshal Badoglio's rule in August 1943 seemed to him incontestable proof of the qualities of Fascism, Fascism, that is, in its noblest form. "In the press and in the acts of the new government the base, poisonous, anti-Fascist, defeatist vindictiveness continues. The result is an

---

[1]Soffici-Prezzolini, *Diari 1939-1945,* Milano, 1962, pp. 51-52.
[2]See *infra,* p. 238.
[3]Papini did not adhere to the Republic of Salò. His refusal to commit himself was condemned by both the partisans and Fascists. In May 1944 he wrote in his diary: "Before 1914 I complained about the mediocrity of the times and the bourgeois dullness of events. These last thirty years have fulfilled and punished my yearning for excitement. Events which not even a madman would have imagined in his folly are now daily history: the face and spirit of the world are changing in an infernal whirlwind. And, as if fate were replying to my youthful mania, nowhere on earth is the tragedy more acute and desperate than in Italy." (G. Papini, *Diario,* Firenze, 1962, p. 187.)
[4]C. Alvaro, *op. cit.,* p. 272.
[5]Soffici-Prezzolini, *op. cit.,* p. 43.

inexpressible disgust and a spiritual reaction in favour of the past régime—its mistakes and faults are blamed, of course, but it is pointed out that the new government is merely repeating them the other way round. Mussolini had a great, generous, heroic, fundamentally Italian idea, and he tried to put it into practice. The idea was betrayed by his men: he was overthrown, kidnapped, and replaced by these mediocre quibblers, incapable of doing what he did, and determined to ruin Italy ideally, politically and historically."[1]

On November 28, Soffici wrote an article in *Il Corriere della sera* stressing the importance of a return to the origins of Fascism, repeating Papini's idea of the poorer nations warring against the plutocrats, and asserting the necessity for Italy to expand her territory. It was not long, however, before Soffici grew disillusioned. He had hoped that Mussolini would allow the press a degree of liberty. Instead, the new Fascist Party was more dogmatic than ever before. Pavolini unleashed the most brutal punitive expeditions throughout the Republic. The Minister of the Interior, Buffarini-Guidi, even more corrupt than Ciano, earned quantities of money by "Aryanizing" his Jewish acquaintances, and allowed a network of autonomous police organisations to develop, many of which tortured, for the first time in the history of Italian Fascism, with a sadism worthy of the Gestapo. "Liberty," concluded Soffici in June 1944, "is at the origin of every nation, and man's dearest aspiration . . . A people without liberty is no living people, it is a mere populace."[2] But he also expressed that reluctant admiration for Stalin which we find in the last writings of Drieu La Rochelle : "Roosevelt's and Churchill's loquacity, the form and substance of their speeches, invariably increase our respect for Stalin. We respect Stalin's seriousness, his simplicity, and the quiet, tough energy with which he gets to the point . . . He had his people fighting with the style worthy of a serious tragedy . . . The truth is that the Russians have fought with the spirit of a people who have fully accomplished their revolution . . . If the Axis were not to win, most true Fascists who escaped the flail would pass over to Communism and form a bloc with it. We would then have crossed the gap which separates the

---

[1] *Ibid.*, p. 197.
[2] *Italia e Civiltà*, June 23, 1944; see also Carlo Frankovich, *La Resistenza a Firenze*, Firenze, 1961.

two revolutions. A process of exchange and mutual influence would lead to the fatal fusion."[1]

A few Italians of repute adhered to the Republic of Salò for personal reasons : Graziani accepted command of the Republican army largely because he hated Badoglio, and the journalist Luigi Barzini agreed to direct the Fascist press agency, the Agenzia Stefani, out of gratitude to Mussolini.[2] Perhaps the most pathetic figure of those last months of Italian Fascism remains Giovanni Gentile. In the summer of 1943, a month before Mussolini's arrest, Gentile was one of several intellectuals to be asked to make an appeal to the nation. He was the only one to accept, and, on June 24, from the steps of the Campidoglio in Rome, he had delivered his *Discorso agli Italiani*—an appeal to patriotism and faith in victory.

The news of Mussolini's arrest shocked him, but although he felt the Duce had been betrayed, his loyalty went primarily to the King. When Leonardo Severi, who had been his secretary in 1922, was appointed as Badoglio's Minister of Education, Gentile wrote to congratulate him. Severi replied privately to his letter, thanking him, but at the same time wrote to *Il Giornale d'Italia* saying he wanted nothing to do with a man who had served the Fascists for so long. Gentile indignantly resigned from the directorship of the *Scuola normale superiore* in Pisa and the Italian Institute for the Middle and Far East, and moved to Florence to look after his publishing firm, Sansoni, determined to have nothing more to do with politics. On the strength of Severi's letter to *Il Giornale d'Italia* the Fascists on Radio Munich accused him of trying to collaborate with Badoglio.

---

[1] *Italia e Civiltà*, June 17, 1944.

[2] In 1940 his son, Luigi Barzini junior, after a riotous evening at the British Embassy, is said to have told members of the Embassy staff that the Italian secret service knew the British code and deciphered their messages. In doubt as to whether to believe him, the Embassy decided to send a message reporting Barzini's indiscretion: if the Italians knew the code they would arrest him. It so happened that Barzini had told the truth. He was duly arrested and was only spared the death sentence as a personal favour from Mussolini to his father; see *Dovrebbero schiaffeggiarsi almeno una volta al giorno* in *Il Secolo*, September 2, 1962. In these circumstances Luigi Barzini senior, could hardly refuse Mussolini's invitation to direct the *Agenzia Stefani,* although he never even entered the press agency buildings. His other son died at Buchenwald when the Italian troops were deported to Germany after the armistice.

Eager to surround himself with moderate elements capable of opposing the pressure exerted on him by the extremist followers of Farinacci and Pavolini, Mussolini hoped to make Gentile president of the new Academy to be formed in Florence. In November, therefore, he persuaded him to come to Gargnano. Gentile found the Duce aged, ill and humiliated by the weeks spent in prison. It was out of pity, personal affection, and an idealistic hope of being able to prevent the imminent civil war that he accepted the presidency of the Academy. In December he wrote in *Il Corriere della sera* deploring the violence of Fascists and partisans. On the staff of his review *La Nuova Antologia* he tried to assemble both government supporters and anti-Fascists, "as long as they are sincere and loyal Italians". Giovanni Preziosi accused him of protecting the Jews, and the attacks on Radio Munich resumed.

Gentile had few illusions about the new régime. The historian Gioacchino Volpe had visited him in 1943 and told him that he was remaining loyal to the King : Gentile appeared stunned and frightened. "Don't go on, don't go on!" Gentile begged him. "I don't want to be confused." Just as it had been important for Gentile to believe in his ideal Fascism, it was now essential for him to believe in the unlikely event of an Italian military victory. "I want Italy to resurrect with honour," he wrote to his daughter. "I want my Sicily, at my death, to be the Italian Sicily in which I was born and where my parents are buried . . . To remain at home and wait is the only way to compromise events. We must march as our conscience dictates. This is what I have preached all my life. I cannot deny it now that I am about to die."[1]

Ugo Ojetti, bed-ridden in his Florentine villa overlooking the Duomo, regarded the Allies as an army of vandals about to destroy every monument in Italy. "Each morning, as soon as my windows are opened, I look at Brunellesco's cupola. It stands there, intact, as it has stood for over five hundred years, and it might stand there for ever, provided America does not intervene."[2] Gentile shared this view, which was confirmed for him by the bombing raids on Florence. However much he hated the Germans, he now felt they would save Italy from destruction. "Wretched are those who do not see that the fall of Rome means not only the destruction of

---

[1] Giovanni Gentile, *la vita e il pensiero, IV,* Firenze, 1951, p. 40.
[2] *Corriere della sera,* December 9, 1943.

the capital, but the progressive destruction of the whole of Italy, because it is in the logic of things; and to curse the Germans or the Fascists is childish folly. If the devil himself were at Cassino and Nettuno instead of the Germans, we should wish him victory."[1]

In March 1944 Gentile made a speech before the Academy in which, for the first time, he publicly stated that it was important that Italy be allied to Germany. "Mussolini's resurrection was necessary," he affirmed, "like every event in the logic of history. German intervention, unacknowledged by the traitors, was also logical . . . Thus Italy found herself through Mussolini, and was assisted to her feet by the Leader of great Germany, whom Italy awaited at her side . . . fighting in the formidable battle for the salvation of Europe and western civilisation, together with her courageous, tenacious, invincible people. Mussolini has revived the Italy of Vittorio Veneto . . . the Leader's voice still rings, for it is the voice of immortal Italy."[2] A month after his speech Gentile was assassinated on the orders of the Italian Communist Party as his car drew up at the gates of his villa.

Gentile died, the martyr of a cause which he was almost alone in revering. It was in a way fortunate for him that he did not live to witness the farcical termination of Fascism in the spring of 1945 and the unheroic death of its founder and leader. But there was something else which Gentile was spared : the most obvious proof of the superficiality of Fascism's influence on Italy. Apart from the consequences of the war and the rhetoric of anti-Fascism which replaced the rhetoric of Fascism, the country emerged unaffected by a régime which had claimed to be revolutionary and which had lasted for over twenty years. There was little nostalgia for the man whose popularity in 1935 had been unparalleled. His former supporters eagerly ridiculed him and frequently found consolation in another revolutionary movement. Many of the younger men joined the Italian Communist Party, while Malaparte, who had managed to join the American forces in the south of Italy in 1943 after spending the first half of the war performing small security missions in the Balkans for Ciano and reporting on the Italo-German armies on the eastern front, died in 1957 with the personal blessing of the Pope, leaving his villa in Capri to the Chinese government.

[1]G. Gentile, *op. cit.*, p. 54.
[2]*Nuovo Giornale*, March 20, 1944.

H

GERMANY

Section Two

The unification of Italy and the proclamation of the Third Republic in France suggested that in these two countries liberalism had triumphed at least temporarily; but in Germany 1871, the year of national unity, had been preceded by the definitive end of liberal government. On September 3, 1866, two months after the defeat of the Austrian army at Sadowa, the Prussian parliament, by a large majority, had granted Bismarck an indemnity for the unconstitutional collection of taxes, thereby renouncing its sole means of control over the Prussian crown—its right to regulate the monarch's expenditure of money for military purposes. The monarch, William I, Bismarck, and the Junkers, were henceforth free to rule Prussia, and later Germany, unencumbered by Parliamentary control.

Parliament's loss of power resulted in a loss of interest in parliament. There ensued a tendency to avoid political responsibility, to leave decisions to those few, all-powerful men who ran the state—Bismarck, William II and his ministers, Caprivi and Hohenlohe, then Bülow and Bethmann Hollweg, and finally the High Command of the German army. From the material point of view this had certain advantages. It meant that men who might in other circumstances have sought a career in parliament concentrated, instead, on business, or, as the historian Werner Sombart said in 1903, on "economic life". It led to a speed of economic and industrial development unprecedented in any other country in the world. "German industry," wrote A. J. P. Taylor, "was 'forced' as vegetables and rhubarb are forced: exposed for centuries to the frost of disunity and absolutist rule, it was brought suddenly into the hothouse of the new Reich and shot up in luxuriant, unnatural growth." And by 1910, Germany, with as many large industrial cities as the whole of the rest of Europe, was "a runaway horse or, more truly, an overpowered steam engine out of control . . .

Runaway in economic development, with steel production now twice as great as British, German exports passing the British mark, and German national wealth well above that of either Britain or France. Runaway in population with the sixty-five million mark passed in 1910 and more than sixty per cent of the population living in towns. Runaway in armaments . . . Runaway in political ambitions. . ."[1]

In such overdevelopment and the almost universal reluctance to assume political responsibility after national unification lies one of the reasons for the unrealistic or "escapist" aspects of German Nationalism between 1871 and Hitler's rise to power. But to this we must add other causes. Until 1871 Germany had been a collection of independent states and principalities, often opposed to one another, and nearly all opposed to Prussia. In order to hold them together and to fulfil his ambition of imposing the Prussian Junkers on the rest of Germany, it was necessary for Bismarck to play on the spirit of nationalism, to get as many men as possible to identify their own prosperity with the greatness of the nation. Italy was in an analogous position, but there was a major difference between the two Nationalisms : Italian Nationalists *could,* and the more liberal ones *did,* have as objects of their admiration figures like Mazzini who had believed in rationalism, equality and individual liberty. German Nationalism, on the other hand, was directed *against* liberty, equality, fraternity and the rationalism of the French philosophers. It developed in the first decade of the nineteenth century as a reaction against the Napoleonic armies which invaded German territory—and what these armies represented were the "rights of man". The German Nationalists' aim had been to evict the invader, purge Germany of foreign influences (particularly of the foreign ideology introduced by the French) and restore ancient German traditions.

Two themes constantly recur in German Nationalist thought: one is the Führer, the traditional military and political leader,[2] and the other the Reich, a Germany supreme in Central Europe. The point of the Reich, however, is not so much *what* it is as *where* it is, for, geographically, the Reich was indefinitely expandable. Founded by Charlemagne in 800, it was indeed an

---

[1]A. J. P. Taylor, *The Course of German History,* Hamish Hamilton, 1945, pp. 124, 160.
[2]See *infra,* p. 120.

ancient institution. At its largest it could be taken to include all the territory occupied by German-speaking minorities in Europe—it would, of course, cover Austria and Bohemia. It could include much of Hungary and most of Poland. It might even stretch as far as Transylvania and the Balkans—everywhere to the costs of local (particularly Slav) Nationalism. But a Reich of these dimensions was an unrealistic proposition: it would be virtually impossible to govern.

It was a mark of Bismarck's genius that he should have decided on "Little Germany". Only a small Germany, he realised, could be comfortably run by the Prussian Junkers. So, again in the interests of the Junkers, the only foreign "Nationalism" which Bismarck was eager to suppress in order to protect those Germans who might be threatened by it, was that of the Poles. By the Alvensleben convention in 1863 he secured the East Prussian border and Russian friendship at the expense of Poland. He resisted the temptation to amalgamate Austria, Trieste and Bohemia and showed no alarm at the legendary "Slav menace" in Central and South-Eastern Europe. His sole concessions to the Nationalists' yearning for the Great Reich were the annexation of Alsace and Lorraine and the conquering of colonies in Africa.

Yet German Nationalism survived Bismarck. The idea of Greater Germany was treasured by writers and historians throughout the 1890s. It was constantly in the minds of many of those intellectuals under the Weimar Republic with whom I shall be dealing, and Hitler's determination to fulfil it was to be one of his qualities which appealed most to the German electorate in the early thirties. On the level of practical politics the German government committed itself to the Greater German policy by deciding to enter the Great War on the side of Austria-Hungary in August 1914. The declaration of war by Austria on Serbia signified the failure of the Habsburg system, and it was the Habsburg monarchy alone, the guarantee of Austro-Hungarian independence, which Bismarck had shrewdly and carefully avoided destroying, that formed a bulwark against Germany's advance into Central Europe.

If we examine the writings of some of the artists who supported Germany's entry in the war and justified the violation of Belgian neutrality in the belief that the Austrian and German armies were defending a cultural tradition on which their existence as artists depended, we find the same convictions that induced the German

Nationalists to decry the Napoleonic invasion at the beginning of the nineteenth century. I shall deal with Thomas Mann not only because he admirably expressed those widespread feelings which were to undermine the Weimar Republic from the start, but because he himself decided to stand by the Republic in 1922, as soon as he realised what the triumph of those principles he had held before and during the Great War would entail.

Like dozens of other intellectuals in France, Italy and England Thomas Mann welcomed the war as an end to a period of complacency, "a ghastly world, which is now over, or will be over once the great storm has passed! Was it not teeming with vermin of the spirit as with maggots? Was it not fermenting, reeking of the decay of civilisation?"[1] The war, according to Mann, was a conflict of ideas : the "culture" of Germany was opposed to the "civilisation" of France and England, art to intellect, Frederick the Great to Voltaire. Battle itself, he believed, was essentially artistic. "That victorious, war-like principle of today, organisation, is the basic principle, the essence of Art . . . Endurance, precision, circumspection, boldness, courage in the face of hardship and defeat in the battle with solid matter; contempt for what is known as 'security' in bourgeois life . . ., the habit of a dangerous, tense, attentive existence, . . . all these things are both military and artistic."[2]

Two months after writing these lines, in January 1915, Mann ended an article entitled *Friederich und die grosse Koalition* in which he supported Germany's invasion of Belgium by pointing out the necessity of Frederick the Great's violation of Saxon neutrality in 1756 in self-defence. Two men who had opposed the war from the outset replied indignantly. Romain Rolland attacked Mann in *Au-dessus de la mêlée*, while Mann's brother, Heinrich, riposted with an essay on Emile Zola. Wounded by Heinrich's deliberate contrast of Zola, the defender of Dreyfus, to the militaristic ruler of Prussia, Thomas Mann wrote his *Betrachtungen eines Unpolitischen* more as an answer to his brother than to Romain Rolland.

The book appeared in 1919 and the case which Thomas Mann put in favour of the aristocratic intellectual seems more justifiable in the light of modern totalitarianisms than it seemed to the democrats of the Weimar Republic. Mann saw democracy as the com-

---

[1]T. Mann, *Politische Schriften und Reden, II,* Frankfurt a/M, 1968, p. 10.
[2]*Ibid.*, p. 8.

pulsory political participation of every individual and this, he considered, was fatal for the artist. As he had formerly equated art with war he now equated it with political reaction and opposed the "artist" to the "intellectual". "Art will always 'turn back', it will always be reactionary. It is with good reason that it has always been included, like religion, among the anti-democratic forces; and to compare the artist with the 'intellectual' is democratic humbug. Never will art be moral in the political sense. Never will it be virtuous; never will progress be able to count on its assistance. Art has a basically unreliable, treacherous streak; its delight in scandalous irrationalism, its love of that 'barbarity' which produces beauty is ineradicable. Even if one wanted to call this love hysterical, unintellectual, immoral to the point of endangering the world, it remains an immortal fact. And if one wanted to, if one could extirpate it, one would both be freeing the world from a grave danger and ridding it of art—and few people want to do that."[1] In Thomas Mann's eyes the reactionary "artist" was the product of German "culture", while the intellectual was a democratic product of civilisation. Germany, the champion of the "musical", artistic spirit, needed a reactionary régime, insisted Mann. He was "fully convinced that the German people will never love political democracy for the simple reason that they cannot love politics. . . I want a monarchy, I want a tolerably independent government, for that alone will guarantee political freedom in the spiritual and economic sphere."[2]

Mann's political writings are filled with contradictions, the contradictions inherent in his own personality. By proposing a rational defence of irrationalism he was defeating his own purpose. And even *he* had to admit that he was too much of a *Zivilisationsliterat* to be able to identify himself convincingly with the pure German cause which he sustained. Indeed, he was proud of his Brazilian blood inherited from his mother and liked to observe within himself the conflict between Nordic irrationalism and Southern practicality which was to be the subject of *The Magic Mountain*. By the time he had finished *The Magic Mountain*, in 1924, he had decided to support the Weimar Republic: in his case, at least, Settembrini,

---

[1] T. Mann, *Politische Schriften und Reden, I,* Frankfurt a/M, 1968, p. 295.
[2] *Ibid.,* pp. 23, 194.

the liberal intellectual who endeavours to save Mann's hero, Hans Castorp, from the influence of Naphta, had won. But as far as Hans Castorp was concerned the question of victory remained open, and if Mann had consciously and rationally committed himself to Weimar, as a writer, on an artistic level, he could never truly resist those romantic forces he associated with Germany.

In the summer of 1918 Germany's military position still seemed good. The Bolsheviks had signed the Treaty of Brest-Litovsk in March, and from March to mid-July the German armies scored a succession of victories in the west. It was not until August that the British broke through the German lines on the Western Front and September that Bulgaria fell in the east. Germany's military dictator, General Ludendorff, relinquished his supreme powers, after ordering constitutional monarchy and agreeing to the necessity of signing a peace treaty on the basis of President Wilson's Fourteen Points. Prince Max von Baden became constitutional Chancellor and early in October the German government informed the nation that it was suing for peace.

Nevertheless German troops remained on foreign territory in the west, while the Brest-Litovsk treaty would seem to guarantee the security of the Eastern Front. On hearing of the government's decision to request peace a great many Germans believed, in all good faith, that they had been betrayed. Even Ludendorff, who had ordered peace negotiations in the first place, thought he could renew the war in October when he at last realised what the Fourteen Points, which he had not previously read, implied. But the position was untenable. Ludendorff was dismissed on October 26. The Allies refused to treat with the Emperor, William II, and continued to advance. In Berlin the Spartacist, Karl Liebknecht, was preparing to proclaim a Soviet Republic. The only way to meet these two threats, the advance of the Allies on the one hand and the rise of the Spartacists on the other, was for the government to announce the Emperor's abdication and proclaim a German Republic. Max von Baden announced the abdication on November 8, and the next evening William II left for exile in Holland. On the same day Baden handed his Chancellorship over to the Social Democrat Friederich Ebert, while the other Social Democrat in Baden's cabinet, Phillip Scheidemann, hurriedly proclaimed the German Republic at Weimar. Two days later, on November 11, the German armistice commission, led by Matthias Erzberger, a Catholic Centre

Party Deputy, came to an agreement with the Allies to end the war.

At the moment of the armistice revolution seemed inevitable. On October 28 sailors had mutinied in Kiel; the Spartacists under Liebknecht and Rosa Luxemberg all but held Berlin; and on November 8, Kurt Eisner, an Independent Socialist,[1] proclaimed himself Prime Minister of the Bavarian Republic. On November 10, however, Chancellor Ebert agreed with General Groener, Ludendorff's successor, to support the German army in its efforts to restore order at home and combat Bolshevism. A few months after this formal alliance between the army and the new government—an alliance to which the Weimar Republic owed its survival—the Minister of Defence, Noske, sanctioned the *Freikorps,* bodies of volunteers, for the most part former officers and unemployed youths with high ideals or a taste for violence. Their purpose was to quell Bolshevik uprisings in Germany and to fight against the Russians, Poles and various independence movements on Germany's eastern borders.

In January 1919 the army broke the Spartacist rebellion in Berlin and Rosa Luxemberg and Liebknecht were murdered on the orders of a group of officers. The Bavarian ruler, Eisner, was shot by a right-wing fanatic, Graf Arco, on February 28. The workers retaliated with a general strike; the Social Democratic government under Johannes Hoffman collapsed on April 6; and, in considerable confusion, a Soviet Republic was proclaimed in Munich. Despite the excellent intentions of its leading ideologists, Erich Mühsam, Gustav Landauer and Ernst Toller, the Soviet régime was an ill-organised and brutal business which proved decisive in turning the Bavarian bourgeoisie irrevocably against the left-wing. The Communists took a number of citizens as hostages and when Munich was stormed by government troops and *Freikorps* at the end of April, the hostages were put to death.

The Republican government of Germany did all it could to restore order. Indeed, there was nothing revolutionary about it. It had adapted itself as well as it could to the existing system—the system it had inherited from William II. It had enlisted the support of the army and proved ruthless in quelling risings from the

---

[1]The Independent Socialists and the Spartacists were the only factions of the German Social Democratic Party to have opposed the war.

left. What the Nationalists could never forgive, however, was the proclamation of the Republic in the moment of defeat, its acceptance of the Allied armistice, and, above all, the signature of the Treaty of Versailles. Republican admission of defeat came to be known as the *Dolchstoss*, the stab (in the back), and the régime came to be associated with the betrayal of German honour.

The Treaty of Versailles was signed by the Social Democratic Foreign Minister, Hermann Müller, on June 28, 1919. Germany agreed to pay large sums of money as reparation of the damage she had caused the Allied powers, plead guilty to causing the war and surrender her "war criminals". She lost all her colonies, Alsace-Lorraine to France, West Prussia, Upper Silesia and Posen to Poland and small areas to Belgium. Danzig was to be a free city, while East Prussia was separated from the rest of the country by the "Polish corridor". The left bank of the Rhine was occupied by Allied troops and the German army was to be reduced to 100,000 men and disarmed. Finally, Germany had to give up, once and for all, any hope of uniting with Austria.

Within a relatively short time the attempted *coups d'état* and the political assassinations came from the Nationalists. In March 1920 Ludendorff and a Prussian bureaucrat named Wolfgang Kapp attempted to seize power in Berlin, but the Berliners ordered a general strike, paralysed the city and Kapp was forced to resign as "Chancellor" four days later. Matthias Erzberger, the Minister of Finance, was assassinated in August 1921 by two former officers, and in June 1922, Walter Rathenau, the Foreign Minister and signatory of the Treaty of Rapallo which cancelled the terms of the Brest-Litovsk treaty and secured the friendship of the Soviet Union, was shot in the streets of Berlin by members of the *Freikorps*.[1]

Continuous Nationalist agitation, the Germans' refusal to reduce their army to the size stipulated by the Treaty of Versailles, and, above all, Germany's failure to pay the reparations promptly, induced the French Prime Minister, Poincaré, to decide to occupy the Ruhr. In January 1923 French and Belgian troops marched into the centre of German industry, and for the first time Germany was faced with the direct consequences of defeat. Foreign troops penetrated deep into German territory. These troops were French,

---

[1]See *infra,* p. 128.

soldiers whose military capacity the Germans despised profoundly, and they included coloured regiments. The German government ordered "passive resistance". Every office, factory, bank and mine in the Ruhr closed. Inflammatory pamphlets were written about the atrocities committed by the occupants, and Communists and Nationalists united in defence of Leo Schlageter, a German terrorist shot by the French.

Nearly all the Germans, however liberal their politics, were outraged. "We are glad to hear that you received our cards from Spain," Thomas Mann wrote to Ernst Bertram in June. "Much has been lost, and this, like so many worse crimes, is the fault of the French. A ghastly nation, ghastly, ghastly. I can say no more. But their mixture of infamous cruelty which undoubtedly has sexual undertones and the veneer of humanitarian and sentimental phraseology which they put before the eyes of Europe, have aroused all the impersonal, mythical antipathy of which I am capable in addition to a truly shattering disgust."[1] And in November he wrote to his brother Heinrich: "We are assured that the details of the Ruhr have not been exaggerated, but are even slightly less than the truth. The wrath that has been aroused is appalling—deeper and more widespread than that ever caused by Napoleon. One cannot foresee what will happen. And the worst of it is that a French failure, however desirable, would entail the triumph of Nationalism at home."[2]

The strikes in protest against the occupation completed the destruction of the German economy. There had been growing inflation since the end of the war, but it reached its climax between Rathenau's assassination and the end of 1923. By the beginning of November the rate of exchange with the dollar had risen from a million marks in August to a hundred and thirty thousand million. "I have known days," Stefan Zweig recalled in his memoirs, "when I had to pay five thousand marks for a newspaper in the morning and a hundred thousand in the evening. . . On streetcars one paid in millions, lorries carried the paper money from the Reichsbank to the other banks, and a fortnight later one found hundred-thousand-mark notes in the gutter; a beggar had thrown them away contemptuously. . . The unemployed stood around by

---

[1] *Thomas Mann an Ernst Bertram: Briefe aus den Jahren, 1910-1955,* Pfullingen, 1960, p. 121.
[2] Thomas Mann, *Briefe,* 1889-1936, p. 204-205.

the thousands and shook their fists at the profiteers and foreigners in their luxurious cars who bought whole rows of streets like a box of matches."[1]

With inflation at its highest point Germany, or at any rate middle class Germany, was crushed. "Instead of taxing the rich," I quote A. J. P. Taylor, "Germany paid her way and paid off all the costs of the war by destroying the savings of the poor and middle classes. . . (The inflation) stripped the middle classes of their savings and made the industrial magnates absolute dictators of German economic life. . . The former rentiers . . . became resentful of the republic to whom they attributed their disaster; violent and irresponsible; and ready to follow the first demagogic saviour, not blatantly from the industrial working class. The inflation, more than any other single factor, doomed the republic; its cause was not the policy of the Allies, but the failure to impose direct taxes on the rich."[2]

Yet the combination of the occupation of the Ruhr and the destruction of the national economy had results which were by no means negative. In August 1923 the Chancellor Cuno was replaced by Gustav Stresemann, the leader of the former National Liberals, and, on November 12, he appointed Dr. Hjalmar Schacht as special commissioner to restore the German currency. Largely at the instigation of the British the Dawes Plan was drawn up; Germany was accorded substantial financial loans by the United States; and by the summer of 1924 inflation had ended. By the Locarno Pact the inviolability of the Franco-German and Belgian-German frontiers was guaranteed, and the French gradually withdrew their troops. From 1924 to the Wall Street crash Germany enjoyed a period not only of stability, but of relative prosperity.

National Socialism played on the fears and prejudices of the lower middle classes. It exploited the losses they had suffered during the inflation and preyed on the terror left by the Soviet Republic of Munich. Not only was the attraction of the National Socialist German Workers' Party initially restricted mainly to Bavaria, but it was more petty bourgeois than Italian Fascism had ever been. It had no such colourful and anarchistic intellectual sponsors as the Futurists. Indeed, as far as this study is concerned,

---

[1]S. Zweig, *The World of Yesterday,* Cassell, 1941, pp. 237-238.
[2]A. J. P. Taylor, *op. cit.,* p. 196.

one of the most obvious differences between the early history of the National Socialists and that of the Italian Fascists is the singular lack of appeal which National Socialism had for intellectuals. Most of the men I shall be writing about, however extreme their nationalism or however similar in many respects their views to those of the Fascists, looked down on the Nazis.

The twenty-five point Party programme, drawn up in 1920 by Anton Drexler,[1] Gottfried Feder, the economist, and Adolf Hitler, who, after leaving the army in April, rapidly became the most important figure in the Party, aimed at the protection of the middle classes. It called for the nationalisation of trusts and large companies, the abolition of unearned income, the confiscation of war profits, the expropriation of land required for national purposes, the abolition of ground rents and prohibition of land speculation. Big department stores, it said, were to be communalised and rented to small tradesmen. With regard to foreign policy it stipulated the abrogation of the Treaty of Versailles, and demanded the fulfilment of the Greater German programme, the union of Germany with Austria and the Sudetenland. Finally, catering to men for whom anti-semitism was, as we shall see, a superstition rather than a prejudice, it stated that Jews were to be excluded from German citizenship and office, while those who had entered the country since 1914 were to be extradited. Any inferiority the lower middle classes might feel was to be compensated for by the knowledge that they were Aryan, members of the Germanic master race.

One of the greatest paradoxes to emerge from a study of Nazi Germany is the Germans' attitude to anti-semitism. Research done both in the Third Reich and after the Second World War, has shown that by no means all the members of the National Socialist Party were in agreement with Hitler's policy towards the Jews. When, in 1934, six hundred National Socialists sent autobiographical histories to the American sociologist Theodore Abel, sixty per cent of them made no mention of anti-semitism in giving their reasons for joining the Party. What usually attracted them was

---

[1]Anton Drexler, a Bavarian locksmith, and a journalist named Karl Harrer, founded the German Workers' Party in January, 1919. In February 1920 Hitler, who had been put in charge of the Party's propaganda, announced that it was henceforth to be called the National Socialist German Workers' Party, *Nationalsozialistische Deutsche Arbeiterpartei* (NSDAP).

the idea of a Führer and Greater Germany.[1] Nevertheless, the consequences of Hitler's hatred for the Jews, and the indifference with which the Germans watched these consequences, were not altogether fortuitous.

Broadly speaking two types of anti-semitism existed in Germany. There was, on the one hand, a fashionable and aristocratic disdain for the Jews which we find amongst the German upper class throughout the nineteenth century. Although the Jews only formed about one per cent of the population their relatively swift rise in science, the arts, business and the liberal professions after their legal emancipation had been confirmed in 1871, stimulated prejudice. Even here, of course, anti-semitic propagandists exaggerated the Jewish advance. According to censuses taken in 1910, 1925 and 1933, "the highest Jewish percentage was among the lawyers, where it was 16.25; among doctors 10.88; among State-appointed lawyers (judges, magistrates and prosecutors) the percentage was only 2.75. The percentage of Jews in universities was 2.64; among teachers in the elementary and secondary schools 0.53. The figures given in the cultural field show a Jewish percentage among theatrical producers of 5.61, among actors and dancers 3.00, musicians and singers 2.04, booksellers 2.5, painters and sculptors 2.44, editors and authors 5.05."[2] However that may be, in the German Empire orthodox Jews were rarely received in court, and were not admitted to the nobility (even to the rank of *von*), or to high posts in politics, the army or academic life.

At the same time there was a far more sinister type of anti-semitism—anti-semitism as a superstition. The idea of some sort of Jewish conspiracy had existed in Central Europe for hundreds of years, but it took the unification of Germany, the violent awakening of a national consciousness, and the economic crisis which succeeded German unity to give this idea the power it assumed. The first indication of such a development was the crisis of 1873 which followed the boom after the Franco-Prussian war. A

---

[1]See T. Abel, *Why Hitler Came To Power,* New York, 1938; M. Müller-Claudius, *Der Antisemitismus und das deutsche Verhängnis,* Frankfurt a/M, 1948; W. S. Allen, *The Nazi Seizure of Power: the experience of a single German town, 1930-1935,* Chicago, 1965.

[2]*The Yellow Spot, the outlawing of half a million human beings: a collection of facts and documents relating to three years' persecution of German Jews, derived chiefly from National Socialist sources, very carefully assembled by a group of investigators,* Victor Gollancz, 1936, p. 18.

wave of resentment against the Jews broke out in two sections of
the lower middle classes, the artisans and small retailers. The
inevitable victims of the speedy advance of German industry and
capitalism, embittered and insecure, they watched enviously the
Jews who succeeded both in the liberal professions and in certain
trades.

Tradesmen were encouraged in their prejudice, and many
university students converted to it, by the writings of a
number of intellectuals who, no longer able to have that influence
on politics to which German writers had formerly been accustomed, turned to extravagant philosophies of history. And, like
the petty tradesmen, they sought a scapegoat for their loss of status.
Paul de Lagarde, an orientalist of high repute, pointed out in his
Deutsche Schriften, which appeared in 1878, that the Jews were
impeding the unity of the German *Volk,* that only after they had
been destroyed "as speedily and thoroughly as possible" could this
unity be achieved. In 1881, Eugen Dühring, lecturer in economics
and philosophy at the University of Berlin, depicted the Jews,
in his *Die Judenfrage als Rassen-, Sitten- und Kulturfrage,* as the
most evil element of humanity, a race whose very blood was wicked.

Such were the writings which strengthened the theories of the
völkisch Nationalists, those baleful products of the Napoleonic
invasion of Germany, who looked back to an archaic world of
peasants bound together by their blood and their race, and united
in the worship of the sun god. The return of this world, for which
the *völkisch* Nationalists longed, depended on the defeat of the
Jews, for it was, they believed, the Jews, the powers of evil, who
had destroyed the primitive, happy German society, partly by
supporting such symbols of modernity as capitalism, liberalism,
democracy, Socialism, and the urban way of life in all its forms,
but above all by inventing Christianity.

The German military defeat, the proclamation of the Weimar
Republic, the economic crisis and the inflation, the influx of Jewish
refugees from Russia,[1] all served to increase a prejudice which
found complete justification in the *Protocols of the Elders of Zion,*

---

[1] Here again the statistics "reveal that instead of hundreds of thousands, the total number of Jewish immigrants into Germany (both
from East and West) between 1910 and 1925 did not exceed 31,000.
Between 1925 and 1933, 9,000 of them had left the country again."
The Yellow Spot, pp. 17-18.

I

published in 1920. This document was proof of a Jewish conspiracy to secure world domination. It showed that, according to a Jewish plan, every Gentile institution, religion, monarchy, aristocracy was to be undermined. Authority was to be destroyed by a succession of wars and economic crises. When the resistance of the Gentiles had been broken the Elders of Zion, who already controlled most political organisations, were to emerge as rulers and impose Judaism as the sole religion.

The *Protocols* initially met with a certain amount of credence all over the world. In England both *The Times* and *The Spectator* took them seriously, and it was not until a year after publication, on August 18, 1921, that *The Times* printed a long article proving that the document was a forgery, two-fifths of which were plagiarised from an obscure work by a French lawyer, Maurice Joly—*Dialogue aux Enfers entre Montesquieu et Machiavel,* published in Brussels in 1864. The forgery itself was mainly concocted by Pyotr Ivanovich Rachkovsky, one of the heads of the *Okhrana,* the Tsarist secret police.[1] Only a few ardent anti-semites in England continued to believe in the *Protocols* after this revelation—one of them was Lord Alfred Douglas, who had founded a weekly review, *Plain English,* in which to express his anti-semitic views, another was Lord Sydenham. In France Jacques Bainville of the *Action Française* suggested that to say the *Protocols* were a forgery proved nothing, while Céline[2] was later to use them as an important source of inspiration. The most steadfast believers, however, were the Germans. Ludendorff, for example, firmly sustained the authenticity of the *Protocols* which were reprinted twice within a month of publication and sold 120,000 copies within a year.

Hitler himself was not as fanatically anti-semitic as Julius Streicher, the editor of *Der Stürmer,* or as Alfred Rosenberg, who succeeded that hero of early National Socialism, Dietrich Eckart, as editor of the party paper, *Der völkische Beobachter,* in 1923. Yet he did have an emotional hatred for the Jews which he appears to have developed in Vienna before the First World War. In Vienna, too, he became aware of the possibilities of exploiting the anti-semitism of the lower middle classes, and observed atten-

---

[1]Norman Cohn, *Warrant for Genocide, The Myth of the Jewish world-conspiracy and the Protocols of the Elders of Zion,* Eyre & Spottiswode, 1967.
[2]See *infra* p. 198.

tively the methods of two men who had a considerable influence on his political formation—Georg von Schönerer, the leader of the Pan-German Nationalists, and Karl Lueger, the head of the Christian Social Party. Lueger, who had once said "I decide who is a Jew", was entirely cynical in his anti-semitism, but he put it to such good use that he became not only mayor of the Austrian capital, but the leader of the strongest party in the Austrian parliament.

Hitler's hatred for the Jews, however, was genuine—far more so than Lueger's, but, from the most important statement of his beliefs, *Mein Kampf*, which he wrote in 1924, it also becomes apparent that he regarded anti-semitism primarily as a means of mobilising the masses. He did indeed regard the Aryans as the "custodians of culture" and thought it essential for the survival of humanity that the Aryan race be protected and purified. Yet he also believed the sheer negative force of virulent anti-semitism to be the best way of arousing that irrational side of the masses which would enable him to control them. "Whoever wants to win the masses must know the key to the door of their hearts. It is not objectivity, which is weakness, but will power and strength . . . Our masses can only be nationalised successfully if, along with the positive battle for our people's soul, its international poisoners are extirpated. . . Without a clear recognition of the race problem—and of the Jewish problem, the German people will never rise again."[1]

Like Mussolini, Hitler had one aim: to rise to power. All his life he continued to believe that anti-semitism was a good method of seizing power and an excellent way to keep it—in this, at least, he was consistent. When it came to biding by the other points of the 1920 party programme, however, he was just as cynical as the Duce, and according to Baldur von Schirach, the leader of the Hitler Youth, even the Führer's ideas on what should actually be done with the Jews were extremely vague. A few days before Hitler was appointed Chancellor, in January 1933, Schirach asked him: "How would you solve the Jewish problem when you came to power?" "We'll see about that," Hitler replied, and added a little later: "It's too primitive to think that I want to throw all the Jews out. That's the sort of thing Streicher raves about. I simply don't want any Jews employed by the State. They can keep their shops and businesses: but they must clear out of politics and the

---

[1] A. Hitler, *Mein Kampf*, München, 1938, pp. 370-372.

law." "How about our party programme?" asked Schirach. "Should Jews be German citizens?" "We'll see about all that. Don't you worry about it. What will our party programme matter to us once we're in power?"[1]

Of the men who did so much at the end of the nineteenth century to foment anti-semitism and elaborate a doctrine of the supremacy of the German race, one had the fortune to meet Hitler and inform him personally of his admiration—Houston Stewart Chamberlain. His book *Die Grundlage des neunzehnten Jahrhunderts,* which appeared in 1900, had an immense influence on the ideology of National Socialism. Like Lagarde and Dühring before him, he believed it essential for the good of humanity that the Germans should triumph over the Jews. Only thus would a new world emerge in which modern technology could be combined with the traditional, rural and hierarchical Germanic culture.

As anti-English as he was anti-semitic, Chamberlain was a naturalised German, though the son of an English admiral. He associated England with an unpleasant period in a boarding school and the Edwardian "decadence" that struck him on his rare visits. "A victorious England," he wrote to his brother in October 1914, "would now be terrible, a catastrophe for the whole world, while I would see the hope of a necessary moral and political rebirth in a defeated England."[2] Chamberlain had spent most of his early life in Vienna, and then moved to Bayreuth where he married one of Richard Wagner's daughters. Convinced that *völkisch* Germany was the only country capable of reinvigorating Europe, he saw the proclamation of the Weimar Republic as the victory of Jewry. Shortly after this unfortunate event he expressed a sentiment fully shared by the *völkisch* Nationalists and the anti-semitic wing of the National Socialists : "One can maintain with no exaggeration that what we are experiencing in Germany today is the supremacy of the Jews; when the newspapers tell of eighty to a hundred Jews in the so-called government, this is inaccurate, for among the remaining twenty there are very many half-breeds. . . The only hope for a future victory of the Germanic genotype would be if the Germans learnt from the present bitter experience to see the danger of this dual of humanity, and, with a courageous hand, not

---

[1]Baldur von Schirach, *Ich glaubte an Hitler,* Hamburg, 1967, pp. 164-166.

[2]H. S. Chamberlain, *Briefe, 1882-1924, I,* Munich, 1928, p. 245.

kill or even harm the Jews, but give them the status of foreigners and exclude them from all public services. Any Jew who continued to rebel would be immediately extradited like any other unwelcome foreigner."[1]

Four years before his death, in 1923, Chamberlain met Hitler in Bayreuth. His enthusiasm was unbounded. "You are not as you were described to me," he wrote to the Führer, "you are not a fanatic. I could almost say the opposite. A fanatic wants to persuade people. You want to convince them, just to convince them —and that is why you succeed. . . Your eyes have hands, they capture people and hold them in their grip. . . And your hands are so expressive when they move that they compete with your eyes. Such a man can administer peace to a poor tortured soul. My belief in Germany never wavered, but I must confess that my hopes were at a low ebb. You have transformed my state of mind with one stroke. That Germany should give birth to Hitler in her hour of need proves that she is still alive . . ."[2]

What little intellectual support Hitler initially managed to gather came mainly from the *völkisch* Nationalists, whose artistic production was to flourish when he came to power. Their leading representative, to whom Hitler accorded a visit in 1925, was Adolf Bartels, the poetaster and critic from Schleswig-Holstein. "Everyone agrees that one of my greatest merits," Bartels was to claim in 1935, "is to have completed the distinction between Germans and Jews in the history of German literature."[3] And indeed, it was Bartels' intent to discredit Heinrich Heine for, "however well he handles the German language and German poetical forms, however much he knows about the German way of life, it is impossible for a Jew to be a German."[4] Although North German National Socialism tended to be less reactionary, less violent in its anti-semitism than that of the Bavarians, the *völkisch* aspect of the party policy did have a curious appeal for a number of Bartels' compatriots from Schleswig-Holstein. Such a one was the Expressionist painter Emil Nolde: the first German painter to join the National Socialist Party, in 1920, he was the first to be proclaimed

---

[1] H. S. Chamberlain, *Briefe 1882-1924, II,* Munich, 1928, p. 71.
[2] *Ibid.,* p. 124, see also H. S. Chamberlain, *Lebenswege meines Denkens,* München, 1919.
[3] *Völkischer Beobachter,* February 3/4, 1935.
[4] *Ibid.*

degenerate by Rosenberg's *Kampfbund für deutsche Kultur* in 1929.[1]

Their mediocre literary production, their primitive anti-semitism, their philistinism and narrow-mindedness were some of the reasons which led the other groups of Nationalists to regard their *völkisch* counterparts with contempt. And their contempt increased when it came to assessing National Socialism. For one thing Adolf Hitler was neither a gentleman nor a German : he was the son of an Austrian petty customs official and had not risen above the rank of corporal in the First World War : he was, as Thomas Mann put it, a mere "foreign vagabond"[2], and, as long as a *coup d'état* seemed possible, in the first years of the Weimar Republic, there were men a great deal more eligible than Hitler to whom to look—officers, artistocrats, gentlemen, above all, *German* gentlemen. Yet there was also another factor which made Hitler unacceptable, especially to the younger Nationalists[3] : this was his determination to seize power at the head of a political party. The older Nationalists were more tolerant towards this aspect of National Socialism, for they, too, tended to join a party, the German National Party. But the younger men refused allegiance to any political organisation which, by the very fact of being organised, implied some form of compromise with the established order.

German Nationalism in its traditional form was well represented by a man who was born in 1880 and saw in the Weimar Republic the collapse of everything which had seemed of value to him in Imperial Germany. As far as Oswald Spengler was concerned the Emperor's abdication was followed by anarchy. Living in Munich, he experienced the discomfort of the Soviet Republic in April 1919, and, looking back on it that May, described it as "nothing but hunger, looting, filth, danger and rascality without parallel."[4]

Before we proceed to an examination of Spengler's political ideals we should glance briefly at the work which made his name and his fortune, *The Decline of the West*. The purpose of the book was to provide a "morphology of history", to examine the course of

---

[1]See *infra*, p. 152.
[2]T. Mann, *Politische Schriften, II*, p. 258.
[3]See *infra*, p. 119.
[4]*Spengler Letters*, translated by Arthur Helps, G. Allen & Unwin, 1966, p. 80.

past historical cycles and thereby determine the future. The revival of the cyclical theory was one of many fruits of the revolt against positivism. Held by the Hebrews, the Greeks and the Romans, sustained in the twelfth century by the German monk Joachim of Floris, it recurs in the work of Vico and of Nietzsche. Before, during and after the First World War it emerged in the writings of such men as Pareto, while lesser minds like Malaparte used the idea that the time had come for a revival of heroic values as a justification of Fascism[1]. According to Spengler history consisted of thousand yearly cultures which accomplished an organic life cycle. Although each of these cultures was different from the other, "the inner structure of one corresponds strictly with that of all the others", allowing the historian to draw certain irrefutable conclusions. The mainspring of history, for example, was "life", irrational and instinctive. And the last stage of decay of each culture was "civilisation", a stage which the Western or "Faustian" culture reached after 1789. The West, therefore, dominated by money and materialism, was condemned. Spengler confidently announced that this final stage would be the age of Caesars, each of whom, with his militia of devoted followers, would struggle with the other for world supremacy while the rest of humanity looked on helplessly. The Westerner should resign himself to this fact, give up the idea of ever producing a great work of art, and concentrate on technical achievement. "We are civilised, not Gothic or Rococo people; we have to reckon with the hard cold facts of a *late* life . . . Of great painting or great music there can no longer be, for Western people, any question. Their architectural possibilities have been exhausted these hundred years. Only *extensive* possibilities are left to them. Yet, for a sound and vigorous generation that is filled with unlimited hopes, I fail to see that it is any disadvantage to discover betimes that some of these hopes must come to nothing . . . And I can only hope that men of the new generation may be moved by this book to devote themselves to technics instead of lyrics, the sea instead of the paint-brush, and politics instead of epistemology. Better they could not do."[2]

The first volume of *The Decline of the West* appeared in April 1918. In 1922 Spengler completed a further volume, and by 1927

---

[1] See *supra*, p. 53.
[2] O. Spengler, *The Decline of the West, I,* translated by C. F. Atkinson, G. Allen & Unwin, 1926, pp. 40-41.

100,000 copies had been sold. The gloom of the book had an appeal all over the world, but nowhere more than in Germany. Reading the ambitious proposals in the introduction was to pull aside the curtain of the fortune-teller's tent, and the assertion that Germany was not the only country in the Western world to be in decline was found highly encouraging. Oswald Spengler, an unhappy, lonely bachelor, misogynous, misanthropic and irritable, the victim of migraines, a weak heart, poor eye-sight and insomnia, had given up his career as a school-master in order to write his book. He wrote it in penury during the First World War, and, within a few months of the appearance of the first volume, he had become one of the most famous and influential figures in Germany. Of a retiring disposition, Spengler never answered his critics and rarely appeared in public. Fond of identifying himself with Herostratus and Tiberius, symbols of the frustrated megalomania, self-hatred and impotence which obsessed him, he envied "everyone who *lives*. I have only brooded, and whenever I was really offered the possibility of living I drew back and let it pass, only to regret it bitterly as soon as it was too late."[1] Owing to his ill health his life as a man of action was a continual frustration. He was considered unfit to enlist during the war, and the "rapture of battle", the pain and the violence which he had longingly described in his short story *Der Sieger* in 1910, were destined to remain in his imagination.

One of Spengler's most perceptive critics was Thomas Mann. Mann basically disliked Spengler, and Spengler, who had little respect for any of his contemporaries, certainly had none for Mann. In 1922 Mann referred to him as Nietzsche's "ape"[2] and, in *Ueber die Lehre Spenglers,* called him "a defeatist of humanity", a snob with bourgeois ideas. Resenting Spengler's materialistic statement that twentieth-century man could no longer hope to produce a work of art, Mann wondered what would become of men like Spengler if intellectuals ceased to exist. Yet he was aware of Spengler's qualities. "His *Decline,*" he wrote, "is the product of immense force and will-power, far-reaching and knowledgeable. It is an intellectual novel of great entertainment value, reminiscent... of Schopenhauer's *World as Will and Idea*."[3]

---

[1]A. M. Koktanek, *Oswald Spengler in seiner Zeit,* München, 1968, p.1.
[2]T. Mann, *Briefe 1889-1936,* p. 202.
[3]T. Mann, *Politische Schriften, II,* p. 121.

Spengler's interest in politics had been aroused by the Second
Moroccan Crisis in 1911 when Germany seemed on the verge of
war with France over conflicting claims in North Africa. It was then
that the idea of *The Decline of the West* came to him, but it was
only in 1919 that he decided to take an active part in politics himself. The result was disastrous, for Spengler, whose long term
prophecies often came true, failed almost invariably in his short
term predictions. Until 1918 he was confident that Germany would
win the war. Although he foresaw the rise of totalitarianism and
Russia's ascent to world power, he initially stated that Bolshevism
would be short-lived. So with German politics between the wars.
The men he backed proved unrealistic or incapable.

The essence of Spengler's political ideas after the defeat is contained in a letter of December 1918. "I see that the German revolution is following the typical course," he wrote, "slow abandonment
of the existing order, violent disturbances, wild radicalism, subver-
sion." His hope was that the monarchy would be strengthened by
the crisis, for he was in no doubt about the fact that it would
be restored. "What will be accomplished by the programme of
present day Socialism," he went on, "is precisely what the
Hohenzollern state has always desired : the organisation of production and of communications by the State; everybody to be a servant
of the State; that is to say illiberal and authoritative forms of the
most extreme kind. I foresee that the old Prussian element with its
incalculable treasures of discipline, organizing power and energy
will take the lead, and that the respectable part of the working
population will be at its disposal *against* anarchism in which the
Spartacus group has a remarkable relationship with the left
liberalism of the Jewish newspapers, pot-house pamphlets, jobbers
and doctrinaires." But this was to take time. First Germany must
be punished for the disgrace brought on the monarchy and for the
military defeat. She must be punished "until finally . . . the Terror
has brought to a head such a degree of excitement and despair, that
a dictatorship, resembling that of Napoleon, will be regarded
universally as a salvation. But then blood must flow, the more the
better . . . First of all force, then reconstruction, not through the
agency of the dilettantism of political majorities, but by the superior
tactics of the few who are born for and destined to politics." He
concluded with the wish that "the upheaval will have also so
severely affected the Western powers that the reconstruction of

central Europe from us will create the position which is our destiny and in which I steadfastly believe."[1]

Although *Preussentum und Sozialismus,* which appeared in December 1919, was not nearly as successful as the first volume of *The Decline of the West,* it is important in that it illustrates the points both of agreement and divergence between the older and younger Nationalists. Nearly all the Nationalist groups, from the National Socialists to the National Bolsheviks[2], claimed, at one moment or another, to implement what they called "Prussian Socialism", the only form of Socialism suitable for Germany. Where Spengler departed from the younger Nationalists was in his insistence that this Prussian Socialism could only be realised under a hereditary monarch. Where he met them was in the description of the hierarchical form this Prussian Socialism would take. His concept of the ideal society was of a pyramidal structure in which each man knew his place. Although a gradual evolution, a gradual improvement of each man's lot would come about, this structure would remain. It would contain "local corporate bodies organised according to the importance of each occupation to the people as a whole; higher representation in stages up to a supreme council of state; mandates revocable at any time; no organised parties, no professional politicians, no periodic elections."[3] The ideal of this society was to be the traditional Prussian submission to a leader, a *Führer.* "Prussian society," Splengler maintained, was founded "on the distinction between command and obedience," so, not unnaturally, he described the father of Frederick the Great, Frederick William I, as the "first conscious Socialist".

Despite the small sales of the book Spengler received numerous letters of admiration. Admiral von Tirpitz wrote that he wished Spengler's "ideas could find response in the Marxist infected working classes"[4] and Spengler was more than ever determined to resort to political action. It is difficult to establish the precise nature of the political rôle he would like to have played. His best connections were in the German National Party and in 1921, after meeting the industrialist Paul Reusch, he had hoped, vainly, to influence

---

[1] *Spengler Letters,* p. 69 *ff.*
[2] See *infra,* p. 124.
[3] O. Spengler, *Preussentum und Sozialismus* in *Politische Schriften,* München, 1932, p. 64.
[4] *Spengler Letters,* p. 93.

the newspaper *Münchener Neueste Nachrichten* which Reusch was partially financing. Through Reusch Spengler met further industrialists and financiers, and tried, equally vainly, to direct a group of newspapers. He even considered forming a party of his own which would unite all the right-wing elements. Above all, however, he regarded himself as a political adviser whose destiny it was to guide the guileless Republican politicians. In 1918 he had sent a copy of *The Decline of the West* to Walter Rathenau, but his attempts to meet him failed and he turned against him as soon as Rathenau championed the Republic. In September 1923 he wrote to the new Chancellor, Stresemann, suggesting that he should be used to establish contact with General Smuts, the only man influential enough to revise the terms of the reparations and withdraw the "war guilt" clause from the Treaty of Versailles. He demanded an interview with Stresemann, but it came to nothing.

Spengler's natural pessimism had increased that January with the occupation of the Ruhr : this step, he believed, was taken by the French in order to reduce Germany to a military base from which France could strike at England. As the last and worst year of the post-war crisis, 1923 was the year which saw the last and most brutal attempts to overthrow the Republic. Spengler's political ambitions flourished and ended, and one of his first great disappointments was the decision of the Commander-in-Chief of the German army, General Otto von Seeckt, to give Stresemann his unconditional support. To Spengler (and to many other enemies of the new government) Seeckt had seemed the best man to overthrow the régime, and indeed, he was one of the few who were truly in a position to do so. But Seeckt was shrewd enough to see that it was ultimately in the interests of the army to support the Republic. Enraged by this decision and piqued by Stresemann's refusal to take his advice, Spengler wrote in October that "the replacement of the Stresemann-Seeckt dictatorship by an unparliamentary one is necessary if everything is not to go to pieces . . . Since the fall of Cuno, instead of a foreign and economic policy, all we have had is a struggle for position between noisy factions. The Rentenmark will collapse as a result . . ."[1] Believing that Stresemann had profiteered during the inflation in association with the

---

[1] *Spengler Letters*, p. 139.

firm of Wolff, Spengler was sure that both he and Seeckt were instruments in the hands of international finance and represented that materialistic stage of civilisation which he had described in *The Decline of the West*. It was time for the monarchy to be restored and Spengler now looked to the conservative Bavarian State Commissioner, Gustav von Kahr, whose aim it was to put on the throne Prince Rupprecht, the eldest son of Ludwig III of Bavaria.

Kahr, Lossow (the commanding officer in Bavaria) and Seisser (the head of the State police) thought that they could use Hitler and his storm-troopers, the S.A., ex-servicemen and former members of the *Freikorps* who had been brought into the Nazi party by Captain Röhm, to overthrow Stresemann's government. Hitler, on the other hand, hoped to overthrow the government with their and General Ludendorff's assistance, and dictate his terms to them once he was in power. In the Munich Bürgerbräukeller on the evening of November 8, Spengler assisted at the ridiculous failure of Hitler's putsch. After a convincing speech Hitler had to leave the beerhall to settle a quarrel which had started when some of his S.A. men tried to occupy the Engineers' barracks. The spell he had cast broke in his absence; Lossow, Kahr and Seisser departed unobstrusively; and the next day the S.A. were routed by the local police in the Odeonsplatz.

Sickened by the failure of the plot, Spengler attributed it solely to the inexperience of the National Socialists. On February 26, 1924 Hitler was tried for treason,[1] and in a lecture "on the political duties of German youth" that same day, Spengler deplored the National Socialists' amateurish adoration of flags, parades and facile slogans. "These things undoubtedly satisfy feelings, but politics are something else."[2] "The wretched Hitler case", as he described the trial, confirmed his view that Hitler was no potential Caesar.

When he surveyed Europe Spengler was agreeably surprised by the turn events had taken in Italy. Initially he may well have been prejudiced against Mussolini in view of his support of French occupation of the Ruhr. As early as June 1923, however, Spengler mentioned a "circle round Mussolini . . . evidently beginning to

[1]He was sentenced to five years in prison, of which he served less than nine months.
[2]O. Spengler, *Politische Schriften*, p. 148.

form a front against France"[1] and in February 1924 he stated that the *Camelots du Roi* of the *Action Française* and the Italian Fascists bore the mark of the armies of the future. Besides, "Fascism has at least realised the importance of reaching an understanding with the governing economic powers . . . It counts on results rather than programmes and parades."[2] The next year he visited Italy for the first time since the war and sent Mussolini five of his works, and, in the period that followed, only slightly modified his admiration of the Italian régime. Fascism, he was to say in *The Hour of Decision* in 1933, was *on the way* to the Caesarism of the future. But it was too left-wing. It courted favour "in the streets" and was in reality little more than "the socialistic ideology of the last century", an imitation of Bolshevism. "This all belongs to the past . . . What anticipates the future is not the being of Fascism as a party, but simply and solely the figure of its creator. Mussolini is no party leader, although he was formerly a labour leader; he is the *lord* of his country."[3]

After Hitler's trial the National Socialist Party was outlawed and the party paper, *Der völkische Beobachter,* banned. While the Führer was in prison, the most active member of the movement was Gregor Strasser. A representative of the left wing of National Socialism Strasser was an upholder of the nationalisation of heavy industry and large estates. In view of his anti-capitalism it is strange that he should have at first been the only National Socialist to get in touch with Spengler. Writing to him for the first time in 1925, Strasser described *The Reconstruction of the German Reich,* which had appeared in the previous year, as "a mine of highly constructive and practical policy, in which I see a far-going relationship with our aims."[4] After going to considerable lengths to inform Spengler of what these aims were—the introduction of German Socialism with forceful and practical means—he begged him to contribute to a National Socialist monthly magazine. Spengler rejected this offer, but remained in correspondence with Strasser until 1934. Did he hope to influence Hitler through him? It is possible. Unfortunately only two letters of the correspondence

---

[1]*Spengler Letters,* p. 124.
[2]O. Spengler, *Politische Schriften,* p. 153.
[3]O. Spengler, *The Hour of Decision,* translated by C. F. Atkinson, Allen & Unwin, 1934, p. 187.
[4]*Spengler Letters,* p. 181.

remain. Otherwise, as he wrote in 1927, "I have not only stood aloof from the National Socialist Movement which led to the Munich putsch, but actually, unfortunately in vain, done my utmost to prevent it . . . I am of the opinion that politics should be based on sober facts and considerations and not on a romanticism of the feelings."[1]

In *Preussentum und Sozialismus* Spengler did indeed emphasise the superiority of the Germanic race; he did indeed believe in an élite. But he had no time for the "petty, superficial, limited and unworthy" anti-semitism of the Nazis. "The most dangerous anti-German characteristics," he wrote, "the tendency to dream of internationalism and pacifism, the resentment of authority, power and success, are deeply engrained in the *German* character. Members of one's own race are more dangerous than those of another. A minority always prefers assimilation when offered the choice."[2] To the National Socialists such an attitude was clearly unacceptable. In one of the few literary contributions to National Socialist ideology *The Myth of the Twentieth Century*, Alfred Rosenberg condemned Spengler outright : "He does not see racial-spiritual forces forming the world, but fabricates abstract schemes to which we are all subjected 'fatally'. Ultimately this brilliantly presented doctrine denies race, personality, intrinsic value, every real, culturally productive impulse of 'the heart of hearts' of the Germanic mind."[3]

Although most of the aspirations of the German Nationalists were based on irrational premises and, except in the case of the jurist Carl Schmitt, rarely on an intelligent critique of the Weimar system, the new Republic had defects which justified criticism. The constitution itself was weak. The aim of the Republican government had been to put an end to the supremacy of Prussia over the other federal German states, but this raised the problem of centralised rule. In Prussia the Social Democrats were supreme, largely as a result of the universal suffrage which had followed the proclamation of the Republic, and the Social Democrats were eager for Germany to be a unitary republic. But they were opposed both by the Nationalists, who wanted the federal states to retain a certain

---

[1] *Spengler Letters*, p. 217.
[2] O. Spengler, *Neubau des deutschen Reiches*, München, 1924, p. 18.
[3] A. Rosenberg, *Der Mythos des 20. Jahrunderts*, München, 1934, p. 404.

autonomy as an obstacle to democratisation, and by the Independent Socialists who were horrified by the idea of a united Germany and the power it might wield. The compromise between these attitudes allowed the states to retain their autonomy but also ensured their powerlessness. "The result," according to A. J. P. Taylor, "was to be expected: Reich governments of the left, anxious to avoid constitutional disputes, dared not interfere with state governments of the right; Reich governments of the right, caring nothing for the prestige of the constitution, did not hesitate to overthrow state governments of the left. In other words, the constitution became an instrument for crippling the democratic elements in Germany, if they ever attempted to defend it against its enemies."[1]

The Republican government met with opposition on every level of administration. The civil servants on whom it depended for carrying out its reforms, tended to associate it with the military defeat. Judges, prosecutors and magistrates made no secret of their sympathy for the extreme right, and proved unnecessarily harsh in their dealings with all elements from the left. In the Reichstag itself after 1921 there was never a majority which sincerely upheld parliamentarianism. Even the Social Democrats were aware of this and in 1926 the former Bavarian Minister of Justice, Müller-Meiningen, admitted that "the most dangerous enemies of the parliamentary system are the parliaments themselves : their lack of discipline, their pettiness, their narrow-mindedness, their provincial party spirit, their arrogance, their garrulousness and lack of concrete action! Quarrelsomeness and party strife are the most dangerous enemies of parliament . . . From the outbreak of the Revolution till now the German Reichstag has given its citizens the worst example of political dignity and understanding . . . So far its proceedings have been closer to the goings on in a lunatic asylum than to those in a national parliament."[2]

Few of the Nationalists had any more practical solution to offer than an aggressive foreign policy. All they could do was to call for the end of liberalism and parliamentarianism. Demanding the abolition of political parties, the young Nationalists preferred the idea of *Bunde,* unions on which some of the Youth Movements were based. They wanted an organic state, a people's community untroubled by class warfare. They called for the Führer and the

---

[1]A. J. P. Taylor, *op. cit.,* p. 185.
[2]Müller-Meiningen, *Parliamentarismus,* Berlin, 1926, p. 18.

Third Reich, but the interpretation of these terms varied considerably. The Führer was a traditional German idea, implying loyalty, obedience and the fulfilment of duty on the part of his inferiors. For Wilhelm Stapel the Führer was a combination of the "sovereign, warrior and priest", for Julius Binder he was "the spirit of the nation", who had understood his people's history and knew and willed himself to be a Führer. For some he was a warrior, for others a Messiah. In every case he was the one leader figure who would replace parliament and act alone in the name of the people. The concept of the Third Reich was still vaguer. It varied from Spengler's *"Germanic ideal, an eternal tomorrow . . . arrows of yearning for the other bank of the river . . .",* Moeller van den Bruck's, "always promised . . . never fulfilled . . . perfection that can only be attained in the imperfect", and Thomas Mann's "synthesis of power and spirit", to the more concrete proposals of Giselher Wirsing, a contributor to *Die Tat*[1], who saw it as the traditional German supremacy in Central Europe.

A number of the younger Nationalists had welcomed the original proclamation of the Republic: what turned them against it irremediably was the signature of the Treaty of Versailles. In theory the Republic, preceded by the deposition of the Emperor, was revolutionary : but they did not accept this revolution. Too attached to certain traditional institutions, too nationalistic to accept the internationalism of the Communists, they wanted a revolution of their own. "Old Nationalism," wrote Kurt Sontheimer, "meant the continuation of the old conservative traditions of a national state in the altered circumstances of the new Republic. New Nationalism, on the other hand, was something really new; it did not fit into the traditional parliamentary classification, and took as its point of departure the World War which it regarded as the beginning of a new era."[2]

While the old Nationalists, the men of Spengler's generation, hoped for a return of the pre-war days, the *Kaiserzeit,* Edgar Jung, and the young "Conservative Revolutionaries", went back still further for their ideals. They aimed, not unlike the *völkisch* Nationalists, to eliminate the traces of the French Revolution and restore "eternal values". "We call the conservative revolution the

---

[1] See *infra,* p. 131n.
[2] K. Sontheimer, *Antidemokratisches Denken in der Weimarer Republik, Studienausgabe,* München, 1968, p. 26.

Oswald Spengler

Ernst Jünger

restoration of all those elementary laws and values without which man loses contact with nature and God, and can no longer build up a true order. Equality will be replaced by inner quality, social principles by assimilation in a graduated society, mechanical election by the organic development of the Führer, bureaucratic tyranny by the inner responsibility of real self-management, the happiness of the masses by the rights of the people's community (*Volksgemeinschaft*)".[1]

The spokesman of yet another group, the Revolutionary Nationalists, was that authoritative young writer, Ernst Jünger. His political thought was based on his experiences in the Great War, and the organisation on which his revolutionary state was to be modelled was the army. For ever in search of adventure, Jünger ran away from home to join the Foreign Legion when he was seventeen, but after he had been for a few weeks in Sidi-Bel-Abbes his father reclaimed him and he returned to Germany to volunteer in 1914. Jünger's conduct in the Great War was more than distinguished : wounded several times, he was one of the few soldiers to be awarded the *Pour le mérite* (Erwin Rommel was another). By 1918 he was an officer in the *Stosstruppen,* the gallant and pampered élite of the German army, and in 1920 he published his war diary *Im Stahlgewittern.* In his war books Jünger did not merely describe the comradeship and sense of accomplishment which he felt on the battle-field : he shared Thomas Mann's fascination for decay and, with the same scientific precision frequently to be found in Mann, analysed the emotions of pain and fear.

Yet there were two Ernst Jüngers. There was the elegant stylist who went to war with a copy of *Tristram Shandy* in his pocket, and there was the hysterical pamphleteer. Only those men who had participated in the heroic but morbid experience of the German trenches, he and his brother Friederich Georg believed, were worthy to form the élite of the revolutionary State, and they were determined to sustain the revolutionary spirit by a rhetorical exaltation of trench warfare. "Modern Nationalism . . . wants the extraordinary. It does not want moderation . . . but its basic productive quality, spiritual strength . . . The father of Nationalism is war. What our literati and intellectuals say about it is of no

---

[1]Edgar Jung, *Deutschland und die konservative Revolution* in *Deutsche über Deutschland,* München, 1932, p. 380.

K

importance. War is the experience of blood, so all that matters is what *men* have to say about it . . .War is our father, it has given birth to us in the glowing womb of the trenches as a new race, and we recognise our origins with pride. Thus our values should be heroic values, the values of warriors and not of shopkeepers who want to measure the world with their yardstick. We do not want what is useful, practical and agreeable, but that which is necessary and desired by fate."[1]

After the armistice in 1918 Jünger stayed on as a lieutenant in the army. He contributed to a manual on infantry tactics and was posted in various garrisons throughout the country until his demobilisation in 1923, when he took up residence in Leipzig and embarked on the study of zoology. As an officer with a distinguished career and a writer of considerable quality he was much in demand in Nationalist circles. In Leipzig, before his demobilisation, he had represented Lieutenant Rossbach's *Freikorps* in Saxony for one month, and by 1925 he was contributing to the *Stahlhelm* paper, *Die Standarte*.

The *Stahlhelm,* founded by Franz Seldte in 1919, was the largest ex-servicemen's organisation in Germany, its conservative principles bearing a certain resemblance to those of the *Croix-de-Feu* in France.[2] Like all the other semi-legal military organisations founded to save Germany from Bolshevism it was outlawed after Rathenau's murder in June 1922, but was reinstated the following year. Its aims, which it hoped to accomplish legally, were to overthrow the Republican régime, revise the Treaty of Versailles and install a dictator. The supplement of *Die Standarte* to which Jünger contributed, had been founded by the *Stahlhelm* leaders, Seldte and Düsterberg, to let the organisation's younger members express their more radical views, and in it Jünger attacked every facet of democracy—universal suffrage, elections in general, legality, any form of compromise with the Weimar system. "Revolution, revolution! This is what must be preached permanently, vindictively, systematically, mercilessly . . . In the Great War a new, dangerous type of man has developed and this type must be set into action."[3]

---

[1]Ernst Jünger, *Vorwort* in Friederich Georg Jünger, *Der Aufmarsch des Nationalismus,* Leipzig, 1926, p. 11

[2]See *infra,* p. 192.

[3]*Die Standarte* May 20, 1925, see also H-P Schwarz, *Der konservative Anarchist, Politik und Zeitkritik Ernst Jüngers,* Freiburg i/B, 1962.

Die Standarte had a circulation of 150,000 and Jünger's ideas were considered dangerous. The paper was temporarily suppressed, but in April 1926 Helmut Franke, the editor, was allowed to start a further supplement. Yet within five weeks this too was withdrawn, following an article in praise of Leo Schlageter and the murderers of Erzberger and Rathenau. Jünger and Franke then proceeded to take over a Munich paper, *Arminius,* financed by the *Freikorps* hero, Captain Ehrhardt,[1] an individual who owed his influence among the young Nationalists to the sinister rôle he had played in the first years of the Republic. He had been behind nearly every *coup* and political assassination. He had led the finest brigade into Berlin at the time of the Kapp putsch in 1920, and then fled to Munich where he appears to have founded the "Organisation Council", a mysterious body whose activities were never clear, but which may well have organised the assassinations of Erzberger, Gareis and Rathenau.[2] In 1926, however, Ehrhardt joined the *Stahlhelm* and committed himself, if only briefly, to the course of legality, thereby gaining the support of Seldte and Düsterberg.

Although Jünger had attacked Ehrhardt's policy in the *Stahlhelm,* he hoped, through *Arminius,* to unite all the Nationalist movements. It is this that explains his initially favourable attitude to Hitler : in 1925 he had stated that the National Socialists "had more fire and blood than the so-called revolution has been able to produce in all these years."[3] He even sent Hitler dedicated copies of his war books: only one survives, a copy of *Feuer und Blut* dedicated "to the national leader Adolf Hitler". In his turn Hitler sent him a copy of *Mein Kampf,* and in 1927 offered him a National Socialist seat in parliament. This Jünger refused. He rejected parliament as totally as he did parties. He had disapproved of Hitler's decision to adopt legal methods in 1925 and by the late twenties feared that National Socialism would betray the purity of National Revolutionary ideals. A party based on Italian Fascism, he believed, would never do in Germany, for Fascism was no more than "a late form of liberalism . . . at the same time a brutal stenography of the liberal

---

[1]It was through *Arminius* that Jünger first met Goebbels. A number of other contributors also rose to important posts in the Third Reich: Hans Friederich Blunck, Alfred Rosenberg, Hanns Johst.

[2]See R. G. L. Waite, *Vanguard of Nazism,* Harvard, 1952.

[3]*Die Standarte,* November 1, 1925.

constitution . . . Fascism is as little suited to Germany as Bolshevism . . ."[1]

Jünger's most important work of this period, *Der Arbeiter,* appeared in 1932. One of the major effects which the Great War had had on him was to make him aware of the potentiality of modern technology. Warfare had been transformed by technical discoveries and now demanded the concentration of every means of production in the country on armament and the improvement of the national fighting force. It was in this state of "total mobilisation" that Jünger envisaged the Germany of the future, run by the worker-warrior, the heroic technocrat formed in the trenches of the First World War. This was the main theme of *Der Arbeiter,* and through it ran Jünger's contempt for the "bourgeoisie" and anyone who hoped to avoid living in a state of mechanised militarisation. "Like many others," Spengler wrote to him, "you have not been able to free the idea of the worker from Marxist phraseology. The official, the peasant, the contractor, the officer, is a worker as much as the artisan. The only one today who works to the limit of his powers is the peasant, and it is he who is defrauded by the division into bourgeoisie and proletariat. But the peasantry are still a force in Germany . . ."[2]

Jünger's intolerance towards the bourgeoisie brought him progressively closer to the last group of anti-democrats, the National Bolsheviks. They formed the cusp of opposing ideological circles, but what ultimately placed them nearer to Bolshevism than to Hitler's National Socialism, was their policy towards Russia. Hitler was consistent in two points: he was consistently anti-semitic and he was consistently determined to crush the Slavs. Germany, he stated in *Mein Kampf,* needed to expand. "We put an end to the perpetual Germanic march towards the south and west of Europe and turn towards the lands of the east. We put an end to the colonial and commercial policy of before the war and pass on to the territorial policy of the future. But when we speak of new territory and soil in Europe today, we can only think of Russia and the border states subject to her. Destiny itself seems to wish to point out the way for us here . . . This colossal empire in the east is ripe for dissolution."[3] By expanding eastwards the Germans would not

---

[1] *Süddeutsche Monatshefte,* September 12, 1930.
[2] *Spengler Letters,* p. 272.
[3] A. Hitler, *op. cit.,* pp. 742-743.

only obtain the *Lebensraum,* the "vital space" which Hitler considered essential for them: they would be able to assert their own racial superiority at the expense of the Slavs.

Germany's greatest statesmen, however, had always been aware of the importance of friendship with Russia if Germany were to enjoy any measure of security in the east. This was what induced Bismarck to sign the Alvensleben convention in 1863, and this was one of the ideas behind the Treaty of Rapallo which Rathenau had signed in 1922. But in addition to the practical advantages of an alliance with Russia, there were powerful emotional ties between the two countries. Thomas Mann had always claimed that the "eastern" irrationalism of Russian literature made Russia far closer to Germany than any of Germany's Western neighbours, and another supporter of this view was a minor, but none the less influential writer, Arthur Moeller van den Bruck, who had some part in the intellectual formation of National Bolshevism. Germany, Moeller insisted, was not a Western country. The West represented a decadent civilisation, admirably described by Spengler, and alien to the German spirit. Germany's only hope of salvation, as far as he could see, was an alliance with Russia against the West, against democracy and Republicanism.

In 1919 Moeller founded the *Juniklub* whose aims were to impose a nationalistic, Socialist corporative state with a strong anti-Western foreign policy.[1] Hitler's appearance at the club in 1922 was a failure. "You have everything I lack," he told Moeller. "You create the spiritual framework for Germany's reconstruction. I am but a drummer and an assembler. Let us work together." But Moeller took against him strongly. "That fellow will never grasp it," he told a colleague, and, according to Brüning, said: "I would rather commit suicide than see such a man in office." After the Munich putsch, however, he modified his views: "There are many things that can be said against Hitler. But one thing one will always be able to say : he was a fanatic for Germany . . . Hitler was wrecked by his proletarian primitivism. He did not understand how to give his National Socialism any intellectual basis. He was passion

---

[1]The members included Hans Grimm, the author of the *völkisch* novel *Volk ohne Raum* and Heinrich von Gleichen, who later led the *Herrenklub,* which replaced the *Juniklub.* Spengler himself visited the *Juniklub,* and meetings were attended by Otto Strasser and the future Chancellor, Heinrich Brüning.

incarnate, but entirely without measure or sense of proportion."[1]

In view of Moeller's scorn it was his misfortune that Hitler should take the title of his book, *The Third Reich* which appeared in 1923, as the name of Nazi Germany, and that numerous National Socialists should have hailed him as the precursor of their movement. Yet this was something that Moeller did not live to see. Of neurotic disposition, he was grieved by his lack of success as a writer and by his hatred for the Weimar Republic. Field-Marshal von Hindenburg's election as President in the spring of 1925 gave him some slight hope, for Hindenburg, he felt, represented the triumph of Nationalism, and, in his last political message, he said that he had "been immensely pleased by the Hindenburg election and . . . I must ask the people to forgive my pessimism. It was a victory of sentiment over utility and there is no purer victory."[2] A few days later, however, still suffering from the effects of a nervous breakdown, he committed suicide.

National Bolshevism was, as I have said, the meeting point of many of the conflicting ideologies of the Weimar Republic.[3] In its extreme "anti-bourgeois" form it meant not only admiration for the Soviet Union, but belief in a national Communism, and, although they were strictly against the principles of the Communist International, tendencies towards such an ideology, represented variously by Laufenberg, Wolffheim, Heinz Neumann and Scheringer, had existed within the German Communist Party. The leading figure in the National Bolshevik movement, however, was a former Social Democrat, Ernst Niekisch. He had sat in the Bavarian parliament immediately after the armistice, initially participated in the Soviet Government of Bavaria, and although he was soon disappointed by the behaviour of the Communists, he remained on good terms with

---

[1]Fritz Stern, *The Politics of Cultural Despair,* University of California, 1961, pp. 237-238. Moeller's contempt for Hitler was in contrast to his admiration for Mussolini. "The Italian people," he wrote immediately after the March on Rome, "live in the conception of their freedom, independence and unity. The Germans do not possess this tradition." (*Das Recht der jungen Völker,* Berlin, 1932, p. 123.) And in January 1924 he referred to "the men of the fascio who finally made a reality of a State that had hitherto only existed in poetry." (*Gewissen,* January 28, 1924.)

[2]Fritz Stern, *op. cit.,* p. 266.

[3]For the combined responsibility of the left and right wing extremists in overthrowing the Weimar Republic, see Otto Ernst Schüddekopf, *Linke Leute von Rechts,* Stuttgart, 1960.

Ernst Toller and Erich Mühsam. Subsequently he joined the Independent Socialists and in 1925, after serving a prison sentence for his part in the Soviet Republic, joined another dissident branch of the Socialist Party, the Old Social Democratic Party.

In fact Niekisch's beliefs were remarkably close to those of the Italian syndicalists. He hoped to liberate the proletariat from the bonds of capitalism, and thought that the workers would only manage to overthrow the bourgeoisie if they developed a national consciousness, within a strong State. His main complaints against the Weimar Republic were the acceptance of the reparations clause in the Treaty of Versailles, and the agreement to the Dawes and Young reparations Plans, which he considered to the advantage of the industrialists and the detriment of the working classes. Nor did his nationalism, which separated him from the Communists, diminish his admiration for the Soviet Union. He had welcomed the Treaty of Rapallo and believed, as had Moeller van den Bruck, that Russia and Germany should ally against the Western plutocracies.

On his paper *Widerstand,* which he founded in 1926 to advocate a policy of friendship towards the Soviet Union and German acceptance of her rôle as an Eastern power, he managed to assemble members of every Nationalist group. One was Ernst Jünger, whom he had met through the philosopher Alfred Bäumler in the autumn of 1927. Another was the Conservative Revolutionary Friederich Hielscher, a young lawyer who had fought in the *Freikorps* and who was to write one of the vaguest definitions of the German Reich a couple of years later. And with Hielscher Niekisch met Ernst von Salomon.

As Salomon admitted in his memoirs, *Der Fragebogen,* he was not made for a bourgeois life. Indeed, this applies not only to him but also to the other members of his family : one of his brothers, Pfeffer von Salomon, became the commander of Hitler's S.A.; the other, Bruno, later joined the Communist Party. Educated in the Royal Prussian Cadet School, Ernst von Salomon had been too young to fight in the Great War, but had identified himself with the cause and honour of the German officers. After seeing the Spartacists assault soldiers in the streets, and watching the return of the defeated German army in the winter of 1918, he decided to enlist. Yet police duty in the Weimar Republic, at the service of a government he despised, was too inactive an occupation for him, so, on April 1, 1919, he and a group of fellow soldiers, "deserting Weimar and our division, left for the Baltic States"[1] to fight the Bolshevik forces near Riga. Salomon prided himself on being one of the notorious "Freebooters", the *Freikorps* soldiers who chose to continue fighting on Germany's eastern borders in defiance of the orders from the Republican government. Their aims, however, were confused. "What we wanted we did not know," he wrote, "but what we knew we did not want. To force a way through the prisoning wall of the world, to march over burning fields, to stamp over ruins and scattered ashes, to dash recklessly through wild forests, over blasted heaths, to push, conquer, eat our way through towards the East, to the white, hot, dark, cold land that stretched between ourselves and Asia—was that what we wanted? I do not know whether that was our desire, but that was what we did. And the search for reason was lost in the tumult of continuous fighting . . . We felt that we were the last survivors of the German race. We were almost grateful to the Government for shutting us out of the country. For since the connection had been officially severed, our action need not be influenced by troubles at home . . . We had a fresh source of strength, of hope, and we were freed from the burden of piteous claims which had accompanied us day by day and step for step. Outcasts, exiles, homeless and beggars—we held our torches high."[2]

When he finally returned to Germany Ernst von Salomon found that the only men he could respect were the soldiers who still had the courage to challenge the Republic—Ehrhardt, and Rathenau's murderer, Kern. Salomon's own accounts of the reasons for Rathenau's murder differ considerably from those that emerged during the subsequent trial. When Ernst Techow, one of the assassins, was interrogated in court, he maintained that Kern had told him "that Rathenau had himself confessed, and boasted, that he was one of the three hundred Elders of Zion, whose purpose and aim was to bring the whole world under Jewish influence. . ."[3] Rathenau's assassination, in this case, would be the first step in an attempt to exterminate the Jews on the orders of the fanatical believers in the spurious *Protocols*. According to Norman Cohn,

[1]E. von Salomon, *The Outlaws*, translated by Ian F. D. Morrow, Jonathan Cape, p. 58.

[2]*Ibid.*, pp. 65, 100.

[3]Quoted in Norman Cohn, *op. cit.*, p. 146.

Rathenau had been "offered up as a human sacrifice to the sun-god of ancient Germanic religion. The murder was timed to coincide with the summer solstice; and when the news was published, young Germans gathered on hilltops to celebrate simultaneously the turning of the years and the destruction of one who symbolised the powers of darkness".[1] But according to Salomon, the fact that Rathenau was a Jew had nothing to do with his murder. Both he and Kern, he claimed, were admirers of the Foreign Minister—"the man who is greater than all those who surround him", Kern is supposed to have said.[2] Salomon himself was fascinated by Rathenau's writings, "just the kind of thing that it seemed . . . necessary and right to read at the present time . . . lighted with a serene optimism being tempered by a gentle melancholy".[3] It was precisely because of their admiration for him, Salomon wrote, that they believed him to be by far the most dangerous figure in the Weimar government: Kern "couldn't bear it if once again something great were to arise out of the chaotic, the insane, age in which we live"[4] and therefore took the decision to assassinate him.

In effect the ideals of Salomon and Kern in the early twenties corresponded (always according to Salomon) to those of the National Bolsheviks. In *The Outlaws* Salomon reported a conversation with Kern about Communism : "I said excitedly: 'But it's a matter of war against the West, against capitalism. Let's become Communists. I'm ready to make a pact with anyone who will fight my battles. I have no interest in protecting the propertied classes, since I am not one of them.' 'It isn't a matter of interest. The Communists are concerned with interests. If we quarrel with them about it, it's not because it's theirs, but because we can recognise no other interest than that of the nation. If instead of "Society" or "Class" we speak of the "Nation", you will understand what I mean.' 'But that represents Socialism in its purest form.' 'It does, as a matter of fact, represent Socialism and only in its present form; that is to say in the Prussian form.' "[5]

---

[1] Norman Cohn, *op. cit.*, p. 169.
[2] E. von Salomon, *op. cit.*, p. 275.
[3] *Ibid.*, p. 180.   [4] *Ibid.*, p. 270.
[5] *Ibid.*, p. 268. After Rathenau's murder, in June 1922, Kern was shot by the police; Fischer, another of the assassins, committed suicide; Techow was sentenced to fifteen years' penal servitude, and Salomon, whose part in the affair was minimal, to five.

As the twenties drew on it became increasingly obvious that the National Socialist Party was deeply riven. Unlike Mussolini, Hitler never bothered to alter the 1920 programme, but ever since his release from prison in December 1924 he had been prepared to make those very compromises which the Duce, the politician whom he admired more than any other, had made in Italy. In January 1925 he met Dr Heinrich Held, Minister-President of Bavaria and leader of the Catholic Bavarian People's Party, and admitted that the beer-hall putsch of 1923 had been an error. He also stated that he did not share the hostility which Ludendorff and the North German *völkisch* leaders, Reventlow and Graefe, displayed towards the Catholic Church. The purpose of the meeting with Held was to show that National Socialism was essentially respectable, ready, above all, to help the government defeat Marxism. Thus, Hitler hoped, the Minister-President of Bavaria would raise the ban which had been passed on the party and *Der völkische Beobachter* a year earlier, and Held, though reluctant, agreed. Hitler, therefore, had decided to rise to power legally, within the framework of the constitution—the idea of a revolutionary *coup d'état* was set aside.

Later in the year there was a disagreement between Hitler and the Strasser brothers as to whether the former German royal houses should lose their possessions to the various German states. The Strasser brothers demanded expropriation—but Hitler, who was receiving a large allowance from the Duchess of Sachsen-Anhalt, decided to the contrary. The Strassers, backed by a young journalist named Joseph Goebbels, presented a programme still more radical than that of 1920, and insisted that the party should accept it, but by summoning a meeting in Southern Germany where he had consolidated his position as undisputed leader of the party, Hitler managed to foil the Strasser plan. Nevertheless the Strassers and the North German faction of the party presented a serious threat to Hitler's authority. Not until three years later could he overcome it.

In 1929 Hitler supported the leader of the German National Party, the industrialist Alfred Hugenberg, in his campaign to have the Young Plan and the new reparations settlement which it contained rejected by a plebiscite. Although the campaign was a failure, it enabled Hitler to meet and obtain temporary subsidies from men who agreed with his opposition to the Young Plan and were prepared to back him on the strength of it. Recent research has proved, however,[1] that, similarly to the Italian industrialists and the *Partito nazionale fascista,* the heads of German industry were initially most unwilling to give funds to a party with as radical a programme as that of the National Socialists. There were certain exceptions like Fritz Thyssen, the chairman of the United Steel Works, but even most of these threatened to withdraw their money in April 1930 when Otto Strasser supported a strike in Saxony. Hitler had to dissociate himself from so dangerous a colleague, and, after a lengthy discussion with Strasser, totally repudiated the idea of nationalising industry. "It would be the end of German economy," he said. "The capitalists have worked their way to the top through their capacity, and on the basis of this selection, which again only proves their higher race, they have a right to lead." When Strasser asked him what would happen to Krupp's industry if he came to power, Hitler replied that he "should leave it alone. Do you think that I should be so mad as to destroy Germany's economy? Only if people should fail to act in the interests of the nation, then—and only then—would the State intervene. But for that you do not need any expropriation, you do not need to give the workers the right to have a voice in the conduct of the business: you need only a strong State."[2]

Shortly after this conversation Strasser was expelled from the party and in June founded his own Union of Revolutionary National Socialists, which later came to be known as the Black Front. The victory was Hitler's, and, one by one, the other anti-capitalists in the Nazi Party sacrificed their principles to the Führer's interests. Strasser was forced into the large but ineffectual crowd of Conservative Revolutionaries, Revolutionary Nationalists and National Bolsheviks. For, after the Wall Street Crash in 1929, the younger Nationalists certified their hatred of the bourgeoisie by becoming fervent opponents of the entire capitalist system.[3]

Capitalism and the Soviet Union were not the only issues

---

[1]Henry Turner, Jr., *Big Business and the Rise of Hitler* in *American Historical Review,* October 1969, pp. 56-70.

[2]Alan Bullock, *Hitler, A Study in Tyranny,* Penguin Books, 1962, p. 158.

[3]The first serious critiques of capitalism had come from the contributors to *Die Tat,* a paper founded by Hans Zehrer, and were mainly the work of an economist, Ferdinand Fried, whose influential *Das Ende des Kapitalismus,* was published in 1931. (See Kurt Sontheimer, *Der Tatkreis* in *Vjh. für Zeitgeschichte, Jg.* 7, 1959.)

which turned the Nationalists against Hitler. By 1930 many young revolutionaries from both the right and the left had realised the possibility of mobilising the German peasants for a national revolution. The most promising area for such a mobilisation was Schleswig-Holstein where, in 1928, the peasants had united to protest against the import of foreign foodstuffs and the system of credit distribution. Two years later the economic depression caused the banks and institutes of credit to push their claims for repayment and threaten the peasants with expropriation. Further demonstrations ensued, accompanied by strikes and acts of terrorism. The Nationalists, Otto Strasser's left wing of the National Socialist Party, and even the Communists rallied to the peasants' support. Bodo von Uhse and Ernst von Salomon's brother, Bruno, left the National Revolutionaries for the Communist Party and tried to persuade the peasants of Schleswig-Holstein to vote for the Communist candidate, Ernst Thaelmann. Jünger, Niekisch, Hielscher and Otto Strasser, on the other hand, united with other right-wing and centre movements to support the candidature of the peasant leader Claus Heim, who was serving a prison sentence for bomb throwing. Hitler, it was thought, would join them. Yet he refused. Fearful of alienating the bourgeoisie by association with so disreputable a figure, he committed what the young Nationalists regarded as the ultimate betrayal, and dissociated himself from the whole issue.

If Hitler's compromises and the ever more violent anti-capitalism of the young Nationalists were grounds for strife a seemingly contradictory phenomenon was also taking place. 1930 was the year of Hitler's first great electoral success.[1] It suddenly grew clear that if any Nationalist movement was to overthrow the Republic it was National Socialism. For one thing it was a political party. Indeed, it was the only "young Nationalist" party. As we have seen, the other young Nationalists despised it precisely because of this, but now that the discontent caused by the economic Depression provided an opportunity for political action they all had to admit that only a political party was in a position to take this action. Grudgingly, therefore, the young Nationalists began to support National Socialism, not for itself, but because they thought it would serve to end the Weimar

---

[1] See *infra*, p. 142.

régime and then make way for them. It would allow them to implement their ideas, for, they firmly believed, *they* were the ones who had the ideas, not the Nazis. "The spiritual conditions necessary for the German revolution were created *outside* National Socialism," wrote Edgar Jung in June 1932. "National Socialism has really only taken over the idea of a people's movement (*Volksbewegung*) from the combined revolutionary forces. It has built it up splendidly and has become a strong power. We are not only pleased about this : we have contributed ourselves to this growth. It is we who have done the spade-work, especially among the educated classes, in order to prepare for that day when the German people elected a National Socialist candidate. This task was all the more heroic because it did not aim at success or publicity. I respect the primitiveness of a people's movement, the fighting strength of the victorious Gauleiters and Sturmführers. But their success does not give them the right to regard themselves as the salt of the earth and underestimate their spiritual champions."[1]

In the years immediately preceding Hitler's nomination as Chancellor, from 1930 to 1933, it was Joseph Goebbels who, more than Hitler, attempted to enter the intellectual circles of Berlin. Himself the author of a novel, an admirer of Moeller van den Bruck and Ernst Jünger, Goebbels does not appear to have joined the National Socialist Party until 1924, when he worked as assistant editor of the paper *Völkische Freiheit*. He started in the left-wing Strasser faction, and in 1925 even demanded "that the petty bourgeois Adolf Hitler" be expelled from the party. After hearing Hitler speak in February 1926, however, he deserted Strasser and proclaimed himself Hitler's man, though his attitude towards the Führer remained somewhat ambiguous until the S.A. purge in 1934. In November 1926 Goebbels was appointed Gauleiter, or party representative, in Berlin, where his talent for public speaking and his capacity for organisation proved invaluable to the progress of the National Socialists. He and Hermann Göring were elected as deputies to the Reichstag in May 1928, and in November Goebbels was appointed Hitler's propaganda chief.

Goebbels' best connection in the literary world of Berlin was Arnolt Bronnen, a writer whose work was in every way as uneven

---

[1]*Deutsche Rundschau*, June, 1932.

as his character. The play which made his name, *Vatermord*, was written in 1920 and performed in 1922. The protagonist, Walter Fessel, is an indecisive figure, hovering on the borders of homosexuality and incest, continually provoked and beaten by his alcoholised father who wants him to study law and fight for the rights of the workers. But Walter's sole desire is to escape, to work the land and leave, once and for all, his squalid home. In the last scene of the play, after his mother has tried to seduce him and his father has threatened him with a gun, Walter stabs his father. "I have enough of you," he shouts to his mother. "I have enough of everything. Go and bury your husband, you are old. But I am young, I no longer know you, I am free."[1]

The principle underlying Bronnen's form of anarchy was determination to slay the "old world", to flee from the bonds represented by the established order. As a theatrical device it succeeded in *Vatermord*, which still remains one of the best examples of Expressionist drama. It failed, however, in Bronnen's later plays, *Geburt der Jugend, Die Excesse, Anarchie in Sillian, Rheinische Rebellen*, and *Ostpolzug*, and contributed to the mediocrity of his narrative writing, *O.S.* and *Rossbach*, when a "new world" was offered as a solution—a youthful Germany inebriated by Nationalism.

Although there was some justification in the critic Alfred Kerr's description of Bronnen's plays as "empty din", and "noise for the sake of noise", Bronnen was a master of stage effect, and to such a talent Expressionist theatre lent itself admirably. Yet, as Jürgen Schröder pointed out in a recent study, "Bronnen was the Judas of the self-betrayal immanent in Expressionism. All the most dubious and dangerous tendencies of this movement were unleashed by Bronnen and put on the stage. Expressionism turned to exhibitionism, pathos to rhetoric . . . tension to heaviness . . . the revolutionary turned out to be a provocateur, the programme to be propaganda . . . extremes turned to excess, anarchy emerged from the sadistic orgies, commitment became a fashion . . . and the precise dramatic structure, the bold theatrical experiment owed their very existence to a refined stage technique".[2]

---

[1]A. Bronnen, *Vatermord*, Berlin, 1925, p. 96.

[2]Jürgen Schröder, *Arnolt Bronnen* in *Expressionismus als Literatur, Gesammelte Studien*, herausgegeben von Wolfgang Rothe, Bonn, 1969, pp. 585-586.

Because of its many adherents and the extent of its influence in painting, architecture, sculpture, the cinema and literature, it is almost impossible to give a concise definition of Expressionism, the movement that all but dominated German art in the first twenty years of this century. Like Futurism in Italy and Vorticism in England Expressionism had its origins in that impatience with bourgeois life that permeated intellectual circles before the Great War. It was an attempt to free art from the conventions and hypocrisy by which it was gripped, to give it a greater spontaneity or "naturalness". "Expressionism," concluded Gottfried Benn, "was something completely natural—as far as art and style can be natural."[1] I shall later be dealing with Gottfried Benn's attitude to politics,[2] but here a few words should be said about his work. Benn's revolt against the world in which he was brought up ran far deeper than that of most of his fellow Expressionists. He set out to criticise and destroy rational Western thought since Kant, to sweep away the entire positivist tradition of the nineteenth century, but rather than celebrate those Utopias of the future which we find in the writings of Marinetti, Benn put all his talent to exploring the decay of his surroundings. He was the first German poet to write poems about sheer ugliness, to formulate aesthetics of ugliness. And in so doing he stepped perilously close to the trap whose bait so many Expressionists were unable to resist. What had originated as "something completely natural" became totally stylised. A morbidly sensitive form of art became a coarse caricature. In Benn's case his obsession with the rotten, his conviction of the imminent collapse of Western civilisation, made him welcome the ideas of Spengler, and led him, as we shall see, to revel in that form of apocalyptic thought on which National Socialism liked to play.

Nor was Benn alone in this. For Expressionism often pointed to political commitment. It desired the new and scorned the old. As a movement it provided neither ideology nor discipline, and it was in search of these that such men as Johannes R. Becher and Bertolt Brecht turned from it to Marxism. The playwright Hanns Johst, on the other hand, recanted his early artistic principles and yielded himself, sentimentally and romantically, to the German

---

[1]G. Benn, *Einleitung zu Lyrik des expressionistischen Jahrzehnts*, München, 1962, p. 9.
[2]See *infra.*, p. 149.

Volk and National Socialism. And so, more cautiously, did Arnolt Bronnen.

Born in Vienna in 1895, Bronnen retained his Austrian nationality until the *Anschluss* in 1938. During the Great War he had fought on the Italian Front, where he was taken prisoner. He subsequently settled in Germany in order to have *Vatermord* performed, and, in Berlin, he was befriended by Bertolt Brecht. When Brecht tried to direct his play, however, he was so rude to the actors that Heinrich George threw the script into the stalls and Agnes Straub wept. Eventually *Vatermord* was performed in Frankfurt under the direction of Berthold Viertel, and aroused the interest of the publisher Ernst Rowohlt, who agreed to subsidise Bronnen's future works.

Bronnen was singularly susceptible to personalities stronger than his own. First it had been Brecht, later it would be Goebbels, but in 1927 his meeting with Ernst Jünger drew him to the world of the young Nationalists. "I came, saw and was conquered," he wrote in his memoirs. "Ernst Jünger was exactly the sort of individual for whom I had always had the strongest sympathy. The dark, slim, small and wiry man aroused in me . . . the same fascination that Bert Brecht had had for me five years earlier."[1] A natural provocateur, Bronnen retained the anarchical, somewhat destructive cynicism he had once shared with Brecht. The colourful but not always reliable diarist, Count Harry Kessler, reported his meeting with him in the German Embassy in Paris in 1926. "Bronnen, whom I met for the first time, made a strange impression on me: informal, unsure of himself, blasé, with bad breath, in day clothes (when everybody else was in tails), but with a monocle in his eye. He was a drawing-room revolutionary . . . An obviously subordinate, weak, nervous character who wanted to affect superiority . . . a perverted petty bourgeois, shallow, limited, pathologically vain, in short *un grand homme de province* who hadn't got much behind him."[2]

After shocking the bourgeoisie with *Vatermord* and his other plays, Bronnen proceeded to shock the liberals with a novel about the German patriots who tried to resist the plebiscite in Upper Silesia in 1921, *O.S.* When the book appeared in 1929, his left-wing friends of his Expressionist days had no alternative but to repudiate

[1] *Arnolt Bronnen gibt zu Protokoll,* Hamburg, 1954, p. 188.
[2] H. Kessler, *Tagebücher 1918-1937,* Frankfurt a/M, 1961, p. 487.

Martin Heidegger

Arnolt Bronnen

him, particularly after Goebbels had written in his paper *Der Angriff* that "Bronnen's *O.S.* is as if it had been written by us all." And Goebbels' esteem was confirmed when Bronnen set about writing the biography of the *Freikorps* veteran and S.A. leader, Gerhart Rossbach, in a sycophantic tone.[1] Like Ehrhardt, Rossbach had participated in most of the putsches of the Weimar Republic. He was known for his cruelty, his courage and his homosexual proclivities; after quelling nationalist uprisings in the Baltic provinces he joined the National Socialist Party, took part in the Beer Hall putsch, fled to Salzburg, but later returned to Munich on Hitler's orders and helped to organise the S.A. Yet Bronnen's book was no eulogy of National Socialism. As he proudly pointed out in his autobiography, he barely mentioned Hitler, and spelt Göring's name wrong (Göhring).

In 1930 Bronnen arrived in Goebbels' flat to interview him for the paper *Der Querschnitt*. He had heard Hitler speak in Munich in 1923, and he knew the Strasser brothers, but Goebbels, he found, was the most attractive personality. "Here was neither the anti-semitic youth movement attitude of Otto Strasser, nor the petty bourgeois atmosphere of Gregor Strasser's pharmacy, neither Adolf Hitler's guttural medley of dialects nor the stubborn, rowdy fanaticism of Streicher and Rosenberg. Here, I thought, was intellect, the traces of intellect—only later did I discover that it was the remains of intellect."[2]

At the time Bronnen was living with a Russian actress, Olga Förster, who had acted two years earlier in the "National Socialist theatre", Goebbels' attempt to replace the "Jew-ridden" plays by a form of true peasant drama. In 1930, however, Goebbels was more than a failed theatrical director and the representative of a small Nationalist party. He now held one of the most important posts in a party which was gaining votes day by day. Besides, Olga Förster shared Bronnen's taste for violence and one of her favourite pastimes was to watch the battles between the S.A. and the Communists. The co-operation between the Bronnen couple and Goebbels was therefore in many ways ideal. Bronnen admitted Goebbels into literary circles and could, on occasion, serve as a spearhead for the S.A. to disrupt left-wing meetings. In October

---

[1]A. Bronnen, *Rossbach,* Berlin, 1930. The book was in fact commissioned by Ernst Rowohlt.

[2]*Arnolt Bronnen, gibt zu Protokoll,* p. 234.

L

1930 Thomas Mann gave a lecture in the Beethoven-Saal in Berlin, his *Deutsche Ansprache, ein Appel an die Verunft,* a warning to the Germans of the danger of approaching Fascism. With the intention of starting an open discussion with Thomas Mann, Bronnen bought tickets for the lecture, but when Goebbels heard of this he dispatched twenty Storm troopers attired in dinner jackets to provide Bronnen with support. Mann spoke hurriedly, nervously, and, at the end of the lecture, retreated through the stage door into Bruno Walter's motor car while his supporters insulted his opponents in the auditorium.

The invasion of the Beethoven-Saal had unpleasant consequences for Arnolt Bronnen. The newspaper *B.Z. am Mittag* printed a series of articles in which he was reminded that he was a Jew. This was a decisive moment in his life for, from 1930 until the Second World War, he spent much of his time trying to prove that his mother's husband, the Austrian professor Dr. Ferdinand Bronner, was not his father. Bronnen's mother seems indeed to have admitted on various occasions that Ferdinand Bronner was not responsible for Arnolt's conception, but the matter was further complicated after the *Anschluss* in 1938 when Dr. Bronner himself had to prove that *he* was not Jewish.

As long as Bronnen's friendship with Goebbels lasted the two men seemed to be playing a game with each other, and, in the case of Bronnen, a game at the expense of his friends. He tried to introduce Goebbels to Ernst Rowohlt, Ernst and Friederich Georg Jünger, Hielscher and Niekisch, but Bronnen's *Diskussions-Abende* were baleful events. Niekisch, who almost struck Goebbels, described them : "Bronnen enjoyed organising soirées at which the guests were especially picked . . . so as to hate each other. He usually brewed some cup and when the alcohol took effect chaos ensued. Normally, angry discussions would start after midnight and end in brawls. Bronnen sat sprawled in a chair in a corner and watched the disorderly events with interest. He would pass a remark which frayed tempers still more and produced further scenes of violence. Ernst Jünger was a frequent guest at his house, for, like Bronnen, he enjoyed such excesses, took no part in them, but looked on in silent pleasure."[1]

At this point the most progressive section of the National Socialist Party was still constituted by its revolutionary *force de frappe,*

[1]E. Niekisch, *Gewagtes Leben,* Köln-Berlin, 1958, p. 201.

the S.A. Although the S.A. never succeeded in doing as much damage to the left-wing before Hitler's rise to power as the Fascist *squadristi* before Mussolini's, they were an impressive organisation, numbering 400,000 members by the end of 1932. Sharing a hatred of capitalism and uncompromising opposition to the Republic, the S.A. and the German Communist Party had a persistent exchange of members in the years of the Depression. Arnolt Bronnen, who, like Niekisch, believed in an alliance with the Soviet Union, thought that he could use the Berlin S.A. to implement *his* form of National Bolshevism. They were, he said, "a group of unemployed, ill-organised revolutionaries who basically despised Hitler and wanted to see 'facts'. It was the illusion of my friends and myself to use these S.A. men to split the North German National Socialist Party away from Munich and form a large right-wing radical revival movement with Eastern sympathies and Goebbels at the head of it to constitute a front against Western imperialism."[1]

The S.A. revolt had been planned by the former police captain Walter Stennes and had been caused mainly by Hitler's order, issued on February 20, 1931, that the S.A. should refrain from street-fighting. In thinking that Goebbels could be persuaded to join in the putsch, Bronnen was under an illusion. Hitler found out about the plot in time, and replaced Stennes by Edmund Heines, one of Rossbach's former *Freikorps* men, while Stennes himself, who appears to have been in collusion with Otto Strasser, joined the Black Front. Bronnen's relations with Goebbels grew strained and deteriorated still further when Goebbels took less interest in Bronnen's wife. After marrying Magda Quant, Hitler's propaganda chief moved, on her money, from his one and a half room flat in the proletarian quarter of Steglitz, to a twelve room flat in Charlottenburg. But despite his money and his ever greater power, Goebbels still had some use for Bronnen who worked for the Berlin radio : it seems to have been largely owing to him that Goebbels could broadcast his electoral speech in June 1932. According to Bronnen their last meeting took place that winter at a dinner in Goebbels' flat for Leni Riefenstahl. When Goebbels tried to get in touch with him the day after Hitler's appointment as Chancellor, Bronnen could not be reached.

---

[1] A. Bronnen, *op. cit.*, p. 264.

October 1929 has possibly been the most decisive—and disastrous —month in the history of modern Germany. It was the month in which Gustav Stresemann, the greatest statesman in the Weimar Republic, died, and in which the stock market crashed in Wall Street. Within less than a year what prosperity Germany had enjoyed after 1924 came to an end. Between 1925 and 1928 the national income had risen by twenty-five per cent, but from 1929 to Hitler's rise to power the Germans again found themselves in almost as pitiful an economic position as in 1923. The capital which had been flowing into Germany from the United States ceased, and the American loans on which German economy relied were withdrawn. The number of *registered* unemployed rose from about one and a half million in September 1929 to three million in September 1930, from four and a half million in September 1931 to six million early in 1932 and 1933. But, according to recent research, "the actual figure was considerably higher because many people who were without jobs after years of unemployment no longer received support and were no longer included in statistical records. We shall not go far wrong if we assume that in 1932 one in every three of the working population had no job. And even those who still retained their jobs were under constant threat of dismissal because everyone was replaceable; there were vast numbers of competitors ready to take their place, and thus their whole existence was threatened."[1]

Germany presented a sinister spectacle. The unemployed settled in encampments on the outskirts of Berlin; intellectuals sang for *Groschen* in courtyards and railway stations; there were beggars in every street. "Whoever strolls through the residential areas of the Berlin west end," wrote a reporter of the *Vossische Zeitung,* "through those clean, quiet, elegant streets, will find that at every step an elderly man or woman (or rather lady or gentleman, for they wear the same clothes as we do), comes up to him and begs for money. Some of them rush up to one with a smile, as though they were greeting an old friend; others beg apathetically and vacantly; so far none of them have developed the professional beggars' whine. The worst are those who do not speak. In the daytime they sit forlornly on the benches in the wide streets; later they prowl past the restaurants, stop and stare at the diners without speaking, without begging, without moving."

---

[1] Dieter Petzina, *Germany and the Great Depression* in *Journal of Contemporary History,* vol. 4, no. 4, October 1969, p. 60.

Again it was the lower and the middle classes who were the victims. The Weimar government had never had the courage to nationalise the major industries, as it had intended, while cartelisation had enabled the industrialists to increase their hold on the national economy to an unprecedented extent. When Brüning became Chancellor at the end of March 1930 his government was influenced solely by the right, the aristocracy and the army, and his economic policy was to the exclusive advantage of the bankers and industrialists. "It proposed the 'encouragement of capital accumulation', the reduction of taxes on production and the 'removal of uneconomic obstacles', that is, cutting down social expenditure. The industrialists demanded particularly urgently higher indirect taxation—which is borne mainly by the mass of the workers—and at the same time lower taxes on employers and on capital."[1]

With the Depression the lower classes tended to remain loyal to their traditional parties, the Communists or even the Social Democrats, and were satisfied with the Marxist interpretation of the Wall Street Crash as the inevitable outcome of the capitalist system. This, they believed, would be righted by the triumph of the workers. The middle classes, on the other hand, repudiated Marxism with its internationalist foreign policy and its threats to nationalise private property at home. The right-wing parties, they believed, no longer represented their interests. The conservative attitude of Brüning's government hurt them just as much as it did the workers. Instinctively, therefore, they looked for something more radical. Patriotically, they attributed their misery to the cruelty of the Allies, the Treaty of Versailles and the reparations plans,[2] and to the Weimar government which had been cowardly enough to accept these plans. In Hitler they saw a man unsullied by compromise with Weimar, determined to abrogate the Treaty of Versailles, and consistent in his opposition to Marxism. They were prepared to overlook his deals with the industrialists and his anti-semitism. He did not insist on the acceptance of any dogma—all he had was a party, youthful, vital and astonishingly well-organised in view of the confusion that reigned in Germany.

In 1930 the middle classes—farmers, shopkeepers, artisans,

---

[1]Dieter Petzina, *op cit.*, p. 66.

[2]Germany, it must be pointed out, ceased paying reparations after the Conference of Lausanne in July 1932.

tradesmen, white-collar workers, civil servants and professional classes—constituted one-third of the German population and it was primarily from them that the National Socialists won their six and a half million votes at their first great electoral victory in September and over thirteen and a half million votes in the summer of 1932.[1] The four and a half million votes polled by the Communists at the 1930 election merely served to increase middle class fear and antagonism. The other Nationalist groups, as we have seen, were in no position to offer a solution. Hugenberg's German National Party was too conservative and synonymous with capitalism to have a mass appeal. For those who repudiated the Communists and refused to vote for any of the left-wing or centre parties, National Socialism was the only possibility.

Even Spengler again took an interest in politics. The unemployment and poverty did not disturb him and he believed the problem would be solved by a general lowering of wages and abolition of social security. Early in 1932 the presidential candidates were Hitler, Duesterberg of the *Stahlhelm*, Hindenburg, who was supported by all the Weimar parties from the Socialists to the German Nationalists, and the Communist Ernst Thaelmann. When asked whom he would vote for, Spengler replied: "If I vote at all, then it'll be for Hitler . . . Only Hindenburg and Hitler can be taken into consideration—if only Hitler were at least clever enough to take good advisers—he'll certainly do that. He's far too sure of his own incompetence."[2] In April Duesterberg had withdrawn and Spengler voted for Hitler. "Hitler is a fool," he maintained, "but one must support the movement."[3]

Hindenburg won the elections and replaced his loyal supporter, Chancellor Brüning, by Franz von Papen. "It will interest you that recently, in conversation with Reichskanzler von Papen," a friend wrote to Spengler, "I happened to talk about you and found in him an unconditional supporter of your belief in an impending period of Caesarism."[4] As Hitler and his followers paraded through Munich after the elections Spengler and his sister hung flags with swastikas from their windows, claiming that: "When one has a chance to

---

[1] At the Reichstag election in May 1928 Hitler had only polled 810,000 votes.
[2] A. M. Koktanek, *op. cit.*, p. 246.
[3] *Ibid.*, p. 427.
[4] *Spengler Letters*, pp. 273-274.

annoy people one should do so." In the July elections he again voted for Hitler. After Papen's dissolution of parliament, however, the National Socialists began to lose votes. Irritated by the continual elections, Spengler said in a foreword to his *Politische Schriften* in October that he saw no real Caesar in Germany. He complained of the Nazi's refusal to master reality, of the same love of parades he had deplored in 1923. The leader, he said, must be "a hero, not an heroic tenor" and the young should "understand *the art of statesmanship*."[1]

In the November elections of 1932, Hitler lost two million of the 13,745,000 votes he had polled that summer, but he still remained the leader of the largest party in Germany when President Hindenburg appointed him Chancellor on January 30, 1933. As with Mussolini in 1922, few people could tell what the new government would do, or how long Hitler would remain at the head of it. "The democratic centre and left sought consolation in the hope that the National Socialists, who owed their growth to the mere rejection of the *status quo*, would start to lose supporters as soon as they participated in the political responsibility. This idea was the result of political experiences with the Weimar parliamentary democracy and rested on the assumption that, once they were in power, the National Socialists would do little to alter the essence of the Republic."[2] The members of the National Party, on the other hand, were convinced that Hitler was under their control. Hindenburg reassuringly remained President. Franz von Papen, more certain than anyone else that the situation was in his hands, was Vice-Chancellor. Two of Hindenburg's men, Freiherr von

---

[1] Nor was Spengler the only one to be sceptical. In 1932 Ernst Niekisch attacked Hitler in his pamphlet *Hitler—ein deutsches Verhängnis*. When he showed the illustrations to Ernst Jünger, Arnolt Bronnen and Carl Schmitt, "Bronnen immediately pronounced himself against the whole book: he felt himself wounded by the attack on National Socialism and warned me of the serious consequences entailed by publishing it . . . Schmitt exclaimed that he had never seen anything so impressive . . . Jünger withheld judgement. He knew well, he said, that I had thought everything over and considered the consequences. He found the illustrations good and effective and said the pamphlet would make a great impression." (E. Niekisch, *op. cit.*, p. 189.)
[2] Sontheimer, *Antidemokratiches Denken in der Weimarer Republik*, p. 296.

Neurath and General von Blomberg, were Foreign Minister and Minister of Defence; Hugenberg held the Ministries of Economy, Food and Agriculture, and Seldte of the *Stahlhelm* was Minister of Labour. Apart from Hitler the National Socialists only occupied two posts : Frick was Reich Minister of the Interior and Hermann Göring Prussian Minister of the Interior.

On February 27, however, the Reichstag was burnt down. Hitler claimed to have discovered a Communist plot[1] and Hindenburg declared a state of emergency: the police could arrest anybody connected with the Communist Party or suspected of endangering the government, and the guarantees of individual liberty under the Weimar Constitution were suspended. These police powers made Hitler and Göring practically omnipotent : they meant that they could arrest enough people for them to be sure of a majority in parliament and pass any measures they pleased. In March, elections were held again and the National Socialists obtained forty-four per cent of the votes. Although this was not as much as Hitler had hoped it secured his position. The Enabling Bill, passed a few weeks later, secured his dictatorship. It enabled the Chancellor to draft any law to be enacted by the government, made the government independent of parliament and allowed it to deviate from the Constitution. In a characteristically conciliatory speech after the Bill, Hitler assured the nation that he would not abuse his power.

In the following months Hitler completed the process of *Gleichschaltung*, coordination, by which the entire organised life of the country was submitted to the National Socialist Party. In April the first anti-semitic laws were passed, and "public servants not of Aryan stock", lawyers, scientists, professors and doctors with as little as *one* Jewish grandparent were dismissed. Only ex-combatants and those who had held office since August 1, 1914 were exempted. The S.A., whose confidence had increased immeasurably after the March elections, had started to boycott and persecute Jews, and opponents of the régime. In May they occupied trade union offices all over the country, intimidating the trade unionist leaders to such a degree that they were in no position to oppose the merger of their unions in the German Labour Front which was placed under the control of Robert Ley. By the end of the month a law was passed which put an end to collective bargaining and appointed Labour Trustees

---

[1] It now seems almost certain that the Nazis organised the fire themselves.

under the Government's orders to settle working conditions. True to Nationalist principles, the Nazis destroyed all other political parties. The Communists had been powerless since the Reichstag fire. The Social Democrats had had their offices and party buildings occupied in May, and in June their party was banned. The Bavarian People's Party announced its own dissolution in July, after its leaders had been arrested. The democrats and the Nationalists did the same in June, and the Centre and People's Parties in July. The *Stahlhelm* was incorporated in the S.A. at the end of 1933 and dissolved two years later.

Hitler, who was realistic enough to see the danger of any economic experimentation after the sort of crisis his country had just experienced, soon put paid to the anti-capitalist aspirations of such National Socialists as Otto Wagener, Adrian von Renteln and Gottfried Feder. Wagener, the head of the Party's Economic Section, was dismissed at the end of June and replaced by Wilhelm Keppler. Two of the leading German industrialists, Krupp von Bohlen and Thyssen, retained all their power, Krupp remaining president of the Reich Corporation of German Industry and Thyssen becoming chairman of the North-Western Employers' Association and the Association for the Preservation of Economic Interests in the Rhineland and Westphalia (the *Langnamverein*). Hugenberg was replaced as Minister of Economy and Trade by the director of the Allianz insurance company, Dr Schmitt, who made it manifest that there were to be no further experiments in corporativism. With the assistance of Schmitt and the President of the Reichsbank, that same Hjalmar Schacht who had been invaluable to Stresemann, Hitler solved some of the economic problems which had faced the country in January 1933. By spending large sums of money on the improvement of national resources and public works, the government managed to decrease the number of unemployed from six to two and a half million in less than two years.

On October 14, 1933 Hitler announced Germany's withdrawal from the League of Nations, which she had joined under Stresemann in September 1926. The excuse for this step was the question of disarmament. Hitler maintained that Germany had disarmed after the war in accordance with the agreement of Versailles, but the other nations of the League had refused to follow suit. When Germany offered to sign any pact of non-aggression, give up her army and weapons on condition that her neighbours did the same, the French showed that they had no intention of accepting such a proposal. This enabled Hitler to represent Germany as a martyr surrounded by armed inquisitors. For the Germans withdrawal from the Disarmament Conference and the League seemed the first attempt to reassert the nation's prestige since the Great War, and when Hitler submitted his decision to a plebiscite on November 12, ninety-five per cent of the voters confirmed that they were in favour of his policy.

After Hitler's decision to withdraw from the League of Nations the greatest philosopher in Germany, Martin Heidegger, exhorted his students to support the Führer's foreign policy. "It is not ambition which made the Führer leave the League of Nations," he informed them, "nor a passion for glory, nor blind obstinacy, nor a desire for violence: it is nothing but the clear wish to be unconditionally responsible for assuming the mastery of the destiny of our people."[1] That April Heidegger had been nominated Rector of Freiburg University and, at the beginning of May, at the request of the Minister of Education, he had joined the National Socialist Party: never before had he publicly expressed a political view or sympathy.

In his correspondence with Professor Karl Vossler, one of the few German professors to refuse to take the oath of loyalty to Hitler in the autumn of 1933, Benedetto Croce compared Heidegger to Giovanni Gentile.[2] Indeed, Heidegger accepted the Rectorate at Freiburg as optimistically and idealistically as Gentile had accepted the Ministry of Education in 1922, believing that he would be able to implement some necessary reforms. He hoped to overcome the class barriers which rose high in every German university, to facilitate the entry and progress of poorer students, and, despite his own allegiance to Hitler, he wanted to keep university professorships open to every intellectual irrespective of his political convictions. "What then induced me to accept my unanimous election as Rector, was not only my belief, subsequently so bitterly dis-

---

[1] *Freiburger Studentenzeitung*, November 10, 1933.

[2] "Oh, this Heidegger!" complained Croce. "I knew him for what he was six years ago, when his Italian pupils and admirers gave me his works to read, and I foresaw that he would end the way he did. One should introduce him to his Italian predecessor, Gentile. But maybe Heidegger, with his pure philosophy, will be able to keep further away from politics than Gentile, with his pure action. In practical politics the Italians are always infinitely superior to the Germans: they are less naive." (*Carteggio Croce-Vossler*, p. 340.)

appointed, in Hitler. Equally decisive was the hope that I could win over the university professors and persuade them to turn National Socialism into *national socialism* and to develop the spiritual, intellectual powers of the movement. But this expectation was also disappointed. The university did not change, and showed no understanding of the political situation in the world. Today the position is similar. Many demands made by the students of today had already been advanced by the academic youth of 1933."[1]

Heidegger, who was born in the Black Forest, of peasant stock, felt as strong an attachment to rural Germany as he did an aversion for the centres of German industry. "At the most the townsman is 'stimulated' by his stay in the country," he wrote, "but my whole work depends on the world of these mountains and peasants."[2] A "return to the land" was an important part of Nazi propaganda, and, like Mussolini, Hitler employed certain devices which, though affecting a minority, were given great publicity. The most successful (but least original) of these was the Labour Service, the *Arbeitsdienst*. Founded under the Weimar Republic to alleviate unemployment, this organisation had been originally boycotted by the National Socialists:[3] once they were in power, however, they put it to good use. The *Arbeitsdienst*, by which students spent a few months a year doing some form of manual labour, brought them into contact with workers and peasants, and constituted a means of physical training for the young. It was this, of all Hitler's practical accomplishments (or, at this stage, we should still talk of promises), that aroused Heidegger's enthusiasm. He encouraged his students to volunteer, thinking that the Labour Camps would produce a "new man", the intellectual labourer. "In the Labour Camps there is a new reality. The fact that our high school should be open to the new educational powers of the Labour Service symbolises this new reality. Camps and schools intend to gather . . . the educational powers of our people in order to obtain that new unity in which the nation will drive towards its destiny under the State."[4]

---

[1] Letter from Professor Heidegger to Monsieur Palmier, dated January 10, 1969.

[2] *Der Alemane,* March 3, 1934.

[3] See David Schoenbaum, *Hitler's Social Revolution,* Weidenfeld & Nicolson, 1967.

[4] *Freiburger Studentenzeitung,* June 20, 1933. This, and Heidegger's other appeals, are reproduced in Jean-Michel Palmier, *Les Écrits Politiques de Heidegger,* Paris, 1968.

Heidegger's political attitude was similar to that of most of the Nationalists. He wished for the strong State which would discredit the Marxist concept of the class struggle and this, he thought, was what the National Socialists would bring about: "Knowledge and the possession of knowledge, in the sense in which National Socialism understands these words, does not divide into classes— on the contrary, it unites them and binds the members of the Fatherland and the State in the sole, great will of the State." Hitler's Germany, Heidegger believed, was to combine ways of life which had hitherto been incompatible : the warrior would merge with the worker and the scholar, and something similar to the State described in Jünger's *Der Arbeiter* would emerge.[1] Resting on Jünger's concept of the modern technocracy, Heidegger regarded National Socialism as the only ideology suitable for the masters of technology if they were not to yield to Marxist materialism. Thus in 1935, after he had left the Party, he referred to "the works which are being peddled about nowadays as the philosophy of National Socialism but have nothing to do with the inner truth and greatness of this movement (namely the encounter between global technology and modern man). . ."[2]

As Rector of Freiburg University Heidegger did his best to modify the more unpleasant aspects of National Socialist policy. He retained anti-Nazi professors on his staff, refused to allow anti-semitic notices to be pinned up in the precincts of the university and prevented certain books from being burnt.[3] At the end of February 1934, when Rosenberg's representative told him to dismiss two of his deans, his predecessor von Möllendorf and Erich Wolf, Heidegger left the National Socialist Party, and lost his post as

---

[1]Jünger was one of the few writers for whom Heidegger expressed an admiration in his lectures, and in 1939 he formed a study group to discuss *Der Arbeiter*.

[2]Heidegger, *An Introduction to Metaphysics*, translated by Ralph Manheim, Yale University Press, 1959, p. 199.

[3]The various rumours spread about Heidegger have been discredited. The wife of the philosopher Ernst Cassirer falsely accused him of anti-semitism because of certain philosophical disagreements with her husband. On February 7, 1966, *Der Spiegel* published an article in which Heidegger was accused of having signed a document forbidding his friend, the great philosopher Edmund Husserl, entry into the university because he was a Jew. No evidence was ever provided to substantiate this claim. Not until 1942 was the dedication to Husserl omitted, on the publisher's insistence, from *Sein und Zeit*.

Rector. From then on he was subjected to the attacks of the two leading philosophers of the régime, Alfred Bäumler, Rector of Berlin University, and Ernst Krieck, Rector of Heidelberg. This together with the apparent success of Rosenberg's *Myth of the Twentieth Century*, finally disenchanted him. "People read that Rosenberg nonsense," he was to tell his friends after 1935, "It doesn't contain a single thought."

Gottfried Benn had lived in Berlin since 1904, and in November 1917 had opened a surgery for skin and venereal diseases. As an ill-paid, overworked doctor, and a writer of high repute, he was accorded much the same view of the German capital as Céline was of Paris—a view which led to total scepticism and resulted in a refusal to believe in the benefits of progress, political or technical; a refusal to believe in the power of the individual to resist the stream of history; a willingness to submit oneself to the stream and measure its authenticity in terms of its horror.

In 1914 Benn enlisted, and, after a brief period on the Belgian front, spent most of the war as military doctor in Brussels. He later described an episode there with that same scientific objectivity which we find in Ernst Jünger: the trial and execution of Nurse Edith Cavell. As the only doctor present he had to establish her death, close her eyes and lay her in her coffin.

When he returned to his surgery in the Belle-Alliance Strasse he continued to frequent the heterogeneous members of the Berlin intelligentsia—Johannes R. Becher, George Grosz, Carola Neher, and Paul Hindemith (for whom he wrote the text of an oratorio performed in 1931). But as his acquaintances started to join the Communist Party Benn came to be regarded as a somewhat suspicious outsider. He was no Communist. He abhorred the Marxist idea of intellectual commitment and devoted himself ostensibly to the cult of pure aesthetic theory. Yet he was also dissatisfied with the Weimar Republic, or rather with his existence as a doctor under the Republic, and "resented the failure of the government, which in his view supported hordes of party hacks and incompetent bureaucrats, to find him more secure employment or to allow him some alleviation of taxes."[1]

---

[1]Gordon A. Craig, *Engagement and Neutrality in Weimar Germany* in *Journal of Contemporary History*, vol. 2, no. 2, April 1967, p. 61.

His fellow intellectuals found such aristocratic aestheticism, which they associated with the reactionary figure of Stefan George, unacceptable. When, in 1929, Max Herrmann-Neisse praised a work of Benn's in *Die neue Bücherschau*, the paper's two Communist editors, Becher and Egon Erwin Kisch, resigned, and wrote a series of articles against all that Benn stood for. In his reply Benn rejected Communism as a vain attempt to alter the world. "The workers have always wanted to climb up and the rich have never wanted to fall . . . I wonder whether it is not more radical, more revolutionary, and far better suited to the strength of a true, hard man, to teach humanity that this is how you are and you shall never be otherwise. This is how you live, have always lived, and will always live. Whoever has money will live well; whoever has power will be right; whoever has strength will dictate the law. History has no sense, no ascendant curves, no decline of race, no more illusions, no more bluff . . . Of course I can hear the great question of the hour : Myself or the community? Should I surrender to the social union or the formation of the self, to politicisation or to sublimation? To what extent is it permissible to split away, to draw back in order to live one's own aristocracy, to drive oneself to the top? But I have no other answer than what life has taught me: all is permissible that leads to experience."[1]

Benn defended irrationalism as an artistic stimulus much in the way that Pirandello and Thomas Mann had done before the First World War. "The artist ('art bearer', *Kunstträger*)", he wrote in 1934, "is statistically asocial . . . He is cynical and does not claim to be otherwise . . . Art grows on paradoxical ground, and logic and biology fail before it." Benn considered himself both an artist and an "intellectualist"—and intellectualism takes the place, in Benn's case, of Ernst Jünger's microscope. "It is the cold observation of the earth; for too long we have observed it warmly, idyllically, tritely, uselessly. Intellectualism is the belligerent attack on decomposing human substance, its drainage and defence from body-strippers,"[2] which was to produce the creative artist of the twentieth century.

The muddled theories with which Benn was to justify his allegiance to National Socialism have a background of political squabbles which preceded and accompanied Hitler's rise to power. In April Benn's retaliation against left-wing attacks in *Das Tagebuch*

---

[1]G. Benn, *Gesammelte Werke IV*, Wiesbaden, 1961, pp. 208-211.
[2]*Ibid.*, pp. 51, 55.

contained some equally contemptuous remarks about Goebbels and his paper, *Der Angriff*. And in August he broadcast a lecture on "the new literary season", giving as a reason for his anti-Communism the social realism of the Soviet writer Tretyakov, which he saw as the very negation of art.

It is conceivable that Benn really did think that the German Communist Party, which had polled over six million votes in November 1932, presented a danger. In any case anti-Communism was one of his motives for turning to National Socialism, and it was without regret that he saw Becher, Kisch, Döblin, Arnolt Zweig and Brecht leave the country after the Reichstag fire. Above all, however, Benn believed that National Socialism was the herald of an "intellectualistic" age in which *his* aesthetics would be defended against those of Tretyakov. In Italy the two writers he admired most, d'Annunzio and Marinetti, were treated as national heroes. He assumed the same would happen in Germany : Expressionism would become the official art, like Futurism in Italy.

Even if Benn was not anti-semitic he does refer, in his many writings at the time of Hitler's rise to power, to the mysterious term "race", *Rasse* and *Zucht*. For Benn this meant a national "élite" in the Nietzschean sense of the word. "The quality of the new youth is power. May it fulfil its destiny! May the tide of the race bear it over the years, houses, fields and trenches until the inextinguishable German form is joined by the new form, the form which is now dawning in us for the first time! Only then shall we finally realise the meaning of Nietzsche's statement, as yet so obscure, about the sole justification of the world as an aesthetic phenomenon."[1] He believed, he was later to add, "in a genuine innovation of the German people which would find a way out of rationalism, functionalism and the torpidity of civilisation. I believed in an innovation which would serve Europe, guide its development, leave religions and races to themselves, and make the most of what was best in them."[2]

On May 9, 1933 Klaus Mann wrote to Benn asking him why he had not left the German Academy at a time when Heinrich Mann had been forced to leave it and Thomas Mann refused to return to Germany. Benn broadcast his reply on the Berlin radio in the same month. ". . . The German workers are better off than ever before.

---

[1]*Ibid.*, pp. 64-65.
[2]*Ibid.*, p. 78.

You know that as a doctor, as a panel doctor, I come into contact with many circles, with many workers, also with former Communists and members of the Socialist Party: there is no doubt about it, everybody tells me he is better off than before. Workers are treated better at work, the supervisors are more careful, the staff managers are more polite, the workers have more power, are respected more, work in a more cordial atmosphere, an atmosphere of citizenship, and what the Socialist Party could never obtain for them has been provided for them by this new national form of Socialism: a feeling of vitality and energy . . . I shall continue to respect what I used to find exemplary and edifying in German literature, I shall continue to respect it as far as Lugano and the Ligurian coast, but I personally declare myself in favour of the new State, for it is my people which has found its way. Who am I to exclude myself? Do I know of a better way? No !"[1]

National Socialism never provided the cultural policy for which Benn had hoped. Expressionism was not publicly acknowledged as the true form of German art: on the contrary, Expressionist poems, books, plays and paintings were considered of unsurpassed decadence. Benn himself had been appointed head of the poetry section of the Academy in February 1933, but was replaced by the more orthodox Hans Friederich Blunck in June.

The first attempt to formulate a National Socialist cultural policy was made by an organisation founded by Alfred Rosenberg in 1927. Originally called the *Nationalsozialistische Gesellschaft für deutsche Kultur*, it changed its name to *Kampfbund für deutsche Kultur* in 1929. Its aims were to "instruct the German people in the connections between race, art, science, and moral and military virtues",[2] and its most prominent members were Hans Grimm, Adolf Bartels and Hanns Johst. Later Rosenberg prided himself on the fact that the *Kampfbund für deutsche Kultur* presented the first and only co-ordinated effort to regulate National Socialist cultural policy until Goebbels' *Reichskulturkammer* was founded in November 1933, nine months after Hitler had been in power. Indeed, Rosenberg's boast was to become all the prouder—and more desperate—as he grew aware of the extent of Goebbels'

---

[1] *Ibid.*, pp. 244-246.
[2] Hildegard Brenner, *Die Kunstpolitik des Nationalsozialismus*, Hamburg, 1963, p. 8.

power and the opposition which Goebbels cynically, opportunistically, but no less cleverly, put up against his ideals.

Rosenberg and his *völkisch* followers rejected anything modern. They found Expressionism and Futurism decadent, subversive and un-German, and produced lengthy lists of writers and painters whom they termed "enemies"—Brecht, Tucholsky, Toller, Zweig, Arnolt Bronnen, Thomas Mann and countless others. Goebbels, on the other hand, was eager to salvage those remnants of Weimar culture which could be put to good use by National Socialist propaganda. He tried to persuade Thomas Mann to return to Germany. On July 12, 1933 he celebrated the birthday of Stefan George and founded, as the highest National Socialist literary award, the Stefan George Prize. But George himself had left for Switzerland on July 8 and died there in December without making any comment on the honours which the new régime bestowed on him.

There was a time when Goebbels protected Gerhart Hauptmann and Richard Strauss, to the fury of Rosenberg who detested them. After the performance of Strauss' opera *Die schweigsame Frau*, with a libretto by Stefan Zweig, Rosenberg wrote bitterly that "the *Kampfbund für deutsche Kultur* was formed amid the most violent political battles with the intention of tending the cultural side of the movement and finding people who could later develop this cultural interest. At the time hardly anyone had thought of the cultural aspects of National Socialism, not even you, Dr. Goebbels, for it was the time when you preferred the company . . . of Arnolt Bronnen . . ." Goebbels' reply was curt: "Dr Goebbels hardly ever saw A. Bronnen, and when he did it was usually in his office. Their meetings concerned the radio. Herr Bronnen used to provide reports from the *Rundfunkhaus*."[1]

The capacities of both the *Reichskulturkammer* and the so-called *Amt Rosenberg* were ill-defined and further confused by another organisation founded in April 1934, Philip Bouhler's *Parteiamtliche Prüfungskommission*. In September Hitler himself publicly expressed his displeasure at the petty discussions with which his officials wasted their time, referring to both Rosenberg's and Goebbels' protégés as dangers to National Socialism.

Nevertheless the power to protect remained in the hands of those

---

[1]Both letters are reproduced in Léon Poliakov and Josef Wolf, *Das Dritte Reich und seine Denker*, Berlin, 1959, pp. 32-36.

M

closest to the Führer—Goebbels, Göring and Himmler. Rosenberg, whose cultural office was officially subordinated to Goebbels' *Reichskulturkammer* in 1936, remained a figure of fun. He was not even respected as the principal ideologist of National Socialism. *The Myth of the Twentieth Century* sold half a million copies between 1930 and 1940, and Baldur von Schirach described its author as "a man who sold more copies of a book no one ever read than any other author."[1] Hitler, in his *Table Talk* in 1942, was equally deprecating: "I must insist that Rosenberg's *The Myth of the Twentieth Century* is not to be regarded as an expression of the official doctrine of the Party. The moment the book appeared, I deliberately refrained from recognising it as any such thing. In the first place, its title gives a completely false impression. There is, indeed, no question of confronting the conceptions of the nineteenth century with the so-called myth of the twentieth. A National Socialist should affirm that to the myth of the nineteenth century he opposes the faith and science of our times . . . It gives me considerable pleasure to realise that the book has been closely studied only by our opponents. Like most of the Gauleiters, I have merely glanced cursorily at it. It is in any case written in much too abstruse a style, in my conception."[2]

It was through a network of intrigues and private squabbles that the most prominent German writers made their way in the Third Reich. They were courted on one side, attacked on another. Benn, as we shall see, was attacked by members of the S.S. and defended by Himmler, Hauptmann attacked by Rosenberg and defended by Goebbels. Every effort was made to win over Oswald Spengler. In March Goebbels vainly begged him to speak on the radio and in July Hitler accorded him an interview. The meeting, arranged by Frau Else Knittel in Bayreuth, lasted an hour and a half, and the two men found that they agreed about German policy towards France and that they both regretted the mediocrity of all the leading figures in the Evangelical Church. The interview ended with Hitler's assurance that he "considered it of great importance for people outside the party to be won over to a German policy."[3] He hoped, he said, to be able to have further encounters with Spengler in Munich.

[1]William L. Shirer, *The Rise and Fall of the Third Reich*, Secker and Warburg, 1961, p. 149.
[2]Hitler's *Table Talk*, Weidenfeld & Nicolson, 1953, p. 422.
[3]*Spengler Letters*, p. 290.

With a combination of condescension and respect Spengler
described Hitler as "insignificant—but he wants something and he's
doing something and one can say something to him." "A very
decent fellow," he went on, "but when one's sitting opposite him one
doesn't feel for a second that he's significant."[1] Three weeks later
he sent the Führer a copy of his latest book, *The Hour of Decision,*
but this was hardly tactful. It was the introduction to the book
which gave Hitler such offence, for Spengler maintained that the
National Socialist victory had not overcome the dangers facing
Germany; he referred again to the policital amateurishness of
"these same everlasting 'youths' . . . clinging fantastically to some
theory or other."

The Hour of Decision was still more successful than *The Decline
of the West,* selling almost 100,000 copies in two months. Spengler
received countless letters of admiration, from National Socialists,
aristocrats, and members of the "right-wing opposition" like Carl
Friederich Goerdeler. Yet he was also attacked, more violently,
possibly, than he had ever been attacked before. A young man
named Gründel told him how disgusted he was that Hitler should
not have been mentioned in the book, while Johann von Leers,
Leader of the Division of Foreign Policy and Information in the
German High School for Politics, claimed that Spengler was a
dangerous opponent of National Socialism, a reactionary who
jeopardised Germany's relations with Japan by including the
Japanese amongst the coloured races endangering the whites in *The
Hour of Decision.* It appears to have been Goebbels who instigated
the slow and ill-organised banning of Spengler's book. When he
asked Spengler for an article to be used in the National Socialist
electoral campaign in October, Spengler replied that he had never
taken part in electoral propaganda, and would not write a word
for German newspapers, unless the attacks against him ceased.
Were they to cease, he said, he would be willing to write "on
important occasions of foreign policy, such as the withdrawal from
the League of Nations, which I consider to be diplomatically
thoroughly correct."[2]

The rapidity with which Hitler secured his position as dictator
of Germany and "co-ordinated" the country forced those intellec-

---

[1] A. Koktanek, *op. cit.,* p. 441.
[2] *Spengler Letters,* p. 290.

tuals opposed to him to reach a decision about the attitude they were to adopt at an early stage. Heinrich Mann and the draftsman Käthe Kollwitz were the first artists to leave the Academy in February 1933, after proposing that the Socialists should unite with the Communists to combat National Socialism in the March elections. On February 27, the night of the Reichstag fire, Carl von Ossietzky, the Jewish editor of the left-wing *Weltbühne*, was arrested and sent to a concentration camp. In March further writers, including Thomas Mann and Alfred Döblin,[1] were expelled from the Academy, and on April 13 the German students announced their intention of publicly burning books regarded as not in keeping with the national spirit. On May 10 works by Marx, Kautsky, Heinrich Mann, Ernst Glaeser, Kästner, Freud, Förster, Emil Ludwig, Hegemann, Remarque, Kerr, Tucholsky, Ossietzky, Theodor Wolff and Georg Bernhard were ceremoniously burnt in every university town in Germany.

The decision to leave Germany, for a writer who was neither a Jew nor a Communist, was a difficult one. Although other German-speaking countries, Switzerland and Austria, were prepared to offer political asylum to distinguished refugees, exile, in the case of a writer like Thomas Mann, meant breaking with a nation and a tradition to which he owed much of his inspiration. Mann left Munich on February 11, 1933 on a lecture tour of the European capitals. He appears to have been confident that Hitler would be defeated at the next election and there is no indication that he did not intend to return. Indeed, on March 29 he wrote to his friend Ernst Bertram, a supporter of the National Socialists, saying: "We wanted to return after the elections, but were dissuaded by urgent warnings."[2]

The first attack on Mann was in the form of a protest against the lecture he had been giving, in Brussels, Paris and Amsterdam, on Richard Wagner. It was an insult, Mann's opponents implied, to associate Wagner with Mann's "aestheticising snobbery". Printed in the *Münchener Neuste Nachrichten* on April 16, the protest was

---

[1]The others were Leonhard Frank, Ludwig Fulda, Georg Kaiser, Alfred Mombert, Alfons Paquet, René Schickele, Jacob Wassermann, Franz Werfel, Fritz von Unruh, Rudolf Pannwitz and Bernhard Kellermann.
[2]*Mann-Bertram, op. cit.*, p. 176.

signed, amongst others, by Richard Strauss and Hans Pfitzner.[1] His two eldest children, Klaus and Erika, warned Mann that there could be no guarantee of his safety if he returned to Munich, and he chose to remain abroad. In marked contrast to his later attitude, however, he showed an understanding for the predicament of the writers obliged to live in Germany : "Those writers who live outside the German borders," he wrote to Eduard Korrodi, "should not, in my opinion, look down with indiscriminate disdain on those who wish to, or who are obliged to stay at home, and should not bind their artistic judgement to those inside or outside. They are suffering, but the writers living in Germany are also suffering, and the exiles should beware of self-righteousness which is all too often an expression of suffering."[2] Not until April 1935 did Mann resign himself to the idea that Hitler would not fall, and publicly attack the National Socialist government.

The one body in the National Socialist Party which retained revolutionary aspirations after Hitler's rise to power was, as we have seen, the S.A. And indeed, in breaking the trade unions and the opposition parties the S.A. had unquestionably been of value to Hitler. Yet, like Mussolini's *squadristi,* the Storm Troopers were dangerous. Their violent treatment of the Jews, their perpetual thirst for action, above all the ambitions of their leader, Ernst Röhm, to take over the German army, antagonised large sections of German society. Hitler well knew that if he were to stay in power and fulfil his policy of national expansion the consent and support of the Reichswehr were essential, while the Reich Minister of the Interior, Hermann Göring, combined a boundless jealousy of Röhm with a strong affection for the institution of the Reichswehr, of which President Hindenburg had made him a general in August 1933. Furthermore Göring had a powerful ally in Heinrich Himmler, the head of the Bavarian police, whom he had appointed chief of the Prussian Gestapo. Through Himmler,

---

[1]That the composer Hans Pfitzner should have turned against him in this way was particularly wounding, for Mann, who had been introduced to him by Bruno Walter before the First World War, had written at length about Pfitzner in *Betrachtungen eines Unpolitischen,* praising *Palestrina* as the last great romantic opera.

[2]Quoted in Kurt Sontheimer, *Thomas Mann und die Deutschen,* München, 1961, p. 113.

the Reichsführer of the S.S.,[1] he could count on this highly disciplined force of men who had originated as Hitler's bodyguard, were
bound by an oath of personal loyalty to the Führer, and loathed
the boisterous Storm Troopers.

The purge of the S.A. was organised more by Himmler and
Göring than by Hitler but when the Führer heard of it he raised
no objection. On the night of June 29, 1934, claiming to have
discovered a plot against the régime, Himmler's S.S. started
murdering the leaders of the S.A. They killed for two days,
butchering not only the S.A. leaders, Röhm, Heines, von Krausser,
Schneidhuber, Karl Ernst, Hayn, Rossbach and von Haydebreck,
but a mass of other individuals whom they considered undesirable
—Gregor Strasser, General Kurt von Schleicher, the seventy-three
year old Gustav von Kahr, Papen's assistants von Bose and the
Conservative Revolutionary Edgar Jung, Erich Klausener, the
leader of Catholic Action, and an inoffensive music critic, Dr Willi
Schmidt, whom they had mistaken for someone else.

The purge put an end to any fear of a permanent revolution on
the part of the S.A. and greatly tranquillised the Reichswehr.
From then on the S.S. remained supreme but were always compliant to the Führer's orders. Yet it was also the most obvious
display of Nazi brutality. The assassination of Edgar Jung was
taken as a blow against the young Nationalists, the murder of
Kahr against the old. All the Nationalists had lost friends in the
massacre. Spengler, who had known Kahr, Strasser and Willi
Schmidt, hurriedly burnt his correspondence with Strasser and
turned irrevocably against National Socialism. "I have been informed that you are taking an attitude of strong opposition to the
Third Reich and its Führer," Friederich Nietzsche's sister, Elisabeth
Förster-Nietzsche, wrote to Spengler in October 1935. "Now I have
myself experienced your speaking with great energy against our
highly honoured new ideal. But that is exactly what I do not understand. Does not our sincerely honoured Führer have the same ideals
and values for the Third Reich as you have expressed in *Prussianism
and Socialism*?"[2]

Gottfried Benn was appalled by the news of the purge. "I can no
longer go along with them," he wrote in August 1934. "Certain
things have been the last straw. A horrible tragedy . . . It started

[1]*Schütz Staffel* or Protection Echelon.
[2]*Spengler Letters*, p. 304.

off as something so great and now looks so foul."[1] And yet Benn's commitment to National Socialism had made him so many enemies abroad that there was no question of his emigrating. In 1935 he gave up his practice in Berlin and again joined the army, which he described as "the aristocratic form of emigration." Indeed, in Hanover, where he was stationed, he found himself in the company of officers who disapproved of the régime as much as he did, and protected him from the attacks which the Nazi newspapers launched against him. In May 1936 the S.S. paper *Das schwarze Korps* and *Der völkische Beobachter* implied that he was degenerate, Jewish and homosexual, and in the summer of 1937 a member of the S.S., Wolfgang Willrich, lampooned him in a book entitled *Säuberung des Kunsttempels*. The violence of Willrich's attack, however, shocked not only Benn. It drew a sharp reprimand from Heinrich Himmler himself: "I am well acquainted with the case of Benn and consider it unnecessary of you to bring it up again. The Führer's opinion about art is as follows:

"The artists had four years in which to change, to cease producing works of art representing decay and to create real art. From a nationalist point of view Benn's behaviour has been impeccable since 1933, and even earlier. I consider it unnecessary and pointless to run amok against this man who has whole-heartedly supported Germany on an international level. I have forbidden my entire department to have anything to do with the case . . . I repeat my conviction, of which I have previously informed you, that it would be more important for you to go on painting good pictures than to persecute to the point of destruction some individual who painted or wrote something stupid in 1918-19 or even later."[2]

In their determination to cleanse the country of all that was decadent, of all that was "non-Aryan", of all that might undermine the régime, the National Socialists drove any literature of quality abroad or underground. In 1938 even Gottfried Benn was forbidden to have his work published. "In the Third Reich," wrote George Mosse, "the central task of culture was the dissemination of the Nazi world view. What was the place of intellect in this culture? The National Socialist world view was based upon the rejection of

---

[1]G. Benn, *Ausgewählte Briefe Wiesbaden*, 1957, p. 58.
[2]Joseph Wolf, *Literatur und Dichtung im Dritten Reich*, Gütersloh 1963, p. 123.

rationalism, and any emphasis upon man's reason was thought to be 'divisive', destructive of the unity of the emotionally centered ideology which the whole Volk could understand."[1] The books offered the German public were *völkisch* novels, stories of peasants and of German history, old Germanic legends and accounts of the heroic exploits of the early members of the Nazi Party, together with the coarsest anti-semitic propaganda.

Hitler never managed to impose a perfect totalitarianism. Not only did the Nazis lack a coherent ideology, but they were split into a mass of rival factions held together solely by the personality of their leader, who increased his power by playing them off against each other. What Hitler did manage to impose, however, was a régime characterised by the cruelty of its secret police, the Gestapo, and by the complete perversion of justice—judges, magistrates and prosecutors were nothing but the servants of the Party. The individual liberties guaranteed by the Weimar Constitution had been suspended after the burning of the Reichstag, and were never restored. Opposition to the régime was reduced to the minimum. Not only was there no alternative to the National Socialist Party, but the punishments for those who expressed their distaste were more horrible than integrity was worth.

In the years following the S.A. purge the anti-semitic laws became harsher. The Nuremberg Laws, the "Reich Citizenship Act" and the "Act for Protection of German Blood and German Honour" were released on September 15, 1935. By the first of these acts the Jews were formally barred from "Reich citizenship"—they became "second-class citizens" and were no longer entitled to any political right. At the same time those Jewish ex-combatants and Jews who had been in public service since August 1914, exempted from the Civil Service Act passed in April 1933, also became the objects of discrimination : Jewish ex-combatants were superannuated after December 31, 1935 and granted a temporary pension, while the others lost their pension rights. By the "Act for Protection of German Blood and German Honour" marriage and extra-marital relations were forbidden between Jews and pure blooded Germans and it became an offence for a Jew to employ an Aryan woman under the age of forty-five in his house. Between 1935 and 1938 a succession of orders were issued by which it was made increasingly difficult for Jews to teach in

---

[1]George L. Mosse, *Nazi Culture,* W. H. Allen, 1966, p. 133.

schools, to obtain doctorates, to look after Aryan patients, to work in the legal profession, frequently to find any form of employment, and on October 5, 1938 they were obliged to have the letter J stamped on their passports.

The first great pogrom took place on the night of November 9, 1938, after the German legation secretary in Paris, Ernst von Rath, had been assassinated by a seventeen-year-old Jewish boy, Herschel Grünspan. On what came to be known as the *Reichskristallnacht*, Crystal Night, "synagogues throughout the length and breadth of Germany were burnt to the ground and over 7,000 Jewish shops were destroyed. On top of that a fine, originally of one billion, but eventually amounting to a total of one and a quarter billion marks, was imposed on the Jews and insurance payments to which they were entitled in compensation for the damage caused was confiscated by the State. On 11 November Heydrich (Himmler's chief lieutenant) sent a telegram to Göring reporting the death of thirty-six Jews—a later reckoning by the Party high court made the total ninety-one dead. The perpetrators went scot free—unless they had committed 'race pollution' or had overstepped the bounds of 'discipline'."[1]

After Crystal Night some 30,000 Jews were arrested by the S.S. and sent to concentration camps. Government orders excluded all Jews from German schools, obliged them to sell their firms and real estate, stipulated the withdrawal of driving licences and prohibited Jews from visiting theatres, concert halls, museums, sport stadiums and swimming pools. In February 1939 they were made to surrender all their jewellery, except for their wedding rings, to the state, and, with the outbreak of war, a curfew was imposed, their radios were confiscated, telephones cut off, and clothing coupons withheld. In October Hitler gave orders for the deportation of Jews from German occupied territory in Central Europe, and, by March 1941, he "issued his secret decree—which never appeared in writing though it was mentioned verbally on several occasions—that the Jews should be eliminated."[2]

How did the Germans react to the various stages leading to the Final Solution? When Michael Müller-Claudius asked forty-one members of the National Socialist Party about their reactions to

---

[1]Helmut Krausnick, *The Persecution of the Jews,* translated by Dorothy Long, in *Anatomy of the S.S. State,* Collins, 1968, pp. 40-41.
[2]*Ibid.,* p. 60.

Crystal Night, twenty-six expressed indignation, thirteen hesitated to commit themselves, and only two approved. Late in 1942, at a time when the entire Jewish population of Germany was gradually being deported to concentration camps, Müller-Claudius repeated his enquiry. Of sixty-one party members, sixteen were upset about the predicament of the Jews, forty-two were indifferent, and three in favour of extermination. "Expert examination of 1,000 German prisoners of war over the period 1942-44," wrote Norman Cohn, "showed twenty-four per cent to be more or less critical of the régime; sixty-five per cent to have the kind of attitude which suggests that, if they had been asked about the Jews, they would have reacted with indifference; and eleven per cent to be fanatically Nazi."[1] The truth is that the majority of the Germans simply closed their minds to the fate of the Jews. The extermination itself was carried out by a small group of men and, as we shall see, a man of Ernst Jünger's political awareness only heard unsubstantiated rumours of it when he was posted on the Eastern Front in December 1942. The individual was at liberty to believe or to disbelieve such rumours, and in most cases he found it more convenient to disbelieve them.

As far as most Germans were concerned, Hitler's treatment of the Jews until the war was a point of minor importance for which he compensated fully by transforming Germany into a country both feared and respected. Those who visited the Third Reich were nearly always impressed by the enthusiasm of its citizens—a singular contrast to the despair during the Depression. Martin Heidegger was not the only man to admire the effects of the *Arbeitsdienst*. In spite of all his prejudices against National Socialism, William Shirer admitted that "the young in the Third Reich were growing up to have strong and healthy bodies, faith in the future of their country and in themselves and a sense of fellowship and camaraderie that shattered all class and economic and social barriers. I thought of that later, in the May days of 1940, when along the road between Aachen and Brussels one saw the contrast between the German soldiers, bronzed and clean-cut from a youth spent in the sunshine on an adequate diet, and the first British war prisoners, with their hollow chests, round shoulders, pasty complexions and bad teeth— tragic examples of the youth that England had neglected so irresponsibly in the years between the wars."[2]

---

[1] N. Cohn, *op. cit.*, p. 211.
[2] W. Shirer, *op. cit.*, p. 256.

On an economic level there is no doubt that National Socialism, even if it did not fulfil those promises contained in the 1920 party programme, entailed some degree of protection for the small business men and farmers. Department stores were submitted to restrictions and taxes; the training of skilled workers was improved; and Hitler's first public works schemes were mainly to the advantage of the smaller contractors. The farmers were organised in a community of food-producers, the *Nährstand,* a moratorium was granted the smaller farmers on land debts, while a new inheritance law meant that they could be sure of keeping their land within their own family. Though industry and large business concerns certainly prospered under Hitler, government intervention meant the loss of that independence which they had known under the Weimar Republic. The industrial workers, on the other hand, though they had forfeited the right to strike and lost their freedom to move from one job to another, were, on the whole, satisfied with the new régime. To be a worker in the Third Reich "was no longer to be a member of a dangerous, alienated group . . . It was to be a member of the Labour Front, to be flattered in the press, to be offered mass jollity in the form of *Kraft durch Freude* and government-sponsored benevolence on the part of employers competing for Nazi industrial honours as leaders of the *Volksgemeinschaft.* Above all, there was work, even if real wages were low. The Third Reich was not a workers' state, but it at least gave higher status to working men than the empire of Wilhelm II had done."[1]

Finally Hitler did what he had always promised the Germans: he carried out the Greater German programme. In March 1938 his forces marched into Vienna, and in October into the Sudetenland. A year later they invaded Poland. By agreement with Stalin Poland was partitioned between the two powers and the German borders at last stretched as far as Russia. The price, however, was a world war —a war which hardly any German, not even Hitler, seems to have wanted.

For those writers who were not considered degenerate, philosophers like Krieck and Bäumler, playwrights like Johst, poets like Blunck and Binding, there were prizes, awards, and high salaries. At his trial after the war the actor Emil Jannings turned to the judge

---

[1] A. J. Nicholls, *Germany* in *European Fascism,* edited by S. J. Woolf, Weidenfeld & Nicolson, 1968, p. 80.

and said : "Your honour, I happen to have on me one of the contracts I signed before making a film. It is a good example of all the
film contracts I signed between 1933 and 1945. Please consider the
sum I earned . . ." Jannings handed the contract to the judge. "So
allow me to ask, would *you* have refused such a sum?"[1]

The case of Gerhart Hauptmann confuses his biographers as
much as it confused the National Socialists at the time. Was Hauptmann to be considered degenerate? After seeing one of his plays in
1893 the Bavarian statesman Prince Chlodwig zu Hohenlohe-
Schillingsfürst had described it as "a monstrous wretched piece of
work, social-democratic-realistic, at the same time full of sickly,
sentimental mysticism, nerve-racking, in general abominable. Afterwards we went to Borchard's to get ourselves back into a human
frame of mind with champagne and caviar."[2] By the time Hitler
came to power, however, Hauptmann was the most distinguished
playwright in the country, Aryan, nationalistic, who could be of in-
estimable value for propaganda purposes, and he soon made it clear
that, whatever government was in power, he had no intention of
leaving the Academy. "I am delighted that Hauptmann should
agree with me," wrote Rudolf Binding on April 6, 1933, "that we
serve the nation to which we belong and have no reason to leave the
Academy when the régime changes. The Academy has to safeguard
the freedom of artistic creation, not the freedom of political obser-
vations."[3] Three weeks later, on May 1, Hauptmann hung a swastika flag from his window, and when Harold Nicolson met him at
Max Beerbohm's in February of the following year, he found him
optimistic, sure that Germany would "liberalise itself" as Italy had
done.[4]

Yet attacks on Hauptmann had already started, notably in the
Deutsche Kultur-Wacht and *Die Brennessel* in September 1933,
when he proclaimed himself in favour of Hitler's withdrawal from
the League of Nations. And from 1934 to 1939 he was officially in
disgrace. In November 1937 a celebration on the occasion of his
seventy-fifth birthday was forbidden. On meeting the Hungarian
writer Ferenc Körmendy in Rapallo the year after, Hauptmann
told him : "This filthy Austrian painter's assistant has ruined

---

[1]Arno Breker—unpublished memoirs.

[2]Peter Gay, *Weimar Culture, The Outside as Insider,* Harper &
Row, 1968, p. 3.

[3]R. Binding, *Die Briefe,* Hamburg, 1957, p. 182.

[4]H. Nicolson, *Diaries and Letters, 1930-1939,* Collins, 1966, p. 166.

Germany, but tomorrow it'll be the world! This bastard has robbed the Germans of all we had of value—he's made us a nation of slaves! But that's not enough for him. This scum will bring war to the whole world, this miserable brown comedian, this Nazi hangman is rushing us into a world war, into destruction!" "But if that's what you think," Körmendy interrupted him, "why don't you emigrate? Like Mann, Zweig and the others, Jews and non-Jews? Why remain in Germany?" "What are you saying?" said Hauptmann. "Why don't I leave Germany? Because I'm a coward, do you understand? I'm a coward, do you understand? I'm a coward."[1]

William Shirer's description of Hauptmann as "the most popular playwright" in the Third Reich is an exaggeration, for Hauptmann was so hated by Rosenberg that a substantial faction of the National Socialist Party did all in their power to prevent his plays from being performed too frequently. Nevertheless in 1939 he was again in favour. Shirer recalls seeing him at the first night of his play, *The Daughter of the Cathedral*, "a venerable figure with his flowing white hair tumbling down over his black cape," (he) "strode out of the theatre arm in arm with Dr. Goebbels and Johst."[2] In 1942 his eightieth birthday was officially celebrated at the Pallavicini palace in Vienna by Baldur von Schirach, and he was presented with a huge vase decorated with a swastika from Hitler.

The national preoccupation with the war led to the virtual cessation of attacks against individual writers, and put an end to hopes of formulating an original cultural policy. Hauptmann was therefore honoured again, and Goebbels hoped to use him and various other intellectuals who had had uneasy relationships with National Socialism (Hans Carossa, Pfitzner, Richard Strauss, Furtwängler) as exhibits for the belligerent Reich. For other writers there was the possibility of a career in the army. Ernst Gläser, whose books had been burnt and who left Germany in 1933, returned in 1939 to become editor of the army newspaper *Adler im Süden*, and even Ernst Jünger felt that in the Reichswehr he could relive the myths of his youth.

While Carl Schmitt and many other former Nationalists soon supported National Socialism a certain number of Jünger's old

---

[1] *Die Welt*, November 10, 1962, F. Körmendy, *Warum ich Deutschland nicht verlasse.*
[2] W. Shirer, *op. cit.*, p. 243.

acquaintances withdrew with courage and dignity. They were all mistrusted. After the burning of the Reichstag Jünger, Hielscher and Niekisch had their houses searched, and Ernst von Salomon was arrested together with the novelist Hans Fallada. Nevertheless, Ernst Niekisch was allowed to edit *Widerstand* until December 1934, when the paper was banned. In 1935 he visited Rome where he alluded to his opposition of the régime to the German Ambassador, von Hassel, and was accorded a personal interview with Mussolini. The Duce, who found Niekisch agreeable, stressed the left-wing origin of his, and Niekisch's, ideas and told Niekisch how foolish he considered it of Hitler to contemplate aggression towards the Soviet Union. Subsequently Niekisch met the Italian Consul General in Germany, Scarpa, who questioned him about German opposition movements. In 1937 he was arrested by the Gestapo and kept in prison until the end of the war. On this occasion Ernst Jünger intervened in favour of his family, but there was nothing he could do to rescue Niekisch himself.

It is hard to assess the extent of protection which Jünger enjoyed in the Third Reich. Former friends and admirers of his occupied high posts: Werner Best was a leader of the S.S. and Alfred Bäumler Rector of Berlin University. That the National Socialists were eager to obtain his services is indubitable, but Jünger would have nothing to do with them. In November 1933 he refused the offer to join the Academy, and in May 1934, when *Der völkische Beobachter* printed a passage from his book *Das abenteuerliche Herz*, he wrote a letter to the editor stating that the excerpt had been published without his knowledge, and entirely dissociating himself from the paper. Jünger withdrew from public life. The Revolutionary Nationalist was replaced by the student of zoology, the pamphleteer by the intellectual, who studied the events around him coldly and objectively. When he met Ernst von Salomon in 1937 outside a cinema in Nuremberg, he told him that he had "chosen a high place from which I can watch people eating each other up like bugs"[1]: a keen observer of insect life, Jünger became increasingly interested in the way in which National Socialism was reducing the Germans to insect status.

Auf den Marmorklippen, published in the autumn of 1939, was an allegorical attack on dictatorship and the danger which Jünger

---

[1]E. von Salomon, *Der Fragebogen,* Hamburg, 1961, p. 246.

believed Hitler was bringing to Germany and the world. As a disguised attack on National Socialism the book was influential, and it can only be considered surprising that the censor allowed the novel to appear. At the beginning of September, however, Jünger had been called up. Unlike Gottfried Benn he had refused to "emigrate" into the Wehrmacht earlier, maintaining "There is no place for me in an army in which Göring is a general."[1] But the prospect of war made Jünger, the captain of an infantry company on the Western Front, hope for the chivalrous tournament of which Montherlant was dreaming in France. In a way Jünger saw the war as a duel between himself and Montherlant, a clean war, a gallant war, in which he, at least, behaved well. As he marched through France he treated his vanquished opponents with respect. He lived up to his ideals and in Paris in 1941 he planned his political essay, *Die Friede,* which was to have served as an ideological basis for a new Europe well rid of Hitler.

In Paris Jünger served on General von Stülpnagel's staff. He recorded his encounters and experiences in his diary—the execution of a German deserter, the rumours of mass shootings on the eastern front, lunch with Paul Morand and Jean Cocteau—all with the same detachment. Yet he also realised that the war which was being fought around him was not the war he and Montherlant had wanted. Technology was being put to purposes which appalled him, and the German Army, in which Jünger had once had such hopes, was participating in a total destruction of human values. "In the Rue Royale," he wrote on June 7, 1942, "I saw, for the first time in my life, the yellow star, worn by three young girls who passed me arm in arm. . . . In the afternoon I saw the star more frequently. . . . I suddenly felt embarrassed to be in uniform."[2]

When he was temporarily transferred to the Russian front in the winter of 1942, Jünger again heard of the crimes of the Gestapo. "We celebrated New Year's Eve at headquarters. Unfortunately the usual conversation set me in a bad humour. General Müller told us of the appalling atrocities committed by the Security Services after the conquest of Kiev. Mention was also made of the tunnels of poisoned gas into which trainloads of Jews were driven. Those are rumours, although there must be mass murders in

---

[1]Karl O. Paetel, *Ernst Jünger in Selbstzeugnissen und Bilddokumenten,* Hamburg, 1962, p. 66.

[2]E. Jünger *Werke,* vol. II, p. 351.

quantity. I thought of Potard's wife in the Rue Lapérouse and of his anxiety. When you see individual cases and then come to know of the quantity of murders in these slaughter houses, you are suddenly faced with the prospect of such potentiality of suffering that you let your arms fall in despair. In such moments I am overcome by nausea before the uniforms, the shoulder straps, the decorations, the wine, the weapons whose gleam I once loved. The old chivalry is as dead as the nobleman who existed in the Napoleonic wars, who existed even in the First World War. Wars are waged by technicians. So man has reached that stage which has long been foreshadowed and which Dostoevsky describes in Raskolinkov. He sees his fellow men as lice and vermin, and he must beware of that if he does not want to degenerate into the insect world himself."[1]

When he had returned to Paris in 1943, Jünger saw Freiderich Hielscher, who told him of the Polish ghettoes and the crematoriums. A year later, after the Stauffenberg plot about which Jünger knew but in which he refused to participate, Hielscher himself was arrested, and Jünger's commanding officer, Stülpnagel, executed. Finally, in November 1944 Jünger received the news of his son's death in Carrara. It was with relief that, living with his wife in Kirchhorst, he heard the rumour of Hitler's suicide confirmed, for, he noted in his diary, he feared to see Hitler exposed in a cage and the country fall under his influence again.

---

[1] *Ibid.*, p. 493.

FRANCE

Section   Three

Though the followers of Hitler and Mussolini liked to describe democracy as a French invention, we should not forget that it was from France that they derived many of their ideas—from Gobineau, from Sorel, even, it would appear, from Gustave Le Bon. In France democracy had always had influential opponents, yet it is difficult to assess the extent of their influence under the Third Republic since they never actually triumphed—not, that is, until one of the most humiliating military defeats in French history induced the government to give plenary powers to an army officer. In retrospect the dominant figure of the Nationalist opposition, the son of a tax collector from Provence, Charles Maurras, seems curiously isolated—isolated by his deafness, by the rigid consistency of his ideas and by his baleful sobriety in moments of national inebriation. It was as a deliberate reaction against him that many of his followers deemed it necessary to found or join movements other than the *Action Française*. His overpowering personality, his constancy and his gloom were his attraction, but above all his undoing. While the course of events in the first half of the twentieth century caused most people to change some of their ideas, Maurras never consented to alter his, for he refused to admit that he might once have been mistaken. Determined to be always right, he was equally set on maintaining the purity of his ideals. Were he to resort to political action, they might be compromised; were he to attempt the *coup d'état* he always spoke of, he might fail. He was therefore reluctant to act in any way whatsoever, and it was this, more than anything else, that disenchanted his disciples.

The principal object of Maurras' detestation was the French Revolution of 1789. In this year he believed that three insidious myths had been imposed on France, which had never ceased to mislead her since—Liberty, Equality and Fraternity. Tracing human development from birth to middle age, Maurras established, with-

171

out great difficulty, but also without great originality, that men were neither free nor equal. They were destined, all their life, to be dependent on others or to have others dependent on them. Necessity and inequality, he claimed, were fundamental to the human condition, fundamental, above all, to the formation of any individual. And yet there were certain natural institutions which protected man and to which he owed allegiance: the family, the region, and the nation. It was Maurras' belief that politics should be directed towards the conservation of these units, and this was precisely what French politics were failing to do. With the birth of the Third Republic in 1870 the only force which he regarded as being capable of holding the nation together, the monarchy, had been definitively defeated. One of the main reasons for this defeat was the incapacity of the two factions of monarchists, the Legitimists, who supported the claim of the Comte de Chambord, grandson of Charles X, and the Orleanists, who supported Louis Philippe's descendant, the Comte de Paris, on whom to restore to the throne, but this Maurras was prepared to overlook. All he could see was the triumph of a mass of warring parties set on disrupting national unity, and abetted in this by the "four confederated states", the Jews, the Protestants, the foreigners or *métèques,* and the Freemasons, who were in true control of the Constitution.

When he was twenty-eight, in 1896, Maurras visited Athens to report on the Olympic Games. He was struck by the evidence of German influence in Greece and the power which Britain had been able to establish in the Mediterranean. He was appalled, moreover, by the insignificance of France, and, on his return to Paris, his hatred of the Republic was confirmed and increased by the revival of a case which was to have a determining influence on French politics over the next ten years, *l'affaire Dreyfus.* The theory of Maurras and the other *anti-Dreyfusards* was not so much that Captain Alfred Dreyfus, the Jewish officer on the General Staff who had been sentenced to life imprisonment on a charge of espionage in 1894, was innocent, as that even if he were innocent, he should be condemned. To question his guilt was going further than to question the validity of the army as an institution : it was to question the validity of the French State.

Ever since the sentence, members of Dreyfus' family had been vainly attempting to establish his innocence and prove the guilt of Major Ferdinand Walsin-Esterhazy, a somewhat disreputable figure saved only by his good connections. But in January 1898, Emile Zola, in an open letter to Clemenceau's *Aurore,* charged the French General Staff with having deliberately convicted an innocent man, and *l'affaire Dreyfus,* which had temporarily been smothered, revived with the trial of Zola himself. Within the next months Esterhazy gave some indication of the blackness of his conscience by fleeing the country and a certain Colonel Hubert Henry was arrested on the insistence of the more objective members of the Intelligence Bureau and charged with forging a letter in order to clear Esterhazy's name. Henry admitted his guilt and committed suicide in his cell.

At this point Maurras declared in the Royalist paper *Gazette de France* that Henry was a heroic patriot who had sacrificed his life for the honour of the French army and whose only fault was to have been revealed as a forger. France was divided : on the one hand there were those who believed in the innocence of Dreyfus and the truthfulness of Zola, and supported the founders of the *Ligue des Droits de l'Homme.* On the other there were Dreyfus' equally impassioned opponents. They, too, founded organisations, with the primary intention of combating the *Ligue des Droits de l'Homme.* In the spring of 1898 two "patriotic" Republicans, Henri Vaugeois and Maurice Pujo, had set up the small *anti-Dreyfusard Comité d'Action Française,* and in the winter the *Ligue de la Patrie Française* was formed. Before Dreyfus' official pardon had come through, in the autumn of 1899, Maurras joined Vaugeois and Pujo, whom he converted to royalism within a year, and a new movement developed around the three men known as the *Action Française.*

Although Maurras himself was an atheist, he believed that France under a monarch would have to be a Catholic France, Catholicism being in the French tradition and national tradition providing the sole criterion of what was good for a country. By defending Catholicism Maurras managed to enlist such powerful support for his movement that even the Vatican was alarmed. Nor did this support come solely from the more reactionary sections of the French Catholics, from those who regarded the Third Republic as the triumph of the anti-Christ, the reign of the Jew and the Protestant, and who feared the damage which French revolutionary ideals might do to the influence of the Church. It came also from those many Catholics horrified by the growing anti-clericalism of the Republican government: in July 1904 France broke off diplomatic relations with the Vatican, and in December of the following year a law was passed separating Church from State. "Church and State," in the words of David Thomson, "were torn apart, not neatly separated."[1] The property and buildings which had belonged to the Church were expropriated with ruthlessness; Church schools were submitted to State inspection and supervision, and the number of children attending them dropped drastically over the next twenty years. Nevertheless more conciliatory movements than the *Action Française*, like Marc Sangnier's *Sillon*, did exist, and the Pope himself was unwilling for the breach with the Republic to be as radical as Maurras would have it. From the start, therefore, the *Action Française* bore a slight stigma of heresy which, deepening over the years, was to end in the Papal condemnation of 1926.[2]

Anti-semitism was an unfortunate aspect of French Nationalism, French royalism and, sometimes, French Catholicism. Sanctioned by the leading aristocrats of the land, blessed by princes of the Church, accorded scientific and philosophical justification by the treatise of Gobineau, *L'Essai sur l'inégalité des races humaines,* fomented both in its emotional and economic form by Edouard Drumont's paper, *Libre parole,* and his books, *Le Secret de Fourmies* and *La France Juive,* it became a smart prejudice adopted by young men whose only aim was to be in fashion. It was considered a sign of patriotic Germanophobia, for many of the Jewish immigrants who had come to France after 1870 had German names, and Germany, from the Franco-Prussian war to the Second World War, was widely regarded as France's main enemy. French artisans and petty tradesmen resented the intrusion of the Jews and watched their success jealously, while the royalists, concerned principally with the defence of real estate, were alarmed by the growing importance of movable property which was frequently in the hands of Jews and foreigners. "As the importance of capital grew, as the existing social order began to shift, the umbrage of those whom economic change endangered focused upon the Jews. The Jews, like the Protestants, had played an important part in the

---

[1]David Thomson, *Democracy in France,* Oxford University Press, 1958, p. 143.
[2]See *infra,* p. 185.

creation and in the politics of the Republic and of the new society, the new world of which the Republic was the political incarnation. Not only in the banks, but also in the University, in letters, the theatre, and in the press, throughout the complex society of Paris, their rôle seemed increasing and increasingly obvious. Not surprisingly, the once-privileged social groups found it easy to blame them for their loss of position, their dwindling incomes from land or careers in the public service, their bad financial investments, their losses in crashes and speculations, in which the dealings of Jews were always prominently featured."[1]

The *Action Française* soon appeared as the only important organisation of the extreme right in France. The *Ligue de la Patrie Française* disintegrated in 1904 after its secretary, Gabriel Syveton, had committed suicide the day before he was to be tried for having sexual relations with his stepdaughter and embezzling the *Ligue's* funds. The other large movement, Paul Déroulède's *Ligue des Patriotes,* lapsed into insignificance at about the same time. In 1908, therefore, thinking, or pretending to think, that the time to take action had come, Maurice Pujo organised the body which was to restore the monarchy with a *coup de force*—the *Camelots du roi.* Like Mussolini's *squadristi,* the *Camelots* contained an incongruously progressive element. "We were not right wing," wrote Georges Bernanos, who, as a *Camelot,* was imprisoned for rioting in 1909. "We preferred risking a workers' revolution to compromising the monarchy with a class which had for a century been totally alien to its ancestral traditions, to the profound meaning of our history, a class whose selfishness and cupidity had managed to establish a form of servitude more inhuman than that once abolished by our kings."[2] And indeed, the *Camelots,* whose main task was to sell copies of the *Action Française* newspaper at church doors on Sunday, and to disrupt Socialist rallies, found that they agreed on many points with their political adversaries whom they encountered in prison. They were, in their own way, revolutionaries. Above all, they were active rebels who, rather than sit at home and preach right-wing doctrines, took to the streets and fought.

It was also in 1908 that the *Action Française* founded its own daily newspaper. "French by birth and by heart, reason and

---

[1]Eugen Weber, *op. cit.,* pp. 197-198.

[2]G. Bernanos, *Les Grands Cimetières sous la lune,* Paris, 1938, p. 48.

will," the members of the movement declared in the first issue, "I shall fulfil all the duties of a conscious patriot. I undertake to combat the Republican régime. The Republic of France is the reign of the foreigner. The Republican spirit disrupts national defence and favours religious influences directly hostile to traditional Catholicism. France must have a French régime. So our only future is in the monarchy personified by H.R.H. the Duc d'Orléans, the heir of forty kings who created France over a thousand years. Monarchy alone insures public welfare. Responsible for order, it prevents the public evils denounced by the anti-semites and the Nationalists. . . ."[1] The policy which the paper advocated was that of Maurras—a monarchy with a decentralised government which could see to the well-being of each region and a corporative economy. For the myths accompanying the Republic, Liberty, Equality, Fraternity, the *Action Française* substituted the myth of Joan of Arc, the symbol to the people's call to a king as the only unifying force in a divided country.

In 1913 there appear to have been only about 7,600 subscribers to the paper and a nonsubscription circulation of 20,000,[2] but the figures rose notably during the Great War, for, in this period of national crisis, the *Action Française* laid more stress on patriotism than on royalism. Its speciality was to spot traitors and defeatists in the French ranks, and it headed a veritable witch-hunt against politicians, industrialists, or even tradesmen with foreign names. It led the campaign against Joseph Caillaux, the Minister of Finance, and another Radical-Socialist, Louis-Jean Malvy, the Minister of the Interior, accusing them of subsidising Miguel Vigo-Almereyda, the editor of the left-wing *Bonnet rouge* who was suspected of espionage. All three men were arrested—Vigo was found hanged in his cell, and Caillaux and Malvy were tried and convicted, and only amnestied some years after the war.

The hatred which the royalist paper had for Germany was unequalled. Maurras' had been one of the first voices to clamour for German payment of reparations, and after the armistice he demanded the partitioning of the country. This, too, was a popular

---

[1] *Action Française,* March 21, 1908.
[2] Between 1920 and 1926 the subscription figures range from 20,000 (in 1921) to 48,000 (in 1925), while the nonsubscription circulation from 1923 to 1926 runs from 41,000 to 55,000.

stand. The *Action Française* came forward to defend every French-man who had suffered some material loss in the war. It increased the conviction that the Germans alone were responsible for the hostilities and that they alone should support their former victims. Encouraged by the widespread agreement with which they met and the popularity of their paper, which appears to have had a record circulation of 156,000 in 1917 and an increase of 7,262 sub-scribers, the leaders of the *Action Française* took a step which was to lose them their revolutionary members and ultimately precipitate their decline—they decided to run for parliament as the *Union Nationale* in the 1919 elections. This amounted to nothing short of compromise with the Third Republic, and the conciliatory inten-tions of the movement were confirmed by its relatively moderate programme which made no mention of the restoration of monarchy. The main points were that there should be no amnesty for crimes of treason in the war, that some legislation should be introduced to regulate immigration and that a campaign should be launched to increase the declining national birth-rate. The military service period of three years was to be reduced, adminis-trative and economic decentralisation brought about, relations with the Vatican re-established and some agreement reached with the Pope about the various religious problems at hand. Finally, every measure interfering with the Church, religious orders and Church schools was to be abolished. The programme was decidedly popular, and some thirty candidates "who could be considered close to the *Action Française*",[1] including Maurras' fellow-editor, Léon Daudet, were elected.

Like all movements which made it their policy to denounce the evils of democracy, the *Action Française* thrived in times of crisis —when the blame could be put on democracy—and wilted in moments of prosperity. From 1918 to 1923, though stable in com-parison with Italy and Germany, France did have a small share of the social disorder which spread through Europe. By the begin-ning of 1919 the franc was weak and the cost of food was rising rapidly. In January there were public transport strikes; in February an attempt was made to murder Clemenceau; in March there were difficulties with employees in the civil service; and on May day there were clashes between strikers and the police which resulted in numerous casualties. All these incidents were to the advantage

[1]E. Weber, *op. cit.*, p. 129.

of Maurras, who never ceased to emphasise the danger of a *coup* from the left. On the other hand, the *Action Française* found itself, surprisingly often, in agreement with the policy of the French government. In September 1920, the government abandoned the idea of an official celebration on the occasion of the fiftieth anniversary of the Republic, largely on account of right-wing pressure; a little later diplomatic relations with the Vatican were resumed; and in January 1923, Raymond Poincaré, who was known to sympathise with Maurras, decided, with the whole-hearted support of the *Action Française*, to occupy the Ruhr. This, Daudet and Maurras believed, was a sign of true patriotism which, Daudet thought, might even lead to his own nomination as Minister of the Interior.

It was at the time of the occupation of the Ruhr, however, that public opinion began to turn against the *Action Française*. On January 22 a young anarchist named Germaine Berton had assassinated the secretary general of the *Camelots du roi* and the *Ligue de l'Action Française*, Marius Plateau. The *Camelots* retaliated by sacking the offices of three left-wing newspapers, *L'Oeuvre, L'Ere Nouvelle* and *Bonsoir,* and on May 31, they further antagonised public opinion by assaulting three Republican politicians, Marc Sangnier, Maurice Violette and Marius Moutet, who were on their way to a left-wing meeting of protest against Poincaré's German policy. The result of these attacks was a far more determined and coherent opposition to the extreme right in the Chamber of Deputies, and, indeed, in the country at large; and, as the French economy recovered and the general situation improved, there was a temporary swing to the left. Alexandre Millerand was replaced as President of the Republic by the Moderate Radical, Gaston Doumergue, in June 1924. Daudet failed to be re-elected as deputy. Many of the Socialists and Radicals who had been convicted during the war, including Caillaux and Malvy, were pardoned; the railroad workers who had been suspended after their participation in the 1919 strikes were again employed; and there was again a predominant anti-clericalism in parliament, confirmed by the Cartel Majority's vote to abolish the French Embassy to the Vatican in February 1925.

At the same time, politics became less and less the concern of the individual. The anxiety of the early twenties gave way to the feeling of relief that the Great War, the war to end all wars, was over and won. "An unparalleled prosperity," wrote Maurice Sachs, "was to give us seven years of extraordinary euphoria during which the shops were crammed, the theatres full, and the streets packed with visitors. It was an incredible period when books were written, printed and sold everywhere, when pictures were painted, exhibited and flogged in a flash. . . Easy money put an ephemeral effervescence into the arts and subjected them to a superficial infatuation which it was later difficult to forgo. Finally, a certain hypocrisy which had camouflaged man's natural instincts during the war, had been rejected like an importunate veil; those who had suffered least were advised to entertain the others; widows were advised to remarry so as to ensure the studies and holidays of the orphans; in short there was a tacit law that we should enjoy ourselves to the full."[1]

But despite the indifference to politics, the pranks of the Surrealists, and the elegant introversion of André Gide and Paul Morand, which characterised the French literary world of the mid-twenties, we must keep in mind that the *Action Française* had once enjoyed immense prestige in intellectual circles and continued to have an influence on a great many young writers. In 1917 Proust and Rodin had taken it regularly; both Gide and Apollinaire had written to Maurras expressing their admiration; and Anatole France had maintained that it was the only paper written in good French. This was due in part to Léon Daudet, Maurras' witty but obstreperous fellow-editor, and in part to Maurras himself: even Romain Rolland, who opposed nearly all his ideas, had described him in 1913 as "the greatest representative of the traditional French spirit".[2]

Maurras was a classicist. He had always regarded romanticism as a foreign import which distorted the French spirit, a barbarous and confused patchwork of ideas and emotions. The French, he claimed must return to *their* tradition, to the classical tradition, in which order, hierarchy and discipline were essential. But still more than Maurras' balanced, classical ideal, it was the importance he attached to will-power as man's only way of ruling "that obscure physical realm where the tides and tumult of our blood are stirring", and of imposing himself on matter, which commanded the

---

[1] M. Sachs, *Le Sabbat,* Paris, 1946, pp. 88-100.
[2] R. Rolland, *Un beau visage à tous sens, choix de lettres, 1886-1944,* Paris, 1967, p. 118.

respect of such young men as Bernanos, Montherlant, Drieu La Rochelle and André Malraux—young men in search of heroism and action. In view of his later commitment to the left wing it is interesting to recall the preface which Malraux wrote to Maurras' pamphlet, *Mademoiselle Monck,* in 1923, when he was still unsure of the direction his political allegiance was to take. "To go from intellectual anarchy to the *Action Française* is not to contradict, it is to construct," he wrote. "(Maurras') work is a series of structures designed to create or maintain a harmony. He appraises everything and makes one admire order, because all order represents strength and beauty. . . Reason succumbs to sensibility : it is only with the help of one emotion that it can modify other emotions, and for Charles Maurras this emotion is the love of France. . . Charles Maurras is one of the greatest intellectual forces of today."

As an intellectual force Maurras remained strong until the Second World War : it was as a political force and as a human force that he failed. For Georges Bernanos, who believed, as he wrote to Louis Salleron in 1939, that "God created me to devote myself to one man", who needed "to see the eyes, to hear the voice of him who commands", who thought that "the only true banner is a living prince",[1] the heroic aspect of the *Action Française,* which he had joined largely under the influence of his confessor, Dom Besse, vanished with its entry into Republican politics, while the heroic side of Maurras was somewhat obscured by his continued efforts to be elected to the *Académie Française.* For his part Bernanos would accept no honour from the French Republic, refusing the *Légion d'honneur* three times, in 1927, 1938 and 1946. Royalism, as he saw it, was a crusade, directed primarily against the comfort-loving bourgeoisie, whom he never tired of shocking. It was more for the sake of the scandal it might cause than out of sincere anti-semitism that he wrote the book that his admirers prefer to ignore, *La Grande Peur des Bien-pensants,* a eulogy of Edouard Drumont and an obituary of "the idea of heroism which, still more than the idea of the fatherland, seems to be the price that has been paid for the war."[2] "In reality," he asserted, "present day society, so-called modern society which is a society of transition and compromise, has no plan, no definite aim other than to survive as long as possible thanks to the disgusting empiricism that it

---

[1] *Georges Bernanos, Cahiers de l'Herne,* Paris, 1967, p. 127.
[2] G. Bernanos, *La Grande Peur des Bien-pensants,* Paris, 1931, p. 413.

has used hitherto."[1] For such rebels as Bernanos, Maurras, whom they now identified with "modern society", was losing his fascination.

Mussolini's seizure of power in Italy increased the impatience of Maurras' followers. Needless to say, the French were eager to emphasise the debt which both the Italian Nationalists and Fascists owed to the royalist leader, but the Italians were more sceptical : when Georges Valois[2] informed Mussolini that "the *Action Française* was the nest of Fascism", the Duce replied: "Yes, but I put the baby in the cot."[3] And the baby, it had to be admitted, was very different from anything Maurras himself could have conceived. In its original form Fascism was both Republican and anti-clerical, and it came to terms with the Church and the monarchy with some distaste. Anti-semitism played no part in its ideology until the late thirties, and even the more reactionary members of the party, like the monarchist Gioacchino Volpe, regarded the *Action Française* as excessively conservative. Finally, as Eugen Weber stated, the *Action Française* was "as resolutely doctrinal and rationalistic" as Fascism was "churlishly anti-intellectual".[4]

Even when Fascism had become a régime—a régime which retained the monarchy and respected the Church, Mussolini embarked on a process of deliberate centralisation of government which was in direct contradiction to the regionalism of the *Action Française*. But though Léon Daudet stressed immediately after the March on Rome, that the most interesting aspect of Fascism was "recognition of the fact that in modern times a dictatorship can only be beneficial as a support of monarchy or as a passage to monarchy",[5] his admiration for Mussolini was sincere, and he referred to him in a letter to Giovanni Preziosi in December 1934 as "one of the greatest politicians of all times".[6] At a still later date, in 1937, even Maurras lavished praise on the Italian régime, "Socialism freed of democracy, syndicalism liberated from the bonds to which the class struggle had submitted Italian labour".[7]

[1]*Ibid.*, p. 430.

[2]See *infra.*, p. 182.

[3]Yvon de Begnac, *Palazzo Venezia, storia di un regime,* Roma, 1950, p. 185.

[4]E. Weber, *op. cit.*, p. 134.

[5]*Action Française*, October 31, 1922.

[6]G. Pini & D. Susmel, *Mussolini, L'Uomo e l'Opera, III*, p. 312.

[7]C. Maurras, *Mes idées politiques,* Paris, 1937, p. 62.

Mussolini, he went on to say, had instituted a corporative system in true national tradition; he had formed a national State which brought about "friendship and union instead of arousing hatred and schism, as the democratic electoral State had done". "Italy," he concluded, "needed a dictatorship. The genius of the dictatorship and the dictator has calmed, pacified and revived a country which had previously been feverish or languishing. It has returned to its destiny an ardent, intelligent, patient and courageous race. It has managed more than once to adapt potential evils to the common good. However deep the differences between the centralisation adopted by Italy, which has only been united since 1870, and the local liberties due to a nation unified as long as our own, we must admit that Fascism has spared the peninsula the damage of Communism and the disappointments of Socialism. It is absurd to maintain that this has been at the cost of crushing the people. The Italian workers have long enjoyed a statute the likes of which does not exist in France."[1]

The first major split in the *Action Française* was the work of a man who preferred the determination of Mussolini to the inertia of Maurras. Georges Valois was a former syndicalist, single-minded in his opposition to the plutocracy he thought was dominating the world, who had joined the *Action Française* in 1906 in the belief that it was possible to conciliate the workers with royalism. Like Bernanos, he regarded the monarchy as a unifying force in a country which could then adopt as progressive a social and economic policy as it pleased and the pretender to the throne, the Duc d'Orléans, seemed to him ideally suited to this purpose. *"Il était très prince et très peuple,"* he was to write several years after his break with the royalists, "a man with whom the Republicans could well have fought against plutocracy."[2]

Unlike most of the other members of the *Action Française,* Valois had some knowledge of economics and had come forward with more than a vague critique of the current system. He proposed to revolutionise organisation and production, and introduce a form of corporativism by which both employers and employees would be acknowledged as producers and divided into groups according to their occupation or their region. Each group would send a repre-

---

[1] *Ibid.,* pp, 63-64.
[2] G. Valois, *L'homme contre l'argent,* Paris, 1928, pp. 111, 112

sentative to a national economic council, and in what Valois called an Estates General of French Production, every institution in French society would be represented—the families, the provinces, even the Church. The Estates General would ensure the co-ordination of all national forces; it would revive the sense of traditional hierarchy and authority by emphasising the rôle of the leader—of the head of the family and the head of the State. But the true institution on which Valois' system was modelled was the army, and the true spirit which he hoped would prevail was the fighting spirit, the comradely heroic and idealistic mood he had known in the trenches during the Great War.

The similarity between Valois' principles and those of the Italian revolutionary syndicalists was considerable, and when Valois visited Rome in 1923 as a delegate of the *Action Française* it was the ubiquitous Malaparte who acted as his guide. Malaparte, Valois recalled, "a Republican and a Socialist by origin, culture and sentiment, was the sort of Fascist I liked".[1] As Valois pointed out, however, there was no question of his having derived any of his ideas from the Italians: they had derived theirs from a Frenchman, Georges Sorel. Indeed, he was irritated when two of the Italian Nationalists he encountered, Corradini and Coppola, implied that if Italy was naturally drawn to Fascism, France was by nature a democracy. Nevertheless Valois was pleased by what he saw in Italy and delighted by his meeting with Mussolini. Two years later he told an Italian journalist that Fascism and Communism were the only positive forces in the world. "Whichever wins and conquers the other, Communism in Russia and Fascism in Italy will have similar results. No parliament, no democracy, a dictatorship, a nation which forms itself on its own. Once the bourgeoisie has been ousted the alliance between State and people will oblige everyone to march in national discipline. . . Fascism has taken all that is best from the *Action Française* and Socialism. Fascism in Europe is becoming the synthesis of all positive anti-democratic movements. All honour is due to Italy and to Mussolini for having baptised the movement."[2]

For some time Valois had been mistrusted by the leaders of the *Action Française*. To start with certain industrialists had

---

[1] *Ibid.*, p. 48.
[2] *Popolo d'Italia*, October 18, 1925.

shown an interest in his corporative theories, which did appear as a possible solution to the industrial unrest and the tyranny of the C.G.T. His proletarian origins made him one of the most likely members of the royalist movement to enlist the support of the workers, and in 1920 he had succeeded in launching a corporatist organisation, the Confederation of French Intelligence and Production which turned into the Union of French Corporations four years later. But when the radical implications of his theories became clear he lost the support of French industry, and all that remained was royalist jealousy and suspicion.

In February 1925, with the financial assistance of the perfumer François Coty[1], Valois founded his own newspaper, *Le Nouveau Siècle*, and in April he formed his own legions of ex-servicemen. He left the *Action Française* in October, and founded a movement, *Le Faisceau*, the following month. With its blue-shirted legionaries as its *force de frappe*, the principles of *Le Faisceau*, according to Valois, were to criticise "the individualistic bourgeoisie" and to exalt "the heroic spirit of the soldier and the revolutionary worker" as opposed to the prevalent spirit of "mercantilism and parliamentarianism". By the end of the year Valois had not only repudiated the anti-semitism and royalism of the *Action Française*, but had become an outspoken detractor of Maurras. "You are no leader," he told him, "neither you nor any members of your movement have ever had a precise idea about how to seize power. So none of you ever attempted it."

Valois' support came from unexpected sources. A revolutionary above all else, he counted on an alliance with the Communists, and succeeded in attracting Marcel Delagrange, the Communist mayor of Périgueux, and the trade unionist Henri Lauridan, while as many as 2,000 members of the *Action Française* seem to have defected to the *Faisceau* in January 1926. Yet the relentless enmity of the royalist leaders, which increased when their own followers started to desert them, was one of the causes for the failure of Valois' movement, and soon led to skirmishes between the *Camelots* and the Blue Shirts. Then there was the sudden hostility of Coty, who, claimed Valois, motivated principally by his hatred for Horace Finaly, the director of the Banque de Paris et des Pays-Bas, was working for the British intelligence services. He was

---

[1]*See infra.,* p. 191.

Otto Abetz (*left*) & Robert Brasillach

Jean Cocteau (*left*) & Arno Breker

acting "as a liaison agent between London, Paris and Rome in order to unite the French and Italian right-wing against a German-Soviet bloc".[1] He wanted, in short, to make France the slave of England before Finaly made her the slave of the United States. But Valois would have nothing to do with these plutocratic intrigues. In 1926 Coty withdrew his financial support and *Le Faisceau* turned further and further to the left. At this point, however, two of its leading members, Marcel Bucard and Philippe Lamour, whom Valois believed to be working for Coty, proved themselves in disagreement with Valois' policy and the movement began to disintegrate. In March 1928, a month after Valois had denounced the reactionary nature of Italian Fascism, his paper, *Le Nouveau Siècle*, ceased to appear, and *Le Faisceau* came to an end. Valois returned to his revolutionary syndicalism and was later deported for his part in the Resistance during the Second World War, while Lamour, after trying vainly to form his own Revolutionary Fascist Party, developed the same revulsion for Fascism as a political régime as his former leader, and stood as candidate for the *Front Populaire* in 1936.

Suffering defections for political reasons on the one hand, the *Action Française* saw the growth of an "internal opposition" for religious reasons on the other. One of the first signs of this was the foundation, in 1924, of *La Gazette française* by Amédée d'Yvignac under the influence of the Abbé Lallement and the neo-Thomist philosopher, Jacques Maritain. D'Yvignac hoped to formulate a "Christian policy" which would restore "the notion of the Right of God in society and State", and which, he believed, Maurras had neglected. Not until two years later, however, did he leave the *Action Française*, and the reason for his (and Maritain's) departure was the Vatican's decision to place the newspaper, together with all Maurras' work, on the Index.

Vatican policy had been at odds with the *Action Française* throughout the early twenties : Pope Pius XI had not only opposed the occupation of the Ruhr in 1923 and preached conciliation and peace with the fallen enemy; he had also advised co-operation with the Third Republic and had showed himself favourable to Marc Sangnier's *Le Sillon*. Besides, suspicion that Vatican sympathy lay

---

[1] G. Valois, *op. cit.*, p. 295.

O

with the *Action Française* had done the Church ineffable damage
in the eyes of the French workers, who associated the movement so
narrowly with the Vatican that they identified the most progressive
priests with reaction. But above all the Pope had good reason to be
jealous of Maurras: the influence he exercised in Catholic circles
both in France and Belgium, was immense, and he was far from
being obedient to Papal orders. At the time the motive advanced
by the Vatican for the condemnation of the *Action Française*—that
the paper should be putting religion at the service of a political
movement—seemed unsatisfactory to most of Maurras' followers,
and indeed, it was a poor excuse for remedying a state of affairs
which seemed on the verge of getting out of hand. Nevertheless the
effect of the ban was catastrophic. Within four years the *Action
Française* lost nearly half its readers. True to his contradictory
nature, Bernanos was one of Maurras' few old supporters who
returned to the movement as proof of his defiance—but, as we shall
see, he only stayed a short while. Maritain's departure was most
damaging for he was accompanied by a host of younger members
or sympathisers who now searched for political and religious guidance elsewhere. Many of them followed Maritain, others the more
extreme political movements which were soon to arise and, in view
of the influence they were to have on the ideology of these movements and of Pétain's *Révolution nationale,* I shall briefly examine
some of their aims.

"The non-conformists of the thirties"[1] demanded "a break with the
established disorder".[2] To the French left, they were all Fascists, and
Denis de Rougemont of the *Ordre Nouveau* found himself described
in the Soviet paper *Izvestia* as "one of the leaders of the avant-
garde of French Fascism." They would not accept Marxism, and

---

[1] I use the title of Jean-Louis Loubet del Bayle's study, *Les non-
conformistes des années 30,* Paris, 1969.

[2] They fell into three main groups. To the left were the contributors
to *Esprit* which had been founded by Emmanuel Mounier, Georges
Izard and André Déléage in 1931, and included Pierre-Henri Simon
from Taittinger's *Jeunesses Patriotes,* Jean Lacroix, Aldo Dami and
André Bridoux. Like the founders of the *Gazette française* they were
influenced mainly by Maritain. In the centre there was the *Ordre
Nouveau,* started by Robert Aron, Robert Dandieu, Alexandre Marc
and Daniel-Rops, and to the right, closest and most loyal to the *Action
Française,* were the young royalists known as *La Jeune Droite*—Jean
de Fabrègues, Thierry Maulnier, Jean-Pierre Maxence, Maurice
Blanchot and Robert Brasillach. Their papers were *Les Cahiers, La
Revue Française, Réaction, La Revue du siècle,* and, later, *Combat.*

they were looking for an alternative to capitalism. But although a number of them were later to join "Fascist" parties—Jean-Pierre Maxence the *Solidarité française,* Robert Loustau the *Croix-de-Feu* and then the *Parti Populaire Français,* Robert Francis, the *Parti Populaire Français*[1]—they were trying, in the early thirties, to find a path which was in theory as far from Fascism as it was from Communism. Too young to have fought in the Great War, they rejected the myth so dear to the followers of Mussolini and Hitler—the myth of the heroic trench fighter. The Great War and all that resulted from it were, they believed, the fruits of an anachronistic form of nationalism. "We do not bear the remotest responsibility for the war," claimed the *Ordre Nouveau* in a letter congratulating Hitler on leaving the League of Nations. "We do not consider ourselves bound by the imbecile and murderous treaty which our delegates—and yours—drew up. We refuse to recognise the face of our country in the frozen image of a system in which justice is betrayed behind the appearance of legality. The business deals and base policies underlying the Treaty of Versailles are as repugnant to us as they are to you. The Treaties of 1919 are as alien to us as the Treaties of London or Unkiar Skelessi, whose dates and terms we read about in our history books; relics of the nineteenth century, they express the inane ideology of the principle of nationalities. For us they are null and void."[2]

Spurning Nationalism, which they distinguished from patriotism, *Esprit,* the *Ordre Nouveau* and the *Jeune Droite* demanded a federation of European regions with a corporative economic system. Only thus, maintained the *Ordre Nouveau,* would the "eternal bases" of man be revived : the family, the commune, the profession and the region. For the object of the bloodless revolution propagated by the non-conformists, and which only France, a country "which was not in a state of acute crisis", was in the position to accomplish, was the supremacy of man, his enfranchisement from the machine and the process of productivity, from capitalism, liberalism and the "American cancer".[3] "Against capitalist disorder and Communist oppression, against homicidal Nationalism and powerless internationalism, against parliamentarianism and

---

[1] See *infra,* p. 218.

[2] *Ordre Nouveau,* November 1933.

[3] R. Aron & A. Dandieu, *Décadence de la nation française,* Paris, 1931; *Le Cancer américain,* Paris, 1931; and *La Révolution nécessaire,* Paris, 1933.

Fascism, the *Ordre Nouveau* puts all institutions at the service of the personality and submits the State to man."[1]

Although the non-conformists repudiated Italian Fascism and Soviet Communism, they acknowledged both movements as the only "revolutionary" attempts to change the existing order of things. They repudiated the Marxist concept of the revolution as the inevitable product of an historical movement and found that historical materialism reduced the Communist experiment to as materialistic a level as capitalism. Their attitude to Fascism, however, was more complex. Emmanuel Mounier rejected the possibility of any conciliation between his ideas and those of Mussolini or Hitler. The *Jeune Droite*, on the other hand, inherited a degree of Maurras' admiration for the Italian dictator, but also the *Action Française* hatred for all manifestations of German Nationalism. The group that took the greatest interest in the various forms of German Nationalism remained the *Ordre Nouveau*. Alexandre Marc had been in touch with members of Otto Strasser's Black Front and the contributors to *Die Tat* with whom he shared a repugnance for Hitler, and he had even toyed with the idea of supplying them with arms to prevent a National Socialist seizure of power. Above all, however, Marc and the other non-conformists subscribed to the young German Nationalists' opposition to capitalism, and when Ferdinand Fried's *Das Ende des Kapitalismus* was translated into French, in 1932, it became almost as influential as it had been in Germany.

Clearly, of course, Fascism "in practice" was incompatible with the ideals of the non-conformists. They who had always decried the strong State found themselves confronted by political systems in which the State grew to unprecedented strength. The main accomplishments of Mussolini and Hitler were to have mobilised the young (and the non-conformists never failed to emphasise that their revolution would have to be the work of youth) and to have destroyed the liberal State, parties and parliament. Otherwise, as René Dupuis and Alexandre Marc wrote, "Fascism claimed to free man from the slavery of materialism, but by making the State the supreme expression of the material and spiritual life of the nation, it has reduced the spiritual values which it claimed to incarnate to a distorted form of materialism, because the cult of the state, in its

---

[1]*Ordre Nouveau*, May 1933.

absolute form, is nothing but the political transposition of materialism."[1]

It took over two years for the Depression to have a direct effect on France, and when it did the damage was by no means as severe as in Germany, the United States or even England. The unemployment figures were incomparably lower: 60,000 in 1931; 260,000 in 1932; 335,000 in 1933; and 465,000 in 1935. Yet foreign trade was hit by the devaluation of sterling in September 1931; industrial production went into a decline which reached its nadir in May 1932, and, after a brief revival, sank again at the end of 1934; and the international situation was distressing for even the most dispassionate spectators

The resentment of all the French taxpayers was aroused in July 1932 when, by the Conference of Lausanne, an end was put to German payment of reparations. For the French had hoped that Germany would really compensate for the damage caused by the Great War; they had believed themselves entitled, if not to prosper, at least to survive economically at the expense of their former aggressor. The government's agreement to the various plans to alleviate Germany's obligations had angered them, especially since taxes in France had risen steadily, and the Conference of Lausanne was found all the more loathsome when the French realised that they still had to pay *their* war debt to the United States of America. When the payment fell due, in December 1932, the *Action Française* was presented with an admirable opportunity of demonstrating against government policy. And when the Finance Minister, Henri Chéron, attempted to cut budgetary expenses, "indifference to politics became hostility. Taxpayers refused to pay their taxes; in Burgundy, Normandy, and Languedoc rebellious farmers and vintners ran tax inspectors out of towns and farmsteads; veterans met to cry down proposed pension cuts; students demonstrated against the suspension of competitions and examinations, burned fat Chéron in effigy, and clashed with the police. By mid-January 1933 the Latin Quarter was seething, and the Law Faculty, a stronghold of integral Nationalism, was in something like a state of

---

[1]Quoted in J. Loubet del Bayle, *op. cit.*, p. 306. When Robert Aron, Chevalley, Dupuis, Marc, Mounier, André Ulmann, Jean de Fabrègues and Thierry Maulnier attended a congress in Rome in May 1933 they were the only members to express their reservations about the Fascist corporative system.

siege."[1] Every measure taken by the government increased the grievances against "politicians"—the decision, in the winter of 1932, to retain the large salaries of the members of parliament, the vote to accord Austria 350 million francs credit—and all this while "at the barracks gates in Paris, every freezing night, long lines of people who had never begged before, waited, shivering, for scraps of food left by soldiers."[2]

It was with a shudder that the embittered bourgeoisie recalled a number of incidents which proved the dishonesty of their politicians and their sinister contacts with an intangible world of finance. In 1928 Clemenceau's former Minister of Finance, Louis Klotz, had been arrested for signing dud cheques, and the fraudulent deals of Marthe Hanau, an able woman with numerous friends in the government, had been revealed. In 1930 the Oustric scandal had brought about the resignation of Péret, the Minister of Justice, and the fall of Tardieu's government. Then, at the end of 1933, the Stavisky scandal[3] became public knowledge. Could it be, the French began to wonder, that the corrupt institution known as parliamentary democracy did not work? Three ministries succeeded each other in the first half of 1932, and five in the course of 1933. Such incapacity to remain in power suggested a weakness which France could ill afford after Hitler's nomination as Chancellor of Germany, and the triumph of an aggressive form of German Nationalism of which, as we shall see later, Hitler had boasted that France would be the first victim.

Men were haunted by the fear of an imminent apocalypse. Even the least political of writers found it necessary to comment on the disquieting "news in the papers". "The old capitalist world is crumbling," Julien Green wrote in his diary on June 14, 1931. "A new world is beginning. It is time, high time for us to leave with our prejudices, our police, our army, our flags and anthems."[4] "Maritain's visit depressed me," he added on October 1. "According to him the world is about to end. What am I saying? We are already sliding toward the abyss. We are there. The mystics all agree about this. If there isn't a war there will be a revolution which will destroy us. Everything is collapsing." By February 1932

---

[1] E. Weber, *op. cit.*, p. 308.
[2] *Ibid.*, p. 307.
[3] See *infra*, p. 193.
[4] J. Green, *Journal 1928-1958*, Paris, 1961, p. 40.

André Gide, whose interest in Communism had been growing since his visit to the Congo in 1925, had "begun to wish whole-heartedly for the rout of capitalism and all that crouches in its shade— abuse, injustice, lies, monstrosities."[1] The alternative was a totalitarianism which would provide the discipline he had formerly associated with monarchy.

Before discussing the Stavisky scandal and the subsequent riots of February 6, 1934 it is necessary to glance at the right-wing participants in these riots, at the movements which had either developed, or had gained strength during the Depression. The oldest, after the *Action Française,* was the *Jeunesses Patriotes,* founded by a Bonapartist deputy, Pierre Taittinger, in 1924, and recruited mainly from middle class students. The members of the organisation, anti-semitic and anti-democratic, had as their uniform blue raincoats and blue berets and specialised, like the *Camelots du roi,* in fighting Communist demonstrators. The size of the movement is almost impossible to gauge : after February 6, 1934 Taittinger claimed to have 240,000 members, but police reports suggest that the figure was closer to 90,000.

Behind the other Nationalist movements stands the capricious and megalomanic, though physically undistinguished figure of François Coty, more famous, undoubtedly, outside France for his talcum powder than for his politics. A Corsican, whose real name was Spoturno, Coty started his career at the end of the nineteenth century as secretary to the Corsican deputy, Emmanuel Arene. In 1900, however, he founded a small perfume industry; five years later he opened a plant at Suresnes near Paris, and during the Great War became one of the richest men in France.

The fact that Coty (and so many other millionaires—Serge André, the oil magnate, Jean Beurrier, the banker, Jean Hennessy, the owner of the brandy company) should have provided the French "Fascists" with financial support, would seem to belie the anti-capitalist claims of these movements. The main attraction of French "Fascism" was, as Robert Soucy pointed out, anti-Communism,[2] and it was precisely in an attempt to remedy the disorder which he imagined the left-wing had caused after the Great

---

[1] A. Gide, *Journal, 1889-1939,* Paris, 1939, p. 1116.
[2] Robert J. Soucy, *The Nature of Fascism in France,* in *The Journal of Contemporary History,* vol. 1, no. 1, 1966, p. 41.

War, that Coty, who claimed to be a Bonapartist, meddled in politics. In 1922 he gained control of the Parisian daily paper, *Le
Figaro,* and was both the owner and director of it from 1924 to
1932. But though he was one of the most generous subsidisers of the
Action Française, Coty's real ambition was to run a large ex-servicemen's organisation. After his quarrel with Georges Valois in 1926,
he first allowed a small "Association of members of the Légion
d'Honneur decorated for risking their lives", under the direction of
Léon Démoge, to take offices in the building of *Le Figaro,* and in
November 1927 encouraged Maurice d'Hartoy to found an association of wounded and front-line soldiers called the *Croix-de-Feu.*
Two years later Coty, who had quarrelled with d'Hartoy, manoeuvred to the presidency of the movement the handsome, gallant
and aristocratic colonel, Count François de La Rocque, under
whom the *Croix-de-Feu* was to become the largest and most powerful veterans' organisation. Yet Coty's friendship for the Colonel did
not last, and he turned his mind to forming a movement of his own.
In 1928 he had founded a newspaper, *L'Ami du peuple,* which was
sold at the price of two sous a copy, cheaper than any other paper
in France. His aim, Coty stated in its columns, was to conciliate
capital with labour, but capitalists, he asserted, were divided into
two categories : there was the good capitalist, like Coty himself,
who had worked hard all his life, and was entitled to be regarded as
a producer, the capitalist "with a fatherland, a home, a name, a
face, who is the accessory and instrument of a *human value*"; and
there was the bad capitalist, the crooked speculator, "an international, anonymous, irresponsible vagabond, lacking a fatherland as
does that bankers' capitalism whose innumerable offices are open
the world over, like so many avid tentacles watching their human
prey."[1]

Owing to his predilection for war veterans Coty gave special
encouragement to two contributors to *L'Ami du peuple.* The first
was Marcel Bucard, a former member of Valois' *Faisceau,* who was,
in November 1933, to found the most intransigent (and least
popular) Fascist party in France, *le parti Franciste,* and whose
admiration for Hitler and Mussolini was immense. And the second
was Jean Renaud, whom Coty appointed as leader of his own
political movement, the *Solidarité Française,* nicknamed *Sidilarité
française* by the *Canard enchaîné* on account of its appeal to

[1] *L'Ami du peuple,* July 10, 1933.

unemployed North Africans. The organisation developed in 1933, the year before Coty's death, and, though never particularly effective as an "anti-Communist" fighting force, it was yet another contribution to the dispersal of strength which undermined the French right-wing. I shall later refer to the antagonism which divided La Rocque, Doriot and Maurras, but little had done as much before February 1934 to disrupt the unity of the French right as the quarrelsome disposition and personal ambition of François Coty.[1]

Not until the Stavisky scandal did the French Nationalists appear to have a unity of purpose which might lead to unity of action. Yet, on closer examination, even this temporary and somewhat fortuitous alliance between the right-wing groups, turned out to be illusory. Thanks to the research of the *Action Française,* the French public was informed that Serge Stavisky, a cosmopolitan adventurer who had already served a prison sentence for fraud, had been able to carry out his dubious activities under the protection of Dalimier, the Minister of Justice. By reproducing two letters from Dalimier to Stavisky the *Action Française* contrived to implicate the whole of the Radical party. A warrant for Stavisky's arrest had actually been signed in December 1933 when enquiries were made into the

---

[1]By 1933 he had quarrelled with nearly all his former *protégés.* He had withdrawn his financial support from the *Action Française* and had even won from Maurras his contrary disciple Georges Bernanos. The issue which caused the split appears to have been Jacques Ditte's political candidature, which was opposed by Maurice Pujo. It led to a series of letters, written by Bernanos for *L'Ami du peuple* and Maurras for the *Action Française,* and the final repudiation of Bernanos by Maurras (see *Bulletin périodique de la Société des amis de Georges Bernanos,* No. 17-20, Noël 1953.) Maurras' description of the break, however, which he gave Xavier Vallat in prison after the Second World War, has different implications: "In 1931 Bernanos was at Hyères and invited me to go and see him . . . He had posted his two boys at his garden gate and told them to greet us with Fascist salutes, which meant nothing to me. He himself greeted Pujo and me with a great show of affection. I invited him to call on me at the beginning of November . . .He came, spent the day with us and made us laugh till tears rolled down our cheeks with his extraordinary imitations of that poor lunatic Coty: Bernanos spared him nothing . . . A fortnight later he returned to Paris, went straight to Coty, and became one of the most violent detractors of the *Action Française.* Coty had an absurd side to him which one could tease, but it wouldn't have been reasonable to make fun, of his money . . ." (Xavier Vallat, *Charles Maurras, numéro d'écrou 8.321,* Paris, 1953, p. 144.)

capital he required for an issue of bonds on behalf of a pawnshop in Bayonne. Eager to avoid a national scandal, however, the Prime Minister, Chautemps, refused to order a parliamentary enquiry into the case. Then Stavisky's corpse was discovered. The official statement, that he had committed suicide in his mistress' flat, was not generally believed, and Chautemps, forced to resign, was replaced by Daladier.

Ever since the Stavisky affair had begun the *Camelots du roi* had rioted nightly in the streets of Paris, with the encouragement, according to the left wing, of the Prefect of Police Jean Chiappe. To appease the Socialists Daladier dismissed Chiappe, whose cause was immediately taken up by the right. On February 6, 1934, when Daladier's new government was to appear in parliament, the right-wing leagues, the *Croix-de-feu,* the *Camelots,* the *Jeunesses Patriotes,* and the *Solidarité française,* together with some gangs of communists singing the *Internationale,* converged on the Palais Bourbon. The police opened fire, fifteen demonstrators were killed and 1,435 were injured. Despite the resignation of Daladier and the confusion of the left-wing the right failed to unite, and in retrospect the February riots seem ineffectual. The only true Fascist movement, Bucard's *Francistes,* took no part in them. The *Jeunesses Patriotes,* the *Camelots du Roi* and the *Solidarité française* participated independently, while Colonel de La Rocque did his best to keep his *Croix-de-Feu* out of the actual fighting. Maurras, in the offices of the *Action Française,* did nothing whatsoever. Lucien Rebatet relates how one young man appeared in Maurras' office on February 7, and shouted at him : "Maître, Paris is in an uproar. There is no government, everybody is expecting something. What shall we do?" Maurras' reply was : "I don't like people to lose their self-control."[1]

To the left, however, the right-wing looked formidable. "I am very alarmed by the disorder and confusion of all left-wing elements," Gide wrote to Roger Martin du Gard on March 9. "The right, on the other hand, is admirably organised. If we are not careful Fascism will come to power in France as easily as it did in Germany."[2] Deeming the danger far greater than it actually was, the left gathered their forces in an anti-Fascist bloc. The Com-

---

[1] L. Rebatet, *Les Décombres,* Paris, 1942, p. 30.

[2] A. Gide-R. Martin du Gard, *Correspondence, 1,* Paris, 1968, pp. 598-599.

munists decided to co-operate with the Socialists and Radicals, and in May 1936 Léon Blum was elected Prime Minister at the head of the *Front Populaire,* the ill-fated and well-intentioned *Front Populaire* which once again provided the Nationalists with the semblance of unity of purpose—to overthrow Blum.

Blum's accomplishments were considerable. He managed to unite the left, Socialists, Radicals and Communists, as no French politician had been able to do since Jaurès. He carried through reforms which had long been recommended by anti-capitalists of every political colour. Workers' delegations were set up to deal with factory managers; workers' wages were raised between seven and fifteen per cent; the armament industry was nationalised; the Banque de France at last brought under government control, and the hold of the capitalist oligarchy, the "two hundred families", weakened. An *office du blé* was established to eliminate speculation in wheat prices, and the forty-hour week, together with compulsory, paid holidays, were introduced. Why, then, did the *Front Populaire* arouse such fear and such vituperation? Why was it one of the main reasons for the transient success of such parties as La Rocque's *Parti Social Français* and Doriot's *Parti Populaire Français?*[1]

France felt more insecure than she had felt for many years. In March 1936 Hitler had occupied the Rhineland and demands for immediate mobilisation had been ignored. Blum came to power in May and in July civil war broke out in Spain. The French right-wing were infuriated by Blum's overt sympathies for the Republicans, while the left were disappointed by his refusal to supply them with arms. Then, as Hitler continued to fortify the Rhineland and it was thought that national energy should be devoted to France's own defences, the forty-hour week was introduced. At the same time there was an ever more genuine fear of Communism. The Franco-Soviet pact, signed in May 1935 and ratified in February 1936, irritated those Frenchmen who saw it as a deliberate provocation of Hitler and those who merely disliked the Soviet Union. "The pact wants to associate us with a state with which we have nothing in common," complained Maurice Blanchot. "It wants to associate us with a peace which is not ours, with a war which cannot be ours. It binds us to our destruction. It is both a vain and a criminal plan,

[1]See *infra,* pp. 204 and 218.

the worst thing possible."[1] Any alliance with Russia was feared as a stimulus to the French Communist Party which had 350,000 members in 1936. And Blum's left-wing government increased these fears. Under the *Front Populaire* seventy-two Communist deputies sat in the Chamber, as opposed to the previous twelve; two million workers occupied the factories to prove their power; menacing processions of Communists marched past the Arc de Triomphe; streets, stadiums and youth organisations were named after the heroes of the Left—Marty, Barbusse, Marx and Lenin; whole quarters of Paris were decked with red flags; and lists of the "two hundred families" were on sale outside the métro stations. The hedonistic existence of the rich bourgeoisie seemed in peril, and the gloomiest economic prophecies were confirmed when, after three months in office, the Prime Minister devalued the franc by a third.

Blum remained in power until June 1937, and while he was Prime Minister, his government struck as hard and as frequently as it could at the Nationalists. In June 1936 the right-wing Leagues were officially dissolved, and in October Maurras was imprisoned for having incited his followers to murder those left-wing politicians who were in favour of the League of Nations sanctions against Italy. The behaviour of the *Action Française* had, it was true, been execrable. On February 13, as Blum and another Socialist deputy, Georges Monnet, were driving down the Boulevard Saint-Germain, their car was stopped by a procession going to the funeral of Jacques Bainville, a prominent figure in the *Action Française* who died on February 9. Blum and Monnet were surrounded by a group of royalists, beaten up and rescued only by some workers who happened to be nearby. On that same day an irate cabinet decreed the dissolution of the *Action Française,* the *Etudiants d'Action Française* and the *Camelots du roi* : all that remained was the newspaper.

Although he had been sentenced for various periods on other occasions, October 1936 was the first time when Maurras actually served a term of imprisonment. His arrest caused an outcry. In England Professor Yvon Eccles protested against the sentence and a collection of university professors from all over the world put up the French royalist leader for the Nobel Peace Prize. In France his friends on the two right-wing reviews, *Candide* and *Gringoire,* conducted a campaign against the man responsible for the "Mas-

---

[1]*Combat,* March 1936.

ter's" arrest, Blum's Minister of the Interior, Roger Salengro. They accused him of deserting in the Great War, and proved so persistent that they contributed, in all probability, to the reasons for Salengro's suicide that November. In 1937 the French pretender, the Duc de Guise, officially dissociated himself from the *Action Française* on the grounds that Maurras' principles were incompatible with the French royalist tradition, but, as it turned out, this decision did more harm to the House of Orléans than to Maurras. For his imprisonment had made him something of a martyr. He was gaining in respectability. In June 1938 he was at last elected to the *Académie Française*; when he visited Spain in the same year he received the personal thanks of Franco for his propaganda in favour of the Nationalist cause and was elected to the Royal Academy of Spain. Finally, in July 1939, the new Pope, Pius XII, lifted the ban on the *Action Française*.

Nor was Maurras the only martyr of the *Front Populaire:* another was Jacques Doriot who in May, 1937, was ousted from the mayoralty of Saint-Denis. The right reacted forcefully. More and more discontented intellectuals became "Fascists" out of perversity. Other men turned away from the Republic because they considered that their most sacred values were threatened. Marxist ideology, they thought, endangered religion; Léon Blum's book, *Sur le Mariage,* chastity; the sit-in strikes, property. The combination of the three endangered the French nation, and the number of Jews in the government, together with the increasing quantity of immigrants from Germany and Central Europe, endangered the French race. Under Léon Blum, therefore, French anti-semitism revived with a violence unprecedented since the Dreyfus case. The *Action Française* of October 8, 1936 contained an article by the novelist Marcel Jouhandeau entitled *Comment je suis devenu anti-sémite.* Affirming his dislike of the Jews working on the *Nouvelle Revue Française* (Maurice Sachs, Léon Pollès and Julien Benda) Jouhandeau attacked Léon Blum, deplored the Jews' hatred of all that was French, and swore that he would continue to denounce every Jew who remained in France without control by special statute. His attitude, he subsequently said, was due to "the inopportunity of the *Front Populaire* which made me attack those responsible for it."[1]

The following year a book appeared which provided the French

---

[1]Eugen Weber, *op. cit.,* pp. 372-373.

reader with sinister information—*Bagatelles pour un massacre.* Basing his statistics on the *Protocols of the Elders of Zion* and other anti-semitic propaganda brochures, Louis-Ferdinand Céline asserted that ninety-eight per cent of the tourists who visited the Soviet Union each year were Jews; there were two million Jews in France; the Jews were behind royalism and Fascism, Communism and capitalism; they controlled the cinema, theatre and literature; they were responsible for the alcoholism which Céline believed was ruining the health of the French. They were trying to cause a world war, but Céline made it manifest that *he* would not fight in it. He recommended, instead, sending all the Jews to the front line.

"France," wrote Céline, "is a colony of international Jewish power . . . the slightest attempt at evicting the Jews is doomed in advance to ignominious failure . . . I'd like to make an alliance with Hitler. Why not? He hasn't said anything against the Bretons or the Flemish . . . Nothing at all . . . He only said about the Jews that he doesn't like the Jews . . . Nor do I . . . Carrying things to their logical conclusion, not being in the habit of distorting, I say quite frankly what I think : I'd rather have twelve Hitlers than one omnipotent Blum. At least I could understand Hitler, but with Blum there's no point in trying, he'll always be the worst enemy, absolute hatred, hatred to death."[1]

In the Great War Céline had had his shoulder broken, his ear drum perforated, and subsequently appears to have undergone a trepanation of the skull. But although he suffered from a permanent buzzing in his head which ultimately led to chronic insomnia, his life after the war was by no means as arduous as he would have his readers believe. He travelled widely and adventurously. As a writer he was a success, and won the *Prix Renaudot* for his first novel, *Voyage au bout de la nuit,* which appeared in 1932. Yet it is also true that his activity as a general practitioner in Clichy and Montmartre caused much of his bitterness, and professional jealousy may well have contributed to his anti-semitism.[2]

"She didn't believe in feelings, she judged low, she judged well,"

---

[1] L.-F. Céline, *Bagatelles pour un massacre,* Paris, 1937, pp. 131, 317-318.

[2] The medical profession was crowded with Jewish immigrants. Partly out of anti-semitism and partly because of the fact that Léon Daudet had been a medical student and used a jargon which appealed to doctors, more doctors joined the *Action Française* in the thirties than any other professionals.

Céline wrote of his secretary in *Mort à crédit,* and this was the attitude he found it convenient to adopt in his protests. For Céline's pamphlets were protests in the tradition of Drumont, *engueulades* in the style of his first and most assiduous supporter, Léon Daudet, and as such his wisest critics judged them. "He has a basic need to say at least one vulgar thing on every page he writes," commented Gottfried Benn, with whom Céline had so much in common. "But that is beside the point. In his second book he rants against the Soviets and the Faculties of Medicine, but also against the Jews. That's his way of expressing himself, his method. In the next book it will be coastal navigation or apprentice gardeners. Excellent subjects."[1] At the time of the *Front Populaire* Céline's anti-semitism was, as Gide pointed out, a joke—an unsubtle joke, maybe, but nevertheless a joke. "Céline excels in invective. He will pin it on anything. Jewry is a mere pretext. It is the most obvious and trivial pretext, the one which denies every nuance, which allows the most summary judgements, the most colossal exaggerations, the least sense of equity, the greatest intemperance of the pen. And Céline is at his best when he is most immoderate." "*If Bagatelles pour un massacre* were more than a game," he concluded, "Céline, for all his genius, would have no excuse for arousing the most banal passions with such cynicism and frivolity."[2]

That Céline's writings tended towards Fascism had not escaped the notice of the vigilant left-wing. Paul Nizan, writing in *L'Humanité* in 1932, could not accept Céline's "profound anarchy, his disdain, his general disgust which does not except the proletariat,"[3] and at the Writers' Congress in 1934 Maxim Gorky found Céline "indifferent to every crime," "since he does not find any way of committing himself to the proletariat and understanding their revolt, he is ripe for Fascism." Indeed, Céline neither believed in nor respected the proletariat. "There is no such thing as 'the people' in the touching sense of the word," he wrote to Elie Faure in 1935. "There are only the expoiters and the exploited, and every victim of exploitation only wishes to exploit. That's all he understands. The heroic myth of the proletariat *does not exist.* It's all a hollow dream. The proletarian is a failed bourgeois."[4]

---

[1]*Louis-Ferdinand Céline, II, Cahiers de l'Herne,* Paris, 1965, p. 141.
[2]*N.R.F.,* April 1938.
[3]*L'Humanité,* December 9, 1932.
[4]*L.-F Céline, op. cit.* pp. 57-58.

One of Céline's first references to Fascism is in a letter he wrote immediately after the February riots. "We are going, we are flying towards Fascism. Who's stopping us? . . . Die for the people? Yes! When you like and where you like. But not for this hateful, wretched, unconscious, vain rabble of patriotic alcoholics and mental layabouts . . . We're becoming Fascist. Too bad—the people will have wanted it—THEY WILL HAVE WANTED IT—they like the cudgel."[1] The physical decrepitude of the French filled Céline with sadness. He had always had a nostalgia for the physically healthy, and the women he admired most, largely on account of their physical accomplishments, were ballet dancers. He visited Germany on various occasions during the thirties, and the health of the young Germans returned from the *Arbeitsdienst* cannot fail to have impressed him. Nevertheless he refuted any political commitment deeper than the references in his books. At heart, as he told Elie Faure, he was an anarchist. "I have never voted, I shall never vote for anything or anyone. I don't believe in men . . . The Nazis loathe me as much as the Socialists and Communists . . . They all agree about vomiting me."[2]

It seems most unlikely, therefore, that Céline departed for Moscow in 1936 with any illusion as to what he would find there. He went to spend the royalties which had accumulated after the translation into Russian of *Voyage au bout de la nuit* by Aragon and Elsa Triolet, and the staff of the Soviet Embassy in Paris expected a positive reaction from him. In this they were, not unnaturally, disappointed. Céline returned more dejected than ever, convinced that "only three things work in the Soviet Union: army, police and propaganda." It was as much against Soviet Communism as against the Jews that his pamphlets were aimed.

Whether he intended it seriously or not, *Bagatelles pour un massacre* was welcomed by the French anti-semites. "Instinctive anti-semitism," wrote Brasillach, "found its prophet in Louis-Ferdinand Céline . . . *Bagatelles pour un massacre* was a torrential, ferociously joyful book, excessive, of course, but immensely vigorous. No reasoning in it, just the 'revolt of the natives'. The success was prodigious."[3] In 1938 Céline had a further book published,

---

[1] *Ibid.*, pp. 53-54.
[2] *Ibid.*, p. 55.
[3] R. Brasillach, *Notre avant guerre*, Paris, 1941, pp. 189-190.

Arno Breker (*left*) & Pierre Drieu La Rochelle

Sacha Guitry (*centre*)

L'Ecole des cadavres. The Aryan race, he now declared, was vanishing. Everybody was Jewish except for Hitler—the Pope was a Jew, La Rocque, whom Céline calls "Colonel Ghetto", even the right-wing newspaper *Candide* was Jewish. Maurras and Doriot had Jewish accomplices because they were insufficiently pro-German. Céline advised the expulsion of all Jews, the prohibition of all masonic lodges and secret societies, and hard labour for life for anyone who was not satisfied. "Personally I find Hitler, Franco, Mussolini fabulously débonnaire, admirably magnanimous, infinitely to my taste, ranging pacifists, in a word, worth 250 Nobel Prizes. The Fascist States don't want war. They've nothing to gain from a war. Everything to lose. If peace could last another three or four years, all the States of Europe would turn Fascist, quite simply, spontaneously. Why? Because Fascist States implement, under our eyes, among Aryans, without gold, without Jews, without freemasons, the famous Socialist programme which the kikes and Communists have always been bragging about but have never carried through . . . Who's done more for the worker? it isn't Stalin, it's Hitler."[1]

The extent to which Céline's form of prejudice existed among the conservative intelligentsia was indicated by the appearance in 1939 of *Pleins Pouvoirs,* a book by Daladier's future Minister of Information, the playwright Jean Giraudoux. The subject matter, as Drieu La Rochelle remarked, was the death of the Frenchman "between the aged and the foreigner"[2] and Giraudoux repeated some of the themes which the Nationalists had been dwelling on for many a year: France must expand demographically if she were to be a great nation; French towns should be cleaner, healthier, better planned; democracy was distorted by the French electoral system; French economy should be directed on lines similar to those adopted by the totalitarian states where, at least, there was mass employment and national enthusiasm. The solution to the problems facing the country was of a "strictly internal order. Render force to our nation, breadth to our imagination, comfort to our life. Have a

---

[1] *L'Ecole des cadavres,* Paris, 1938, pp. 662, 100, 107. In November 1938 the German legation secretary in Paris, Ernst von Rath, was murdered. "Crystal Night" followed and Céline's anti-semitic books were banned in France.

[2] P. Drieu La Rochelle, *Chronique politique 1934-1942,* Paris, 1943, p. 47.

P

policy of demography, town planning, great works and national honesty."[1]

Giraudoux was distressed that France should be overrun by foreigners, whose physical qualities he resented: it would not be so bad if the immigrants were good-looking and in good health, he said, but they were ugly, sick and deformed, and most of them were Jews. He did not, of course, consider himself anti-semitic: on the contrary, he agreed that distinguished Jewish intellectuals, like Freud and Bruno Walter, should be welcomed. What he did not want were migrants from the Central European ghettoes. "Under cover of all the revolutions, of all the ideological movements, of all the persecutions, not only do those handsome exiles of 1830 or 1848 enter our country, those exiles who carried with them, wherever they went, to the United States, Central Europe, South Africa, work, consciousness, dignity and health, but all the extradited, inadaptable, avid invalids. By some mysterious means of infiltration which I have failed to elucidate, hundreds of thousands of Ashkenazim, escaped from Polish or Rumanian ghettoes of which they have rejected the religion but not the characteristics, have entered our country. Accustomed for centuries to work in the worst conditions, they eliminate our compatriots from every handicraft . . . and, living ten in a room, avoid any investigation into their quantity or their work, and evade taxation . . . All these immigrants, used to living on the fringe of the State and its laws, accustomed to avoid all the burdens of tyranny, have no difficulty in avoiding those of liberty. Wherever they go they bring vagueness, conspiracy, confusion, corruption and present a constant menace . . . to the French craftsman. A horde which manages to lose every national right and brave every extradition, and which its precarious and abnormal physical condition forces into our hospitals by the thousand, crowding them to bursting point . . . . If the country can provisionally only be saved by armed frontiers, it can only be saved in the long run by the French race, and we fully agree with Hitler in saying that a policy only assumes a superior form when it is a racial policy, for that was what Colbert and Richelieu thought."[2]

After Mussolini's rise to power there had been a tendency among the more conservative intellectuals in France to admire his accom-

[1] J. Giraudoux, *Pleins Pouvoirs,* Paris, 1939, pp. 209-210.
[2] *Ibid.,* pp. 65-6, 75-6.

plishments. Their enthusiasm increased in the early thirties, when the order that reigned in Italy could be contrasted to the havoc in the rest of Europe. In Italy roads had been built, marshland had been drained, archaeological excavations were being carried out at the Duce's behest : it all made the very best impression. Sacha Guitry, whose plays were popular in Rome, told a journalist in 1934 that "the transformation of the capital was unforgettable. I had previously seen a mere village, and I now found a city, and what a city! My admiration has increased this year : the majestic ruins for everyone to see, ancient monuments at the end of great modern avenues, order, cleanliness, grandeur everywhere. On my last journey I met Mussolini and I gathered and retained the vision of a man who has conceived and performed miracles. The strength and charm of this leader and the immensity of his accomplishments are undeniable."[1] Guy de Pourtalès, Eduard Schuré, Henry Bordeaux, Jacques de Lacretelle—dozens of writers were of Guitry's opinion. "May God grant us too a Mussolini," had exclaimed the eighty-five-year old Schuré in 1926. "And may we once again turn our minds to great art, beauty and true civilisation."[2]

Like that of Paul Morand, Lacretelle's commitment to right-wing politics followed the riots of February 6, 1934. Formerly regarded as a liberal, though an aristocratic liberal, whose masterpiece, *Silbermann,* was a subtle but effective attack on anti-semitism and the hypocrisy of the *grande bourgeoisie,* Lacretelle had now come to consider liberalism "incapable of curing the present sickness of the world", "a perfect philosophical doctrine . . . for periods of ease", but "an agent of decivilisation in troubled periods." "It is precisely because one loves liberty passionately," he wrote, "that one would wish for a little less of it in France today, where it is losing its noble function. By running away from difficulties, liberty has bound itself with personal interest and laziness."[3] A tour of Italy in the company of Mussolini's former Minister of Finance, Count Volpi, led Lacretelle to appreciate the way in which the Duce had conciliated apparent contradictions : the myth of ancient Rome with the Concordat, a progressive social policy with the traditional class structure. Fascism, he found, was more civilised than barbarous National Socialism and more attractive than dreary

---

[1] *Popolo d'Italia,* February 23, 1934.
[2] *Popolo d'Italia,* January 9, 1926.
[3] J. de Lacretelle, *L'Ecrivain public,* Paris, 1936, p. 154.

democratic materialism. "What the layman recalls above all in Italy today is the fine way in which the human mind is manoeuvred. A finger has indicated the sense of greatness to thousands of people. Strength and relaxation, these are the impressions one receives when one crosses the Alps . . ."[1]

At a lunch attended by Paul Morand, Jean Giraudoux and Drieu La Rochelle in 1932 Lacretelle had made the acquaintance of Colonel de La Rocque who, he later said, "demilitarised himself in order to become interested in social problems".[2] And although La Rocque affirmed, on occasion, that he cared nothing for legality, the impression he made on those who met him was of extreme respectability. He was on good terms with the Prime Minister, André Tardieu, and with Pierre Laval. The rallies of his *Croix-de-Feu* were formidable but disciplined, his followers mainly from the upper middle classes. To the *Front Populaire* La Rocque was the incarnation of Fascism, but he never thought of himself as a Fascist. Refusing to unite with any of the other right-wing or "Fascist" movements, he was detested by both Doriot and Maurras.[3] He was highly critical of Mussolini and Hitler, and shared neither the anti-semitism of the *Action Française* nor the violence of the *Jeunesses Patriotes*: until 1934 the most brutal act of the *Croix-de-Feu* had been to break up a pacifist meeting in 1931, and on February 6 La Rocque had proved his moderation by keeping his followers out of the fighting. In 1935 he agreed to disarm his movement, and accepted its dissolution a year later. Even his political programme had been moderate, if only on account of its vagueness: "An immense love of the people, a wish to unite those classes which unpleasant circumstances force into a brutal union, a total respect for every form of work and for the rights obtained by the workers, a reasonable need for authority and stability, and the feeling of what is possible and impossible: those are our aims."[4]

After the *Front Populaire* had ordered the dissolution of the *Croix-de-Feu* in June 1936, La Rocque formed his own party, the *Parti Social Français* (P.S.F.). Robert Loustau of the *Ordre Nouveau* was one of the few intellectuals who had tried to elaborate a social doctrine for the *Croix-de-Feu* in 1934, but it was not until

---

[1]*Ibid.*, p. 156.
[2]Douglas Alden, *Jacques de Lacretelle, an intellectual itinerary*, New Brunswick, 1958, p. 218.
[3]See *infra*, p. 222.
[4]*Le Flambeau*, April 1, 1934.

the foundation of the P.S.F., which guaranteed La Rocque's respectability, that Lacretelle, who had been elected to the *Académie Française* in 1936, decided to put himself at the Colonel's service. His contribution to the party was a forty-seven page pamphlet which appeared in 1937 : *Qui est La Rocque?* The Colonel symbolised, he informed his readers, dignity and magnanimity. La Rocque was no petty demagogue, no fanatic, no potential dictator. He was a tolerant and broad-minded leader who would ensure freedom of expression if he ever became Prime Minister.

The main preoccupation regarding Hitler's rise to power was what his attitude would be towards France. In *Mein Kampf* he had been explicit on the subject. "Germany regards the annihilation of France as a means of providing our people with the necessary territory for expansion elsewhere."[1] His plan was to destroy France in order to prevent her interference with Germany's East European policy, and in view of the hatred the French had suscitated by the occupation of the Ruhr and their insistence on payment of reparations, this remained one of Hitler's plans of which the German people approved most. Once he was in power, however, Hitler found it diplomatic to stress his desire for European unity and peace. To his French admirers he gave conciliatory interviews.[2] "We Frenchmen are pleased to read your declarations of peace," Bertrand de Jouvenel told him in 1936. "Nevertheless we are worried by other less encouraging things. In your book *Mein Kampf* you attack France. This book is regarded as a sort of political bible in the whole of Germany. New editions are sold without any alterations to the passages regarding France." "I wrote the book in prison," replied Hitler. "It was at the time when the French troops were occupying the Ruhr. It was a moment of great tension between our countries . . . But today these is no longer any reason for a conflict. You want me to alter my book . . . But I am not a writer, I am a politician. I plan to alter my foreign policy, which is based on an understanding with France! . . . I make my altera-

<hr />

[1] A. Hitler, *op. cit.,* pp. 766-767.
[2] To Fernand de Brinon in *Le Matin* on November 19, 1933; to Lucien Lemas in *L'Intransigeant* on September 13, 1934; to Jean Goy in *Le Matin* on November 18, 1934; to Madame Titayna in *Paris Soir* in January 1936 and to Alphonse de Châteaubriant in *Le Journal* on September 2, 1938.

tions of the great book of history."[1] Of course, as Eberhard Jäckel has pointed out,[2] this was all untrue. Hitler wrote the incriminating passages in the second volume of *Mein Kampf* at the time of the Treaty of Locarno—that was late in 1925, almost two years after the occupation of the Ruhr and one year after Hitler had been released from prison.

And yet such statements, made both by Hitler and his Ministers, were encouraging : they gave National Socialism a less aggressive aspect and account, to some extent, for the position of Jules Romains. Romains, it is important to emphasise, never approved of National Socialism in itself : as an active and influential member of the P.E.N. club[3] he demanded the exclusion of the Nazi delegates at the Dubrovnik Congress in 1933, and, a former member of the left-wing and pacifist *Clarté* movement, he was known for his anti-Fascism. Nevertheless he appeared ready to set aside his personal antipathy for totalitarian régimes when it came to upholding the one principle he had held ever since 1918—European peace should be preserved at all costs. His very brief experience in an administrative capacity in the Great War had convinced him of the foolishness of all military endeavours and of the incompetence with which armies—especially the French army—were run. "I swear," he had said after the signature of the peace treaty, "that I shall do all in my power to prevent another war."[4]

It was Romains' belief in the importance of European peace and unity which led him to support the League of Nations with such ardour and to take as active a part as possible in international cultural organisations like the P.E.N. club. He visited the Weimar Republic on several occasions and each time repeated his conviction that peace between France and Germany was essential. And when the National Socialists came to power he overcame the repugnance he felt for Hitler and published a series of articles in which he told the French that, in such a moment of crisis, democracy had much to learn from Fascism. "We should not allow a

---

[1]*Paris-Midi,* February 28, 1936.

[2]E. Jäckel, *Frankreich in Hitlers Europa,* Stuttgart, 1966, p. 27.

[3]By 1933 Romains had written some of his best known works—the trilogy, *Psyché* (*Lucienne,* 1922; *Le Dieu des Corps,* 1928; *Quand le Navire,* 1929); and the first five volumes of his *Hommes de Bonne Volonté*—*Le 6 Octobre, Crime de Quinette, Les Amours Enfantines, Eros de Paris,* and *Les Superbes.* His plays, *Knock, Donogoo,* and *Le Dictateur* had been staged by Louis Jouvet.

[4]Madeleine Berry, *Jule Romains,* Paris, 1959, p. 28.

natural antipathy for the outer appearances and many of the aims
of the Fascist revolution in Italy and Germany to prevent us from
realising that it is not merely a return to the past, a completely
negative episode of regression and exhaustion, but also an attempt
to find a possible solution to modern problems, precisely to those
problems which Marxism has ignored or ridiculed."[1] It was time
for hierarchy to be restored, said Romains, and, whatever its defects,
Fascism claimed to restore a "genuine and natural hierarchy of
values".

Another fault of modern society was the lack of what Jules
Romains called "collective euphoria" : modern man was miserable;
the worker regarded his factory as a prison, the bureaucrat his
office as a fortress under siege. The social structure was threatened
by the myth of the class struggle. But this problem, too, Fascism
was attempting to resolve. "It is trying to erect a modern society
in which everyone is in his place and declares himself happy to be
part of it. . . France is not obliged to give up democracy," Romains
concluded. "But she should draw bold and wise ideas from Bolshevism and from Fascism. The day when, by a synthesis for which
our present régime provides the basis, we can show the world that
a democracy can be formed on a hierarchical system, according
to laws other than those of money, and return to euphoria without sacrificing human liberties, we shall again be what we have
been so many times in the past: the guides of other nations and
the founders of the newest order."[2]

Romains' critique of democracy differed little from that of the
"non-conformists", and indeed, after the riots of February 6, 1934,
he founded a group similar to those of the dissidents from the
Action Française, the *Groupe du neuf juillet,* whose aim was to
strengthen France by introducing corporativism. His attitude to
Germany, however, brings out one of the paradoxes of French
opinion between the wars. In the twenties to support Germany
had been a progressive and enlightened decision. While the conservative electorate had been insistent about the payment of reparations and virulent in their hatred of the country which they
believed had caused the Great War, the French Communists
deplored the reparations policy and the Treaty of Versailles; they
had demonstrated against the occupation of the Ruhr in 1923 and

---

[1] J. Romains, *Problèmes européens,* Paris, 1933, p. 177.
[2] *Ibid.,* pp. 183-186.

attacked both the Dawes and Young plans. Even the liberal left-wing tended to countenance the struggling Weimar Republic; they had approved of the Treaty of Rapallo sealing Germany's friendship with the Soviet Union; and they had favoured those few individuals like Romain Rolland who had remained pacifists throughout the Great War and had condemned one side as much as the other.

It was perfectly logical that this benevolent attitude of the left should come to an end with Hitler's rise to power, while the conservatives, on their side, continued to inveigh against the threat of German Nationalism. Even Maurras condemned Hitler's *racisme de peau* (as opposed to the royalist *racisme d'état*), and on July 17, 1935, the *Action Française* contained a front page article by Georges Gaudy describing the inhuman conditions in the S.S. concentration camps. Although the conclusion reached by Maurras' followers was that what Hitler did to the Jews in Germany was his business and that the concentration camps were yet another indication of the basic barbarity inherent in all the Germans (including the Jews), the *Action Française* continued to affirm that Germany was France's main enemy, and Maurras, who thought that the best way of showing the French Hitler's real intentions was to circulate an unexpurgated translation of *Mein Kampf*, warned his readers not to believe the Führer's conciliatory statements to French journalists too readily. For all their disapproval of Hitler's methods, however, the members of *Action Française* were against provoking the Germans by so rash a step as the Franco-Soviet pact. What Maurras and his correspondents advised was the improvement of national defences, the extension of the military service period from one year to two, and an alliance with France's "natural" allies—her Latin neighbours, Italy and Belgium, and (with a little more caution) Great Britain.

The greatest hostility to the Third Reich came, not unnaturally, from the liberal left wing, from some of the most impassioned supporters of the Weimar Republic. They were appalled by Hitler's treatment of the Jews, by his outlawing of opposition parties, by such obvious provocations as withdrawal from the Disarmament Conference. Only a few of them continued to urge co-operation between the two countries, and although these few were nearly all to collaborate with the Germans during the war, their closest connections across the Rhine were men who were, at least at this stage, far from being fanatical National Socialists. On the French side one of the more prominent figures was Jean Luchaire, the editor of *Notre Temps,* who appears to have been on the pay roll of the French Communist Party until shortly before the outbreak of the Second World War. Primarily an ambitious journalist, Luchaire was prepared to turn anywhere for financial support for his newspapers—to the left, to the right, to the Germans during the war. Yet he was also a sincere believer in a Franco-German rapprochement. He took part in a number of French-German youth meetings between 1930 and 1933, and in 1932 his secretary on *Notre Temps* married a young drawing teacher active in the organisation of the German youth movements, Otto Abetz.

When, in his memoirs, Abetz accounted for the love he had always had for France, he quoted Romain Rolland,[1] and, as a result of his Francophilia he was originally suspected by the more orthodox National Socialists of being a French spy. Only in the summer of 1934 did he join the Hitler Youth and meet the man to whom he owed his career, Hitler's future Foreign Minister, Joachim von Ribbentrop. Aware of Abetz's value as a propagandist, Ribbentrop set him to organise meetings of French and German ex-servicemen for the *Deutsch-Französische Gesellschaft* and took him to Paris in December 1938 when he signed the Franco-German friendship pact. But by this time Abetz's support of National Socialism made him as suspect in France as his Francophilia had formerly made him in Germany, and, in 1939, the French government, implying that he was guilty of espionage, issued orders for his extradition.

The French equivalent of Abetz's *Deutsch-Französische Gesellschaft* was the *Comité France-Allemagne* whose president was Fernand de Brinon. Its publication, the *Cahiers France-Allemagne,* was an excellent vehicle for German propaganda in France and the issue covering the Berlin Olympic Games in 1936, the photographs of German athletes and National Socialist rallies, were almost as effective as Leni Riefenstahl's films. The *Comité France-Allemagne*

---

[1]"The experience of the cultural commonwealth of the two countries determined my attitude towards the problems facing them. And a stronger power than all words of hatred was exercised on me by the words in Romain Rolland's *Jean-Christophe à Paris:* 'Germany and France are the two wings of the west—whoever breaks one of them, impedes the flight of the other.' " (O. Abetz, *Das offene Problem,* Köln, 1951, p. 25.)

itself was accorded considerable respectability by the fact that Jules Romains should have remained chairman of the organisation until 1938. In 1934 he had visited Germany, where he had met Abetz, Goebbels and Rosenberg. "If we were stupid enough to wage war," Rosenberg had reassured him, "the Mongol ponies would graze on the ruins of Europe." Romains returned to France convinced not only that France had nothing to worry about, but that it was folly for the Western powers to provoke the Germans by continual re-armament. He urged caution, even if this meant overlooking the persecution of the Jews, and expressed alarm at the increasing number of Jewish refugees in both France and England, who, by "the very sympathy which their lot deserves", were creating an atmosphere in which war might be inevitable.[1]

A number of future collaborators were at first most cautious in their attitude towards the Third Reich. We have encountered Robert Brasillach among the members of the *Jeune Droite* and indeed, Brasillach had shared most of the non-conformists' aspira-tions. But he, more than most of them, had remained under the influence of Maurras. "My first political reflections corresponded to the *Action Française* and Maurras, and have never ceased to do so," he was to write in 1941. "A world of reason, precision and truth suddenly presented itself to me."[2]

By the age of twenty-one, in 1930, Brasillach was writing reviews for the *Action Française,* and in November 1931 he joined *Je suis partout,* a weekly paper owned by the publisher Arthème Fayard which, within four years of its foundation, had become strongly anti-semitic and had as its contributors some of Maurras' most extreme followers—Pierre-Antoine Cousteau, Maurice Bardèche (Brasillach's brother-in-law), Georges Blond, Claude Roy, Claude Jeantet, Alain Labreaux and Lucien Rebatet. Yet Brasillach, owing to his literary virtuosity, remained the paper's most cherished writer. He was a good critic, an excellent poet, and a translator of genius (his anthology of Greek poetry remains a masterpiece). He wrote well, he had taste and a sense of humour which only failed where Fascism was concerned. For, as the thirties drew on, Fascism grew to represent the one thing Brasillach really cared about—youth.

---

[1] J. Romains, *Le Couple France-Allemagne,* Paris, 1934, pp. 76-77. Not until 1938 did Romains oppose a rapprochement between France and Germany. During the war he emigrated to the United States, whence he supported General Giraud (see *infra,* p. 234).

[2] R. Brasillach, *Notre avant-guerre,* p. 27.

He was terrified of growing old; indeed, Brasillach, plump and bespectacled, "dreamy and effeminate,"[1] was terrified of growing up. "There is only one youth in life," he wrote, "and we spend the rest of our days regretting it: nothing on earth is more marvellous and moving . . . If our thirtieth year is the age of serious mistakes, it is because we think we can prolong those minutes, because we think we have not changed . . . because the excessive proximity of youth cheats us and makes us think we are *still in time*."[2] In June 1936 Brasillach met the Belgian Rexist[3] leader, Léon Degrelle, the first of the young Fascists to make him think of the movement as a symbol of youthfulness, and two visits to Italy the following year convinced him that Fascism was "a spirit" "a non-conformist spirit, anti-bourgeois with a dose of irrespectfulness . . . a spirit which opposes prejudice, class prejudice as well as any other . . . the very spirit of friendship, which we would wish to become national friendship."[4]

In the Maurrasian tradition Brasillach was far more sceptical about National Socialism, as he showed when he reviewed a book by the Catholic novelist, Alphonse de Châteaubriant. Thinking that the Germans, with their spirit of self-sacrifice, their heroic myths and their asceticism, were saving the West from the inevitable collapse with which materialism and Bolshevism threatened it, Châteaubriant, one of the many Frenchmen who was to collaborate for reasons of pacifism, had bought a chalet in the Black Forest in 1935. In *La Gerbe des forces*, which appeared in 1937, Germany was presented by him as the only alternative to Russia. He harped on the necessity of Franco-German friendship and assured the French that Hitler's intentions regarding them were excellent. Drieu La Rochelle admired the book, André Breton was enchanted by Châteaubriant's mysticism, and many left-wing papers found his pacifism commendable. Brasillach, however, was contemptuous: "I

---

[1]Maurice Martin du Gard, *Chronique de Vichy, 1940-1944,* Paris 1948, p. 334.

[2]R. Brasillach, *Les Sept Couleurs,* Paris, 1939, p. 145.

[3]The Rexist movement developed around Degrelle in Louvain in the early thirties. Originally composed of Belgian Catholics looking for an alternative leadership after the Papal condemnation of the *Action Française,* the Rexist movement soon drew far closer to Italian Fascism than its French precursor. During the war the Rexists, Degrelle, Robert Poulet, José Streel, collaborated eagerly with the Germans.

[4]R. Brasillach, *Notre avant-guerre,* p. 283.

am distressed," he wrote in the *Action Française,* "to see such a serious, such a vital problem as the relations between France and Germany, treated with such *puerility.* That is the only word one can use for this book, in which the author kneels lower on each page, with religious respect, before all that Germany and Hitlerism represent. I have rarely seen such a ghastly spectacle . . . Supported by his confused and false ideas, Monsieur de Châteaubriant goes in for a series of prophecies of truly shocking ingenuousness. He tells us, for example, that one must choose between Berlin and Moscow . . . But no, Monsieur de Châteaubriant, there is also London, which controls half the planet, and New York, and Tokyo . . ."[1]

That autumn, in the company of his colleagues Blond and Cousteau, Brasillach attended a congress at Nuremberg. He found the Germans tidy, polite and reserved, and yet he felt uneasy. He was upset by the parades of National Socialist women, "not a pretty spectacle: those green skirts, those short brown jackets, are not always attractive. And then, to be quite frank, apart from the grace lacking in ninety-nine per cent of these Bavarian girls, I'm not sure whether this system of forced marches is very good for them."[2] Besides, Germany perplexed him. "I understand Italian Fascism he wrote, "I understand that its immortal qualities will last, even after the fall of the régime. But before this construction of a new man one asks: is it permissible? Is not Hitlerism soon to be no more than a great historical curiosity? . . . Isn't it all *too much?* Is it going to last? . . . Yes, when I try to recall those days which were so full, when I try to recall the nightly ceremonies illuminated by torches and projectors, the German children romping like wolves around their memories of civil war and sacrifice, the leader arousing the spellbound crowd in great waves and plaintive cries, I tell myself that this country is . . . prodigiously and profoundly *strange.*"[3]

A glance at Pierre Drieu La Rochelle's accounts of the Great War leaves us with the impression that he might be a less gifted Malraux or Saint-Exupéry, with the same determination to impose his will, to assert himself as a leader. The following passage from *La Comédie de Charleroi* serves more as an example of his mentality than of his talents as a stylist: "By raising my head I saw nothing,

[1]*Action Française,* July 8, 1937.
[2]R. Brasillach, *Les Sept Couleurs,* p. 120.
[3]*Ibid.,* pp. 124-125.

but I gave the others something to see. They saw me, watched me, called to me . . . I suddenly knew who I was and what life was. *I was that strong, free hero* . . . At times I had felt a surge of hot, young blood, the puberty of courage; I had felt a prisoner within me, ready to rush out. A prisoner of the life that had been made for me, that I had made myself. A prisoner of the crowd, of sleep, of humility. What was bursting out? A leader. More than a man, a leader . . . a complete man, the man who gives and takes with the same spurt. I was a leader. I wanted to take hold of all those men around me, to enhance myself through them, enhance them through me, and to charge across the world, myself at their head . . ."[1]

War gave Drieu the temporary possibility of playing the part of a man of action. He was neither a leader nor a "public character". "His," wrote Lacretelle after the Liberation, "was a female mind which had always allowed itself to be seduced by the myth of strength. Always feeble in his principles and careless as a creator, he searched in politics for the sensation of an energy and greatness which he did not possess by nature . . ."[2] During the Second World War, however, when he heard that Drieu had been appointed editor of the *Nouvelle Revue Française,* Lacretelle gave a very different judgement: "As for Drieu's career as a political writer, it is worthy of respect because it follows . . . a single line: patriotism and the greatness of the country."[3] And both these statements are correct: Drieu was not nearly as inconsistent as his enemies made him out to be.

On one level Drieu's character was a welter of contradictions. Attracted by life, vigour and health, he was obsessed by suicide. Stimulated by war, he was a pacifist, aware of the squalor of modern warfare and frightened of it. "I always wanted to combine contrary ideas: the nation and Europe, Socialism and aristocracy, freedom of thought and authority, mysticism and anti-clericalism."[4] After the Great War he had dabbled in contrary movements. He had joined the Dadaists, came under the influence of Jean Cocteau and Maurras, but remained a "sort of Republican who believes that capitalism will give birth to a fairly Communist aristocracy."[5] He

---

[1]P. Drieu La Rochelle, *La Comédie de Charleroi,* Paris, 1934, pp. 56-58.
[2]J. de Lacretelle, *Libérations,* New York, 1945, p. 25.
[3]J. de Lacretelle, *L'Heure qui change,* Genève, 1941, p. 231.
[4]P. Drieu La Rochelle, *Récit secret,* Paris, 1951, p. 58.
[5]Henri Massis, *Maurras et son temps,* Paris, 1951, p. 254.

was wary of Maurras, considered him too reactionary, yet maintained that he was "the most influential political thinker since
Marx."[1] And he was disappointed by Marx, of whom he wrote a
critique in *Socialisme fasciste*. Solitary and overcritical, he could
find no social thinker whom he truly admired and no group that
appealed to him for long.

Drieu's uncertainty is reflected in his writing—not only in his
political essays but also in his fiction, *Le Journal d'un homme
trompé, Une Femme à sa fenêtre, Le Feu follet, Rêveuse bourgeoisie,
Gilles* and *L'Homme à Cheval*. The reason for which he hated
Brasillach was an article that the latter wrote in 1934 entitled
Drieu La Rochelle ou le feu de paille.[2] Comparing his writing to
the tales in pre-war women's magazines, Brasillach disclosed Drieu's
defects with the spite of which only he was capable. The very slight
promise which Drieu had shown in his first poems, he wrote, had
turned out to be an illusion: Drieu was finished as a writer before
he even started. "We might have let the bad taste, the emphasis,
the confusion pass. We might have overlooked the clumsiness, the
boredom, the digressions, the falsity of every feeling. We expected
all this, but were prepared for certain sacrifices in order to find a
few fine lines. But M. Drieu La Rochelle had chosen the emptiest
and silliest stories. He had taken his sets and characters from M.
Paul Morand, although he lacked the latter's skill and precision
of observation . . . Unlikely heroes in one-dimensional intrigues—
this is how he presented modern youth. To tell the truth M. Drieu
La Rochelle was writing six or seven years too late . . ." The plots,
said Brasillach, were miserably superficial, the characters non-
existent. Drieu tried to describe violence, death, the artificial para-
dise of the drug addict, lust in all its forms, but there was not one
feeling which he could convey and the only impression which the
reader retained was of confusion. Yet Brasillach's judgement was a
little premature, for, however disagreeable his politics, Drieu was a
talented political essayist, and there was one tragedy, one feeling,
which he managed to describe in a masterly manner in the brief
récit written after his first unsuccessful attempt at suicide in 1944 :
the tragedy and sense of his own destruction.

On a political level, too, there were themes which recurred in
Drieu's writings from 1922 to 1944 : opposition to capitalism was

---

[1]P. Drieu La Rochelle, *Le Français d'Europe,* Paris, 1944, p. 147.
[2]R. Brasillach, *Portraits,* Paris, 1935, pp. 227-238.

one, the idea of a federation of European states another. In *Mesure de la France,* in 1922, he had already stated that the only means of reviving Europe, trapped between the United States and the Soviet Union, was to form a federation. Nine years later, in *L'Europe contre les patries,* he repeated his plea, warning against the dangers of Nationalism which could only serve to weaken Europe and turn her into an easy prey for "the continental federations (Russia, America) that threaten her." Aristide Briand had proposed the creation of just such a federation of the United States of Europe to the League of Nations in September 1929. Were it not that they rejected everything and everybody connected with the liberal system, the young "non-conformists" of the *Ordre Nouveau* might have welcomed this proposal. Because of his association with the Republic and his belief in the League of Nations, however, they scorned Briand, and this was where they differed from Drieu La Rochelle. Some ten years older than they, Drieu had fought in the Great War, and he, like so many other Frenchmen, thought that the League of Nations really was going to bring about an era of eternal peace. He believed in it implicitly. Only when its failure to keep peace became clear, after the Japanese occupation of Manchuria in September 1931, only when Drieu grew convinced that capitalism was not "going to reform itself", did Communism and Fascism emerge as the only alternatives. Nevertheless Drieu's decision to commit himself was a slow and inconstant process.

In 1933 he joined the *Front commun,* a movement founded by a Radical deputy, Gaston Bergery, together with Etienne Langevin, Bernard Lecache, Jean-Richard Bloch, and Georges Monnet, in order to unite Radicals, Socialists and Communists against Fascism. Not until after the February riots did he collaborate with Colette's stepson, Bertrand de Jouvenel, on *La Lutte des Jeunes,* a weekly review which intended to form a revolutionary group powerful enough to overthrow the Republic, establish a dictatorship, and replace the capitalist system by a planned economy. From then on Drieu regarded Fascism as an inevitable development. "I have become convinced that Fascism is a necessary stage in the destruction of capitalism, for Fascism does not aid capitalism, despite what the anti-Fascists believe . . . Fascism creates a transitory civilisation, in which capitalism as it existed in its period of greatest prosperity, is led to rapid destruction."[1] And Fascism, Drieu stressed, was

[1] *La Grande Revue,* March 1934.

essentially a left-wing movement. "It is obviously amongst groups traditionally supposed to be naturally anti-Fascist that we find the only men susceptible to Fascism: amongst the young Radicals and the young Socialists and Communists."

Drieu maintained that France had been declining ever since the Middle Ages. With the industrial revolution man had fallen under the domination of the machine, he had lost the use of his hands and body, and Fascism alone, with its emphasis on physical health, discipline and order was to put France on a level with Drieu's favourite country, England, both physically and politically. "The deepest definition of Fascism is this: it is the political movement which leads most frankly, most radically towards the restoration of the body—health, dignity, fulness, heroism—towards the defence of man against the large town and the machine . . . Fascism has done no more than to join, consciously, the instinctive habits of the Anglo-Saxon, Scandinavian, Swiss world."[1] The only party in France which Drieu considered capable of realising such an ideal was Jacques Doriot's *Parti Populaire Français* (P.P.F.).

"Impressively tall, ascetic in his personal habits, marked with the indelible sign of Moscow's tutelage," wrote Gilbert Allardyce, Doriot "became as leader of the Communist Youth a kind of *beau idéal* among the young proletarians who were advancing through the party. In a movement which at the time left the rank and file little to admire beyond intransigence towards the class enemy, Doriot put together a reputation for political extravagance and parliamentary outrage that made him, by the end of the party's first decade, the most popular militant in the organization, 'the living incarnation in France', as one journalist later recalled, 'of the man with a dagger clenched between his teeth'."[2] Doriot had joined the French Communist Party (P.C.F.) when he was twenty-two, and his career in it had, in spite of profound disagreement with both the French leaders and the Comintern, been brilliant. In 1930 he was appointed mayor of the Parisian suburb of Saint-Denis. Here he built schools, kindergartens, a swimming pool and a public library; workers' children were sent to well-organised holiday camps, and, with the most effective system of unemploy-

---

[1]P. Drieu La Rochelle, *Chronique Politique 1934-1942*, Paris, 1943, pp. 50-52.

[2]Gilbert D. Allardyce, *The Political Transition of Jacques Doriot*, in *The Journal of Contemporary History*, vol. 1, no. 1, 1966, p. 56.

ment relief in the country, Saint-Denis soon ranked as the most generous of all the Communist boroughs. Doriot's popularity and prestige were immense. He was a blacksmith's son, vigorous, tough and vital; he spoke well and convincingly, and, after the February riots in 1934, when the leader of the P.C.F., Maurice Thorez, had gone into hiding, he had been the only Communist to organise successful counter-demonstrations.

As far as the leaders of the P.C.F. were concerned the great danger of Doriot was his rejection of party discipline—and the one aspect of party policy which Doriot had opposed for many years was the "class against class" tactic, the prohibition to form a united front with the other left-wing parties, which had been imposed by the Comintern in 1927. This, he, and a great many more docile members realised, did the P.C.F. incalculable damage, and Doriot came into open rebellion against the party leadership when, in February 1934, he proposed the formation of an anti-Fascist vigilance committee in Saint-Denis. Within a matter of months even the most dogmatic Communists were to agree that his proposal had been correct; but Doriot had taken his decision independently: at the time and in the circumstances it appeared as a deliberate provocation of Maurice Thorez. It was therefore suggested that Doriot acknowledge his mistakes before the party and that he visit Moscow in order to settle matters with the International. Refusing both the compromise and the invitation,[1] he was expelled on June 27, 1934.

A few weeks after Doriot's expulsion, the Communists signed the *pacte d'unité d'action* with the Socialists, an achievement which embittered Doriot and determined the political line he was now to take. He found himself excluded from the French left wing. The Communists had expelled him and he could no longer be of interest to the Socialists, who had fulfilled their purpose without him. For the many workers who still remained loyal to him, for his newspaper, *L'Emancipation,* formerly the Communist paper of Saint-Denis, and for himself Doriot had to find something new: what started as opposition to the P.C.F.'s subservience to the Soviet Union turned into sheer anti-Communism;

---

[1] It was rumoured at the time, although it now seems unlikely, that, had Doriot accepted the International's invitation to Moscow he could have replaced Thorez; see Dieter Wolf, *Die Doriot Bewegung,* Stuttgart, 1967, p. 96.

what began as an attempt to "regroup the forces opposed to war" became support of a rapprochement with Germany. For Doriot could see no reason why the French workers should undertake, either by a national alliance or through party loyalty, to fight and die for the Soviet Union. Claiming that "the struggle against Fascism cannot be separated from the struggle against war," Doriot affirmed in April 1935 that "we must maintain the peace, and to do that we must speak with Hitler just as we speak with all the other governments, whatever the régime they represent."

In the course of 1935 Doriot's opposition to Communism grew more and more manifest. In the columns of *L'Emancipation* he and Henri Barbé, who had formerly been in charge of the P.C.F.'s finances, revealed the sums which the French Communists had been receiving from Moscow. At the October elections he withheld the votes of the Saint-Denis delegates from the Communist candidates on the pretext that it was impossible for pacifists to vote Communist, and in December he announced his intention of launching a new programme "for the working class, for the middle class, and for the peasantry; a programme that will rally a popular front of action and of mass, that will enable us to rally forces that we are not accustomed to seeing, forces that want to understand . . . What will be our programme, comrades? . . . Our programme is peace." With these principles, in June 1936, Doriot founded the *Parti Populaire Français,* a nationalistic though left-wing party which purported to unite classes and forces that had hitherto been incompatible.

With a central committee and a political bureau, the P.P.F. was modelled on the Communist Party, and many of its members came from the extreme left. The secretary general was Henri Barbé; Paul Marion, one of the party's leading ideologists, had been editor of *L'Humanité* and had broken with the Communists after an unpleasant sojourn in the Soviet Union in 1929. Victor Arrighi had also been a Communist, Bertrand de Jouvenel a Radical, and the party's two assistant secretaries, Teulade and Abremski, syndicalists.[1] In 1937 fifty-seven per cent of the members seem to have

---

[1]Membership figures of the P.P.F. are unreliable: it claimed to have some 137,000 members in March 1937 and 250,000 in January 1938. A number of writers joined it for varying periods of time—Fernandez, Georges Suarez, Marcel Jouhandeau, Paul Chack, Jacques Benoist-Méchin. The man who devised the Party's social and economic programme was Robert Loustau of the *Ordre Nouveau.*

been workers. Judging by appearances, therefore, the P.P.F. was "progressive", and, the average age of its members being thirty-four, it was youthful. But above all it had Doriot at its head, a figure who, though not necessarily in agreement with the ideology his followers attributed to him, provided them with a leader.

The P.P.F. offered Drieu La Rochelle a means of breaking out of his isolation, of participating in a movement and of taking some form of political action. To begin with he expressed the same adolescent adoration of Doriot which a cub might feel for his scout leader. "Doriot, the good athlete," he wrote, "stands before France not as a fat-bellied intellectual of the last century watching his 'sick mother' and puffing at his radical pipe, but as an athlete squeezing this debilitated body, breathing his own health into its mouth . . . Doriot has that peasant vigour which goes beyond games of words to reach the heart, he has good humour and solid simplicity. Doriot will create a France where thousands of young couples will be happy rushing each season to primitive pleasures, skiing, fishing, camping, swimming. With him the France of the camping expeditions will conquer the France of cocktail parties and congresses."[1]

There was neither strict discipline nor a rigid dogma in the P.P.F., and it is as well to avoid the temptation of taking Drieu's political views for those of Doriot. Doriot did not regard his party as Fascist until after the German invasion : to start with its main object was to attract the bourgeoisie. He pronounced himself against monopolies, large financial trusts and big business concerns, which, he suggested, should be suppressed so that free rein should be given to small private enterprise. He did not specifically want a dictatorship, but a two party system after the English model, and a national hierarchy within a corporative system, based, as Jouvenel put it, "on services rendered at present". Doriot's foreign policy was fluid, his maxim accommodating: *Ni Moscou, ni Berlin!* Although he received money from the Italian government[2] he hesitated to commit himself to any foreign variety of Fascism. During the Spanish Civil War he initially limited himself to pointing out that a Republican victory would mean Communism for Spain,[3] and,

---

[1] P. Drieu La Rochelle, *Chronique Politique,* p. 54.
[2] G. Ciano, *Diario 1937-1938,* Bologna, 1948, p. 11.
[3] In July 1938, however, he went as far as to pay Franco a personal visit.

instead of praising Hitler or Mussolini, merely recommended an alliance with England, Germany and Italy against the Soviet Union.

Initially Drieu, too, was wary of foreign dictatorships. "We are well aware of the excesses of Italian and German Fascism," he wrote in 1938. "If we want to save the principle of authority from the lamentable decline to which parliamentary democracy has let it sink, this does not make us totalitarians."[1] He hoped that the P.P.F. would "rebuild a strong France which could intervene between England and Germany, demand a true alliance with England and undertake firm negotiations with Germany—(thereby) helping England to throw Germany onto Russia and intervene later if needs be."[2] Unlike Doriot, however, Drieu was anti-semitic, or had at least become so by the late thirties. "What I dislike most about the Jews," he wrote, "is that they are bourgeois who make everything they touch bourgeois."[3] While Maurras rejected the biological arguments for anti-semitism, Drieu accepted them, though without going as far as Hitler. He thought that Jews should be offered a choice: they could either be extradited or assimilated after two generations in which they were not to enter the public service or take part in any political activity.

Before the war Drieu's attitude to Germany was of cautious curiosity. He had travelled to Berlin with Jouvenel in January 1934 and had there met Otto Abetz. Eighteen months later he attended the Nuremberg Congress—an event which he found "marvellous and terrible. I am more and more certain that the future holds no tranquility. In any case, it is impossible for France to remain immobile next to this sort of Europe. I have not experienced such an emotion since the Russian ballets. This whole nation is intoxicated with music and dancing."[4, 5] At this stage there was no question of deeper commitment. As late as September 1939 Drieu wrote in his diary that he would

---

[1] P. Drieu La Rochelle, *op. cit.,* p. 164.
[2] P. Drieu La Rochelle, *Récit secret,* p. 101.
[3] P. Drieu La Rochelle, *Chronique politique,* p. 105.
[4] Quoted in F. Grover, *op. cit.,* p. 42.
[5] The Nazi rallies had a similar effect on Sir Neville Henderson : "I had spent six years in St Petersburg before the war in the best days of the old Russian ballet, but for grandiose beauty I have never seen a ballet to compare with it." N. Henderson, *Failure of a Mission,* Hodder & Stoughton, 1940, p. 71.

"never adhere to a régime, whatever my political convictions. The only man I recognised as a brother was Ernst von Salomon in Berlin. He fought in the *Freikorps*, served a six year prison sentence for Rathenau's murder, and yet was no Nazi and refused to participate in Hitler's triumph. Hitler's ideas were close to his own. But there is an abyss between the ideas of an intellectual (*un homme d'esprit*) and a man of action."[1] Indeed, during most of 1939 it looked as though Drieu was going to withdraw from politics for good. He was thoroughly disillusioned with Doriot and, like several other members of the P.P.F., was horrified to discover not only that Doriot was receiving subsidies from conservative millionaires, but that he was getting money from Ciano.[2] Moreover, Doriot, attractive for his asceticism and his opposition to traditional bourgeois habits, was putting on weight : he had been overeating and drinking to excess, spending more and more time at the cocktail parties which Drieu had hoped he would abolish. Finally, he hesitated to take a firm anti-German stand after the Munich agreement in 1938. Drieu, who had previously stated his belief that small nations were destined to be engulfed by larger powers, now came out on the side of Czechoslovakia and expected Doriot to do the same. His hesitation confirmed Drieu's suspicion that he was incapable of action. "You have betrayed us," he wrote to him. "You never wanted to save France. You remained inactive, incredulous and in bad faith. You let those Frenchmen who wanted to escape from the destiny which has been that of France over the last hundred years, who were ready to tear themselves away from it at the least sign of encouragement, be crushed beneath the same doubt and irony which has stifled them for a century."[3] On January 6, 1945 Drieu left the P.P.F. together with Jouvenel, Marion, Fabre-Luce and Pucheu. With the desertion of its leading members, Doriot's movement lost its vitality and its raison d'être. It disintegrated, and with it the hopes and dreams which had surrounded the mayor of Saint-Denis three years earlier.

When confronted with the failure of the various French "Fascist" movements before the Second World War many a modern

---

[1] Quoted in F. Grover, *op. cit.*, p. 96.
[2] The main financial supporters of the P.P.F. appear to have been Pierre Pucheu, the export manager of the *Comptoir sidérurgique de France*, and Gabriel Leroy-Ladurie, the managing director of the Banque Worms.
[3] *Ibid.*, p. 45.

historian has been tempted to conclude that French Fascism never really existed, and has tended to agree with Drieu La Rochelle's statement : "We received the word Fascism from the mouths of our adversaries, from the whole democratic, anti-Fascist clique : we took up this word as a challenge."[1] But was French Fascism merely a fantasy of the left wing? The problem is almost insoluble, for, with the possible exception of Marcel Bucard, none of the leaders of the so-called right-wing movements would accept the title of Fascist— not Maurras, not La Rocque, not Doriot. Not only did they not consider themselves Fascists, but they were most reluctant to admit that their movements had anything in common the one with the other. Doriot was somewhat despised by Maurras and La Rocque because of his Communist past, and he resented La Rocque's refusal to join his *Front de la Liberte contre le Communisme* in 1937. The *Action Française* had come to detest La Rocque after his acceptance of the dissolution of the *Croix-de-Feu* and the formation of the *Parti Social Français,* and in July 1937 a curious alliance was formed between the Communists, the right-wing paper *Gringoire* and the *Action Française* in an attempt to discredit the Colonel by accusing him of receiving money from Tardieu and Laval—an accusation which he never managed to disprove. In December of the same year Ciano noted in his diary that Arrighi, Doriot's emissary, "considers La Rocque a traitor in the service of the *Front Populaire.*"[2]

The most redoubtable product of the French right wing before the war was the *Comité Secret d'Action Révolutionnaire,* known as the Cagoule. Founded by a polytechnician named Eugène Deloncle in 1936, most of its leaders were dissident members of the *Action Française*—Henri Martin, Jacques Corrèze, Joseph Darnand, Jacques de Bernonville and the Jeantet brothers. The purpose of the *Cagoulards* was to establish a dictatorship in order to forestall the Communist *coup* which they believed to be imminent, and for this they hoped to gain the support of the French army. But Marshal Pétain, who was approached, refused to have anything to do with them, and although Marshal Franchet d'Esperey and the retired Air-Vice Marshal Duseigneur favoured them, they had to limit their activity to isolated acts of sabotage and murder, performed with weapons obtained from Italy and Nationalist Spain.

---

[1] *Révolution nationale,* November 20, 1943.
[2] G. Ciano, *loc. cit.*

In 1937 they blew up two buildings in Paris, the *Confédération générale du patronat français* and the *Union patronale interprofessionnelle*, and they appear to have murdered the Russian economist Navashin. Possibly their most notorious crime, however, committed in exchange for an arms consignment from Italy, was the assassination of the two anti-Fascist Rosselli brothers who had settled in France. The life of the *Cagoule* was brief. The police raided their headquarters late in 1937, to discover a large store of weapons: "12,000 grenades, 34 machine-guns, 135 Schmeisser submachine guns, 95 Beretta carbines, 149 army rifles, 151 hunting guns, 50,000 rounds of ammunition, 375 lbs of explosive, and 4,000 assorted revolvers and pistols."[1] Deloncle, Duseigner and some fifty-five other members of the organisation were placed under arrest, and the Third Republic survived, bewildered, but unharmed.

The French "Fascists" failed to bring off a successful *coup* mainly because of their disunity. Many people who might otherwise have joined a more extreme movement were contented to follow the ever more law-abiding Colonel de La Rocque. Yet to lack of unity was soon added a lack of purpose. The main enemy of the right had been Léon Blum: he resigned as Prime Minister in June 1937, to be replaced by the Radical Camille Chautemps, and although the *Front Populaire* itself lasted until January 1938, Chautemps did little to carry out its original programme. In April Daladier formed a new cabinet, which adopted a conservative and authoritarian policy: after crushing a general strike in November, the government took plenary powers, and after the signature of the Nazi-Soviet pact in August 1939, it banned the French Communist Party. As his Minister of Information Daladier appointed Jean Giraudoux, whose political and social views are already known to us, while, to the satisfaction of those many Frenchmen concerned with the decline of the French birth-rate, the government enacted a family code with the intention of boosting it.

Above all, as Dieter Wolf stressed in his study of the *Parti Populaire Français,* France under the Third Republic offered barren ground for a Fascist experiment. "The French middle classes were only perturbed by the riots of February 1934 and the results of the *Front Populaire* : they were not shattered by them. Only during and after the Second World War was the class system truly threatened. In spite of the discontent which appeared on the sur-

[1] G. Warner, *France*, in *European Fascism*, p. 270.

face, the thirties were a period of social stability, and the traditional governing class rarely lost control of the situation. Besides, the Third Republic possessed numerous colonies where men thirsting for action could let off steam. Finally, there was no explosive or aggressive foreign policy, no myth which could mobilise the masses and allow a radical minority to come to power."[1]

The enthusiastic reception given to Daladier on his return from Munich was only one indication of the strong opposition to war with Germany. Another was the quantity of individuals who were placed under arrest in 1939 as potentially dangerous pacifists, not only notorious members of the right like Brasillach and notorious members of the left, such as Lucien Sampaix, but men like Jean Giono, who, with no extreme political sympathy, simply hated the idea of war. The *Action Française,* with wide support, said that they would not fight for the Czechs or the Jews, and Marcel Déat, a former Socialist and Air Minister in Sarraut's left-wing cabinet early in 1936, met with considerable agreement when he declared, in his article *Mourir pour Dantzig?,* that he would not fight for the Poles either. A "France at war", Simone de Beauvoir suggested to Colette Audry, might well be "worse than a Nazi France"[2]; the liberal philosopher Alain warned his compatriots that to contemplate the prospect of war was tantamount to causing it; and the Surrealists concisely summed up their own attitude in the title of their tract *Ni de votre guerre, ni de votre paix!*

In the spring of 1939 the French right lost faith in the ally they had consistently counted on—Mussolini. Italy's claims to Corsica, Savoy, Nice and Tunis were found excessive by the Duce's French admirers, and put an end to any hope of a Mediterranean alliance. "The Italian manifestations wounded me like an insult from an intimate friend whom one has long boasted about"[3] wrote Lucien Rebatet. *Je suis partout* condemned Italian aggression in Albania in April, while Maurras turned the photograph of Mussolini hanging in his study to the wall and started to consider the idea of a rapprochement with England.

The widespread reluctance on the part of the French to fight can be advanced as one of the reasons for the relative ease with which the Germans advanced into France in 1940. "The French

[1]D. Wolf, *op. cit.,* p. 307.
[2]S. de Beauvoir, *La Force de l'Age,* Paris, 1960, p. 367.
[3]L. Rebatet, *op. cit.,* p. 104.

armies," wrote A. J. P. Taylor, "were no doubt badly directed, but most contemporary observers also thought, whether rightly or wrongly, that the French nation had lost the will to greatness. Memories of the First World War hung heavy over the land. The propertied class could not think why they had ever become involved in war against Hitler . . . The ordinary Frenchmen had no faith in their leaders . . . The French had no driving force, no inner conviction which sustained them. They had come to believe that civilisation meant a more comfortable life and particularly two good meals a day. War threatened these comforts, and the French surrendered in order to preserve what they regarded as civilisation."[1] The French right wing would willingly have believed the *Front Populaire* responsible for the defeat on account of their incompetent conduct of national defence, but, at the Riom Trials in 1942[2] Blum, Daladier and Gamelin successfully acquitted themselves by attributing equal responsibility to the General Staff, of which both Darlan and Pétain were members. However this may be, the armistice was signed on June 22. "Defeat has saved us," Giraudoux confided to Maurice Martin du Gard. "It is a miracle of the instinct of self-preservation. If we had resisted a year we would no longer exist."[3]

By the terms of the armistice France was divided by a demarcation line running from the Swiss border near Geneva, west to near Tours and then south to the Spanish border near Pau. The Italians occupied the Alpes Maritimes and Savoy, and the Germans the northern zone. But although the Germans held two million French prisoners-of-war as hostages, the unoccupied zone, its capital at Vichy, retained the fleet and the colonies. On June 18, four days before the signature of the armistice, General De Gaulle had addressed the French from London, announcing his intention of carrying on the fight. In France the government of Vichy was split—split between Pierre Laval who believed that Germany had won the war and that the sooner France came to a satisfactory agreement with the victor, the better it would be, and Philippe Pétain who was willing to bide by the terms of the armistice while continuing negotiations with the Germans and the British.

A. J. P. Taylor, *From Sarajevo to Potsdam,* Thames & Hudson, 1966, p. 166.

[2]See *infra,* p. 234.

[3]Maurice Martin du Gard, *op. cit.,* p. 174.

At first few people questioned the legitimacy of Pétain's government. It was recognised by thirty-two foreign powers, including the Vatican, the United States of America, and the Soviet Union. Admiration for the eighty-four-year-old Marshal was by no means restricted to Maurras, despite the immense influence of the *Action Française* on what emerged as Vichy's ideology : within the first year of his rule François Mauriac, Daniel Halévy, Roger Martin du Gard and Paul Claudel, had all expressed their gratitude to the victor of Verdun for saving the nation. Even if many Frenchmen disapproved of the policy Pétain's government was proposing to put into practice, they were comforted by the sight of the Marshal's dignified figure at the head of it, by the sound of his voice and the content of his speeches, "the appeal," as François Mauriac wrote in *Le Figaro*, "of the Great Nation humiliated."[1]

To everybody who had opposed the Republic, its collapse with the German invasion was a sign that it was still more rotten than its enemies had made it out to be. The signature of the armistice and the formation of Pétain's government seemed an occasion, if not an ideal occasion, for starting afresh, and the ideas that had been developed over the past twenty years now saw some hope of being implemented. "The defeat, was not merely military, it was the defeat of an entire society, the end of a decline which had started many years earlier. This was the interpretation given both by the most lucid supporters of the *Révolution nationale* of Vichy and by the most dynamic elements in the Resistance. Both Vichy and the Resistance were part of the same urge to break the traditional moulds of French political thought which seemed to have failed, and saw the resurrection of the same themes and the same men who had appeared in the thirties."[2]

Pétain did indeed pass many of the measures which the young "non-conformists" had long recommended. Endowed with plenary powers he dissolved the Third Republic and abolished opposition parties. Strikes were outlawed; the main trade unions and employers' associations were dissolved; and the peasants and workers were assembled into corporations. Much was made of the family : divorce became more difficult; married women were not allowed to work in public services and were hurried back to the hearth; and parents of large families were accorded special privileges. Absinthe

[1] *Le Figaro*, July 3, 1940.
[2] J.-L. Loubet del Bayle, *op. cit.*, p. 404.

and other dangerous alcohols were prohibited; sport was encouraged, and attempts were made to enforce religious instruction in schools. In short it was the aim of the *Révolution nationale* to revive health, discipline and, finally, hierarchy. From René Gillouin, who had a considerable influence on Pétain in the first months of the new régime, we have a definition of the form the new State was to take : "Authoritarian and, in a sense, absolute, that is to say free of the bonds of material and financial gain . . . a strong power, but limited in its spiritual functions by respect for religious values and for the human being, and, in its temporal functions by the recognition of such natural groups as the family, the region, the professions, bodies, companies and communities of every sort . . . In a society threatened by total industrialisation it will avoid the deadly errors of the old liberal capitalism. It will no longer consider the workman as an animated tool and his work as merchandise, but will return to labour its material, moral and spiritual significance, end the reign of economics and its immoral autonomy by submitting money and even work to the human being . . . Finally, it will try in every way not so much to improve the condition of the proletariat, as to abolish it, not only through fair distribution of the fruits of labour but by restoring the vigorously organic and generously human elements which existed in the 'spirit' of the old corporations."[1]

It is obvious that the main influence on the Vichyite ideology remained the *Action Française*—obvious from the authoritarian structure to which Vichy aspired and obvious from the reactionary structure which it adopted. "In place of Liberty," David Thomson has pointed out, "Vichy offered the regimentation of a police state . . . In place of Equality, Vichy offered discrimination . . . In place of Fraternity, Vichy offered the cult of leadership, hierarchy, authority."[2] Although the anti-semitic laws of October 1940 were passed in order to please the Germans by Laval, one of Pétain's only Ministers to care nothing for the *Révolution nationale*, they were applied by an old admirer of Maurras, Xavier Vallat: French Jews were excluded from the public service and many professions, and Algerian Jews were deprived of full citizenship. When it came to taking the measures advocated by the Germans, however, Xavier Vallat stood firm: he refused to make the

[1]Quoted in J.-L. Loubet del Bayle, *op. cit.*, pp. 406-407.
[2]D. Thomson, *op. cit.*, pp. 222-223.

Jews of Vichy wear a yellow star, and refused to impose a curfew, with the result that the Germans insisted on his being replaced in 1942 by the unscrupulous Darquier de Pellepoix, who assisted them in deporting the Jews to extermination camps.

Despite its enthusiastic ideologists the *Révolution nationale* failed. Disappointment with the Vichy government was, we shall see, one of the reasons which induced Frenchmen to collaborate with the Germans, for there was no question of its ever abolishing "the condition of the proletariat" through "fair distribution of the fruits of labour" and the restoration of "the vigorously organic and generously human elements which existed in the 'spirit' of the old corporations," as René Gillouin had hoped. The Peasant Corporation which had been set up in December 1940 was soon dominated by the large landowners and government officials; the Organizing Committees founded in order to replace the main trade union confederations, the C.G.T. and the C.F.T.C., were to the advantage of the industrialists and under the control of government representatives who supported the industrialists. When the government tried to enforce religious instruction in the schools, the anticlericalism it aroused was such that it had to abandon its attempts. The only unifying force of the system was Pétain himself, and the ideology of the *Révolution nationale* degenerated into flattery of the Marshal. Moreover, when Laval returned to power in April 1942 he did as little as he could to further Pétain's home policy. He curbed the laws against the freemasons, which were being applied by a former member of the *Action Française,* the biographer Bernard Faÿ, and he prevented the "revolutionary" *Conseil National* from meeting, preferring to concentrate his energy on bargaining with the Germans. Then, in November 1942, the Germans invaded the free zone after the American landing in North Africa, and French hopes of performing their own revolution were thwarted for good.

I shall later be discussing the international events and the constant pressure which the Germans exerted on the government of Vichy and which contributed to Pétain's failure to carry out an original home policy, but to this must also be added the demoralising conditions in which the French were living. Sport and manual labour were to assume great importance in the schools and youth movements of Vichy, yet rations were so low as to make physical exercise almost impossible. The Germans, on the other hand, by disrupting

French agriculture and industry, left, wherever they went, good ground for Allied propaganda. "At Vichy," wrote Maurice Martin du Gard in January 1942, "the *Révolution nationale* is feeling the effects of the general misery and the B.B.C. broadcasts. Even the best enterprises are undermined by doubt. Many plans, even a five year plan, modernised motorways and ports, will remain, it is feared, on paper. In the distance one can hear explosions and gunfire. To his visitors the Marshal talks of good workmen, good bosses, and good children, of the sanctity of family life and of a courteous agrarian civilisation . . . His faith in eternal France remains intact. One wonders whether he is still sane, or whether he alone is sane."[1]

The régime's younger supporters soon started to desert it : Emmanuel Mounier and Jean Lacroix had joined the Resistance by 1942, while Lucien Rebatet and Robert Brasillach saw a better possibility of fulfilling their ambitions in collaboration with the Germans. Older men, like Claudel and Mauriac, tended to support De Gaulle. What many retained in common until late in the war, however, was hatred for England—a hatred which had originated with the idea that the British troops, forced to retreat before the German invasion, had abandoned and betrayed France. In these circumstances it was considered quite possible, by a realist like Paul Morand, that England would come to terms with Hitler and that the only losers would be the French. The obvious determination of the British to keep on fighting might have pierced this illusion, had not a further incident turned ill-founded suspicion into the deepest loathing—the bombardment of the French fleet at Mers-el-Kebir and Dakar in July 1940. This measure, taken to prevent the fleet from falling into German hands, "erected a unanimous France against England."[2] It did almost as much to facilitate German propaganda as German pressure on France was later to do in favour of the Allied cause. If one incident can be held responsible for the temptation felt by Pétain's future Prime Minister, Admiral Darlan, to fight with the Germans against England, it was Mers-el-Kebir. It convinced such jingoist collaborators as the naval historian Paul Chack, who, like Darlan, had never really been able to forgive the English for winning the battle of Trafalgar, that the perfidious British made others fight their battles for them, to reward them with flagrant betrayal.

[1] M. Martin du Gard, *op. cit.*, pp. 245-246.
[2] François Mauriac, *Le Figaro*, July 15, 1940.

Even when it grew clear not only that the English had no intention of coming to terms with Hitler, but that if the French were ever liberated from German rule it would be largely owing to England, the events of 1940 continued to rankle. In this respect the attitude of Charles Maurras, who combined hatred of the Germans with detestation of the British, was typical. A stalwart *attentiste*, as those loyal to Pétain were called, Maurras was again an influential figure in Vichy France. Although he had settled with the *Action Française* in Lyons after the armistice, and seldom visited Pétain's capital, his few meetings with the Marshal were extremely cordial, and Pétain, on whose photograph was written the question *Êtes-vous plus français que lui?* paid him the supreme compliment of referring to him as *le plus français des Français*. Besides, the Marshal was surrounded by former members of the *Action Française* and keen admirers of Maurras—Dumoulin de La Barthète, Raphael Alibert, Paul Baudouin, General Brécard, Henri Massis, René Benjamin and Pierre Caziot.

Germany, according to Maurras, remained France's main enemy. He repudiated all his former colleagues on the *Action Française* who had become collaborators, or even expressed sympathy for the Germans. He would have nothing to do with Georges Suarez, the editor of the Parisian paper *Aujourd'hui*. He refused to associate with Georges Claude, the scientist who became increasingly partial to a Franco-German alliance against the Soviet Union, or with Dominique Sordet, the former *Action Française* music critic who now ran the collaborationist press agency *Inter-France*. Both Brasillach and Lucien Rebatet were turned out of the *Action Française* offices when they went to pay their respects to Maurras, and he never spoke to either of them again. The Germans and the collaborationist organisations regarded him with undisguised antipathy, and in June 1944 his colleague Maurice Pujo and his friend Georges Calzant were imprisoned by the Germans in Fort Montluc.

Nevertheless Maurras ranted against Gaullists and Communists: he considered them bandits and could not forgive the reprisals caused by their acts of terrorism. He referred by name to Jews and Gaullist sympathisers in the *Action Française* at a time when such a denunciation could be to the advantage of the Gestapo, and complained of the inadequacy of the anti-semitic measures of Vichy: not only should the Jews become second-class citizens, he said, but they should lose all their money. Even if he supported Laval's

policy of sending French workers to Germany in return for French
prisoners-of-war, Maurras attacked Laval's efforts to conclude a
Franco-German alliance. Yet he did not prefer the idea of a British
victory dominated by the Communists and the Gaullists to a
German one, and, on occasion, recommended French obeisance to
Germany's most brutal orders. His slogan remained *La Seule
France,* the title of his book which appeared in 1941. Here he
broached the problem of collaboration:

" 'Do you support what the Marshal calls collaboration?'

" 'It is not for me to support it.'

" 'Do you oppose it then?'

" 'Neither.'

" 'Are you neutral?'

" 'No.'

" 'So you allow it?'

" 'It is not for me to allow it, still less to discuss it.'

" 'We are no longer, thank God, under the régime of Discussion
in which everything went to rack and ruin because it could receive
no continuous direction : nothing stood firm, neither authority nor
responsibility. Since we have changed all that, the country must
benefit from it. . . When a State exists, when it performs its task,
our duty is twofold : to allow it to perform its task and to facilitate
its performance."[1]

Such an attitude as that of Maurras was all very well for the
men living in the free zone as long as it remained free. Maurras
said neither yes nor no to collaboration; he in fact never collaborated, but then he had little occasion to do so. The problem was
far more real for the inhabitants of the occupied zone who came
into daily contact with the Germans. Even if they were *attentistes*
at heart—and most Frenchmen were—Pétain himself had ordered
them to collaborate: on October 24, 1940, the Marshal had met
Hitler at Montoire. Although he managed to evade Hitler's proposals that France should ally herself with Germany against
England, he agreed, by way of compromise, to deliver a brief
speech on the radio. "It is in honour and to maintain French unity
. . . within the cadre of constructive activity in the New Order of
Europe that I today enter upon the path of collaboration," he told
his fellow-countrymen six days later. "This collaboration must be

---

[1] C. Maurras *La Seule France,* Lyon, 1941, p. 287.

sincere. It must consist of a patient and trusting effort. For the time being the armistice is not peace. France has numerous obligations to the victor. At least she remains sovereign. This sovereignty makes her defend her soil, quell the differences of opinion, reduce the dissidence within her colonies. This is my policy. It is I who shall be judged by History. So far I have spoken to you as a father. Today I am addressing you as a leader. Follow me. Trust in eternal France."

It was difficult for the average listener to know that Pétain was playing a double game, that he was in contact both with Hitler and with Churchill, and that this speech was a mere concession to the Germans by which he set little score. For most people it seemed an invitation, if not an order, to collaborate. And even when the extent to which the Marshal hated the Germans and Laval became clear to those close to him, it was still hard for the inhabitants of the occupied zone, unable to communicate freely with Vichy, to judge this state of affairs from the intrigues within the government. The Marshal's order remained. Thousands of Frenchmen could justify their collaboration by loyalty to him.

But successful collaboration required two willing parties, and the cause of its failure was that neither the German nor the French leaders were ready to collaborate with each other for any length of time. Hitler had stated in *Mein Kampf* that France was good only for exploitation, and with this his most powerful colleagues agreed. The confusion of the German administrative system in France was such, however, that this basic attitude was frequently concealed. Two of Germany's representatives, Otto Abetz, the Ambassador in Paris, and General Karl Heinrich von Stülpnagel, president of the armistice commission and later military commander of Paris, did truly believe in collaboration, as did the members of another institution designed to forward Franco-German friendship, the German Institute in Paris. Indeed, not only Stülpnagel, but a number of other highly placed German officers hoped for military collaboration with France on an egalitarian basis. But apart from Hitler's own antipathy for the French, a succession of incidents connected with Vichy served to aggravate the relations between the two countries and convince the Führer that the French were neither worthy nor willing to co-operate.

The first of these was the dismissal and arrest of Laval on December 13, 1940. Fully convinced that the Germans had won the war,

Laval had been the first French politician to establish a cordial relationship with Abetz in Paris. Through the intermediary of Fernand de Brinon, Jean Luchaire and another journalist, Jean Fontenoy, he had succeeded in meeting the ambassador in July 1940, and, with his exceptional powers of persuasion and the Latin charm which he exploited far more when talking to the Germans than to his compatriots, Laval had led Abetz to regard his position in the government of Vichy as the surest guarantee of Franco-German military collaboration. Yet Laval's self-assuredness, his cunning, and his overtures to Germany caused Pétain and his fellow ministers, to dislike him deeply, to intrigue against him, and to organise his arrest. No sooner did Abetz have news of this event than he arrived in Vichy with a military convoy and demanded the Prime Minister's release and return to office. His release was granted, but when Pétain and he met in Abetz's presence, Laval was so rude to the Marshal that Pétain refused him a post in his government, and Laval departed for Paris in the company of the German ambassador.

Pierre-Etienne Flandin, Laval's immediate successor, did all he could to resist German demands on French manpower and industry. On February 9, 1941, however, he was replaced by Admiral Jean Darlan, whose "Napoleonic" hatred of England and disgust over Mers-el-Kebir made him initially open to the idea of military collaboration with the Reich. He raised the hopes of the collaborators in Paris by admitting three former members of the P.P.F., Pucheu, Paul Marion, and Jacques Benoist-Méchin, to his cabinet, but the ever more exorbitant demands of the Germans, the continued opposition of Pétain to a military alliance, Hitler's refusal to take any notice of the projects formulated by Benoist-Méchin and Abetz for the introduction of the "New Order" into France, proved the futility of belief in co-operation. And by the end of the year the French themselves had doubts about the advisability of collaborating in view of certain alterations in the military situation: in June Hitler had invaded the Soviet Union and in December, after the bombing of Pearl Harbour, the United States had entered the war. There was no longer any certainty of a German victory. What, then, was the point of collaboration?

When Laval returned to power in April 1942, he thought it possible, in the words of Robert Aron, "to offer Germany French collaboration in order to destroy Bolshevism, and at the same time

R

to remain on good terms with the United States. He anticipated a German victory in the East and a compromise peace between the United States and the Reich in the West signed through his intermediary. By this means France would be no satellite, and would have the rank and position due to her in the new Europe".[1] But his return took place in the most unfortunate circumstances. The Germans were irritated by the outcome of the trial which was being held in Riom since February 19 against Daladier, Blum, Gamelin and three other Republican politicians. For the Germans these men were being tried for having caused the war, for the French they were being tried for having lost it. Faced with an equivocal bill of indictment designed to combine both charges, the defendants succeeded in turning the trial to ridicule, and on March 21 Abetz telegraphed from Paris demanding that an end be put to the proceedings.

A further event, which took place on April 17, the day before Laval's appointment as Prime Minister, increased the ill-humour of the Germans: General Henri Giraud, who had commanded first the Seventh and then the Ninth army before the armistice, escaped from the fortress of Koenigstein on the Elbe where he had been held prisoner for almost two years. Speaking perfect German, he managed to travel unmolested to the Swiss border, engaged in conversation with an S.S. officer he had met in his railway carriage. In his fury at losing Giraud, Hitler gave orders that the treatment of the French prisoners-of-war should deteriorate and broke off negotiations concerning their return to France. These soldiers, Germany's most valuable hostages, her best way of exerting pressure on the government of Vichy and on Pétain, who felt a sense of personal responsibility for them, had long been used to extort manpower from France, one prisoner being promised in exchange for three French labourers. Laval, in despair about the failure of negotiations, begged Giraud to return to prison; Abetz, as keen as ever on improving relations between his country and France, offered Giraud a suite in the Adlon Hotel in Berlin if he agreed to go back to Germany. But Giraud refused. All he agreed to do was write a letter to Pétain on May 4 giving him his word as an officer that he would make no attempt to obstruct the policy which the Marshal and his government were pursuing towards Germany and with which he,

---

[1] R. Aron, *Histoire de Vichy, 1940-1941, II*, Paris, 1954, p. 183.

Giraud, was in full agreement. Six months later, however, after the American landing in North Africa, Pétain received another letter from Giraud, post-marked Marseilles, in which the General informed him that he had kept his word, that he had never attacked the Marshal's policy, but that the time had now come for him to take "the unexpected opportunity of enabling my country to emerge from the war with honour" : he was on his way to Africa, where he was subsequently appointed commander of the French forces and managed to raise 250,000 combat troops with the help of the Americans.[1]

German disapproval entailed a considerably harsher policy to France. The first notice informing the French that the Germans had shot a hostage had appeared in December 1940, but after August 1941, when the French forces of Resistance grew better organised, the shooting of hostages in retaliation for attempts to kill German soldiers became a frequent occurrence. In March 1942 the first trainload of foreign Jews arrested on French soil left for Auschwitz, and on June 7 all Jews in the occupied zone had to wear a yellow star. The intensification of anti-semitic persecution was accompanied by the arrival in France of Fritz Sauckel, the Gauleiter of Thüringen, in charge of obtaining civilian labour for the Reich. German colonisation of France had begun. By the spring of 1942 about 845,000 workers in France were contributing to German armament and defence; the French railway industry and shipyards were operating solely in the interests of the Reich; in Germany herself there were still over a million French prisoners-of-war working on the land and in the armament industry, and by the end of the year nearly a quarter of a million French labourers had been imported. "I'll have you know that only Herr Abetz collaborates," exclaimed Goering, reiterating Hitler's French policy in August 1942. "I don't collaborate. I see collaboration with the French as follows : when they deliver until they have nothing left to deliver, when they volunteer to go on delivering, then I'll say I collaborate."[2] When the Germans occupied the free zone after the Allied landing in North Africa in November 1942 there was no longer any question of voluntary co-operation between France and Germany. Abetz, deemed too compliant to French demands,

---

[1] In 1943 he became co-president of the French Committee of National Liberation together with De Gaulle, but retired in April 1944.
[2] O. Abetz, *op. cit.*, p. 244.

was recalled from the Embassy in Paris, and did not return to France until after Mussolini's fall the following year. But by then the whole idea of collaboration was senseless: Germany had definitely lost the war.

Why did Frenchmen continue to collaborate? What was the attraction of those sinister organisations which resurrected or were formed under German patronage—Bucard's *Francistes,* Doriot's *Parti Populaire Français,* Marcel Déat's *Rassemblement National Populaire* (R.N.P.), Joseph Darnand's Militia which assisted the Gestapo in their hunt for Jews and Resistance fighters? Bucard, Doriot and Déat were mistrusted by Pétain and only manipulated by the Germans as a threat to the Marshal: that Hitler ever contemplated putting the power to govern France in their hands is most unlikely. Among themselves they agreed on nothing except the establishment of the *Légion des Volontaires Français contre le Bolchévisme* in July 1941 which provided the Germans with volunteers to fight on the Eastern Front. Their opportunism, their subservience to German demands, were obvious at every step they took, and it was only when the Germans forced him to do so that Laval reluctantly admitted Darnand and Déat into his government in November 1943, appointing Darnand as Secretary-General for the Maintenance of Order and Déat as Minister of Labour and National Solidarity. And yet the two major collaborationist parties, the P.P.F. and the R.N.P., had their members. A number of Doriot's former followers—Drieu La Rochelle, Fernandez and Sicard—returned to him; Jean Fontenoy, Luchaire, Georges Suarez and Lucien Rebatet joined Déat. "There were five to six thousand people in the Salle Wagram, but not a single workman among them," wrote Jean Guéhenno of Déat's first rally in February 1941. "The majority of them consisted of office workers, shop-keepers, pseudo-intellectuals, the same people who had been in the P.S.F. and the *Cagoule* three years ago. When their old leaders appeared on the podium they applauded. It is neither a national nor a people's movement, we can be sure. . . Only the frantic petit bourgeois with white shirt cuffs was represented. . . Déat spoke. . . Only one passion seems to have inspired him : his hatred for the government of Vichy which would not make him a minister."[1]

_____

[1] J. Guéhenno, *Journal des années noires 1940-1944,* Paris, 1947, pp. 121-122.

What, asked Sartre in 1945, is a collaborator? "Having established *strength* as the source of right and as the prerogative of the
master, the collaborator resorts to *cunning*. He recognises his weakness and this priest of virility and masculine virtues uses the arms
of the weak, of the woman. In all the articles of Châteaubriant,
Drieu and Brasillach we find curious metaphors which present the
relations between France and Germany as a sexual intercourse
in which France plays the woman's part. And there is no doubt
that the feudal relationship between the collaborator and his master
has a sexual aspect. In as far as we can talk of a collaborationist
mentality we find that it has a feminine quality. The collaborator
speaks in the name of strength, but he is not strong : he is cunning, he is slyness resting on strength, he is even charming and
seductive and hopes to exploit the appeal which he thinks French
culture has for the Germans. He represents an odd mixture of
masochism and homosexuality, and indeed, the homosexual circles
of Paris provided numerous and brilliant recruits."[1]

In the third volume of his *Chemins de la Liberté, La Mort dans
l'âme*, Sartre describes the entry of the German army into Paris
through the eyes of one of his protagonists, Daniel. "(Daniel) was
not afraid, he yielded trustingly to those thousands of eyes, he
thought 'Our conquerors!' and he was supremely happy. He looked
them in the eye, he feasted on their fair hair, their sunburnt faces
with eyes which looked like lakes of ice, their slim bodies, their in-
credibly long and muscular hips. He murmured : 'How handsome
they are!' . . . Something had fallen from the sky : it was the
ancient law. The society of judges had collapsed, the sentence had
been obliterated; those ghastly little khaki soldiers, the defenders
of the rights of man, had been routed. . . An unbearable, delicious
sensation spread through his body; he could hardly see properly;
he repeated, gasping, 'As if it were butter—they're entering Paris as
if it were butter.' . . . He would like to have been a woman to
throw them flowers."[2] There is no doubt that this aspect of the
Germans appealed to Pétain's Minister of Education, the Acade-
mician, Abel Bonnard, appositely nicknamed *La Gestapette*. In the
first months of occupation Jean Cocteau "even went as far as to

---

[1] J.-P Sartre, *Qu'est-ce qu'un collaborateur?* in *Situations, III,* Paris,
1949, p. 58.
[2] J.-P. Sartre, *La Mort dans l'Ame,* Paris, 1949, pp. 82-83.

write a series of poems in German"[1] while Paul Léautaud liked to tell his friends that he saw a letter from Gide to Drieu La Rochelle saying that he dare not come to Paris lest he meet too attractive a young German in the offices of the *Nouvelle Revue Française*.[2]

To the love of force Sartre, in his article on collaboration, adds a certain interpretation of history which accounts for the attitude of many of those people who "yielded" to Fascism once it was there, because it was there. This, to the collaborators, was "realism". "For them the domination of the fact is accompanied by a vague belief in progress, but in a headless progress. . . We don't know where we are going, but since we are changing we must be improving. The latest historical phenomenon is the best because it is the latest. . ."[3] Basically, according to Sartre, collaboration was a phenomenon of "disintegration". Those who indulged in it were elements of society who had never been assimilated, a sort of criminal fringe: integration which they had never achieved in a democracy, but for which they had always longed, would only be possible in an authoritarian state which punished the society that had rejected them.

Yet the problem is more complex than it would appear from Sartre's article. I think we can say that there were two forms of collaborators: the revolutionaries and the passive collaborators. The latter accepted the situation and hoped to make the best of it. France had declared war on Germany and she had lost. The German troops initially did all they could to make themselves popular. Far from amputating the hands of the male population of occupied villages, as it had been rumoured they would, they helped old ladies with their suitcases and provided stranded motorists with petrol. To start with France experienced none of the atrocities which the Germans committed in Eastern Europe, and, closing their eyes to the horrors of the Polish campaign, the French could claim to have encountered a humane invader. Indeed, in the first months of occupation more German soldiers appear to have been shot for breaches of discipline than Frenchmen executed for acts of terrorism or sabotage. "The Germans have waged war

---

[1] E. Sprigge and J. J. Kihm, *Jean Cocteau: the man and the mirror*, Gollancz, 1968, p. 153.

[2] M. Martin du Gard, *op. cit.*, p. 346, and Jean Galtier-Boissière, *Mon Journal pendant l'Occupation*, Paris, 1944, p. 58.

[3] J.-P. Sartre, *Situations, III*, p. 53.

causing the least possible damage," wrote Jacques Chardonne.[1]
"They spared us. These conquerors of a new style did not abuse
their absolute powers even in the first confusion of victory. Whatever
happens, I shall never forget this surprise, particularly since it was
we who attacked them."

At the same time French defeat, so swift and so total, seemed
an indication of a deeper evil in the French character : German
domination, it was to be hoped, would provide France with that
discipline which she lacked, and France would be foolish were she to
ignore the victor's lessons. It was largely for these reasons that Gide
justified collaboration in his diary. He had initially disapproved of
Pétain's signature of the armistice, but his disapproval gave way
to pessimistic resignation. "To compose together with yesterday's
enemy is not cowardice," he wrote in September 1940, "but wisdom;
it is to accept the inevitable. *Untersuchen was ist, und nicht
was behagt*, Goethe so rightly said. Whoever kicks against fate is
caught in a trap. What use is there in bruising oneself against the
bars of one's cage? To suffer less from the narrowness of one's jail
one only has to keep in the middle. I feel, in myself, unlimited
possibilities of acceptance : they do not commit the being itself in
any way. The risk is far greater if one lets thoughts be dominated
by hatred."[2] "So you believe one should refuse to play this game?"
he wrote about collaboration in January 1941. "Maybe play it to
begin with; if possible without too much bitterness, but also without
any illusions, so as not to have too bitter a disappointment later.
Shall I tell you what I think? I think it is good for France to submit
herself for a time to this yoke of imposed discipline. Just as she was
incapable, at the point of moral relaxation and decomposition to
which she had fallen, of winning a real victory over an adversary
better equipped than herself, united, resolute, tenacious, fierce and

---

[1] J. Chardonne, *Chronique privée de l'an 1940*, Paris, 1940, p. 210,
cf. "It is easy, after the event, to poke fun at the first two years of
'collaboration'. Certain facts are incontestable. Germany invaded,
without hatred, a France which she had not attacked. She conquered,
without useless massacres, respecting monuments, sparing and sometimes repatriating, with fatherly care, the fugitives of the exodus. For
a moment she was a figure of Order before an hysterical nation.
Others, with more men and more money, will conquer her. Our
relationship will be for ever marked by the memory of this *tête-à-tête*."
(Alfred Fabre-Luce, *Journal de la France, 1939-1944*, Genève, 1946,
p. 493.)
[2] A. Gide, *Journal, 1939-1942*, Paris, 1946, p. 83.

wisely led by a leader determined to pass beyond all those scruples which enfeebled us, all the considerations which encumbered us, so I do not think that France today is capable of arising on her own, with the mere means at her disposal. I say 'today', but in 1914 I wrote: 'We have all to learn from Germany; she has all to take from us.' I still think this."[1]

That March Gide read Jacques Chardonne's *Chronique privée de l'an 1940*. He found Chardonne's justification of collaboration flippant and cynical, which in many ways it was, although Chardonne, an Anglophile and an aesthete, shared a basic conviction with Gide and Montherlant—"Such a defeat," he wrote, "is not military, it is civil. It is an internal, private matter. To recover we must take lessons from our victors."[2] Gide now refused to provide further articles for the *Nouvelle Revue Française* under Drieu La Rochelle's editorship, and broke with Drieu and Alphonse de Châteaubriant, the editor of the collaborationist review *La Gerbe*. Nevertheless he continued to appreciate Drieu's qualities as a writer and even pronounced himself in agreement with his assessment of Fascism printed in the *N.R.F.* in January 1943.

So disgusted was Gide by the state of things in France that he felt the French deserved no liberty whatever. On May 6, 1941, he wrote in his diary: "I even believe German subjection, with its painful humiliations, to be preferable and less detrimental for us, less degrading than the discipline which Vichy proposes."[3] A fortnight later he had planned to give a lecture on the poet Henri Michaux in Nice. That morning, however, he received a menacing letter from the local leader of Pétain's *Légion française des combattants* suggesting that it would be unwise for the author of *Les Nourritures terrestres* to give a public lecture at a time when the Marshal was trying to develop the spirit of sacrifice in French youth. Shortly afterwards he set sail for Tunis.

Henri de Montherlant's attitude was similar to that of Gide. He too believed that defeat meant there was something deeper the matter with France than military unpreparedness. From 1925 to 1932 he had lived abroad. In 1928 he had visited Morocco and, shocked by the injustices of the French colonial system, wrote a severe criticism of it, his novel *La Rose de Sable*. On his return to

---

[1] *Ibid.*, p. 105.
[2] J. Chardonne, *op. cit.*, pp. 118-119.
[3] *Op. cit.*, p. 123.

France he found his country devitalised and debilitated, materialistic and comfort loving. "When one returns from Spain, Italy and
North Africa . . . what strikes one most in the Frenchman's face
is insipidity. . . There is everything you like in the faces of these
men, youths or adolescents : intelligence, vivacity, personality, kindness; one expression is always lacking: energy."[1]

So acutely did Montherlant feel the danger and weakness of his
country's position that he decided not to publish *La Rose de Sable*,[2]
fearing it would only serve to undermine France still further. As for
France's relations with Germany, Montherlant felt that war was
inevitable. Franco-German friendship could be no more than the
salute of two warriors about to fight, and Montherlant, introducing
a lecture by Abetz to the Rive Gauche club in 1936, welcomed the
prospect of war as a swordsman welcomes a duel with a worthy
rival. German vicinity, he hoped, would stimulate France. "(Dictators) prevent the nations which prefer happiness from being incapable nations. There is a low point of virility beneath which one
cannot sink. Germany has been placed near France as Xanthippe
was placed near Socrates : to enable him to surmount himself. They
also induce the friends of liberty to savour it more subtly, they
stimulate the friends of a certain form of culture to unite in order
to defend it : it is a whole moral universe which defines itself by
counterbalance . . . Peace and security must be conquered, not
begged for. The only rights one has are those which one knows
how to defend."[3]

After serving as war correspondent for the left-wing review
Marianne, Montherlant withdrew to the south of France once the
armistice had been signed. The occupation, he found, entailed certain advantages for the artist. No longer pestered by visitors or dis-
tracted by letters, liberated from commitments to publishers and
newspapers, he had an indefinite amount of leisure at his disposal.
Reflecting on German occupation he concluded, in *Solstice de
Juin,* that it was a necessary and possibly beneficial punishment.
Although he was sure that France would eventually be resurrected, in the meantime she "must assume, within a new system,
the place she occupied before the trial of strength : defeat
was only one sign, among many less obvious ones. She must

[1]H. de Montherlant, *Equinoxe de Septembre,* Paris, 1938, p. 206.
[2]*La Rose de Sable* was first published in 1968.
[3]*Ibid.,* pp. 57, 99.

realise that the right of the victor over the vanquished is only limited by the victor's interests : before the modern era, no voices, not even the purest, protested against the rights of conquest any more than against war itself. She must realise that Franco-German relations will only be productive if they evolve in the same revolutionary climate in which Hitler's Germany was born, because what we have lived through and experienced, what we live through and experience, only assumes a significance in terms of the real revolution at stake in the present war. She must at least benefit from the lessons which the victor can give her in many respects."[1]

Solstice de Juin was published in the occupied zone after considerable difficulties, on the insistance of Montherlant's German translator, Karl-Heinz Bremer, the assistant director of the German Institute. Even then it was banned in Holland and Belgium, and by no means appreciated by the pro-German critics : reviewing it for the *N.R.F.* Drieu La Rochelle indignantly refuted Montherlant's identification of Germany with paganism.

Montherlant declined an active rôle in politics. Aware of the mistakes normally made by intellectuals who committed themselves, he maintained that the writer's only duty was to his art. Although he admired Pétain he could not accept the Vichy ideology unquestioningly. He refused to have anything to do with the Vichyite youth movements—even to lecture or write for them, and from 1942 to 1945 worked for the Red Cross. "To remain alone, deliberately, in a society in which it is clearly to your interest, every day more and more, to be assimilated, this is the sort of heroism which I ask you to respect."[2] And this was what Montherlant did : he remained, as he had always been, alone.

France, the more enlightened National Socialists acknowledged, had a cultural tradition which was not to be despised. Despite their decadence as a nation, the French still retained some important artists who might well regale the New Europe with their talents : France's leading sculptors, painters, writers and actors were accordingly invited to the Reich. In the autumn of 1941 Van Dongen, Derain, Despiau, Friez, Vlaminck and Dunoyer de Segonzac travelled to Germany; at the Writers' Congress in Weimar, France was represented by Brasillach, Drieu La Rochelle, Marcel

---

[1] H. de Montherlant, *Solstice de Juin*, Paris, 1941, p. 309-310.
[2] *Ibid.*, p. 240.

Jouhandeau, Ramon Fernandez, Jacques Chardonne and Abel Bonnard; French film stars—Danielle Darrieux, Viviane Romance and Harry Baur (supplied with a document proving he was Aryan) —were welcomed in Berlin, and in April 1942, when the German sculptor Arno Breker visited Paris and gave an exhibition at the Orangerie, the aged Aristide Maillol agreed to emerge from the seclusion of the south of France and inaugurate it. After speeches by Abel Bonnard, delivered in the presence of Jean Cocteau, a magnificent reception was organised for Maillol at the German Embassy.

In an effort to prove his good will immediately after the French defeat François Mauriac dedicated his novel, *La Pharisienne,* to Lieutenant Heller of the *Propagandastaffel,* while many other intellectuals—Cocteau, Paul Morand, Montherlant, Colette—found that German friends of before the war had been posted in Paris. By frequenting them they could sometimes obtain the release of friends in the Resistance who had been captured by the Gestapo, in addition to material advantages for themselves and their families. For rations in France were lower than in any other German-occupied country in western Europe : by the winter of 1940 each person was allowed 360 grammes of meat and 100 grammes of fat substances per week (respectively forty-eight per cent and fifty-six per cent less than what was consumed before the war). As time passed this was reduced still further, and cigarettes and wine rose to prohibitive prices; it was difficult to obtain coal; petrol was rationed; there was a curfew at midnight in the summer and eleven in the winter; and a special permit issued by the Germans was required to drive a car and to cross the demarcation line. Friends in the German army solved these problems. Large consignments of coal would be delivered, food would be available and meals would be provided in the best hotels and restaurants in Paris. Money, too, abounded, as Abel Hermant discovered when, after refusing to edit *Le Temps* for the Germans, he contributed some articles to two German subsidised papers, Georges Suarez's *Aujourd'hui* and Jean Luchaire's *Nouveaux Temps* : the sums he received, he said, exceeded anything he had been paid under the Third Republic.

To fulfil any official function in the occupied zone, it was necessary to have the consent of the Germans, so when Sacha Guitry, the President of the Artists' Union, returned to Paris after the armistice and decided to open his theatre, the Madeleine, he required permission from the head of the *Propagandastaffel*. Then, after the Madeleine had been opened on July 31, Guitry found himself obliged to reserve a certain number of seats at every performance for the German propaganda office—a measure applied to every theatre in Paris. According to Guitry,[1] between five and ten Germans would attend the performances.

Guitry's German admirers visited him in his dressing room, and General Turner had been so impressed by a performance of *Pasteur* that he asked Guitry if there was anything he could do for him. Yes, said Guitry, he could release some French prisoners-of-war. Turner offered him ten, and Guitry obtained the release of eleven. He received further visitors : General Schomburg appeared in his dressing-room to offer his respects; the German Consul General Rudolf Schleier invited him to dinner with Arletty, and Guitry demanded the release of more friends. He asked Schleier to free Tristan Bernard who had been captured by the Gestapo, and, together with Brasillach, persuaded the Germans to liberate Colette's Jewish husband.

On account of his charm, his wit and his attractive house Guitry was regarded as something of a curio. Count Bismarck and Ernst Jünger called on him. When Goering came to Paris he asked to meet him. "You accepted?" the examining magistrate subsequently asked him at his trial. "Out of curiosity," replied Guitry. "You who have met the King of England! You who have been entertained at Windsor, you met Goering!" exclaimed the examining magistrate. "Yes," said Guitry. "And I'll probably lunch with Stalin before you do."[2] Celebrated for his *bons mots,* Guitry entertained Ernst Jünger at a small dinner party at the house of Fernand de Brinon, Pétain's ambassador in Paris, with an anecdote about Octave Mirbeau, the playwright and author of *Le Journal d'une femme*

---

[1] S. Guitry, *Quatre ans d'occupations,* Paris, 1947, p. 161 *ff*. Hitler appears to have given Abetz orders that German censorship in France should not be too strict. "The Germans have a schoolmasterly way of meddling in everything," the Führer told his ambassador. "The censor . . . should simply make sure that press, radio, screen, stage and literature produce nothing which could arouse the French population politically and endanger the security of the forces in occupation." (O. Abetz, *op. cit.,* p. 142.) And in spite of the interminable lists of books which were to be banned, many French writers, Gaullists like Claudel, and prominent members of the left wing, like Sartre, had their works published and their plays performed.

[2] *Ibid.,* p. 358-359.

de chambre. Mirbeau, said Guitry, had died in his arms and his last words had been : *Ne collaborez jamais* ![1]

Céline was more deeply committed. In 1939 he had volunteered for the French army, but had been declared disabled on account of wounds received in the Great War. Appointed ship's doctor on a merchant vessel, he was torpedoed off Gibraltar, and after his rescue, settled in Paris, where his pamphlet *Les Beaux Draps* appeared in the summer of 1941. He now suggested that the French should bring about a Communist revolution without the Jews. Apart from his recommendation that banks, mines, railways, insurance companies, stores and industry should be nationalised, however, Céline's Communism resembled the doctrine of Maurras far more closely than that of Marx. "We need a Labiche type of Communism, a petit bourgeois Communism, with a house, hereditary so it sticks in the family and can never be confiscated, a garden of five hundred metres and insurance against everything. Everyone a small land owner."[2] Again Céline said that the Jews and freemasons were behind everything and the white race was threatened, chiefly, this time, by the black and yellow races. But there was already a tone of defiance, which led the book to be banned both in the free zone and in Germany : "I didn't wait for the Kommandantur to hoist its flag over the Crillon to be pro-German . . . It's under Dreyfus, Lecache, Kéril that we should have shouted 'Vive l'Allemagne !' Now it's the order of the day."[3] This was typical of the remarks Céline was now heard to make. Always a pessimist, he knew he was destined to back the losing side. "Vichy is non-existent, smoke, shadows. What's true is that the Huns have lost the war . . ." he told Rebatet,[4] in October 1940, and in 1943 he informed another friend, "You know, old boy, as long as the Huns are stupid enough to get themselves killed in the East, it's all right. But the day they stop, the Asians will be in Paris, and it'll be ghastly."[5]

For all his scepticism Céline remained as anti-semitic as he had been under the *Front Populaire*. He confirmed this in a letter to *Le Pilori*, a paper which specialised in denouncing

---

[1]E. Jünger, *Werke, III*, Stuttgart, 1962, p. 270.
[2]L.-F. Céline, *Les Beaux Draps,* Paris, 1941, p. 137.
[3]*Ibid.*, p. 156.
[4]*Louis Ferdinand Céline I, Cahiers de l'Herne,* Paris, 1943, p. 46.
[5]*Ibid.*, p. 12.

Jews to the Gestapo, and in March 1941 Abetz mentioned him as a possible member of the *Office Central Juif,* whose other candidates included Darquier de Pellepoix and the notorious Professor Montandon who suggested that all Jews should have their noses amputated. That September Costantini's paper, *L'Appel,* contained a statement by Céline : "Really there's only Chancellor Hitler who knows about the Jews," and in February 1942 he accused Jean Luchaire of being insufficiently anti-Jewish. Later in the year *Je suis partout* received one of his erratic epistles. "I want to be the most Nazi of all the collaborators," he wrote, "and suggest that all the Mediterranean bastards south of the Loire be thrown into the sea." The Provençal members of the newspaper's staff found the joke in doubtful taste, and declined to publish the letter, yet Céline was undeterred. He informed some French workers in Berlin that it was worth collaborating, for Bolshevism was like the plague, while National Socialism was more like cholera. He applauded Doriot's *Légion des Volontaires Français contre le Bolshévisme;* he wrote to the secretary of the *Institut d'Etudes des Questions Juives* to complain that his books were not on sale at the anti-semitic exhibition in Paris, and then proceeded to sabotage a lecture at the same institute by shouting out in the middle of it : *"Et la connerie aryenne, dis, t'en causes pas?"*

For a brief time, in the first months of the occupation, Céline appears to have thought that the Germans would bring about a revolution in France, that they would introduce "Aryan Socialism". But, as early as 1941, he could establish, not without baleful satisfaction, that he was on the verge of experiencing the persecution which had existed only in his imagination before the war. The Jews, he could tell himself, had caused the war : the Germans had lost it : both were unforgivable. The Germans grew to distrust him; the true collaborators watched him with awe as he raged against everyone and everything. In 1944, when the collaborators began to receive overt threats from the Resistance, and Marcel Jouhandeau was sent a miniature coffin by post, Céline heard himself condemned to death on Radio London. His period of exile began shortly after : Berlin, Sigmaringen, Copenhagen, the prison of Copenhagen, and finally a hut on the shores of the Baltic. Only in 1951, after the amnesty, could he return to Paris.

The "revolutionary" collaborators were the men who committed themselves so deeply in the first years of the war that they had no alternative but to collaborate until the end, past all hope of German victory, past the point of opportunism, and, as Alfred Fabre-Luce stated in his diary, there was no question of opportunism after November 8, 1942, the date of the American landing in North Africa. From then on they had almost the whole of France against them. The protection offered them by the Germans was temporary and often inadequate. Despised as traitors by their compatriots, threatened by the growing power of the Resistance, they spent the last eighteen months of the war in France in a justifiably apocalyptic frame of mind.

"I thought it really was a revolutionary war of the Napoleonic type," Jacques Benoist-Méchin said some years later. "I believed in an ideological war. I was sure the Germans had won it. . . In December 1940 or in February 1941 we could not foresee that the United States and the Soviet Union would enter the war. At the time Great Britain could be of no help to us."[1] The true collaborators had all believed that the German armies would bring the New Order with them—a strong Europe, a peaceful Europe, a united Europe, a nationalistic *and* Socialist Europe. They believed that the example of Germany's strength would enable France to recover. The time, Alphonse de Châteaubriant wrote in August 1940, had "now come for a European resurrection. We must begin again and remould ourselves. In the midst of exhausted nations Germany alone gives incontestable proof of ardent life. Europe without Germany is nothing but a free passage for all the great invasions of the future."[2] What hopes they might have had in Vichy faded with the failure of the *Révolution nationale*, and as Pétain's hostility towards Germany became more evident, the collaborators began to loathe the Marshal's government. It was Pétain, they believed, who was obstructing the New Order, who would not accept Germany's sincere offers of friendship. Drieu La Rochelle, whose proposals that a single French party be formed under Jacques Doriot or the former Radical, Gaston Bergery, had been ignored by both Pétain and the Germans, wrote in January 1943 that he could "never forgive the men of Vichy, half-masked Catholics, unwashed democrats, for having ruined France's last chance of recovery and resurrection by maintaining her internal unity at all

---

[1]Saint-Paulien, *Histoire de la collaboration*, Paris, 1964, p. 202.
[2]A. de Châteaubriant, *Cahiers, 1906-1951*, Paris, 1955, p. 186.

costs. It was possible, but it would have been necessary to perform a frank revolution of virile Socialism, to establish the iron rule of the single party."[1]

The most outspoken critic of Vichy remained Lucien Rebatet, the violence of whose anti-semitism, which developed when he had worked as Charles Maurras' private secretary and acted as the *Action Française* film critic under the name of François Vinneuil, was matched by few of his fellow collaborators. "Last winter," he wrote in *Je suis partout* in June 1942, "I said how pleased I was to see the first German Jews branded by their yellow star. It will give me still more pleasure to see this star in the streets of Paris where this detestable race was trampling us to death less than three years ago."[2] For him the absence of Jews was an essential part of Fascism, which was "true Socialism, that is to say Aryan Socialism, constructive Socialism as opposed to the anarchist and Utopian Jewish Socialism". Fascism meant unity— the unity of the nation and the family; the protection of private property and the fruits of labour; and the abolition of the class struggle. None of these qualities could he find in Vichy, which he visited soon after the armistice. "I'd been in Vichy nearly three weeks," he wrote in *Les Décombres,* the book which established his reputation, and, according to *Je suis partout,* sold 20,000 copies in three weeks when it appeared in 1942. "I still wanted to believe that the ridicule, the insanity, the terrifying anachronism which one met at every step were accidental, that the heads which counted remained cool and strong in this most loathsome atmosphere. But I was mistaken. The Vichy of the streets, the drawing-rooms, the bars, the golf-courses where little dandies with ten thousand francs a month pocket money and the daughters of boot polish magnates or illustrious margarine makers sported the *Croix de Lorraine,* fondled each other, met enough little kikes for one to think one-self at the races, that Vichy was the true reflection, the prolong-ation of official Vichy. . . A new State might have been born. But the umbilical cord tying it to the old democratic régime had not been severed. This was doubtlessly due to the weak character of most of the ministers, to their congenital, liberal idiocy, as capable of bringing off a revolution as Maurice Chevalier of acting Hamlet. They couldn't even sign a death sentence without the advice of

---

[1]P. Drieu La Rochelle, *Le Français d'Europe,* Paris, 1944, p. 212.
[2]*Je suis partout,* June 6, 1942.

Charles Maurras

Louis-Ferdinand Céline

twenty-four confessors. . . Vichy has reduced the press, the radio, the speeches to a governmental hagiography of unparalleled shamelessness—well might we mock the publicity of dictatorships! Vichy has sabotaged everything: its Youth statute, its family statute, its Charter of Labour—an amazing mechanism which could only exploit the wage-earner still further—its administrative reforms, finally its Party. But Vichy has succeeded in one thing, the only thing, presumably, on which it had set its heart: it has made the south of France the latrines of Europe. All the excrement evacuated by healthy organisms has found its way there—masons, spies, crooks, mercenaries, parliamentary refuse, the fugitives of five or six routs, Jews and more Jews, petted by all the others."[1]

Although they are usually taken as the archetype of the intellectual collaborator, Drieu La Rochelle and Brasillach were both amongst the more moderate and the first to be disillusioned. Drieu had originally considered joining the British army, and then had thought of escaping to Britain in the event of a German invasion. Yet he stayed in France, and with the establishment of the Vichy government, and the appointment in Paris of his acquaintance Otto Abetz, he once again fell under the illusion that he could "participate" in politics: this was why he had joined the P.P.F. in 1936; this was why he left Vichy for Paris in the summer of 1940 with his unrealistic proposals of a single party under Doriot or Bergery which were as unacceptable to the French as they were to the Germans; and this was why he again joined the P.P.F. in 1942, four years after he had lost all faith in it. Collaboration, he affirmed, was "first and foremost an effort to defend good people from the horror of not being able to do anything."[2] But to participation was added another, more ominous reason: Drieu found the curiously unreal atmosphere of German-occupied Paris exciting. The whole town was palpitating with a sense of destruction—the sense of Drieu's own destruction. The elegant world of the twenties and thirties, the superficial milieu over which the thin characters of Drieu's fiction had skated lightly, eager but unable to thrust their skating boots through the ice, had come to an end, and all that remained was a troubled void, surrounded, not to say permeated by imminent terror, crime, torture and genocide. In this vacuum, too horrible for its reality to be felt or grasped, Drieu was to pre-

---

[1]L. Rebatet, *Les Décombres,* pp. 508, 517, 637.
[2]P. Drieu La Rochelle, *Chronique politique 1934-1942,* p. 291.

S

pare for the event at which his entire life and career had been pointing—his suicide.

He collaborated with an integrity somewhat undermined by his natural kindness and his perpetual sense of self-doubt. Neither a bigot nor a fanatic, after his appointment as editor of the *Nouvelle Revue Française* he obtained the release of his predecessor, Jean Paulhan, who had been captured by the Germans in 1941, and took steps to get Sartre freed from prison camp.[1] "With the Germans he is for the Allies," noted Maurice Martin du Gard, "with the Gaullists he is for the Germans."[2] And the arguments which Drieu advanced for collaboration—the inevitability of a German Empire and the importance of France's acceptance of her place within this empire—sound hollow next to the personal tragedy through which he was living. He had believed, he said shortly before his death, "that Fascism would change from semi-Socialism under the pressure of war. But war did the opposite. It interrupted the social evolution in Italy and Germany (maybe also in Russia) and froze the elements in development into a militarist and bureaucratic state control. Which is why it didn't even occur to Germany to spread her revolution to the other occupied countries. If she had done this it would have transfigured the occupation."[3] By January 1943 Drieu realised that the war was lost, that there was no question of the Germans bringing about the revolution he had associated with their victory. "I was completely wrong about Hitlerism," he admitted to Pierre Andreu. "My views on Germany were far saner in 1933 and 1934. When I committed myself I got confused. Germany is just as much subject to European decadence as the other nations."[4]

In the life of Brasillach the Second World War constitutes a

---

[1] This may be one of the reasons why the Communists accused Sartre of collaborating. He later discovered his name on a black list between Montherlant and Châteaubriant, and when he tried to approach the Communist intellectuals in 1941 he was rejected on the grounds that he owed his release from prison camp to services rendered to his captors, while he had in fact been released because of his health. Not until 1943 was he invited to join the left-wing *Comité National des Ecrivains* and the Communists apologised for their mistake. See David Caute, *Communism and the French Intellectuals, 1914-1960,* André Deutsch, 1964, p. 151; and S. de Beauvoir, *La Force des Choses,* Paris, 1963, p. 16.

[2] M. Martin du Gard *op. cit.,* p. 327.

[3] P. Drieu La Rochelle, *Récit secret,* p. 103.

[4] P. Andreu, *Drieu, témoin et visionnaire,* Paris, 1952, p. 199.

retarded return to adolescence. It started with the period he spent in a German prisoner-of-war camp after the armistice, where he found that spirit of comradeship, that infantile and conspiratorial mentality for which he had retained a nostalgia ever since he left school: he could "gang up" with fellow right-wing officers against the French soldiers who happened to be Jews; he could discuss, late into the night, with an amiable German interpreter, the Europe of the New Order. Prison camp offered every incentive to collaborate—some soldiers did so in order to obtain material benefits for themselves at the time, others to obtain their release, and still others, like Brasillach, because they took a liking to their captors. It was in prison that Brasillach wrote his first article for *Je suis partout*, attacking the British and the Gaullists, and, in the spring of 1941, he was liberated at the specific request of the government of Vichy, supported, in all probability, by Brinon and Abetz. On his return to Paris, he became editor of *Je suis partout*, though remaining, as Maurice Martin du Gard pointed out, one of the more moderate elements of that unsavoury publication.

In the autumn of 1941 Brasillach returned to Germany in order to represent his country at the Writers' Congress of Weimar. The reservations he had had after his visit in 1937 disappeared, and now everything he saw filled him with joy—the architecture, the sculpture, the uniforms—those same German uniforms which he saw in the streets of Paris and which seemed to prove that the international youth movement of which he had always dreamt, had at last come to power. But, unfortunately for Brasillach, forces were conspiring against the youth movement—the British, the Gaullists, soon the Americans, who, if they won the war, would undoubtedly re-install the Jewish gerontocrats of the *Front populaire*. In his articles the plump editor of *Je suis partout* urged his readers to oppose such an event. He begged them not to provoke the Germans and forgo those privileges which their victors had accorded them. He warned against stricter curfews, more brutal reprisals, indeed, against the horrors of war, bombardment, destruction, starvation which France had hitherto been spared. Above all he emphasised the dangers of Bolshevism, and in June 1943, having himself donned a German uniform, he accompanied Brinon to the Russian front, where he reported on the *Légion des volontaires français contre le bolshévisme* and on the massacre of the Polish officers at Katyn.

For all his fancies, however, Brasillach remained a realist and in

July of 1943 he saw clearly that Mussolini's fall in Italy was the end of Fascism, the end of his adolescent dream. "Let us be logical," he wrote to Rebatet. "In 1938 we shouted that we would not get on the same boat that sank with the Czechs; in 1939 Déat poked fun at the people who wanted to die for Danzig. Should we now die so that Danzig remain German? I say no. I am against Bolshevism because it is total death. Otherwise *I am Germanophile and French,* more French than National Socialist, to tell the truth. In case of danger one must stick to one's country. She alone never goes wrong."[1] The owner of *Je suis partout,* Charles Lesca, proceeded to accuse Brasillach of defeatism, and it would seem that the German *Sicherheitsdienst* made plans for his arrest, but that he was saved by Abetz. In all events, he left the newspaper together with Georges Blond and Henri Poulain. "After the fall of Italy it is clear that Germany can no longer win the war," said he. "What remains of the policy of collaboration? The memory of a friendship which neither a dramatic present nor a certain future can efface."[2] All the French could now do was to reach "an agreement with Germany . . . to form a union of losers." In this moment of imminent defeat, however, Brasillach made it plain that realism must prevail over feeling. Feeling, of course, would remain—it was the feeling of the woman ravished, but happy to have been ravished, for "all those who love their country and certain images of man, have more or less slept with Germany."[3] And this Brasillach had indeed done—less passionately than some, but with more passion than most.

Both Brasillach and Drieu La Rochelle refused the Germans' offer to escort them to Germany after the Liberation. While Châteaubriant, Céline, Rebatet and Abel Bonnard assembled with Laval and Pétain at Sigmaringen, Brasillach gave himself up to the French police less than three weeks after De Gaulle's entry into Paris and on February 6, 1945, he was executed.

"There is something more than death," Drieu wrote to his mistress in August 1944, "there is pride. I don't want to recant, I don't want to hide, I don't want to go to Germany, and I don't want to be touched by dirty hands."[4] After two unsuccessful

---

[1] R. Brasillach, *Journal d'un homme occupé,* p. 248.
[2] *Ibid.,* p. 249.
[3] *Echo de Paris,* May 17 1944.
[4] F. Grover, *op. cit.,* p. 59.

attempts to commit suicide, he finally succeeded in killing himself on March 16, 1945. Sartre's obituary was harsh: "He had wanted Fascism for society, when all he needed to do was to apply strict rules of behaviour to himself: he wanted to eliminate the human element in himself and in others by transforming human societies into ant-hills. For this pessimist the advent of Fascism corresponded to the suicide of humanity."[1]

---

[1] J.-P. Sartre, *Situations III*, p. 60.

ENGLAND

Section Four

So far was Fascism from enjoying any measure of popularity in England that it seems absurd to ask why it failed. Between the wars England was the scene of events which might well have led to a violent political reaction in other countries—the strikes between 1918 and 1920, the general strike in 1926, the Hunger Marches in the thirties: the parliamentary system tottered, but it survived. As far as the majority of the English were concerned, Fascism was a foreign creation for use by foreigners. All they were prepared to do was to comment on its success in other parts of the world.

Although the Radical and Labour press had condemned Mussolini's methods from the outset, many Conservatives regarded the Fascist régime in Italy with benign condescension.[1] Some—Winston Churchill, Austen and Neville Chamberlain, even Rudyard Kipling—expressed their admiration for the Duce, while John Buchan, writing in the *Morning Post* on December 31, 1929, affirmed that "but for the bold experiment of Fascism the decade has not been fruitful in constructive statesmanship". Besides, Italy, as James Joyce remarked, was always Italy. "Not to like it because of Mussolini would be just as absurd as to hate England because of Henry the Eighth."[2] Compared with other dictatorships, Mussolini's was clement. The censor, strict where daily newspapers were concerned, was lenient with other forms of literature. "Under the Italian despotism," wrote Hilaire Belloc in 1933, "there is still a great deal of highly intelligent writing going on, though they weary one to death with their continual praise of the régime."[3]

[1]P. G. Edwards, *The Foreign Office and Fascism, 1924-29* and R. J. B. Bosworth, *The British Press, Conservatives and Mussolini, 1920-34* in *Journal of Contemporary History*, vol. 5, no. 2, 1970, pp. 153-161 and 163-182.

[2]Richard Ellmann, *op. cit.* pp. 707-708.

[3]*Letters from Hilaire Belloc,* selected and edited by Robert Speaight, Hollis & Carter, 1958, p. 241.

There appeared to be nothing particularly aggressive about Italian Fascism until the invasion of Ethiopia in 1935, and nothing truly unjust about the régime in the period from Matteotti's murder in 1924 to the anti-semitic measures of 1938. It had, according to H. G. Wells, "something in it of a more enduring type than most of the other supersessions of parliamentary methods". Its intellectual content was "limited, nationalist and romantic"; Mussolini's early methods were deplorable; but "it arose not as a personal usurpation but as the expression of an organisation with a purpose and a sort of doctrine of its own"; "it insisted upon discipline and public service for its members. It appeared as a counter movement to a chaotic labour Communism, but its support of the still-surviving monarchy and the Church was qualified by a considerable boldness in handling education and private property for the public benefit. Fascism indeed was not an altogether bad thing; it was a bad good thing; and Mussolini has left his mark on history".[1]

Towards Hitler, however, the English were less tolerant. "Documentation of the outrages committed by German Fascism came quickly," affirmed Julian Symons, "and it would probably be true to say that the acts themselves seemed less appalling than the deliberate degradation of the small Jewish minority among the German people. The destruction of Jewish art, the ruin and torture of Jewish people, carried out in the service of a 'pure' Nationalism, seemed almost incredible to the liberal mind : and worst of all was the fact that these measures were plainly successful, that Fascism had for many German people an appeal never possessed by the Weimar Republic, that no League of Nations could legislate against it successfully."[2] Even those older writers, like H. G. Wells and Hilaire Belloc, who had shown a positive interest in the Italian experiment, were horrified by Hitler, while the younger men, Auden, Isherwood, Spender, MacNeice, Cecil Day Lewis, turned still further to the left, some towards Communism, believing "strongly that their own infusion of liberal feeling would temper Communist harshness, perhaps even change the nature of Communism in Britain".[3]

---

[1]H. G. Wells, *The Shape of Things to Come,* Hutchinson & Co., 1933, pp. 13-138.
[2]J. Symons, *The Thirties,* The Cresset Press, 1960, p. 40.
[3]*Ibid.,* p. 48.

When *Left Review* asked 148 British writers in 1937 whether they were "for, or against, the legal Government and the People of Republican Spain . . . for or against, Franco and Fascism?" only five supported Franco—Edmund Blunden, Arthur Machen, Geoffrey Moss, Eleanor Smith and Evelyn Waugh. Fifteen, including Norman Douglas, T. S. Eliot, Charles Morgan, Ezra Pound and H. G. Wells, remained neutral; Bernard Shaw's reply was unclassified; and the others pronounced themselves in favour of the Spanish Republic. The English preferred legality to any attempt, especially to any right-wing attempt, to carry off a *coup d'état,* and little is as illustrative of the predominant mood in the thirties as the fate of the British Union of Fascists.

"We have made the acquaintance of the most brilliant man in the House of Commons," Beatrice Webb recorded in her diary in June 1923. " 'Here is the perfect politician who is also a perfect gentleman,' said I to myself as he entered the room. . . Tall and slim, his features not too handsome to be strikingly peculiar to himself; modest yet dignified in manner, with a pleasant voice and unegotistical conversation, this young person would make his way in the world without his adventitious advantages which are many—birth, wealth, and a beautiful aristocratic wife. He is also an accomplished orator in the old grand style; and assiduous worker in the modern manner. . . So much perfection argues rottenness somewhere. . . Is there in him some weak spot which will be revealed in a time of stress—exactly at the very time when you need support—by letting you or your cause down or sweeping it out of the way?"[1]

Formerly a Conservative, then independent, Sir Oswald Mosley joined the Labour Party in March 1924. He had, as Beatrice Webb observed, every advantage : he was rich, handsome, athletic and aristocratic, and he had distinguished himself by his gallantry in the First World War. But although he might appear a perfect member of a Conservative governing class Mosley was too rebellious to accept such a rôle, and it was his misfortune to have been born in a country too conservative to accept his proposals.

In 1930, as Labour M.P. for Smethwick and Chancellor of the Duchy of Lancaster in Ramsay MacDonald's government, Mosley

---

[1]*Beatrice Webb's Diaries, 1912-1924,* edited by Margaret Cole, Longmans, Green & Co., 1952, pp. 242-243.

had a practical solution to the problems facing the country. That January there were over one and a half million unemployed, and by July over two million. MacDonald, Philip Snowden, the Chancellor of the Exchequer, and J. H. Thomas, the Lord Privy Seal, did little more than put forward a small-scale public works plan. Mosley's proposals, on the other hand, were more radical: the expansion of home purchasing power by means of credit policy, planned foreign trade, public direction of industry and control of banks, and the alleviation of the unemployment problem by a large-scale public works plan and such subsidiary measures as raising the school leaving age from fourteen to fifteen and providing insured workers with the option of a pension at sixty. The Labour Party refused to accept his scheme. In May 1930 he resigned from the Government and in February 1931, as the number of unemployed rose to over two and a half million, he broke away from the Labour Party to set up his New Party.

Founded on March 1, the New Party had as its programme the "Mosley Manifesto" printed in the *Daily Telegraph* on December 8, 1930. "An immediate policy," the Manifesto stated, "is required, more drastic and determined than any policy yet formulated by any government in the House of Commons . . . It is impossible to meet the economic crisis with a nineteenth-century parliamentary machine. While the power to maintain or change the government must, of course, be retained by parliament, wide powers to deal with the present economic crisis must be vested in the government of the day for a stated period, subject only to the general control of parliament. The whole organisation of the executive machine, Cabinet, and departmental structure must be adapted to the needs of the present situation. An emergency Cabinet of not more than five Ministers, without portfolio, should be invested with power to carry through the emergency policy . . ." Mosley proposed that import control boards and commodity boards should be adopted for the purpose of "insulating" British economy, together with a system of tariffs. "Centralised" purchase of British foodstuffs was to "give us powerful leverage to secure acceptance of our exports in return". "Excellent opportunities clearly exist for the early conclusion of such agreements in the British Commonwealth . . . The Dominions have for the most part foodstuffs and raw materials to sell, and we have manufactured goods to sell. This natural balance of trade should be developed under a Commonwealth plan of mutual advantage . . . We should aim at building within the Commonwealth a civilisation high enough to absorb the production of modern machinery, which for this purpose must be largely insulated from wrecking forces in the rest of the world . . ." To solve the unemployment problem Mosley suggested "an attack by direct action on the great problems of slum clearance and rehousing", while, on a financial level, he specified a "producers' policy". "In the advancement of this immediate policy," he concluded, "we surrender nothing of our Socialist faith. The immediate question is not a question of the ownership, but of the survival of British industry. Let us put through an emergency programme to meet the national danger; afterwards political debate on fundamental principle can be resumed . . ."

Opinions about the foundation of the New Party were, and are, divided. A. J. P. Taylor recently described it as "the greatest personal miscalculation since the fall of Lord Randolph Churchill". "The rejection by Labour of Mosley's programme," he goes on to say, "was a decisive, though negative, event in British history: the moment when the British people resolved unwittingly to stand in the ancient ways."[1] Writing at the time, Beatrice Webb referred to Mosley's defection from the Labour Party as "an amazing act of arrogance". She saw no hope for him: his egotism would ruin his relations with "the Newspaper Lords"; although a foreign journalist had nicknamed him "the English Hitler", he lacked "genuine fanaticism" and, besides, "the British electorate would not stand a Hitler". A few days later she added that "the Mosley Manifesto is an able document—its argument in favour of a general Plan, and there is much reason for it, is well done. But its proposals are as grandiose as they are vague. From the standpoint of propaganda it is a failure; it falls dead in the No Man's Land between those who wish to keep and those who wish to change the existing order. By its proposal to 'insulate' the British Empire and its trade it offends the dearest aspirations of the Labour Party and invades the field of foreign affairs in which Labour statesmen have been signally successful. The proposal to establish Import and Investment Boards attacks the very stronghold of capitalism. The suggestion of an inner Cabinet of Ministers, without portfolios, to

---

[1]A. J. P. Taylor, *English History 1914-1945,* Oxford University Press, 1965, pp. 285, 286.

dictate policy to their colleagues with departments at their disposal, makes the whole scheme look absurd in the eyes of experienced administrators, whether politicians or civil servants. There is, in fact, nothing in the programme that will *grip* any section of the population—the curious assortment of reforms do not hang together; they are based on no political philosophy; they have no emotional appeal—they excite neither love nor hate—and they are far too pretentious and ill-thought-out to convince the common-sense citizen . . . The New Party will never get born alive; it will be a political abortion . . ."[1]

Ideally the New Party was to bridge the traditional gap between Labour and Conservative policies, between Socialism and mass nationalisation on the one hand, and *laissez-faire* capitalism on the other. It was a "third solution" for Great Britain and few of the men who were attracted to it would have regarded it as Fascist. It drew Moore-Brabazon and W. E. D. Allen from the Conservatives, John Strachey, Allen Young, Bill Risdon, W. J. Brown and Robert Forgan from the Socialists, and Major Dudgeon and Sir John Pratt from the Liberals. Aneurin Bevan, Hore-Belisha and Oliver Baldwin sympathised with it. Even Maynard Keynes told Harold Nicolson "that he would, without question, vote for it" although he objected "deeply" to Mosley's methods.[2] "The Mosley programme," commented T. S. Eliot in *The Criterion*, "though in some respects vague or feeble, contains at least some germs of intelligence; and a pronouncement by men who have had the courage to dissociate themselves from any party must be read with respect. It recognises that the nineteenth century is over, and that a thorough reorganization of industry and of agriculture is essential."[3]

At every suggestion that his party might turn into an organisation based on Italian Fascism—and, judging from Harold Nicolson's diaries, Mosley had this in mind at an early stage—Mosley lost members. When he proposed the formation of a youth movement consisting of tough young men to steward his rallies—his "biff-boys"—and when he specified an anti-Soviet policy, Strachey, Young, and Cyril Joad left him. For only three months, at the end of 1931, did he, or rather the editor, Harold Nicolson, manage to

---

[1]*Beatrice Webb's Diaries 1924-1932*, edited by Margaret Cole, Longmans, Green & Co., 1956, pp. 267-268.
[2]Harold Nicolson, *op. cit.*, pp. 72, 74.
[3]*The Criterion*, April 1931, p. 483

persuade a number of intellectuals to contribute to the party paper, *Action,* which foundered in December.[1]

The disadvantage of the New Party was that it only offered a policy for dealing with the crisis at hand. This came to a head in the summer of 1931. In order to obtain foreign credit the Labour Government saw itself obliged to produce a balanced budget by increased taxation and cuts in expenditure, including a ten per cent reduction of the dole. The Cabinet split over whether to admit these measures; MacDonald resigned on August 24, but he was persuaded by the King to form a Coalition Government. For the Labour Party this was betrayal, yet MacDonald, who proceeded to take the measures necessary to obtain foreign credit, had massive support from the Conservatives and a large section of the Liberals. At the General Election in October he was victorious.

The success of the Coalition Government was a reason why not one of the twenty-four New Party candidates got elected that October. Boycotted by the press and short of money, the New Party saw that it had arrived "too late". To the electorate it seemed to be playing on fears which were no longer relevant. "I am not an alarmist," Harold Nicolson told his constituency, "yet I am convinced that we may be faced within measurable distance by a proletarian revolt. The widespread dissatisfaction prevalent in these islands may at any moment become inflamed. If this danger is to be averted we shall require . . . the Corporate, the Organic State."[2] But Nicolson overestimated national "dissatisfaction", and although "the Corporate, the Organic State" as the sole alternative to the inevitable "proletarian revolt" sounded distinctly Fascist, although *Action* had commended a more tolerant attitude towards Mussolini's régime, this was not really where Nicolson's sympathies lay. In January 1932 he travelled to Italy with Mosley to examine a Fascist government in power. Mosley, pleased with what he saw, decided to take Mussolini as his model, while Nicolson, disillusioned, left the New Party in April. "I joined the party for two reasons," he wrote to Robert Forgan. "1. Personal affection and belief in Tom (Mosley). 2. A conviction that a serious crisis

---

[1]The contributors to *Action* included Peter Quennell, Raymond Mortimer, Peter Cheyney, Osbert Sitwell, Alan Pryce-Jones, Christopher Isherwood, Francis Birrell, Eric Partridge and L. A. G. Strong.

[2]H. Nicolson, *op. cit.,* p. 94.

was impending and that our economic and parliamentary system must be transformed if a collapse were to be avoided. Now I feel that the New Party as such has become too much identified with Hitlerism."[1]

The British Union of Fascists was launched by Mosley in October 1932. Of an earlier attempt to form a Fascist movement in England, made by the eccentric Miss Lintorn-Orman in the early twenties, T. S. Eliot had said, "It seems unfortunate that a nationalist organisation should have to go abroad for its name and symbol",[2] and this remained the attitude of the majority of the country towards Mosley. The number of active B.U.F. members seems to have remained extremely low—just over 5,000 in October 1934 and 3,000 in 1938, the inactive members in 1938 numbering about 15,000.[3] The demonstrations and parades which they organised throughout the thirties did little more than frighten the left-wing and confirm the young liberals' "anti-Fascism".

The foundation members of the B.U.F. comprised Forgan and Risdon from the New Party, while some of the more prominent individuals to join in the first years were Alexander Raven Thomson, the author of *Civilization as Divine Superman*, A. K. Chesterton (G. K. Chesterton's second cousin), and William Joyce. Mosley's aim was to introduce into England a system similar to what Mussolini had imposed on Italy : he wanted a one party state, in which the monarchy would be retained, but in which parliament would have little part. Industry and commerce would be reorganised on a corporative basis, the twenty-four corporations including representatives of the workers, the employers and the government, and regulated by a National Council of Corporations. There would be a progressive rise of wages to enable the English to purchase the fruits of expanding British industry. A public works programme was advanced to solve the unemployment problem, and banks, though not nationalised, would be subjected to strict government control.

Until 1934 a certain ambiguity subsisted about the B.U.F. but in June the public was appalled by the brutality which Mosley's stewards displayed in their treatment of anti-Fascists at a Fascist rally held in Olympia. "We were involuntary witnesses of wholly

---

[1]H. Nicolson, *op. cit.*, p. 97.
[2]*The Monthly Criterion*, February 1928, p. 98.
[3]Colin Cross, *The Fascists in Britain*, Barrie & Rockcliff, 1961, p. 131.

Henry Williamson

Roy Campbell

William Butler Yeats

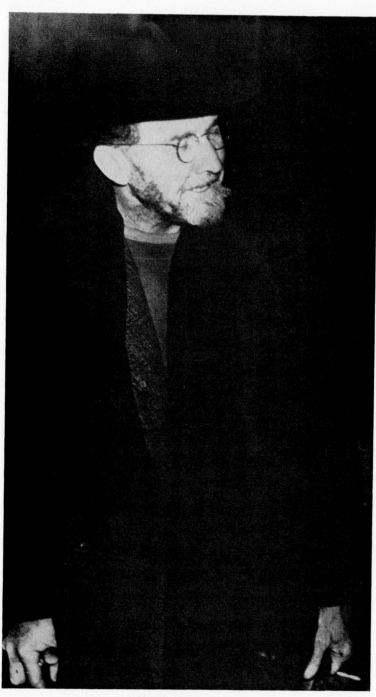

Ezra Loomis Pound

unnecessary violence inflicted by uniformed Blackshirts on inter-
rupters," three Conservative M.P.s wrote to *The Times*. "Men and
women were knocked down and were still assaulted and kicked on
the floor. It will be a matter of surprise for us if there were no fatal
injuries. These methods of securing freedom of speech may have
been effective, but they are happily unusual in England, and constitute in our opinion a deplorable outrage on public order."[1]

Three weeks after the Olympia rally the B.U.F. justified Hitler's
S.A. purge, thereby losing the support of most of their former
Conservative friends, as well as Lord Rothermere, the owner of
The Daily Mail, The Evening News, The Sunday Pictorial and *The
Sunday Dispatch,* who had given Mosley invaluable publicity in
his papers. And by the end of the year the British Fascists further
antagonised public opinion by their attitude towards the Jews.
"From the very outset," Mosley announced at a meeting in the
Albert Hall in October, "we have preserved the principle of no
racial or religious persecution. And we will never have persecution
on racial or religious grounds in the British Empire, because our
Empire is composed of numerous races, a great conglomeration of
the races of the earth bound together in a mighty unity; and any
suggestion of racial or religious discrimination strikes a blow at the
conception of the British Empire . . . And today we do not attack
on racial or religious grounds. We take up the challenge that the
Jews have thrown down, because they fight against Fascism, and
against Britain . . . From every platform and paper which they
control, directly or indirectly, they have striven for the past eighteen months to arouse in this country the feelings and passions of
war with a nation with whom we made peace in 1918 . . . We
fought Germany once in our British quarrel. We shall not fight
Germany again in a Jewish quarrel."[2]

The writer Henry Williamson joined the British Union of
Fascists, holding a grievance which had originally been Mosley's
own. Both men had fought in the Great War and had hoped, on
their return from the trenches, to find a country with full employment for, at least, the ex-servicemen. Lloyd George had led them
to believe in a new era in which the heroes of Flanders would be

---

[1]Quoted in Colin Cross, *op. cit.,* p. 112. The three M.P.s were
W. J. Anstruther-Gray, J. Scrymgeour-Wedderburn and T. J. O'Connor.
[2]Sir Oswald Mosley, *My Life,* Nelson, 1968, pp. 338-339.

T

honoured and rewarded. Instead, all they saw was "the cynical consignment of those who had survived the bloodbath . . . to the unemployment queues."[1] In Mosley Williamson found a man of unquestionable physical and moral courage determined to shake England out of the inertia into which he believed she was sinking. He wanted, as a character in one of his novels says, "to see the money-power controlled by the Government, for the good of the British people in these islands. That is, no capital to be taken out of the country to build factories in Bombay, or Shanghai, using cheap sweated labour to undercut our home industries."[2] Far from regarding Mosley as anti-semitic he considered him "wise and feeling" with regard to the Jews, and applauded his decision to allow them to settle "in the British Empire somewhere", rather than Palestine, which "would upset the Arabs".[3]

In 1935 Henry Williamson visited Germany. The impressions he received were excellent. "No beggars in the streets : there was work of a kind, available to any who applied for it . . . Everywhere I saw faces that looked to be breathing extra oxygen; people free from mental fear. Would there be another war, I asked, again and again, and received the same answer, No : Germany was now strong, and would create her own destiny, no more crowd hysteria or mass panic, no more political parties fighting for power (forty-eight parties between 1918-1933), no more irresponsible newspaper stuff."[4] Hitler, he added in *A Solitary War,* "had freed the farmers from the mortgages which drained the land, cleared the slums, inspired work for all the seven million unemployed, got them to believe in their greatness, each one a German to do his utmost in whatever was his work—in the Arbeitsdienst draining swamp land or making Europe's new autobahnen, stripped to the waist—the former pallid leer of hopeless slum youth transformed into the sun-tan, the clear eye, the broad and easy rhythm of the poised young human being."[5] The disparaging reports in the British newspapers were exaggerations, Williamson believed. There were plenty of prosperous-looking Jews in the streets, shops and restaurants and the police behaved with the utmost intransigence to anyone who attacked

[1]R. J. A. Skidelsky, *Great Britain,* in *European Fascism,* p. 233.
[2]H. Williamson, *A Solitary War,* MacDonald, 1966, p. 347.
[3]H. Williamson, *The Phoenix Generation,* MacDonald, 1965, p. 350.
[4]H. Williamson, *Goodbye West Country,* Putnam, 1937, p. 226.
[5]H. Williamson, *A Solitary War,* p. 365.

these Jews or breached the peace in any other way. From a nation disrupted by anarchy, Germany had turned into a law-abiding community.[1]

What Williamson could never believe about Hitler was that he wanted war : he regarded the Führer as "the only true pacifist in Europe."[2] In the Great War Williamson had developed a comradely esteem and affection for the German soldiers, "brave men who believed in the righteousness of their cause, in the same way as ourselves"[3] and it was inconceivable to him that any of these former soldiers could want to fight in another war which would be to the sole advantage of "Oriental commissars" waiting "like jackals, to grow fat on the killings."[4] But to Williamson's distress the British snubbed Hitler again and again : only Lloyd George had the intelligence to treat him as an equal. In the meantime the international financiers, who saw their investments in Poland threatened by Hitler's perfectly legitimate plans to expand eastwards, were trying to provoke him, to frustrate his "spiritual gifts . . . driving him to do the opposite of his idealistic nature."[5]

In August 1939, therefore, Williamson planned to fly to Berlin to "tell Hitler not to march". "If I could see Hitler, as the common soldier of 1914 who fought the common soldier of his Linz battalion at Ypres," thinks his autobiographical hero, Philip Maddison, "might I not be able to give him, the German common soldier, that amity he so desired from England—to beg him to halt his troops, and to save the two white giants of Europe . . . from bleeding to death, while Oriental Bolshevism waits on, to bring Asia

---

[1]An account of the Führer's grief after the S.A. purge led Williamson to compare him to T. E. Lawrence, "our nearest approach to Hitler" (*Goodbye West Country*, p. 228.) Lawrence's own attitude to Fascism and National Socialism gave rise to considerable speculation. Liddell Hart told him that many people wanted him to be dictator of England, and Lawrence said that the British Fascists had tried to get hold of him, but he refused to help them : only if they came to power, he added, would he agree to be "dictator" of the press for a fortnight. Shortly before his death a friend wrote to him suggesting he meet Hitler. Lawrence wired back saying that he would be delighted, and it was on his return from the post-office on May 13, 1935, that he had his fatal accident on his motor-bike. See Richard Aldington, *Lawrence of Arabia*, Collins, 1955, pp. 286-7.

[2]H. Williamson, *A Solitary War*, p. 364.

[3]*Ibid.*, p. 221.

[4]H. Williamson, *A Phoenix Generation*, p. 349.

[5]H. Williamson, *A Solitary War*, p. 352.

to the chalk cliffs of Normandy?"[1] On Mosley's advice, however, Williamson changed his mind and remained in England. The Second World War was, he concluded, a "two-sided 'brothers' war' in which both sides contributed to what, save for the atom bomb possessed by the Allies, would have brought Asia to the Channel."

For most of the writers who were attracted by Fascism it was an amusing means of provocation, a feather with which to tickle the throats of the English liberals. Yet it must also be admitted that surprisingly few of these writers were English themselves. Yeats and Shaw were Irish, Pound American, Wyndham Lewis and Eliot American-born, Roy Campbell South African, and Hilaire Belloc the son of a French father.

Belloc's attitude to politics was conditioned by his schooling and military service in France. At the Collège Stanislas in Paris he had been surrounded by nationalistic French aristocrats, under whose influence he had developed an admiration for the *Action Française* and an anti-Jewish prejudice which became particularly evident when he was at Oxford at the time of the Dreyfus case, and, to the astonishment and indignation of his fellow students, deplored Zola's intervention on Dreyfus' behalf. In 1902 Belloc became a British subject and two years later he stood as Liberal candidate for South Salford, an industrial suburb of Manchester. Elected in January 1906 he sat in Parliament until 1910. His political views reposed on a mixture of progressive and reactionary principles. He supported Irish Home Rule and free trade, opposed the importation of Chinese labourers into South Africa and disapproved of the enfranchisement of women. As a Catholic he defended the rights of religious minorities in the state educational system and as a French Nationalist he was eager to reveal the machinations of Jews and freemasons.

As Belloc's political career proceeded he became increasingly disillusioned with the democratic system. He found it corrupt and dishonest, and believed that most of the Members of Parliament had no way of enforcing the wishes of their constituents on the executive. Programmes were promised and not implemented. Thus the Liberals in 1906 had promised that the Chinese labourers would leave South Africa—and they had not left. Decisions were taken in secret, and the Legislature had little influence. Belloc's anti-semitism

---

[1] H. Williamson, *The Phoenix Generation*, p. 371.

and his hatred of parliament grew with the Marconi[1] scandal in 1912 and the Peace Conference in Paris in December 1918, when he assumed, with G. K. Chesterton, whom he had converted to the cause of the *anti-Dreyfusards,* that the Jews and the financiers would ensure German supremacy at the expense of Poland.

The one meeting that Belloc had with Charles Maurras, arranged by their mutual friend Yvon Eccles, was complicated by Maurras' deafness, and the two found it impossible to converse. Although he generally agreed with the ideas of the *Action Française,* Belloc entertained some doubts about the monarchy. "There is no doubt that the movement has done an immense amount of good" (he wrote of the *Action Française* in June 1922). "Where I myself hesitate in the matter is on the chief point, which is that of monarchy. I have no doubt that monarchy is what is needed now in every European nation, and by the French most of all because they are the most vigorous; but I do not think that the setting up of an existing dynasty like that of Philip of Orleans would be of the least effect, and I very much doubt in this country whether the present reigning family could ever take on the function. What will save our society when it comes will be some new line of dynasties sprung from energetic individual men who shall seize power. One never sees how things are going to happen, one only sees that they *are* going to happen. The present Parliamentary welter throughout Europe is not *viable.* It is everywhere thoroughly despised and at the same time it is oppressive and dreadfully corrupt. It means in practice government by a few rich men with an absurd preponderance of financial banking and largely Jewish power. That can't last."[2] In the same year, Belloc asserted the impossibility of assimilating the Jews. "The continued presence of the Jewish nation intermixed with other nations alien to it," he wrote, "presents a permanent problem of the gravest character . . . the wholly different culture, tradition, race and religion of Europe makes Europe a permanent

---

[1]Most of the men implicated in the secretive purchase of shares in the Marconi Company happened to be Jews—the company's co-director, Godfrey de Bouillon Isaacs, the Postmaster-General, Herbert Samuel, and Sir Rufus Isaacs, although Lloyd George, the Chancellor of the Exchequer, was also involved. Belloc and Chesterton believed the Ministers to have made a vast profit without the government's knowledge. A parliamentary enquiry was instituted, however, and the whole incident passed over to the government's satisfaction.

[2]*Letters from Hilaire Belloc,* selected and edited by Robert Speaight, Hollis & Carter, 1958, p. 122.

antagonist to Israel." The only solution would be for the host-nations to "openly recognise their [the Jews'] wholly separate nationality, treat it without reserve as an alien thing, and respect it as a province of society outside their own."[1]

Both Belloc and Chesterton, ingenuous opponents of capitalism, believed in a more equal distribution of wealth which they thought the Jews were obstructing and Mussolini was on the way to attaining. Belloc met the Duce in 1924. "He fully understands that Parliament is no longer serious with us," he wrote. "He appreciates the fact that the International Financiers govern us . . . He is not ambitious and that is a great asset in governing men. His driving power is first disgust with Parliamentarianism, which he shares with pretty well everyone in Europe—and next Patriotism. He will do a great deal to confirm the already established religious peace—but I doubt whether he has much faith in himself. The point is that his régime will help it to return to the younger generation"[2]

Although he disagreed with Mussolini's contempt for majority rule, Chesterton, who visited Rome in 1929, approved of his belief in "the civic necessity of Virtue", his respect for motherhood and the Church, and admired certain aspects of Fascist labour policy. Above all he felt that the Liberal governments were in no position to attack Mussolini who "does openly what enlightened, liberal governments do secretly . . . He does and defends what they do and do not defend. They conceal; they effect the same thing, because they think it convenient; but they do not defend it, because they think it indefensible. He is acting with his own principles of Fascism; they are acting against their principles of Freedom."[3] Taking freedom of the press and freedom of political election as examples, Chesterton pointed out that "the British newspapers do in fact belong to two or three men, who have only to agree to suppress something and it is suppressed," while the British elector chooses "between two or three candidates, each provided by a recognised Party Caucus and each supported by an unrecognised Party Fund."

In his eagerness to shock the British Liberals Bernard Shaw went

---

[1] H. Belloc, *The Jews*, Constable, 1922, pp. 3-5.
[2] Robert Speaight, *The Life of Hilaire Belloc*, Hollis & Carter, 1957, p. 434.
[3] G. K. Chesterton, *The Resurrection of Rome*, Hodder & Stoughton, 1930, pp. 275-276.

infinitely further than Chesterton or Belloc. After sending Lenin his latest book with a flattering dedication in 1921 he praised the "inspired precision" with which Mussolini "denounced liberty as a putrefying corpse." "A civilization," Shaw maintained, "cannot progress without criticism, and must therefore to save itself from stagnation and putrefaction, declare impunity for criticism",[1] and to this purpose, the purpose of criticising democracy, he put Fascism. To condemn Mussolini for the assassination of Matteotti was absurd, according to Shaw, for many great statesmen were forced, at one time or another, to murder inconvenient opponents. "It is . . . irrelevant and silly to refuse to acknowledge the dictatorship of il Duce because it was not achieved without all the usual villainies . . . Some of the things Mussolini has done, and some that he is threatening to do go further in the direction of Socialism than the English Labour Party could yet venture if they were in power. They will bring him presently into serious conflict with capitalism; and it is certainly not my business nor that of any Socialist to weaken him in view of such a conflict."[2]

When it came to assessing Hitler, however, Shaw was less benign, for he found anti-semitism as ridiculous as democracy, and the fact that Einstein should be exiled, execrable. "We must not let Adolf give Socialism a bad name," he wrote to Beatrice Webb in June 1940. "We are National Socialists, and for Socialism in a single country as against Trotsky; and we cannot too strongly insist that we are not objecting to German Socialism but to persecution and bogus racialism, which are incompatible with it, and have been attached to it illogically and insanely by the Führer."[3]

Poetry has generally been allowed a freedom denied to other forms of art. Not only does poetic licence cover syntactical distortions, it also provides a certain moral impunity for an aristocracy of artists striving to create a world which becomes ever more secluded with the progress of poetic technique. Any image, however brutal,

---

[1] G. B. Shaw, Preface to *On the Rocks*, Constable, 1949, p. 184.

[2] *Bernard Shaw and Fascism*, London, 1927. Shaw's speeches on Fascism appalled his fellow Fabians, the Webbs, and his articles drew indignant letters from the leading anti-Fascist exiles, Gaetano Salvemini, supported by communications from Filippo Turati, Carlo Rosselli, Ferruccio Parri and Arturo Labriola giving account of Fascist atrocities.

[3] Quoted in Archibald Henderson, *George Bernard Shaw: Man of the Century*, Appelton Century Crofts Inc., N.P, 1956, p. 385.

however opposed to humanitarian principles, has been offered up readily to the building of the ladder which leads to the Mallarmean *azur*. Only recently have poets found it necessary to apologise for their aristocracy, to excuse themselves for their way of expression. Thus W. H. Auden informs us, over thirty years after the event, that his name on the title-page of *The Orators*, which originally appeared in 1932, "seems a pseudonym for someone else, someone talented but near the border of sanity, who might well, in a year or two, become a Nazi." "The central theme of *The Orators*," he continues, "seems to be Hero-worship, and we all know where that can lead to."[1]

The worship of heroes, and its bastard brother, "contempt for the masses", are sometimes an inevitable stage in the journey away from modern society to the poetic universe. To such young left-wing poets of the thirties as Auden, this was deplorable, though they were guilty of it themselves. Often at the expense of their poetry, they yearned for political commitment, and it is partly as a reaction against their taunts that we must interpret the aggressive arrogance of Roy Campbell, a South African, extroverted and obstreperous by temperament. Campbell loathed the literary world of London, and, with a puritanism incongruous in such an admirer of Verlaine and Rimbaud, decried its perversion and effeminacy. He had a predilection for all that was un-intellectual and savoured of violence, liking to surround himself with sailors, cattle-herders, boxers and bull-fighters. For his friends in London he chose the Sitwells and Wyndham Lewis, and vied with them as to who would cause the greatest scandal.

Despite his admiration for the authoritarian politics and classical principles of Maurras, Campbell tended to regard himself as a *poète maudit* in the tradition of Baudelaire. Yet he was a healthy, vigorous *poète maudit*, who preferred riding and bull-fighting to whoring, the mountains and plains of Southern Europe to urban opium dens. Like the late French romantics he was an outsider, but an "outsider on the right",[2] flaunting his taste for hierarchy, his admiration for the institution of slavery, his dreams of an archaic and feudal society in the faces of his left-wing contemporaries. He had nothing but contempt for "the people", "a monster whom the

[1] W. H. Auden, *The Orators*, Faber & Faber, 1966, p. 7.
[2] *c.f.* Bernard Bergonzi, *Roy Campbell: Outsider on the Right*, in *Journal of Contemporary History*, vol. 2, no. 2, April 1967, pp. 133-147.

drunken gods have maimed/ And set upon a road that has no goal". He detested progress, "cobbled with a line of bowler hats", and could admire only "those whose pens or swords have made/ Steep ladders of the broken bones of men."[1]

The interpretation which Campbell gave of Fascism in the first volume of his autobiography, *Broken Record*, in 1934, was characteristically provocative. He took it to be Futurism which "embodies itself in human lineaments, in the love or hatred of a chief and a leader; it is religious, not fanatical; human, not mechanical. The expulsion of renegade intellectuals (those who use their intellect to undermine the intellect itself) is one of the finest reactions of this movement."[2] He was "no pogromite", for he found that the beauty of Jewish women made up "for the ugliness of their men", but he failed "to see how a man like Hitler makes any 'mistake' in expelling a race that is intellectually subversive as far as we are concerned: that has none of our visual sense, but a wonderful dim-sighted instinct for dissolving, softening, undermining and vulgarising."[3]

In 1935 Campbell and his wife were received into the Roman Catholic Church and in the same year decided to settle in Spain. A backward country with a high rate of illiteracy, scarred by the most bigoted Catholicism, Spain, or the reactionary aspect of Spain, came close to Roy Campbell's ideals. When the Civil War broke out in 1936, therefore, there was no doubt in anyone's mind as to which side he would be on. He shared the indignation of most of his fellow Catholics at the Republicans' slaughter of nuns and priests, and appears himself to have been beaten up by the Republican *guardias de asalto*. After escaping with his family from Toledo to the Nationalist lines, he fought briefly, he told a French admirer, in " 'los novios de la muerte' . . . the first regiment of Europe . . . the Spanish legion, the regiment of Cervantes, Lopez and Garcilaso : a few foreigners are admitted, but it's not like the French *foreign* legion with brothels, etc."[4]

As correspondent for *The Tablet*, Campbell was an eloquent supporter of the Nationalist cause. For him it was a crusade.

---

[1] *A Song for the People*, in *The Collected Poems of Roy Campbell*, I, The Bodley Head, 1949, p. 28.
[2] R. Campbell *Broken Record*, Boriswood, 1934, pp. 45-46.
[3] *Ibid.*, p. 156.
[4] *Hommage à Roy Campbell*, Montpelier, 1958, pp. 73-74.

Franco represented the medieval chivalry of his poetry, his make-believe world where industry had disappeared and machines had been replaced by men and horses. The Republicans, on the other hand, stood for all he despised. "The Sodomites are on your side," he wrote in a poem addressed to the President of the Spanish Republic, which appeared in Oswald Mosley's *British Union Quarterly,* "The cowards and the cranks;/ The Devil got you, tortoise-eyed,/ And plus-fours zeppelin in your shanks."[1]

But was Campbell a Fascist? He, at least, never considered himself as such. "It made no difference that one fought as willingly against Fascism as one had done against Bolshevism previously," he complained, after serving in the British army in the Second World War. "So fanatical did the mental goose-stepping of the British intellectuals become, and so gluttonous their fatuous credulity, that, even if you killed ten times as many Fascists as you had previously killed Bolsheviks in self-defence, you still remained a 'Fascist'."[2]

Whether the disgust which T. S. Eliot expressed in his early poems was directed at the day to day existence which lies like a chain on the legs of every poet, or whether it was aimed specifically at modern industrial society, is a debatable point. But when we come to his articles in *The Criterion,* his essays on humanism, his *Idea of a Christian Society* and *Notes towards the definition of Culture,* we see him as a social commentator who had many and definite grievances against the twentieth century. For all his eagerness to assume the role of social commentator, however, he did so as a poet. And yet, he always remained "reasonable". His growing impatience with the English government in the early thirties was tempered by his basically rational approach, his awareness of the incompatibility of purely intellectual ideals with politics.

Eliot found that modern society lacked, on the one hand, a sense of religious values, the feeling that "something must come from above",[3] so essential in his poetry, and on the other, a sense of tradition. Industrialism, he believed, created "bodies of men and women—of all classes—detached from tradition, alienated from religion, and susceptible to mass suggestion : in other words, a

---

[1] R. Campbell, *Hard Lines, Azaña!,* in *British Union Quarterly,* January-April, 1937.

[2] R. Campbell, *Light on a Dark Horse,* Hollis & Carter, 1951. 226.

[3] T. S. Eliot, *Second Thoughts about Humanism* in *Selected Essays,* Faber & Faber, 1932, p. 447.

mob."[1] What Eliot proposed in *The Idea of a Christian Society* was a mild authoritarianism in which the supreme institution would be the Anglican Church. Christian ethics would be enforced on the people by the rulers, while, within this society, there would exist "a community of Christians", "the Church within the Church", "the consciously and thoughtfully practising Christians, especially those of intellectual and spiritual superiority."[2] He devised the same cultural élite which he was to describe almost ten years later in *Notes towards the Definition of Culture* : "What is important is a structure of society in which there will be, from 'top' to 'bottom', a continuous gradation of cultural levels : it is important to remember that we should not consider the upper levels as possessing *more* culture than the lower, but as presenting a more conscious culture and a greater specialisation of culture."[3]

In his assessment of foreign ideological experiments Eliot was cautiously appreciative. Describing himself as a "classicist in literature, royalist in politics and anglo-catholic in religion"[4] he initially esteemed the *Action Française*. "Both Russian Communism and Italian Fascism," he wrote in 1928, "seem to me to have died as political ideas, in becoming political facts." The *Action Française*, on the other hand, was uncontaminated by practice. "Most of the concepts which might have attracted me in Fascism I seem already to have found, in a more digestible form, in the work of Charles Maurras. I say in a more digestible form, because I think they have a closer applicability in England than those of Fascism."[5] Like Maurras, whom he had been reading for eighteen years, Eliot favoured decentralisation of government and a monarchy and aristocracy in the English tradition, which "would protect the humble citizen against the ambitious politician". Fascism, however, seemed merely to have accepted the monarchy "as a convenience", and provided "a powerful dictator and a nominal king" as opposed to "the powerful king and the able minister". Were he obliged to

---

[1]T. S. Eliot, *The Idea of a Christian Society*, Faber & Faber, 1939, p. 14.

[2]*Ibid.*, p. 21.

[3]T. S. Eliot, *Notes towards the Definition of Culture*, Faber & Faber, 1948, p. 48.

[4]T. S. Eliot, Preface to *For Lancelot Andrews*, Faber & Faber, 1928, p. 9.

[5]*The Criterion*, December, 1928, p. 289.

choose between Fascism and Communism, Eliot admitted he would take the former. "I confess to a preference for Fascism in practice, which I dare say most of my readers share; and I will not admit that this preference is itself wholly irrational. I believe that the Fascist form of unreason is less remote from my own than is that of the Communists, but that my form is a more reasonable form of unreason."[1] Of course Eliot agreed that Fascism would never do for England. It was "an Italian régime for Italians, a product of the Italian mind". For Great Britain he recommended a "Toryism" with "not only a doctrine of the relation of the temporal and spiritual in matters of Church and State . . . but even a religious foundation for the whole of its political philosophy."[2]

After the crisis of the *Action Française*, Eliot followed Jacques Maritain away from Maurras.[3] In his poetry the bitter sadness of *The Love Song of J. Alfred Prufrock*, the despair of *The Wasteland*, gave way to a greater serenity, a more positive concern with religion. The "anti-Jewish bias" which John Harrison claims to detect in the early poems,[4] no longer appeared. Even the courteous interest Eliot had shown in Fascism waned. "The fundamental objection to Fascist doctrine," he concluded in March 1939, "the one which we conceal from ourselves because it might condemn ourselves as well, is that it is pagan."[5]

What Frank Kermode calls "eschatological anxiety" is a common sentiment. Few artists have been able to resist the idea that civilisation has reached a point of crisis, that *a* world, whether it be *the* world or *their* world, is about to end. For T. S. Eliot it was to end

[1]*The Criterion*, July 1929, p. 691. Eliot's article was entitled *Mr. Barnes and Mr. Rowes*: James Strachey Barnes, whose book, *The Universal Aspects of Fascism*, Eliot had reviewed in *The Criterion* in December 1928, was a romantic and loyal supporter of Mussolini largely because of his love for Italy. He married an Italian, took Italian nationality and was described by Harold Nicolson as a character out of Stendhal.

[2]*The Criterion*, October, 1931, p. 71.

[3]His ideas came closer to those of the French "non-conformists" see *supra*, p. 186). The groups of *Esprit, L'Ordre Nouveau* and *La Jeune Droite*, he wrote in 1934, "show a valuable determination not to surrender individuality to any of the prevailing tendencies of the hour, at the same time that they avoid the Liberalism that still practises its shrill choruses in England." (*The Criterion*, April 1934, p. 454.)

[4]J. R. Harrison, *The Reactionaries*, Victor Gollancz, 1966, p. 149.

[5]T. S. Eliot, *The Idea of a Christian Society*, p. 20.

"not with a bang but a whimper"[1]. William Butler Yeats saw the end as something more grandiose, "dancing to a frenzied drum"[2], accompanied by a mass of bloody and tortured images. But "crisis", as Mr. Kermode so wisely observed, "is a way of thinking about one's moment, and not inherent in the moment itself."[3] It is, one might almost say, a characteristic of human imagination. Even the most insignificant event can be taken as an indication of imminent crisis : with mathematical acrobatics even the most unlikely year can be shown to mark the termination of an epoch. Yeats chose 1927. It was to be followed by a war, the generator of a new period, an heroic period which Yeats awaited with pleasure.

Although Yeats had elaborated his historical theories by the end of 1917 and did not read *The Decline of the West* until several years later, his view of history remains remarkably similar to that of Spengler. Indeed, he was later to admit that he found "a correspondence too great for coincidence" with the *Decline of the West*.[4] For Yeats liked to visualise history as a pair of interpenetrating cones, or gyres. As the apex of one gyre met the base of the other the historical process from subjectivity to objectivity reversed, and the cycle moved back to subjectivity. In the twentieth century the movement was towards objectivity and civilisation was about to fall under the "antithetical influx" which "obeys imminent power, is expressive, hierarchical, multiple, masculine, harsh, surgical."[5] It could, of course, mean the advent of the most brutal dictatorship, to which Yeats refers in *The Second Coming*; basically, however, he liked the idea of "a bloody, arrogant power" which "rose out of the race/Uttering, mastering it"[6]: he found it aesthetically satisfying.

In his youth Yeats had been briefly attracted by Socialism. Yet his only constant political sympathy was with Nationalism, Irish Nationalism, and his true hero remained the great Irish patriot, Charles Stewart Parnell. By 1922 not only had Yeats' interest

[1]*The Hollow Man* in *The Complete Poems and Plays of T. S. Eliot*, Faber & Faber, 1969, p. 86.

[2]*A Prayer for my Daughter* in *The Collected Poems of W. B. Yeats*, Macmillan & Co., 1965, p. 212.

[3]F. Kermode, *The Modern Apocalypse* in *The Sense of an Ending —Studies in the Theory of Fiction*, Oxford University Press, New York, 1967, p. 101.

[4]W. B. Yeats, *A Vision*, Macmillan, 1961, p. 261.

[5]*Ibid.*, p. 263.

[6]*Blood and the Moon* in *The Collected Poems of W. B. Yeats*, p. 267.

in Socialism been superseded by a passionate belief in aristocracy, but Irish Nationalism had reached a point of crisis. After Easter 1920 Ireland was in a calamitous situation. The Sinn Feiners, determined to obtain Irish home rule, backed by their fighting force, the Irish Republican Army (originally Michael Collins' Irish Volunteers) had started to launch a series of attacks against the Royal Irish Constabulary, loyal to the English Crown, who were supported by English ex-servicemen known as the "Black and Tans". In December 1921, however, Lloyd George granted Ireland dominion status: the problem, for the Irish Nationalists, became whether to accept the English Treaty guaranteeing Irish independence. On this issue they split into two groups, that of Michael Collins who was prepared to compromise with the English, and that of De Valera, who was not, and the civil war continued, this time between the Nationalists themselves, until May 1922. Yeats came down on the side of Michael Collins, for, though he remained anti-British, Yeats, an elderly and revered figure who was nominated to the Irish Senate at the end of 1922, had reached the time of life when he preferred order. A Protestant, he did not share the religious fanaticism of the Irish Catholics. A believer in aristocracy, he felt more akin to the English system than to De Valera's followers. It was in this spirit that he looked to Fascism as an orderly compromise with a revolutionary situation. The civil strife in Ireland, the murder of Michael Collins, strengthened his conviction that "democracy is dead and force claims its ancient right,"[1] and a week after the March on Rome he stated that "the Ireland that reacts from the present disorder is turning its eyes towards individualist Italy".[2]

By this time little filled Yeats with so much horror as the prospect of Marxism, "the spear-head of materialism and leading to inevitable murder."[3] The ideology of Fascism, on the other hand, attracted him. He had the greatest admiration for Giovanni Gentile, who, like Spengler, shared his cyclical theory of history and philosophy. "A similar circular movement fundamental in the works of Giovanni Gentile is, I read somewhere, the half-conscious foundation of the political thought of modern Italy. Individuals and

---

[1] *The Letters of W. B. Yeats,* edited by Allen Wade, Rupert Hart-Davis, 1954, p. 695.
[2] *Ibid.,* p. 693.
[3] *Ibid.,* p. 656.

classes complete their personality and then sink back to enrich the mass. Government must, it is held, because all good things have been created by class war, recognise that class war though it may be regulated must never end."[1] The aim of Fascism was to overcome the class war, but this Yeats did not acknowledge. He saw it as it turned out to be : a conservative counter-revolution dominated by the Nationalists and in which tradition was respected. He spoke enviously of Gentile's educational reforms in the Irish Senate and recommended, in November 1925, "Irish teachers to study the attempt now being made in Italy under the influence of their Minister of Education, the philosopher Giovanni Gentile, the most profound disciple of our own Berkely, to so correlate all subjects of study."[2] In March of the following year he described the Italian educational system as "adapted to an agricultural nation like this or Italy, a system of education that will not turn out clerks only, but will turn out efficient men and women, who can manage to do all the work of the nation."[3]

In 1932 Eamon De Valera succeeded the relatively moderate W. T. Cosgrave as Prime Minister of the Irish Free State, and proceeded to break every link with Britain, going as far, a few years later, to abolish the Irish Senate and distinguish Irish nationality from normal British citizenship of the Empire. At this point Yeats saw Fascism as a highly desirable alternative to the De Valera régime. "Had De Valera eaten Parnell's heart," he wrote in *Parnell's Funeral*, "No loose-lipped demagogue had won the day / No civil rancour torn the land apart."[4] In April 1933 he was trying to work out some social theory to be used against Communism, a form of "Fascism modified by religion", and by July he was "constantly urging the despotic rule of the educated classes as the only end to our troubles". "There is so little in our stocking that we are ready at any moment to turn it inside out, and how can we not feel emulous when we see Hitler juggling with his sausage of stocking."[5] "History," he concluded, "is very simple—the rule of the many, then the rule of the few, day and night, night and day

---

[1]W. B. Yeats, *A Vision*, pp. 81-82.
[2]*The Senate Speeches of W. B. Yeats*, edited by D. R. Pearse, Faber & Faber, 1961, p. 173. Gentile had in fact resigned as Minister of Education in June 1924.
[3]*Ibid*, p. 111.
[4]*The Collected Poems of W. B. Yeats*, p. 320.
[5]*The Letters of W. B. Yeats*, p. 808.

for ever, while in small disturbed nations day and night race."[1]
In that same month of July, Yeats met the man who, he momen-
tarily thought, might overthrow De Valera's government. General
O'Duffy led what was generally regarded as an Irish Fascist movement, the Irish Blue Shirts. He was, according to Yeats, an auto-
crat who directed his movement "from above down as if it were
an army"[2] though, as far as Irish policy was concerned, he was
more moderate than De Valera, hoping for "an independent
Ireland within the commonwealth".[3]

Yeats' interest in O'Duffy was short-lived. In February 1934
he wrote three "marching songs" for the Blue Shirts, but in August
rewrote them so that they should not be sung. When the Blue Shirts
set out for Spain to fight for the Nationalists two years later, Yeats
told his friends that he feared lest O'Duffy should return a hero.
The political position that he finally assumed was of the gloomiest
scepticism. Appalled by the crimes of Nazi Germany, he hesitated "to hold one form of government more responsible than any
other".[4] England herself was so imperfect, he believed, that she was
in no position to criticise any foreign government. "All through
the Abyssinian war my sympathy was with the Abyssinians," he
told Ethel Mannin, "but those feelings were chilled by my
knowledge that the English Government was using those feelings
to help an Imperial policy I distrusted."[5]

There was a brief period, in the years immediately preceding the
Great War, when a group of painters, sculptors and writers living
in England participated in a European movement—or rather, made
their own contribution to the various, but similar artistic movements
in the rest of Europe. They called it Vorticism, and they thought
that they were representing England, yet the leading Vorticists

---

[1]*Ibid.*, p. 813.
[2]*Ibid.*, pp. 811-812.
[3]*Ibid.*, p. 814.
[4]*Ibid.*, p. 851.
[5]*Ibid.*, p. 872. In the hope of forcing the German Government to
release Carl von Ossietzky (see *supra*, p. 156) from concentration camp,
Ernst Toller and Ethel Mannin asked Yeats to put Ossietzky up for
the Nobel Prize. Yeats declined, saying that it would do more harm
than good, and, as it turned out, he was right. Ossietzky received the
Nobel Peace Prize in November 1936. The irate German Government
saw to it that the conditions of his imprisonment should deteriorate
and he died in May 1938 as a result of his ill-treatment.

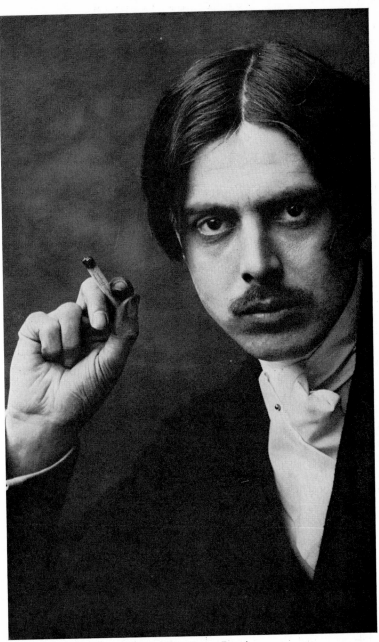

Percy Wyndham Lewis

Thomas Stearns Eliot (*right*)

were a cosmopolitan crowd—a French sculptor, Gaudier-Brzeska, an American poet, Ezra Pound, and an American-born writer and painter, Wyndham Lewis. The influence of the Italian Futurists lay heavily on them, for Marinetti and his followers were active in London at the time.[1] Like their Italian rivals, the Vorticists were determined to cast off traditional values. They were rebelling, wrote Lewis, against "the triumph of the commercial mind in England, Victorian 'liberalism', the establishment of such apparently indestructible institutions as the . . . Royal Academy and so on".[2] Their eulogies of machinery were remarkably similar to Marinetti's manifestos. "Bless all ports," we read in the first number of the Vorticist review, *Blast*, "ports, restless machines of scooped out basins, heavy insect dredgers, monotonous cranes, stations, lighthouses . . . Bless England, industrial island machine, pyramidal workshop, its apex at Shetland, discharging itself on the sea."[3]

Yet the differences between the two groups were in reality considerable. Marinetti's main disciple in England remained C. R. W. Nevinson, while the true precursor of Vorticism was the critic and philosopher, T. E. Hulme. The Vorticists tended far more towards the objectivity and impersonality which form the basis of his aesthetic theories, than to the emotional dynamism of Marinetti. From Marinetti they derived their means of protest, from Hulme their artistic principles. On May 5, 1914, Lewis and "a determined band of miscellaneous anti-Futurists", which included Gaudier-Brzeska, the painter Edward Wadsworth, and Hulme himself, went as far as to disrupt a lecture given by Marinetti at the Doré Gallery in Bond Street. Wyndham Lewis was eager to draw the line between his "Anglo-Saxon" attitude and that of the Italians. "You Wops insist too much on the Machine," he told Marinetti. "You're always on about these driving-belts, you are always exploding about internal combustion. We've had machines here in England

---

[1]Marinetti first lectured in London at the Lyceum Club in 1910. In March 1912 the Italian Futurists exhibited at the Sackville Gallery and in April 1913 Severini held a one-man exhibition at the Marlborough Gallery. From November 1913 to July 1914 Marinetti lectured over ten times in London. See Annamaria Sala, *Some Notes on Vorticism and Futurism* in *Wyndham Lewis*, Special Issue of *Agenda*, vol. 7, No. 3—vol. 8, No. 1, Autumn-Winter, 1969-70, edited by William Cookson, pp. 156-162.

[2]Wyndham Lewis, *Blasting and Bombardiering*, Eyre & Spottiswode, 1937, p. 234.

[3]*Blast*, No. 1, June 20, 1914.

U

for a donkey's years. They're no novelty to *us*." "You have never understood your machines!" exclaimed Marinetti. "You have never known the *ivresse* of travelling at a kilometre a minute. Have you ever travelled at a kilometre a minute?" "Never. I loathe anything that goes too quickly."[1]

Vorticism ended during the Great War. Gaudier-Brzeska and Hulme were killed, Gaudier-Brzeska fighting in the French army, Hulme in the English. Wyndham Lewis fought, with the utmost reluctance, with the British troops, and subsequently established that the experience of the trenches had made his hair fall out. Ezra Pound left England for Paris and then for Italy, and Lewis found himself alone in London, a somewhat eccentric misanthropist, described by Philip Toynbee as "a self-proclaimed bruiser who barged about the place lashing out with hands and feet; then yelled at the top of his lungs when anyone hit back at him".[2] Lewis remained a provocateur and was prepared to go a long way for the sake of giving offence. His contempt for Marinetti led him to despise Italian Fascism, "political amusements of the dago lands, as tiresome as our football and cricket,"[3] and his contempt for English democracy led him to praise National Socialism.

It was perfectly logical that totalitarianism should have an aesthetic attraction for Lewis: resting on Hulme, he believed in a classical revival. The future, he thought, would see the complete separation of man from nature, mechanical precision, an abstract, geometric art. Disciplined states, he hoped, would develop in which every man of quality—and above all, every intellectual of quality, like Lewis himself—would be able to exploit his talents to the full, unharried by the mediocre competitors who abound in democracies. In politics, as in art, Lewis sought something permanent, and permanence could only be achieved by the enforcement of rigid hierarchy.

What, he wondered, could be more preposterous than the " 'democratic' electoral system"? "A person is trained up stringently to certain opinions; then he is given a vote, called a 'free' and fully enfranchised person; then he votes (subject, of course, to new and stringent orders from the press, where occasionally his mentor commands him to vote contrary to what he has been

---

[1] W. Lewis, *Blasting and Bombardiering*, pp. 37-38.
[2] *The Observer*, March 30, 1969.
[3] W. Lewis, *op. cit.*, p. 234.

taught) strictly in accordance with his training."[1] Lewis saw modern society on its way to total effeminacy and total childishness. The increase in homosexuality, the triumphs of feminism, the general desire to be young, to be very young, meant that humanity was lapsing into immaturity and incapacity to assume responsibility. Totalitarianism was the solution, since people wanted to be ruled. For application in the Anglo-Saxon world, Lewis recommended "some modified form of Fascism . . . with as much of sovietic proletarian sentiment as could be got into it without impairing its discipline."[2]

The fact that the National Socialists in Germany should be organising and educating the young was found by Lewis to be especially impressive. He visited Berlin in 1930; in January 1931 a series of his articles on National Socialism began to appear in *Time and Tide*; and in April they were assembled in his book *Hitler*. While he showed remarkable acumen in spotting the importance of the National Socialist party so early, Lewis showed more optimism than accuracy in his assessment of Hitler's intentions and his belief that the obnoxious points of the National Socialist programme would remain dead letters. "If Hitler had his way . . . he would, I am positive, remain peacefully at home, fully occupied with the internal problems of the *Dritte Reich*. And as regards, again, the vexed question of the 'anti-semitic' policy of his party, in that also I believe Hitler himself—once he had obtained power—would show increasing moderation and tolerance. In the *Dritte Reich*, as conceived by Hitler, that great Jewish man of science, Einstein, would I think, be honoured as he deserves."[3]

Lewis admired Hitler's abstinence and the very fact that he was physically so unimpressive. He appreciated his directness, his attempts to moderate the more violent members of his party, and his decision to follow legal methods. The young National Socialists had "the personal neatness, the clear blue eyes, of the police! . . . Everything is strictly legal—*nur legal!*—fair, square and aboveboard to the letter."[4] Sober and respectable, Hitler seemed the only man capable of producing, in a State, a perfect interdependence of community and individuals "conscious of *the identity of interest*

---

[1] W. Lewis, *The Art of Being Ruled*, Chatto & Windus, 1926, p. 111.
[2] *Ibid.*, p. 369.
[3] W. Lewis, *Hitler*, Chatto & Windus, 1931, pp. 47-48.
[4] *Ibid.*, pp. 64-65.

between themselves and their race". The comradeship implied in
the National Socialist doctrine of *Blutsgefül*, the love which only
members of the same culture or race can feel for one another, were,
according to Lewis, "the only sane and realistic policy in the midst
of a disintegrating world", and what he had seen of Berlin in 1930
convinced him that the German capital symbolised European
degeneracy. Not without relish he described the homosexuality, the
prostitution, the strip-tease clubs, flagellation-bars and transvesti-
tism, and the gang warfare which raged in Berlin. Hitler, with his
handsome young followers, would rescue Germany, and by rescuing
Germany, save Europe, from such a decline.

In 1933 Hitler was appointed Chancellor; Einstein fled from
Germany, and it soon became apparent that unpleasant points of
the National Socialist programme were becoming realities. Wyndham Lewis remarked, however, that the National Socialist rise to
power "was the most bloodless revolution on record",[1] and that
the atrocities in the Soviet Union were infinitely worse than anything done by the Fascist dictators. Germany constituted no threat
to the rest of Europe, he maintained : it was the rest of Europe,
notably Russia, England and France, which was menacing Germany, and, if justice were to be respected, Germany should be
allowed to rearm. In *Left Wings over Europe,* published in 1936,
Lewis again stressed the absurdity of democracy in a world which
was clearly governed by money, by bankers and press barons.
Attacking the hypocrisy of the League of Nations' sanctions against
Italy, he concluded "that the industrious and ingenious Italian,
rather than the lazy, stupid, and predatory Ethiopian, should
eventually control Abyssinia is surely not such a tragedy."[2]

In the *British Union Quarterly,*[3] Lewis stated that he was
no Fascist. With Mosley he associated little, but commended his
"great political insight and his qualities as a leader" in an article

---

[1]W. Lewis, *Left Wings over Europe,* Jonathan Cape, 1936, p. 163.
[2]*Ibid.,* pp. 164-5. Evelyn Waugh, who visited Ethiopia before and
after the campaign, agreed. He said that Italian occupation was
"being attended by the spread of order and decency, education and
medicine, in a disgraceful place. . . It can be compared best in recent
history to the great western drive of the American peoples, and the
dispossession of the Indian tribes and the establishment in a barren
land of new pastures and cities". *Waugh in Abyssinia,* Longmans, 1936,
p. 250.
[3]*Left Wings and the C3 Mind,* B.U.Q., Jan.-April 1937.

printed in Germany in September 1937.[1] "Wyndham Lewis used to come to see me in most conspiratorial fashion," Sir Oswald Mosley recalls in his memoirs, "at dead of night with his coat collar turned up. He suggested that he was in fear of assassination, but the unkind said he was avoiding his creditors. I found him agreeable but touchy."[2] When Hitler's intentions regarding world peace became evident Lewis renounced his earlier views. In 1939 two books of his appeared, *The Hitler Cult,* in which he explained his former sympathy and proceeded to attack the German dictator with all the wit with which he had once attacked democracy, and *The Jews: Are they human?*, an indictment of anti-semitism. The Jewish problem, he said, was a Christian invention, and it was up to the Christians to compensate for the damage they had caused. "The particular Bellocian anti-semitism dates as heavily as poke-bonnet."[3]

Ultimately Yeats and Wyndham Lewis were trying to achieve an intellectual integrity untarnished by politics. This cannot be said of Ezra Pound, whose view of "Kulchur" was to become as materialistic as that of the most dogmatic historical materialist. "An expert, looking at a painting (by Memmi Goya or any other)," he wrote in 1942, "should be able to determine the degree of the tolerance of usury in the society in which it was painted."[4]

According to Pound usury, the greatest evil in the modern world, was responsible for all subsidiary misfortune. The very existence of usury was due to the ill organisation of distribution : capital was stagnating in the banks; the consumer lacked purchasing power; credit was accorded to specific individuals and interest charged on it; and cheques could be written out regardless of the services rendered. In short, the whole system was wrong. Yet it could be righted with comparative ease. "The working day," suggested Pound, should be kept "short enough to prevent any one man doing two or three men's *paid* work," while the State should

---

[1]*Insel und Weltreich*, p. 701. quoted in Geoffrey Wagner, *Wyndham Lewis : A Portrait of the Artist as the Enemy,* Routledge & Kegan Paul, 1957, p. 74.
[2]O. Mosley, *op. cit.*, p. 225.
[3]W. Lewis, *The Jews: Are they human?* Allen & Unwin, 1939, p. 22.
[4]E. Pound, *A Visiting Card,* in *Money Pamphlets by £*, Peter Russell, 1950, p. 25.

provide "honest certificates of work done."[1] Thus the unemployment problem would be solved, the ill-intents of the usurers thwarted, and money shared on a fair basis among all those entitled to it.

Pound's ideas on economics were mainly derived from two sources: Silvio Gesell, and the Social Credit system of Alfred Richard Orage and Major C. H. Douglas. Gesell, a German economist, had worked out "a paper-money system by which everyone was obliged, on the first of the month, to affix a stamp on every note he possessed equal to one per cent of the note's face value. . ."[2] By this method Pound thought that inflation, caused by a "superfluity of money", would be remedied and the Treasury constantly refunded the original price of the bank notes which would, according to Gesell's system, consume themselves within eight years and four months of the date of issue.

The belief of Douglas and Orage, on the other hand, was that "financial credit", the credit of the bankers and financiers, controlled "real credit", which was constituted by the people of a nation and their capacity to produce goods. For Orage "this disharmony between Real Credit and Financial Credit lies at the root of our economic troubles. . . Real Credit is a product of Production and Consumption, and . . . its final source is the Community as a whole . . . Financial Credit, that should be, and was designed to be, the handmaid of Real Credit and only exists at all because of Real Credit, is the monopoly of a comparatively few individuals, scarcely more than 1 in 100,000 of the population".[3] This omnipotent minority, Douglas was not slow to imply, consisted solely of Jews. Undeterred by the proof that *The Protocols of the Elders of Zion* were forged, Douglas affirmed that "the authenticity of this document is a matter of little importance; what is interesting about it, is the fidelity with which the methods by which such enslavement might be brought about can be seen reflected in the facts of everyday experience."[4] Indeed, Douglas maintained, and Pound appears to have agreed with him, that the entire modern system, in which usury was predominant, was essentially semitic.

The solution offered by the Social Credit scheme to the problem

---

[1] E. Pound, *ABC of Economics*, Faber & Faber, 1938, pp. 19-20.
[2] Quoted in Charles Norman, *Ezra Pound*, MacDonald, 1969, p. 347.
[3] A. R. Orage, Commentary to C. H. Douglas, *Credit-Power and Democracy*, Cecil Palmer, 1921, p. 165.
[4] C. H. Douglas, *Social Credit*, Eyre & Spottiswode, 1935, p. 146.

of usury was the distribution of national dividends through central banks. Now, although the ideas of Orage and Douglas seem singularly Utopian in retrospect, these two men had some sincere admirers among the English and American intellectuals. Douglas was, in Pound's words, "the first economist to postulate a place for the arts, literature and the amenities in a system of economics", which "ought to endear him to the highbrows, if their foreheads aren't mere façades".[1] And, sure enough, Herbert Read took a considerable interest in the Social Credit scheme. In the *Shape of Things to Come,* H. G. Wells referred to "the too-little-honoured name of that choleric but interesting amateur, Major C. H. Douglas", who was "making it plain that the only possible money for a progressive world must keep pace with the continually increasing real wealth of that world".[2] Even T. S. Eliot, who had the greatest esteem for Orage as a critic, commended his realisation "that any real change for the better meant a spiritual revolution" and "that no spiritual revolution was of any use unless you had a practical economic system".[3]

The great quality of Douglas and Orage was that, by oversimplifying economics, they made them marvellously clear. For everyone resentful of the complication which a scientific study of the subject entailed—and T. S. Eliot was such a one—this clarity was ideal. Eliot, of course, was level-headed enough to be slightly suspicious of the system, "of the possibility, to which we should all be wide awake, of revolutions being side-tracked, manipulated, exploited and degraded".[4] Pound, however, was not. But neither was he prepared to accept the full dogma of the American Social Credit Movement which claimed to be opposed both to Communism and to Fascism. "Even Douglas," he complained in 1935, "seems unaware of the profound harmony between his *economics* and Fascism."[5]

By February 1925 Ezra Pound had settled in Rapallo. "I personally think extremely well of Mussolini," he wrote eighteen months later.[6] "If one compares him to American presidents (the

---

[1]*The Criterion,* January, 1935, p. 299.
[2]H. G. Wells, *op. cit.,* p. 256.
[3]*The Criterion,* January 1935, p. 262.
[4]*Ibid.*
[5]*Ibid,* p. 300.
[6]Pound only appears to have met Mussolini, or "the Boss" as he called him, once, in 1933.

last three) or British premiers, etc., in fact one can NOT without insulting him. If the intelligentsia don't think well of him, it is because they know nothing about 'the state', and government, and have no particularly large sense of values."[1] Not so ingenuous as to think that Mussolini had actually instituted a social credit system on the lines recommended by Douglas, Pound simply believed that he had devised a system preferable to that of the Western democracies and might one day achieve something comparable to Douglas' ideal. "Much as I admire the achievements of the Fascist Quindecennio in Italy," he admitted in 1938, "their tax system is still primitive and monetary knowledge rudimentary. Enlightened by comparison with the bloody and barbarous English methods, than which no greater proof of degradation, personal and national exist."[2]

Where Pound believed that Douglas came close to Mussolini was in his idea of value arising from the cultural heritage : only in a country conscious of its true cultural tradition could a proper sense of value exist. In Italy, Pound pointed out, the parliamentary system was "an exotic, a nineteenth-century fad, imported *ad hoc*, for temporal reasons, a doctrinaires' game in North Italy, a diplomatic accident in the South".[3] The Corporate State, on the other hand, was admirably adapted to the nation. By instituting a council in which the citizens were represented by profession Mussolini had devised the only effective scheme of "ascertaining the will of the people".

Nevertheless Pound also realised that Fascism was only good for Italy : there was no question of its being applied—at least in its Italian form—elsewhere. At the same time he saw Mussolini as a figure within a far broader tradition. Like the Vorticists in 1914 the Duce was aware that the crisis was "OF, not IN the system".[4] Besides, while T. S. Eliot and Wyndham Lewis, though both American-born, regarded themselves as more English than American, Pound considered himself essentially American and, as such, affirmed that Mussolini was continuing the task of Thomas Jefferson. What had they in common? Their attitude to agriculture, the "sense of the 'root and the branch', readiness to scrap the lesser thing for the thing of major importance, indifference to

---

[1] *The Letters of Ezra Pound, 1907-1941,* edited by D. D. Paige, Faber & Faber, 1961, p. 279.

[2] E. Pound, *Guide to Kulchur,* Faber & Faber, 1938, p. 242.

[3] *The Criterion,* January 1935.

[4] E. Pound, *If this be Treason,* Siena, 1948, p. 29.

mechanism as weighed against the main purpose without regard to abstract ideas, even if the idea was proclaimed the week before last ".[1] But if Jefferson was the opponent of usury and the hereditary principle, the believer in a strong but peaceful country, Confucius taught you the importance of order and self-knowledge, the evils of private gain and the benefits of equity. He preached respect of intelligence and urged "a constant renovation". Mussolini, Pound believed, had come near to the Confucian ideal. In Italy liberty existed to a far greater degree than in England, where opinion was manipulated by the newspaper owners, and order, the foundation of strength and civilisation, had been restored.

Largely on the basis of Wyndham Lewis' reference in *Hitler* to National Socialist opposition to Loan capital, Pound assumed that Germany too was tending towards Confucianism. It was, of course, easy for him to associate the Jews with usury, and he did so, in his *Cantos* and in his prose, but always ambiguously. In 1938, for example, he wrote in the *British Union Quarterly,* that "our worst evil is the aryio-kike who is able to take a dirty line and stick to it without deviation or shadow of turning with none of the Jews' moments of pity, excitement or need of opulent display,"[2] and in the same year he described racial prejudice as "the tool of the man defeated intellectually and of the cheap politician".[3] Yet as war approached Pound's articles became increasingly pro-German. "The natural civilizer of Russia is Germany," he wrote in *Action* (which Mosley had revived in 1936). "No less gusty and active people would bother about educating the mujik."[4] Shortly after Italy's military intervention, Pound moved from Rapallo to Rome, where he broadcast on the Italian radio two or three times a week from January 1941 to July 1943, ceasing only for a brief period after the bombing of Pearl Harbour. He appeared to believe that the war "was not caused by any caprice on Mussolini's part, nor on Hitler's. This war is part of the secular war between usurers and peasants, between the usurocracy and whomever does an honest day's work with his own brain or hands".[5] His broadcasts,

---

[1]E. Pound, *Jefferson and/or Mussolini,* Stanley Nott, 1935, p. 64.
[2]B.U.Q., January-March, 1938.
[3]Quoted in Jack Stafford, *Ezra Pound and Segregation* in *The London Magazine,* September, 1969.
[4]*Action,* August 18, 1939.
[5]E. Pound, *L'America, Roosevelt e le cause della guerra presente,* Venezia, 1944.

pronounced in a variety of accents, took the form more of dissertations on literature and economics, interspersed with abuse of international finance and the democratic leaders, than of the propaganda of William Joyce. When Rome fell to the Allies, he returned to Rapallo. In 1945 he was arrested by the American forces in Italy and was subsequently certified insane.

Pound's madness lay in supporting his Utopia until the end. The others, Yeats and Wyndham Lewis, even Roy Campbell, had drawn back in time. There came a moment—for some it was sooner, for others later—when the writers using for their art ideas which could prove monstrous if put into practice, had to go against their artistic principles on a human level, in their day to day existence as men. Few were as aware of this as Thomas Mann. Until the end of the Great War Germanic irrationalism had provided him with a vital source of inspiration, but when the violence of the German Nationalists in the first years of the Weimar Republic was brought home to him, when he saw what men could do by clinging to principles which had once been his own, he acknowledged the "Germanic" spirit as dead food for dreams, and chose what he called "life". His was a rational decision, but Ezra Pound was incapable of such objectivity. With sincerity tinged by provocation, he supported Italy when she was at war with the United States, and the price that he had to pay was high—the price of combining the world of art and "its unreliable, treacherous tendency, its delight in scandalous non-sense, with the world of fact."[1]

---

[1] Thomas Mann, *Politische Schriften und Reden, I,* p. 295.

BIBLIOGRAPHY

In view of the quantity of literature that has appeared on the subject of Fascism, National Socialism and European culture between the wars I shall limit this bibliography to a few of the works which seem to me of particular interest. The most detailed bibliography on Italian Fascism has been compiled by Piero Melograni in *Il Nuovo Osservatore*, No. 50, May 1966 and Nos. 56-57, November-December 1966. For National Socialism and the Weimar Republic I recommend the catalogues issued by the Wiener Library, Institute of Contemporary History, 4 Devonshire Street, London, W.1.

The leading general works on Fascism include:

Arendt, Hannah, *The Origins of Totalitarianism*, Allen & Unwin Ltd., London, 1967.
De Felice, Renzo, *Le interpretazioni del fascismo*, Bari, 1969.
Journal of Contemporary History, vol. 1, No. 1, Weidenfeld & Nicolson Ltd., 1966. *International Fascism, 1920-1945*.
Nolte, Ernst, *Three Faces of Fascism*, Weidenfeld & Nicolson, Ltd., London, 1965.
Rogger, Hans & Weber, Eugen (eds.), *The European Right: A Historical Profile*, London, Weidenfeld & Nicolson, Ltd., 1965.
Weber, Eugen, *Varieties of Fascism*, Van Nostrand Co. Inc., New York, 1964.
Woolf, S.J. (ed.), *European Fascism*, Weidenfeld & Nicolson Ltd., London, 1968.

And on the subject of intellectuals and politics, I recommend:

Hughes, H. Stuart, *Consciousness and Society*, MacGibbon & Kee Ltd., London, 1958.
Joll, James, *Intellectuals in Politics*, Weidenfeld & Nicolson, Ltd., London, 1960.
Journal of Contemporary History, vol. 2, *Literature and Society*, No. 2, Weidenfeld & Nicolson Ltd., London, 1967.

ITALY

Aquarone, Alberto, *L'organizzazione dello stato totalitario*, Torino, 1965.

Arbizzani, Luigi e Caltabiano, Alberto (eds.), *Storia dell'antifascismo italiano*, Roma, 1964.

Bonsanti, Alessandro, *La Cultura degli anni trenta: dai Littoriali all'antifascismo*, Terzo Programma, No. 4, RAI, 1963.

Casucci, Costanzo (ed.), *Il Fascismo*, Bologna, 1961.

Chabod, Federico, *L'Italia contemporanea, 1918-1948*, Torino, 1963.

Cione, Edmondo, *Storia della Repubblica Sociale Italiana*, Caserta, 1948.

Deakin, F. W., *The Brutal Friendship*, Penguin Books Ltd., London, 1962.

De Felice, Renzo, *Storia degli ebrei italiani sotto il fascismo*, Torino, 1962.

De Felice, Renzo, *Mussolini il rivoluzionario*, Torino, 1965.

„   *Mussolini il fascista I*, Torino, 1966.

„   *Mussolini il fascista II*, Torino, 1968.

Fascismo e antifascismo, 1918-1936, Lezioni e testimonianze, Milano, 1962.

Falqui, Enrico, *La letteratura del ventennio nero*, Roma, 1948.

Finer, Herman, *Mussolini's Italy*, Frank Cass & Co. Ltd., London, 1935.

Flora, Francesco, *Ritratto di un ventennio*, Napoli, 1944.

Francovich, Carlo, *La Resistenza a Firenze*, Firenze, 1961.

Gaeta, Franco, *Nazionalismo italiano*, Napoli, 1965.

„   (ed), *La Stampa nazionalista*, Bologna, 1965.

Garin, Eugenio, *Cronache di filosofia italiana, 1900-1943*, Bari, 1955.

Luti, Giorgio, *Cronache letterarie tra le due guerre 1920-1940*, Bari, 1966.

Mack Smith, Dennis, *Italy, A Modern History*, Mayflower Books Ltd., London, 1959.

Melograni, Piero (ed.), *Corriere della sera 1919-1943*, Bologna, 1965.

Melograni, Piero, *Storia politica della grande guerra 1915-1918*, Bari, 1969.

Papa, Emilio R., *Storia di due manifesti—il fascimo e la cultura italiana*, Milano, 1958.

Salvatorelli L. and Mira G., *Storia d'Italia nel periodo fascista*, Torino, 1964.

Sapori, Francesco, *Il Fascismo e l'arte*, Milano, 1934.

Schneider, Herbert W., *Making the Fascist State*, Oxford University Press, 1928.

Seton-Watson, Christopher, *Italy from Liberalism to Fascism*, Methuen & Co. Ltd., London, 1967.

Tasca, Angelo, *Nascita e avvento del fascismo*, Firenze, 1950.
Trent'anni di storia politica italiana 1915-1945, Terzo Programme, RAI, 1962.
Wiskemann, Elizabeth, *Fascism in Italy: Its Development and Influence*, Macmillan & Co. Ltd., London, 1969.
Wiskemann, Elizabeth, *The Rome-Berlin Axis*, Fontana, London, 1966.
Zangrandi, Ruggero, *Il lungo viaggio attraverso il fascismo*, Milano, 1962.
Zurlo, Leopoldo, *Memorie inutili—La censura teatrale nel ventennio*, Roma, 1952.

GERMANY

Allen, W. S., *The Nazi Seizure of Power. The Experience of a Single German Town 1930-1935*, Eyre & Spottiswode Ltd., London, 1966.
Bracher, K. D., *Die Auflösung der Weimarer Republik*, Villingen, 1964.
Brenner, Hildegard, *Die Kunstpolitik des Nationalsozialismus*, Hamburg, 1963.
Broszat, M., *Der Nationalsozialismus*, Stuttgart, 1961.
Buchheim, H., *Das Dritte Reich*, München, 1958.
    ,,   (*et al.*), *Anatomie des SS-Staates*, Freiburg-i-B., 1965.
Bullock, Alan, *Hitler, a study in tyranny*, Penguin Books Ltd., London, 1962.
Gay, Peter, *Weimar Culture, the Outsider as Insider*, Secker and Warburg Ltd., London, 1968.
Hoepke, Klaus-Peter, *Die deutsche Rechte und der italienische Faschismus*, Düsseldorf, 1968.
Hofer, Walther, *Der Nationalsozialismus*, Frankfurt a/M, 1957.
Klemperer, Kl. von, *Germany's New Conservatism*, Oxford University Press, 1957.
Krockow, Chr. Graf von, *Die Entscheidung*, Stuttgart, 1958.
Mohler, Arnim, *Die konservative Revolution in Deutschland 1918-1932*, Stuttgart, 1950.
Mosse, G. L., *The Crisis of German Ideology*, Weidenfeld & Nicolson Ltd., London, 1966.
Mosse, G. L., *Nazi Culture*, W. H. Allen & Co., London, 1966.
Poliakov, Léon & Wulf, Joseph, *Das Dritte Reich und seine Denker*, Berlin, 1959.
Rothfels, Hans, *Die deutsche Opposition gegen Hitler*, Frankfurt a/M, 1958.
Schoenbaum, David, *Hitler's Social Revolution*, Weidenfeld & Nicolson, Ltd., London, 1967.

Schonauer, Franz, *Deutsche Literatur im Dritten Reich*, Olten, 1961.

Sontheimer, Kurt, *Antidemokratisches Denken in der Weimarer Republik*, München, 1962.

Stern, Fritz, *The Politics of Cultural Despair*, Cambridge University Press, 1961.

Taylor, A. J. P., *The Course of German History*, Hamish Hamilton Ltd., London, 1945.

Taylor, A. J. P., *The Origins of the Second World War*, Hamish Hamilton Ltd., London, 1961.

Treue, Wilhelm, *Deutschland in der Weltwirtschaftskrise in Augenzeugenberichten*, Düsseldorf, 1967.

Waite, R. G. L., *Vanguard of Nazism*, Oxford University Press, 1952.

Wulf, Joseph, *Literatur und Dichtung im Dritten Reich*, Gütersloh, 1963.

Wulf, Joseph, *Musik im Dritten Reich*, Gütersloh, 1963.

„ „ *Presse und Funk im Dritten Reich*, Gütersloh, 1964.

„ „ *Theater und Film im Dritten Reich*, Gütersloh, 1964.

FRANCE

Aron, Robert, *Histoire de Vichy 1940-1944*, Paris, 1954.

„ „ *Histoire de l'Epuration*, Paris, 1968-1969.

Audiat, Pierre, *Paris Pendant la Guerre*, Paris, 1946.

Brogan, D. W., *The Development of Modern France 1870-1939*, Hamish Hamilton Ltd., London, 1940.

Caute, David, *Communism and the French Intellectuals, 1914-1960*, André Deutsch Ltd., 1964.

Cotta, Michèle, *La Collaboration, 1940-1944*, Paris 1964.

Heist, Walter, *Genet und andere*, Hamburg, 1965.

Hughes, H. Stuart, *The Obstructed Path*, Harper & Row, New York, 1966.

Jaeckel, Eberhard, *Frankreich in Hitlers Europa*, Stuttgart, 1966.

Lefranc, Georges, *Histoire du Front Populaire 1934-1938*, Paris, 1965.

Loubet del Bayle, Jean-Louis, *Les Non-conformistes des Années 30*, Paris, 1969.

Massis, Henri, Maurras et notre Temps, Paris, 1951.

Plumyène, Jean & Lasierra, Raymond, *Les Fascismes Français 1923-1963*, Paris, 1963.

Remond, René, *La Droite en France, de 1915 à nos Jours*, Paris, 1954.

Saint-Paulien, *Histoire de la Collaboration*, Paris, 1964.

Sérant, Paul. *Le Romantisme Fasciste*, Paris, 1959.

Tannenbaum, Edward, *The Action Française*, John Wiley & Sons Inc., New York, 1962.

Thomson, David, *Democracy in France Since 1870,* Oxford University Press, London, 1964.
Weber, Eugen, *Action Française,* Stanford, 1962.
Wolf, Dieter, *Die Doriot-Bewegung,* Stuttgart, 1967.

GREAT BRITAIN

Benewick, Robert, *Political Violence and Public Order: A Study of British Fascism,* The Bodley Head Ltd., London, 1969.
Cross, Colin, *The Fascists in Britain,* Barrie & Rockcliff, London, 1961.
Graves, Robert and Hodge, Alan, *The Long Week-End,* Four Square, London, 1940.
Harrison, John R., *The Reactionaries,* Victor Gollancz Ltd., London, 1966.
Symons, Julian, *The Thirties,* The Cresset Press Ltd., London, 1960.
Taylor, A. J. P., *English History 1914-1945,* Oxford University Press, 1965.
Thomson, David, *England in the Twentieth Century 1914-1963,* Penguin Books Ltd., London, 1965.
Wood, N., *Communism and British Intellectuals,* Victor Gollancz Ltd., London, 1959.

INDEX OF NAMES

v